BERNARD SHAW

THE DARKER SIDE

ARNOLD SILVER

BERNARD SHAW
The Darker Side

STANFORD UNIVERSITY PRESS, STANFORD, CALIFORNIA 1982

Stanford University Press, Stanford, California
© 1982 by the Board of Trustees of the Leland Stanford Junior University;
The Bernard Shaw texts 1981 by The Trustees of the British
Museum, The Governors and Guardians of the National
Gallery of Ireland, and The Royal Academy of Dramatic Art
Printed in the United States of America
ISBN 0-8047-1091-0
LC 79-92454
Published with the assistance of the Andrew W. Mellon Foundation

Sources of photographs:
pp. iii, 1, 25, 65, 117, 137, 177, 224, BBC Hulton Picture Library;
pp. 15, 145, Raymond Mander and Joe Mitchenson Theatre Collection;
p. 53, Dan H. Laurence;
p. 77, Lady Una Albery (photograph by her father, T. W. Rolleston);
p. 251, Victoria and Albert Museum

Overleaf: Bernard Shaw in about 1906.

To my son DANIEL

ACKNOWLEDGMENTS

I AM GRATEFUL to my colleagues Morris Golden and Alex Page for scrutinizing the manuscript, and to my former teacher Jacques Barzun for his encouragement as well as his astute comments on a late draft. For the opinions herein expressed, I alone bear responsibility.

The MacDowell Colony made available to me, several years ago, the quiet surroundings that first enabled me to hear Shaw's undertones. The Shaw Society of London, and the Shaw Festival Seminar at Niagara-on-the-Lake, Canada, later provided me with forums to test my critical approach. The librarians of the British Museum, the Bodleian, the University of London, the Berg Collection of the New York Public Library, Widener Library of Harvard University, and the Humanities Research Center at the University of Texas at Austin have all been immeasurably helpful. I am obliged to The Society of Authors on behalf of the Bernard Shaw Estate for permission to reprint texts and to include extracts from unpublished manuscripts. Some of the play manuscripts I consulted have now been made available by the Garland Publishing Company. I appreciate the permission of the estate of Mrs. Patrick Campbell to reprint portions of her correspondence. The BBC Hulton Picture Library, the Raymond Mander and Joe Mitchenson Theatre Collection, and the Victoria and Albert Museum have kindly allowed me to use illustrations from their libraries. Lady Una Albery graciously permitted use of the Yeats photograph taken by T. W. Rolleston, and Dan H. Laurence made available the photograph of Alice Lockett and extended other courtesies.

Lillian Silver assisted in very valuable ways in the earlier stages, and Clare Novak helped significantly in the final preparations. Lillian Wittcoff Levy gave me the benefit of her mature judgment and friendship. My son, Daniel, mixed good advice and refreshing diversions in the right proportions. And my wife, Glenise, provided critical acumen, two determined typing fingers, and untiring moral support.

CONTENTS

AN ABBREVIATED CHRONOLOGY

The works in bold type are emphasized in the text. This brief list necessarily omits many of Shaw's lesser plays and political writings.

	BIOGRAPHICAL	PROFESSIONAL
1852	Marriage of George Carr Shaw (b. 1814) to Lucinda Elizabeth Gurly (b. 1830)	
1856	George born in Dublin, July 26	
1871	Serves as clerk in land agents' office	
1873	George John Vandeleur Lee (b. 1831) leaves for London, followed in a fortnight by Mrs. Shaw	
1876	Joins mother in London	
1879–83		Period of Novel Writing: *Immaturity, The Irrational Knot, Love Among the Artists, Cashel Byron's Profession,* **An Unsocial Socialist**
1881	Meets Alice Lockett (b. 1858)	
1884	Joins Fabian Society	
1885–94	Death of father (1885) Death of Vandeleur Lee (1886)	Period of Book, Art, and Music Criticism; *Fabian Essays in Socialism* (1889); *The Quintessence of Ibsenism* (1891); *Widowers' Houses* (1892); *The Philanderer* (1893); *Mrs. Warren's Profession* (1893)
1894		***Arms and the Man; Candida***
1895–98		Period of Drama Criticism
1896	Meets Charlotte Payne-Townshend (b. 1857)	*You Never Can Tell; The Devil's Disciple*
1897	Elected member of St. Pancras Vestry	

Chronology

	BIOGRAPHICAL	PROFESSIONAL
1898	Marries Charlotte, June 1	*Caesar and Cleopatra; The Perfect Wagnerite*
1899	Returns to London and lives in wife's flat at Adelphi Terrace	*Captain Brassbound's Conversion*
1900–1903		**Man and Superman**
1904–7	Vedrenne & Barker seasons at Royal Court Theatre feature Shaw's plays	*John Bull's Other Island* (1904); *Major Barbara* (1905); *Doctor's Dilemma* (1906)
1910		*Misalliance*
1912	Begins romance with Mrs. Campbell (b. 1865) in June	*Androcles and the Lion;* **Pygmalion**
1913	Death of mother (February) End of romance with Mrs. Campbell (August)	
1914		*Common Sense About the War*
1916–23	Publication of Mrs. Campbell's autobiography (1922)	*Heartbreak House* (1916–17); **Back to Methuselah** (1918–20); *Saint Joan* (1923)
1925	Nobel Prize for Literature	
1928–33	Visit to U.S.S.R. (1931) Visit to United States (1933)	*The Intelligent Woman's Guide to Socialism and Capitalism* (1928); **The Apple Cart** (1929); *On the Rocks* (1933)
1934–41	Visit to New Zealand (1934) Death of Mrs. Campbell (1940)	**The Simpleton of the Unexpected Isles** (1934); *The Millionairess* (1935); *scenarios for Pygmalion films* (1934–38); **Revised Edition of Pygmalion** (1941)
1943	Death of Mrs. Shaw	
1950	Shaw dies, November 2	
1952	Publication of the Shaw-Campbell correspondence	

BERNARD SHAW

THE DARKER SIDE

Introduction

A great artist is not a lump of genius to be gaped at, but a combination to be analyzed. Never accept anything reverently, without asking it a great many very searching questions.

Shakespeare must be judged by those characters into which he puts what he knows of himself.

If a man is a deep writer, all his works are confessions.

Bernard Shaw

To the destructive element submit yourself.

Joseph Conrad

Overleaf: Lucinda Gurly Shaw (left), George Carr Shaw (right), George John Vandeleur Lee (seated), and musical associates, about 1863.

*W*HEN SHAW won the Nobel Prize in 1925 he quipped that the world was expressing its gratitude for his unexpected silence, since at least in that rare year he had published nothing. But of course Shaw could not be bought off so easily, and for another quarter of a century until his death at ninety-four he continued to instruct, amuse, and irritate the world with his pen. His career had been marked by versatility and abundance. In addition to more than fifty plays, he had written political tracts, novels, drama reviews, music criticism, and essays on dozens of subjects. Even the thirty-six volumes of his *Standard Edition* omit much, and as each successive tome of his correspondence appears he wins new recognition as a formidable man of letters in a quite literal sense. Yet this harvest of writing would have been still greater had Shaw not also spent his energies as a leader of the Fabian Society and its star lecturer. He gave himself tirelessly to noble causes, and it was as much for this public-spirited activity as for his labors as a writer that Thomas Mann commemorated him as "mankind's friend."

Although nothing can detract from this phenomenal achievement, Shaw in his later years did suffer the fate of many other benefactors of mankind as familiarity wore away the freshness of his ideas and his mode of presenting them. What had been learned from him was taken for granted, and even the enormous rejuvenation he had effected in the theater was undervalued despite the acknowledged indebtedness of fellow dramatists such as Pirandello, O'Casey, and Brecht. The undervaluing was also caused, though more excusably, by resentments against Shaw's latter-day politics and his ostentatious personality; many people were alienated by his antidemocratic views and by the overweening vanity of the G.B.S. public figure. The adulation at the annual Shaw festivals at Malvern in the thirties only quickened the reaction against him, and several young writers of the period, like Stephen Spender, finally came to dismiss Shaw as a mere entertainer. The old iconoclast, now grinning down from his own pedestal, was pelted by a new generation who had fully absorbed the Shavian spirit of irreverence.

3

Both admirers and detractors, however, shared many assumptions about Shaw, all of which he himself first established, as a personality and as a playwright. Certainly few writers in history have imposed on the world a more vivid and original public character. That character named Shaw was unmistakably an intellectual, a man full of fresh ideas and voluble in expressing them. He was a mocking freethinker, impatient with the pieties of the past and confident of the reforms society required. He was a wit and a humorist who personified the rebellion against the Victorian ethos and offered liberating new doctrines about everything, from family life to politics to morality. All of these qualities were evident in his plays. In the first decade of the new century, as an avant-garde dramatist, he helped make theatergoing the invigorating experience it had not been since the days of Sheridan. Life as well as liveliness was being brought back to the stage—contemporary issues were being aired by characters who seemed real and who talked in a current idiom. What the audience gazed at reflected the world outside the theater and provoked thoughts about that world. Slum conditions and prostitution, socialism and women's rights, the ways the Salvation Army ran its shelters or a Balkan officer bungled his campaigns, the ways the Irish talked when Englishmen were absent or doctors talked when patients could not hear them—all this and much more was made to occupy the stage and the audience's mind by a remarkable new dramatist who turned the theater from a cavern where one escaped from life into a mansion where one felt that life was heightened. The young Edwardians who poured from the theater refreshed and stimulated, trying to remember the barrage of jokes and bright lines and new perspectives, discovering that Shaw's talk loosened their own tongues for hours afterward, had reason enough to be joyfully grateful. And for many of them Shaw became a culture hero whose laughter mitigated the guilts that accompany rebellion and in whose seemingly sunlit personality, radiant with assurance and sanity, they were delighted to bask.

After they saw the play they could read its preface, and here too their hero continued his enlightening talk. The prefaces, soon to be as famous as the plays, supplied another platform on which Shaw could play his favorite character. They displayed a man of independent mind, learned and argumentative. Their forceful style, ready with illustration, rhetorical device, and the clinching phrase, bespoke a writer fully in control of his intentions and de-

termined to win assent. True, a reader might at times remain uncertain of the link between the preface and the play that followed,
but would read the play in the spirit induced by the preface, looking for ideas and messages. Occasionally Shaw would disclaim
any desire to control the interpretation of a play; his prefatory
comments, he would say, were only one critic's view of the matter. But he was nonetheless a most persuasive critic, intimately
acquainted with the dramatist and loyally protective of the type
of play that the dramatist wrote. It is easy to forget today—when
Shaw is a staple of the contemporary theater, a now classic dramatist who is not only honored but widely produced—that he
had to fight hard to create an audience for his plays, which were
scarcely regarded as plays at all by several of the most influential
critics of the time, such as A. B. Walkley and William Archer. The
prefaces were to some extent manifestos for a new type of theater
which would be at once more realistic and more philosophical;
and Shaw was training the reviewers to broaden their categories,
to accept the theatrical legitimacy of works by Ibsen or Strindberg or Brieux or himself. He finally succeeded, and then paid the
price of success. The categories and critical vocabulary of the
prefaces came to govern the ways in which his own plays were
discussed. The nature of the plays was agreed upon even while
their value remained in dispute. Ideas were of the essence—the
plays were vehicles of thought, of social comment and suggested
reforms. All else was quite secondary, the means the reformer
used to make an audience attend to his message. Shaw's voice
could be heard everywhere and its tones were at bottom horta-
tory. His admirers did not mind in the least: they liked Shaw's
voice and his ideas, they found the talk and the humor scintillat-
ing, and they felt that he paid sufficient attention to plot and
characterization. His detractors, even when they came to allow
the legitimacy of the plays, found them too cerebral to plumb the
darker depths of human experience, too didactic yet somehow
lacking in seriousness, unsubtle if not cold, with the characters
superficially conceived and the range narrow. Both sides agreed
that Shaw was a highly conscious playwright who calculated his
effects shrewdly, a self-assured man of puritan temperament, an
idealist outraged by social injustice. The plays and the prefaces
were like the man, and they contributed to the making of that
image of a witty, loquacious intellectual called Shaw. Estimates
of him might differ but the assumptions about him could hardly

be questioned. And these assumptions have now solidified into dogma under the pressure of nearly a century of repetition.

In this book I propose to show the inadequacy of these assumptions and to establish the validity of others which will foster a different way of regarding Bernard Shaw. This intention should not be taken to imply an unqualified rejection of the standard view of him or of the many valuable critical works derived from that view. It does imply that further understanding of Shaw has now become blocked by the traditional assumptions about him. Polemically, it was once useful for Shaw's early defenders such as G. K. Chesterton and Desmond MacCarthy to emphasize his programmatic development of a theater of ideas. But today, with that sort of theater firmly established, Shaw's most able recent defenders such as Eric Bentley, Louis Crompton, and J. L. Wisenthal benefit little by following the lead of the prefaces and accepting the public Shaw in his superman outfit as the creator of the plays. This public Shaw was, of course, not wholly a disguise. To some degree it was an extension of the inner man and truly reflected aspects and aspirations of his being. Yet since that being included the host of characters who appear in his plays, Shaw was in himself many people, greater than the sum of his characters, including the public one. The public character undoubtedly helped to write the plays and helped even more to revise them, but the primary creative work was done by a private Shaw whom the world was scarcely allowed to know. And that man, I shall assume, was human enough to have passions and confusions and a fertile unconscious life, to have fierce personal dilemmas that he was trying to resolve even as they pressed for expression. The writer often drew upon the deeply personal experiences of the man; he responded to unconscious as well as to conscious promptings; and he was able to give vitality to the conflicts that define the essence of drama by incorporating his own conflicts into his work. In brief, if we assume that Shaw was a complex man rather than a simple superman, then the paths to understanding him will suddenly become unclogged.

These assumptions about Shaw's inner life, though defensible in principle, are not based upon principle, or upon a desire to apply to him the same explanatory methods as have been used with countless other writers. Nor are the assumptions based upon some of Shaw's own statements, such as his remark that he divined his own meaning in *Candida* only after he had completed the play, or his hint that all his work was confessional, or that it was "a chaos of contradictions." Rather, we are compelled to make these assumptions by conspicuous and often disturbing elements in Shaw's writing which conventional criticism simply disregards. How are we to account for the sharp fluctuations in the quality of Shaw's work—a jagged graph on which the very worst of his plays appears right next to his greatest ones? How do we account for a committed social democrat writing with such ridicule of democracy? How can we comprehend Shaw's support of twentieth-century militaristic dictators when the greatest single hero of his plays is an antimilitaristic Caesar, when *Arms and the Man* satirizes the war hero, when the pacifist Androcles becomes a model of courage? How can we reconcile Shaw's attack on Shakespeare's supposed pessimism with a pessimism of darkest hue in Shaw himself? How—at the level of single plays—are we meant to take the strange preface and postscript to *Pygmalion*, which contradict the meanings of the play? Why did Shaw continually denigrate that play and seek to obscure the many ways in which it is his loveliest masterpiece? Why did he allow *Man and Superman* to turn into two separate plays, only superficially integrated? Such are merely a few of the questions that nag and distract the honest reader and that mark the limits of the assistance provided by critics endorsing the traditional assumptions about Shaw.

At the hands of his commentators, the most influential of whom was the prefatory Shaw himself, Shaw's reputation as a playwright has thus had a history opposite to Shakespeare's. As we know, Shakespeare was for a long time regarded as a wild uncultivated genius with the imagination (according to Voltaire) of an intoxicated savage, the fury of whose fancy (according to Dryden) often transported him beyond the bounds of judgment; it required many years before Coleridge could avow that Shakespeare's judgment was commensurate with his genius, or Carlyle could declare that Shakespeare's was the greatest of intellects. Shaw starts at the other end. He was always pleased to notify the world of the greatness of his intellect and the sanity of his judgment. It may now be profitable to modify that view and to reverse for Shaw the history of Shakespeare criticism—not in order to turn him into a barbarian playwright but to see how far it takes us if we commence thinking about him as an inveterate fantasist whose dreams often sprang from primitive and childish and sexual impulses, from dark compulsions, and from more than a normal touch of madness. The god of the theater is after all Dionysus, who would not have allowed Shaw to win the laurels without receiving due homage, and indeed the playwright was often so embarrassed by the urge to pay this homage that he would then rush to Apollo's shrine and deposit an expiatory preface. (The critics huddle over the offering, examine its entrails, and then pronounce from afar on the meanings of the play.) Explaining his compulsive addiction to writing, Shaw used to imply that it was almost hereditary, that he worked as his father drank. But the parallel extended further. His alcoholic father always insisted on the virtues of temperance and boasted of being, essentially, a teetotaler; Shaw, after writing most of his plays in almost a creative frenzy, and releasing tensions and animosities, then insisted in his prefaces on the sober virtues of reason and sought to display a man who was, essentially, high-minded. In fact this double impulse, which broadly may be thought of in Nietzschean terms as Apollonian and Dionysian, frequently appears in the plays themselves and determines their very structure.

To speak of creative frenzy belies our usual impression of Shaw, which he cunningly established with the help of his critics. Yet this master of paradox can best be approached through paradox, and the one we are now considering is by no means the greatest one we will later encounter. Talk and humor seem the hallmarks of a Shaw play, feelings and emotions seem secondary. But talk can of course carry a strong charge of feeling and can indicate an attempt to master or hide or counter other feelings. And humor can serve identical ends. To be sure, the talk and humor in Shaw is not all of a kind. It often seems thin and stimulates only yawns. At such times we conclude that Shaw is being merely frivolous or garrulous, not feeling what he says or else determined to avoid emotion. But elsewhere, in his better plays, the talk and the humor ride the crest of strong feelings or seek to keep them under control, thereby creating a dramatic interplay between thought, humor, and emotion. The talk in *Saint Joan* or *Major Barbara* is fraught with intensity, and we shall see that in *Man and Superman*, where we have the longest straight debate in all of the plays, very urgent and troubled emotions run beneath a sparkling comic surface. More times than they realize, Shaw's detractors allege a play lacks emotion in order to avoid its disquieting effect. And as a result it now seems paradoxical to ascribe to Shaw that most familiar of human experiences, the conflict between the mind and the passions.

Introduction

Once we grasp that the public Shaw was only the playwright's most famous creation and that he himself was a far more complicated personage, once we allow him shadows and depths that the public figure lacked, then several new perspectives come into view. His plays and their characters will be seen to possess more complexity and depth. No longer will it be easy to claim that all of the characters talk like Shaw, a quite erroneous claim which only confirms the power of the traditional Shavian persona. In the best sense, to be sure, the characters *do* sound like Shaw—as Shakespeare's sound Shakespearean or Dickens's Dickensian. Like any other memorable writer, Shaw had a distinctive manner and tone, and though his range was far narrower than Shakespeare's or Dickens's, he created within it figures as nicely differentiated from one another and from his own public self as, say, Eliza Doolittle and Candida and Barbara and Joan, or Caesar and Undershaft and General Burgoyne and Captain Shotover. The magnitude of Shaw's achievement in creating characters has been insufficiently appreciated, in part because when a writer's characters seem real we almost assume that they were found rather than created, and in larger part because Shaw's reputation as an intellectual makes us think too quickly of his characters' ideas rather than of their achieved reality. Moreover, new perspectives come into view on his personal reasons for giving his characters life at all. Far more than being an intellectual, Shaw was a man with an imperatively dramatic imagination, the Proteus-like urge to shape himself into the many people who live out the fantasies of his plays. Writing plays became a necessity for him, as he himself acknowledged. The characters and situations he conceived enabled him to project diverse feelings that struggled pell-mell for dominance. The characters, rather than serving merely as mouthpieces through which he expounded his philosophy, were the means by which he released the pressure of his own inner conflicts and explored them. His humor was the means by which he sought to make those conflicts tolerable.

Furthermore, and apart now from the plays, restoring depths to Shaw as a man will open fresh perspectives for us on the nondramatic writings and especially the prefaces. From what has been said earlier, the inference might be drawn that the "real" Shaw wrote the plays and the public Shaw wrote the prefaces. The matter is unfortunately not that simple. Once when praising Mozart's operas, Shaw attributed to the composer "the unscrupulous moral versatility of a born dramatist," and he added that this could easily be mistaken for cynicism. To display his own scruples and to thwart any charge of cynicism, Shaw wrote those postscripts known as the prefaces; and here the born moralist tried to counteract the work of the born dramatist and to create the image of a man confident of his ideas, altruistic, fully rational, and wholly adult. The prefaces, more guarded and self-conscious than the plays, therefore tend to be linear, the plays multilinear. Yet when all these differences have been duly noted, we must also recognize that the prefaces were written by the same individual who wrote the plays; both reflect, albeit in varying proportions, the same elements of a very complex man. And once we accept the assumption that the man was human enough to have inner conflicts, then we will be prepared to see them hidden beneath the assured style of the prefaces too. We will further see that a play and its preface are often engaged in a secret dialogue, the former raising questions that the latter seeks to settle. We will see that the play often throws more light on the preface than the other way round precisely because Shaw reveals more of himself as playwright than as essayist. To comprehend Shaw as fully as possible, we must finally trust the playwright rather than the author of the prefaces, and we must break free of the powerful spell of Shaw the critic and use the prefaces warily. But they can indeed be used, with proper cautions, to suggest and confirm certain ways of interpreting the plays.

Ours is not a biographical inquiry. Shaw's work as a dramatist will be our main concern. But his life and character must nevertheless receive attention in order to correct that misleading image of him which has hitherto controlled our ways of perceiving his plays. Any excursion into biography, however, has obvious dangers and unrecognized difficulties. The dangers lie in reducing the dramatist's work to the personal experiences that may have served as inspiration or actual material for his plays. The difficulties stem from the peculiar nature of the many books about Shaw's life. Some of these, especially the three volumes by Archibald Henderson, to which all subsequent studies are heavily indebted, are copiously detailed and very informative. But Henderson's books are a species of hagiography; and two of them were supervised by Shaw himself as part of his continual public relations campaign. On certain central matters, such as Shaw's childhood and his relations with women, these books are oddly reticent. On their hero's character they are reverently superficial.

Even Frank Harris, slapdash and gossipy, scarcely strikes out on an independent line, and his book too was carefully varnished by Shaw before being issued. In a word, Shaw has not yet found his biographer, and until that person appears—possessed of a strong mind and a steady gaze—students of Shaw's work will labor under a sizable handicap.*

These generalizations admit of one exception germane enough to our inquiry to deserve more than passing notice. B. C. Rosset's volume *Shaw of Dublin: The Formative Years* is a thoroughly researched study of young George's family life, which had long been recognized as an unusual one, even by Shaw himself, but whose important effects he and his biographers sought to minimize. Most of the prime facts about the early years were familiar enough before Rosset's book appeared. We had known that George's mother, Lucinda Elizabeth Gurly, had at the age of twenty-two contracted a marriage of convenience to a well-connected though incompetent merchant of thirty-eight named George Carr Shaw. He had dismissed the Gurlys' charge of being a drunkard by solemnly assuring Lucinda that he was a convinced and lifelong teetotaler. Yet on the honeymoon itself she chanced to open her husband's wardrobe and to find it full of empty bottles. As Shaw later wrote, "I can only imagine the hell into which my mother descended when she found out what shabby-genteel poverty with a drunken husband is like." From this "tragedy," he continued, her only "salvation came through music. She had a mezzosoprano voice of extraordinary purity of tone; and to cultivate it she took lessons from George John Vandaleur Lee, already well established in Dublin as an orchestral conductor, an organizer of concerts, and a teacher of singing. . . . He not only made my mother sing by a method that preserved her voice perfectly until her death at over eighty but gave her a Cause and a Creed to live for." Her children (two daughters and a son) were largely left to fend for themselves while she busied herself with her varied activities as Lee's devoted adjutant and made her house the center around which musical life in Dublin revolved. According to Shaw, Lee "at last became a member" of the household, creating "no friction" with George's father, and "certainly no unpleasantness." This joint household and "blameless *ménage à trois*," as Shaw later termed it, existed from George's tenth to his seventeenth year, when Lee left to pursue a career in London, and was

---

*Michael Holroyd is currently writing a new biography and gives promise of being the right person for the job.

followed within two weeks by Mrs. Shaw, who took along her fatally sick daughter Agnes, and was soon joined by her other daughter, Lucy. George himself also left for London at the age of twenty, leaving his father, as Shaw later remarked, in a state of "blessed relief" to be unburdened of his family.

Now Rosset, continuing the work of an earlier scholar with whom Shaw developed an extremely acrimonious relationship, delves into this family situation and unearths facts that cast doubt upon Shaw's bland latter-day accounts. It was not, for instance, solely the father's drinking habits that produced the estrangement between the Shaws and the other members of the family, proud Protestants with a jealous regard for their aristocratic distinction—one of the members being a baronet. Quite as offensive was that most of the participants in the musical activities of the Shaw–Lee household were Catholics, as was probably Lee himself, according to Rosset's findings. Moreover the family clan was distressed by the irregularity of the ménage, which may have been as innocent as Shaw later claimed it to be, but which nevertheless may have appeared to prove that Mr. Shaw was appallingly submissive to his headstrong young wife with her artistic ambitions. Yet was the ménage something other than innocent? Did Lee value Lucinda Shaw as his prima donna in more than a musical sense? Was she his mistress as well as his choirmistress? Had their relationship begun before George was born? And, finally, was Lee the real father of George Bernard Shaw? These are in effect Rosset's central questions—and his answer to all of them is affirmative. We need not accept the conclusiveness of his answers, which he is somewhat too eager to establish, in order to grant cogency to the evidence he marshals. It is undoubtedly interesting to learn from Rosset's researches that Lee and the Shaws lived in very close proximity for many years before the joint household was established; to learn that the music lessons possibly began before George was born and that Lee gave Mrs. Shaw the present of a cottage overlooking Galway Bay and lived in it with the Shaws for a year before their permanent ménage was begun; to learn that the household of which, according to Shaw, Lee "at last became a member" was in fact a house which Lee had already owned for two years, and that despite the impression Shaw conveyed, his family at last became members of Lee's house and the rent was paid by Lee; and to learn that while Shaw would publicly imply that his father's relations with Lee were almost cordial, he privately acknowledged that his father certainly did not like Lee "and would not have tolerated the arrangement if he could have afforded a decent house without it, or if he could have asserted himself against my mother." Rosset also catalogs dozens of references to illegitimate births in Shaw's novels and plays, noting Shaw's lifelong sensitivity to the subject, his evasions and inconsistencies when dealing with it in regard to himself, and his curiosity (extending even into his nineties) to discover through discreet inquiries more information about that man Lee.

The question of Shaw's paternity will in all likelihood never be settled, and it is really not important that it should be, since the crucial matter is Shaw's own doubt about his paternity; and Rosset does at least prove that there were ample grounds for Shaw to be haunted by this intensely embarrassing issue throughout his lifetime. To be sure, despite Rosset's implications, all of Shaw's literary references to illegitimacy cannot be ascribed to personal anxiety—bastards as we know found a welcome home in the fiction of the nineteenth century—yet the frequency of Shaw's use of this motif does indicate an uncommon degree of interest in parentage. That interest, moreover, was expressed in far more subtle ways than can be suggested by any mere counting of bastards in the author's work. Rosset also reasons rather crudely when he concludes that Shaw hated his mother because of her alliance with Lee: such a purported hatred is impossible to reconcile with Shaw's decision to live with his mother for over two decades after his arrival in London. Rosset in sum goes too far in claiming that Lee was George's father, and not far enough in exploring the manifold ways in which George was influenced by his unusual family situation and the resulting ambivalences of feeling toward his father and his mother and Lee. Adapting the image of a man being boxed in, we may say that Shaw was locked in the family triangle during his formative years and never entirely broke free of it. His life and writings both show the effects of this traumatic experience, and indeed every one of his major plays reveals at least traces of it.

Shaw himself recognized the shaping power of some of this experience far more than have his biographers and critics. He acknowledged in one of his *Sixteen Self Sketches* that his "discovery that [his father] was a hypocrite and a dipsomaniac was so sudden and violent that it must have left its mark." And to the actress Ellen Terry he said that this discovery sowed the seeds both of his skepticism—"I have never believed in anything since"—and of his irreverence—"then the scoffer began." But Lee's mark on him he was less aware of or less willing to divulge, though his own contrasting descriptions of the two adult males in the household make it easy to understand why Lee's influence must have been substantial. On the one side was an "impecunious and unsuccessful" father, unable "to shake off his miserable and disgraceful tippling," moving about the house "full of self-reproaches and humiliations when he was not full of secret jokes and . . . either biting his moustache and whispering deep-drawn damns or shaking with silent paroxysms of laughter," an object of his wife's contempt, a source of mortification to his children; on the other side was the dynamic Lee, "an energetic genius," "a conductor of genius," trim and bright-eyed, graceful and darkly handsome, his hair worn long in the current fashion of poets and artists. We can easily understand why Matthew McNulty, George's closest boyhood friend, declared many years afterward that George "hated and despised his weak and inefficient father [and] had a great admiration for Professor Lee . . . whose most striking characteristic was a volubility of language." We can also understand why George, though protecting his own legitimacy and his mother's virtue by downing his suspicions that Lee might have been her lover, nevertheless may have harbored a longing for Lee to be his father. And perhaps some echo of this can be heard in Frank Gardner's manner of dealing with his father in the early play *Mrs. Warren's Profession*, for the elder Gardner, despite his "clamorously asserting himself as [a] father," is unable to command the respect of anyone, especially his son, who instead views the artistic Mr. Praed with "romantic admiration" and declares to him in front of the blustering Mr. Gardner, "Ah, if you had only been my father instead of this unworthy old man!"—and we recall that a central and unresolved issue of this very play is the true paternity of one of the leading characters.

In a childhood deficient in any other living men to emulate, George found in Lee, who was sixteen years younger than Mr. Shaw, a hero of "mesmeric vitality" (the phrase is Shaw's), and he patterned himself on Lee and sought rivalry with him in more ways than he probably realized. To Lee's influence Shaw ascribed only his own preference for brown bread and for sleeping with the windows open. But Lee's vegetarianism, religious skepticism, and antipathy toward doctors seem to have laid the basis for Shaw's own later attitudes. Like Lee, Shaw became an expert in musical matters, and then a better music critic than Lee had

Shaw in 1874 (seated), with friend Matthew McNulty

ever been. Like Lee, Shaw developed an extraordinary interest in the sounds of the human voice and in teaching voice control and enunciation to women. And equivalent in its way to Lee's vaunted system of singing was Shaw's latter-day devotion to a system of spelling English phonetically, toward whose promulgation he left in his will the bulk of his considerable estate. Lee's presence also haunted Shaw's own relations with women. As an adult Shaw developed the habit of becoming the third member of a ménage à trois, which though it remained platonic—as if to prove that it could remain platonic?—did not exclude attempts to detach the woman's affections from her husband. We shall hereafter have occasion to examine the ways in which Shaw's own strange marriage, as well as his romantic attachment to the actress Mrs. Patrick Campbell, shows the influence of Lee. In addition, the gnawing possibility that the artistic Lee might have seduced his mother helped to create Shaw's ambivalence toward sexuality, and also toward art and artists, including his own activities as a literary artist. A secret exasperation with the entire issue of parentage conditioned Shaw's public views on the family. It also may have contributed to his attitude toward Christianity, his resistance to the claims made for a Heavenly Father, and his advocacy of a religion that omitted God or located God only within the individual. Finally, Lee must also be considered in any attempt to explain why Shaw changed his name from the early George Shaw to the later Bernard Shaw. George was the first name of both the older Shaw and of Lee, and Rosset conjectures that Mrs. Shaw had had her music teacher in mind when she named her male child since it was uncustomary for the Shaws to pass on their Christian names to their first sons. While we cannot really know what was in the mother's mind, we do know that she had contempt for her husband from the first week of their marriage onward and that the son grew to hate the name vehemently, calling it "horribly ugly" and "detestable"; and the effort to rid himself of it was perhaps derived from uneasiness over the entire problem of which George he was named after, as well as from a desire to establish his own selfhood once he began to make a name for himself as a writer.

It is I think incontestable that George Vandeleur Lee, more than any other man, exercised a seminal influence upon Shaw, and that this influence bears as greatly upon Shaw's literary work as upon his life. What created misery for the boy and uncertainties for the man provided rich material for the writer, and it is puzzling to find recent commentators so loath to assimilate Rosset's valuable data into their own studies of the dramatist—puzzling until we realize that these critics are merely continuing to follow Shaw's own method of discussing his plays and are assuming those plays were written by the public man. It may also seem more dignified to talk of Shaw's work in connection with the ideas, say, of Schopenhauer or Nietzsche or Butler rather than with the conditions of Shaw's childhood or the vicissitudes of his marriage, though ironically all three of these thinkers insisted on the importance of private experiences in shaping an individual's ideas.

Unhappy childhoods are of course common enough among

writers, but the constellation of circumstances in Shaw's case made for rather singular kinds of misery and helped to form a rather singular kind of person. Like many another imaginative and unhappy boy, George escaped into a fantasy world, yet he himself later recognized a peculiarity in his fantasies: their heroes invariably were foundlings. Peculiar too was young George's idolization of the devil, whose picture he drew on his bedroom wall and whose traditional facial features he would later try to adopt in his own appearance even while cultivating diabolism as a theme in his writings. Living with a hated father and with a mother he worshiped despite her neglect of him, George came to defend himself with a self-sufficiency that bordered on a desperate narcissism. Yet the pains of his childhood were never forgotten, and occasionally the boy's pain can be seen living on beneath the mature man's composure. At the age of forty-one he admitted to Ellen Terry that his had been "a devil of a childhood, Ellen, rich only in dreams, frightful and loveless in realities"; thirty years later he acknowledged, "Except in my secret self I was not happy in Dublin, and when ghosts arise up from that period I want to lay them again with the poker"; at eighty-six he wrote of the way he had been brought up "or rather not brought up!!! It doesn't bear thinking of"; and a year before his death, receiving the news that his admirers had put up a commemorative plaque on his old Dublin house, he snarled, "I would see it blown to smithereens without the faintest regret, in fact, with exultation."

These remarks, it is important to notice, were made only in unguarded moments of correspondence, for the anger still present in the ninety-three-year-old man does not appear in any of his public comments on his early years. In these he talks about his childhood with amusement, determined to squeeze out as much comedy as he can from a family situation that had been predominantly grim. And this indicates a characteristic Shavian device, albeit one shared with many other notable humorists whose high spirits and comic manner were means of triumphing over personal sorrow. Shaw learned early that laughter could check tears and could trivialize occasions that might make for grief. It is proper to honor Shaw as a writer who gave the world a great deal of healing laughter, but we should keep in mind that he was in the first instance seeking to heal himself. And if the scar tissue of Shaw's frightful and loveless childhood was still livid in the very old man, it had been at least equally so during the intervening decades of his writing career; and anguish stirs beneath the many situations in his plays dealing with parents and children, as it stirs too beneath other plays that wring humor from the painful experiences of his adulthood.

Shaw's emotional life as a boy, limited in nourishment from his parents, was nevertheless fed by the perpetual music and singing that sounded through the house. George developed an extensive acquaintance with the works of major composers, especially those of opera. He also frequented museums and read widely—in Shakespeare, Bunyan, Shelley, Dickens, and the current writers on science and religion. The arts exercised his mind as well as his emotions and his imagination. They provided a larger world into which he could move at will and take refuge from the sight of his pathetic father and the indifference of his preoccupied mother. He became a young intellectual even while remaining a middling schoolboy, constitutionally resistant to any authority. And this self-education in the arts and in ideas was added to those other resources he used to create a sense of himself: the fantasy life, the humor, and the narcissism. All were later to be combined in that distinctive blend of intellectual comedy which he fantasized for the stage, often with himself as the hero.

That Shaw was an unusually autobiographical writer has long been recognized. From his first novel written when he was twenty and appropriately entitled *Immaturity*, to one of his last plays entitled *Shakes versus Shav*, he often wrote fairly directly about himself. Scenes from his first affair with a woman were almost literally transcribed into his early play *The Philanderer*, and scenes from his affair with Mrs. Campbell were inserted into his late play *The Apple Cart*. Newly married, he wrote in *Man and Superman* of the wiles a woman uses to capture a husband, and to make it clear that he was talking about himself he specified that the hero Tanner should look as much as possible like the playwright. These and other avowed self-references are often duly noted by critics, who then hasten along to more philosophical ways of dealing with the plays. Sometimes, however, in their haste or perhaps embarrassment, they ignore even the most blatantly autobiographical references. Thus for instance Louis Crompton, in his learned study *Shaw the Dramatist*, attaches no significance whatever to Tanner's resemblance to the playwright and talks instead about H. D. Hyndman, a radical politician who in some minor respects, as Shaw later said, served as a model for Tanner. Crompton's readers may be grateful for the information on Hyndman while still remaining uncertain of the playwright's reasons for dressing the supposed Hyndman figure on opening night in a red beard of Shavian cut and the Shavian Jaeger suit, and for then attributing to him in the stage directions a Shavian fluency of speech and sense of humor. Crompton, shying away from the personal element, thereby excludes from his view large areas of meaning in *Man and Superman*, an omission we shall try to restore in our later consideration of the play. Yet this is only an extreme instance of a practice common among other good contemporary critics such as Maurice Valency and Bernard Dukore. They avoid the danger of reducing Shaw's work to his life, but they thereby deprive themselves of certain insights into the work itself; and they succumb to a less obvious sort of reductivism which sees the work chiefly in terms of its explicit ideas and the ideas of those nineteenth-century thinkers and playwrights who may have influenced Shaw. Accordingly, and despite the erudition they bring to bear, these critics imitate Shaw's own reductive manner of dealing with his plays, and they end up ringing variations on the tunes of the prefaces.

And yet Shaw himself, by stating that his work was one long confession, acknowledged his awareness of the interrelationship between his life and his plays. He implied the same awareness also, if more teasingly, in a challenge to his critics that has gone unheeded:

My plays are interludes, as it were, between two greater realities. And the meaning of them lies in what has preceded them and in what follows them. The beginning of one of my plays takes place exactly where an unwritten play ended. And the ending of my written play concludes where another begins. It is the two unwritten plays [the critics of the world] should consider in order to get light upon the one that lies between.

Now Shaw's unwritten plays are somewhat difficult to discuss, but in dealing with the written ones we can follow his advice to the extent of attending to his other nearby writings and nearby personal experiences—the plays he lived rather than wrote. These constitute the matrix of thought and feeling beneath the existing plays. Moreover, by keeping in mind Shaw's biography, or more especially his character and what he made of his experiences, we are enabled to see beyond any particular play to the overarching patterns of his work as a whole. The abundance and variety of Shaw's writings have discouraged attempts to seek such patterns, other than in his formal philosophical and political positions, and these attempts have not been notably successful because of the many contradictions within those positions, and between them and the plays. There is scarcely a topic upon which one cannot find Shaw expressing opposite views, and this has given rise to the notorious difficulty of not knowing what he means or when he is being serious. In consequence, many people would probably agree with Jacques Barzun's opinion that Shaw "eludes our grasp and measure like a man in a fog"—a curious fate for one of the clearest writers in the language. The difficulties and the fog can be dispersed, the components within the chaos of contradictions can be named even if not harmonized, if we attend to the work in relation to the life and to the conflicts within Shaw himself that energized the plays. Probing to the deeper layers of those plays while connecting them to the deeper layers in his life—this perhaps brings us as close as we can come to the center of Bernard Shaw.

Yet we run no risk, let us be assured, of complete understanding of Shaw or his work. The mystery of his creativity will remain intact, as will the vitality and therefore the changefulness of his better plays. No series of formulas, even the unusual ones we shall arrive at, can encompass a writer of Shaw's scope. No synthesis can be more than provisional. And these, I believe, are inherent limitations in any study of the man, however lengthy. But Shaw's wonderful productivity confronts those who write about him with additional limitations. They can examine with some pretense of thoroughness a single aspect of his work—his politics or his philosophy or his strictures on medicine or on aestheticism, his novels or a particular play or a particular phase of his drama. They can on the other hand attempt a broad view of his entire output, gaining range at the cost of depth. Books of varying quality along all these lines have been written, and I am indebted to all of them even when compelled to disagree with many of their conclusions. The method adopted here seeks to combine the merits of each type of approach—to examine, from both literary and biographic angles, one novel and four plays spanning some fifty years of Shaw's writing career. Many other representative works would have been equally suitable in illustrating my theses, and I was particularly loath to exclude such outstanding plays as *Caesar and Cleopatra, Major Barbara, Heartbreak House,* and *Saint Joan.* These will receive full consideration in future volumes of this study.

A different kind of omission here, it had best be understood, is any full discussion of Shaw's social setting. Never a reclusive writer, he was always alert to the cultural and political currents of his time, and since he lived for nearly a century his work reflects the events of an entire era. Any complete view of Shaw would require attention to those events, and some critics have already attempted to relate the man to his times. The difficulty of such an undertaking can be gauged by the substantial length of Stanley Weintraub's book on Shaw's activity during only World War I. Yet restrictions of space alone did not dictate my general avoidance of the larger social background. I believe that we must understand Shaw himself better before we try to see him in relation to his era (though of course they interacted), and the plays are the gateway to such knowledge. Despite appearances to the contrary, Shaw was preoccupied in the plays with a set of private and unusually tenacious problems that he began grappling with in his earliest years and continued to grapple with right into old age. The critics' attention to his public life, which was encouraged by his voluminous writings on the issues of the day, has distracted attention from the nature and even the existence of these obsessive personal problems.

Yet we seek here to increase our understanding of the playwright as a man chiefly to broaden our understanding of his plays, and I hope that the practical consequences of this book will be new ways of staging the plays under review. These ways I have not ventured to suggest except here and there in passing, but they are implicit in the new interpretations themselves. And I would like to believe that this study will stimulate fresh productions of other Shavian works, for the staging of all the plays has been too bound by traditions based not only on practices initiated by Shaw's own directorial hand but also on the conventional assumptions about the man and the nature of his drama.

And now finally two invitations to the reader. In each critical analysis, the question may arise whether Shaw himself was conscious of the meanings I ascribe to a particular work. This question is unanswerable. Although at times I find it necessary to assume Shaw's consciousness of these meanings, no proof is available, and therefore I have in general avoided speculation on the matter and invite the reader to do likewise. Even the best writers on Shaw crawl far behind his darting intelligence, and it is safe to assume that he saw much that his critics will never see, though for the reasons given earlier he refrained in the prefaces from telling all that he saw. Still, even if we cannot set limits to Shaw's self-knowledge, we can be certain that his mind had a fertile unconscious life. Recurrent themes and concerns appear in the totality of his work, which he was always too busy enlarging to contemplate in any prolonged way. With these recurrences our speculations can be moderately indulged and our talk of Shaw's unconscious can be less illegitimately introduced. And here naturally, when dealing with the unconscious, we may feel it appropriate to use some elementary Freudian conceptions to see if anything can be learned about the particular psychological aspects of the play or its creator. The methods we will use in discussing Shaw have of course no other justification than in what they yield.

I also invite the reader to fasten his mental seat belt, for on the ride we are about to take through Shaw's old and familiar funhouse some alarming surprises await us: skeletons will jump out unexpectedly, the lighting will turn lurid, and the face of the wizard who runs the show will grin at us in disconcerting ways. Metaphor aside, for anyone who likes Shaw there is much herein that will test that liking to the utmost, much that is distressing. I know this because my own liking for Shaw was tested while writing this book, and I was pained at some of the conclusions to which the evidence drove me. Our age is perhaps too greatly in need of heroes for anyone to appear to besmirch the few that are still available. Yet we are also in need of truth, and what I have to say about Shaw seems to me to include some unnoticed, if at times unpleasant, truths. Shaw's admirers have for many reasons taken too comfortable a view of him, preserving for themselves a saintly hero who would have been capable of writing only mediocre plays. Saints may talk eloquently to birds but they do not make good dramatists, and we could not have gotten Shaw's best plays cheaply or from a Saint George Bernard. Adapting if we will Shaw's famous quip that as a young unemployed writer he did not throw himself into the struggle for existence, he threw in his mother, we may have to throw Shaw the man into the mud of life, to uncover the rag and bone shop of his heart, if we are to rescue the complexity of the playwright.

To introduce the reader at once to Shaw's darker aspects, the next chapter will break the chronological order otherwise followed and deal with one of the late plays, *The Simpleton of the Unexpected Isles*. Though little known, and usually treated by the critics with an embarrassed silence, it will starkly confront us with some of the themes we will thereafter pursue. This play was written in 1934, nine years after Shaw had won the Nobel Prize.

And we may perhaps appropriately conclude by noting that Shaw designated an Anglo-Swedish foundation to use his prize money for the production of plays by August Strindberg, whose greatness Shaw had been one of the first men in England to proclaim. Of Strindberg's severe symptoms of paranoia, the critic Robert Brustein justly remarked, "His ability to transform these symptoms into art constitutes one of the most thrilling triumphs of modern drama." I hope that in time we may come to honor Shaw's contribution to modern drama in a similar way, fully recognizing that his darker side, too, played its part even in his most shining triumphs.

2

The Simpleton of the Unexpected Isles

DEFINING THE CONFLICT

Anger rises from sadness, and, having wrought vengeance, terminates in joy.

Aquinas, *Summa Theologica*

Making life means making trouble. There's only one way of escaping trouble; and that's killing things. Cowards, you notice, are always shrieking to have troublesome people killed.

Henry Higgins in *Pygmalion*

Overleaf: The Shaws boarding ship for New Zealand. 1934.

*T*HE CHIEF VALUE of Shaw's late plays lies in what they can tell us of Shaw himself. Only *The Millionairess* among the eight full-length works written in his old age can remotely hold its own with the average work of his prime. The rest, even such stageable pieces as *Too True to Be Good* and *The Apple Cart*, require that allowances be made for their author's advanced years. Yet these late plays offer readier access than the earlier ones to certain aspects of Shaw's mind. The humor and wit have become attenuated, the fusing power of his imagination impaired; but the unfused components of his thought and the main tendencies of his temperament are more visible. This is especially evident in that strangest of all the late plays, *The Simpleton of the Unexpected Isles*.

The Simpleton was written in 1934, one year after *On the Rocks*, a despairing satire of contemporary English political life. Apparently Shaw sought at the age of seventy-eight to recover a mood of hopefulness by turning away from home affairs and writing a fantasy, and he composed the play while on a voyage to New Zealand with his wife Charlotte. This circumstance may help to account for the work's oddly unlocalized quality: it takes place in a kind of limbo and floats in and out of allegory, farce, fable, and tract. A nonrealistic play, it allows for the presence of angels and of characters who fall in love with magical swiftness and change with suddenness. Events occur unexpectedly, years fly by between the acts, plot lines dangle before us for a moment and then vanish. The bizarre incidents are matched by the play's form: a lengthy prologue, divided into three scenes, is followed by two acts, the second twice as long as the first. Shaw said he wrote the work "without any premeditation whatever," and there is not the slightest reason to doubt this. Nor is it doubtful that in spite of some promising moments and mildly amusing passages, it is one of his worst pieces—badly flawed in structure, slipshod in details, confused in meaning. Edmund Wilson rightly called it a silly play, and one champion of the late works was driven to the desperate reply that Shaw's intent was to write a silly play so as "to provoke a revulsion against silliness." Yet the particular nature of its failure repays consideration.

27

The Simpleton

I

Structurally the play is pulled apart because it moves in opposite directions, first toward the presentation of a utopia and then toward the enactment of a Day of Judgment. Shaw's initial impulse seems to have been to avert his eyes from the tormenting present world—still in the throes of an economic depression that saw over 20 percent of the workers in Britain unemployed—and to create for our contemplation "a beautiful and good world," as one of the characters puts it. The guiding spirits of the play's miniature utopia, located on a tropical island outpost of the British Empire, are an Indian priest named Pra and his priestess wife, Prola, each handsome and physically irresistible. In the prologue, they lure four English nationals into a group marriage in order "to open people's minds on the subject of eugenics and the need for mixing not only western and eastern culture but eastern and western blood." In Act I, twenty years later, we rejoin the little polygamous community and its four offspring, two girls and two boys aged seventeen to twenty, all of them beautiful but supposedly devoid of any moral sense. Suddenly a young English clergyman, nicknamed Iddy, arrives on the scene, having been cast ashore by pirates. He is soon enticed into a polygamous marriage with the two daughters, Maya and Vashti, for the parents hope that his highly developed conscience will offset the young women's amorality in the creation of an ideal future race. At the beginning of Act II, several years later, we learn that Iddy is sterile and that the eugenic experiment is terminated.

Now this is by far the better of the two sections of the work. The mood is consistently light even though the humor is often knockabout and labored; perhaps the humor is at its best when Maya angrily rejects Iddy's offer of marriage because as a proper English clergyman he refuses to marry Vashti also:

MAYA [with a flash of rage, springing up]: Wretch! [Calmly and conclusively] You are free. Farewell [She points his way through the house].
IDDY [clutching at her robe]: No, no. Do not leave me. I love you—you. I would die for you. That sounds like a word picked up in the street; but it is true. I would die for you ten times over.
MAYA: It is not true. Words, words, words out of the gutter. Vashti and Maya are one: you cannot love me if you do not love Vashti: you cannot die for me without dying for Vashti.
IDDY: Oh, I assure you I can.
MAYA: Lies, lies. If you can feel one heart throb for me that is not a throb for Vashti; if for even an instant there are two women in your thoughts instead of one, then you do not know what love can be.

IDDY: But it's just the contrary. I—

VASHTI [*who has entered silently, sits beside him and throws an arm round his shoulders*]: Do you not love me? Would you not die for me?

IDDY [*mesmerized by her eyes*]: Oh DEAR!!! Yes: your eyes make my heart melt: your voice opens heaven to me: I love you. I would die a thousand times for you.

VASHTI: And Maya? You love Maya. You would die a million times for Maya?

IDDY: Yes, yes. I would die for either, for both: for one, for the other—

MAYA: For Vashti Maya?

IDDY: For Vashti Maya, for Maya Vashti.

VASHTI: Your lives and ours are one life.

MAYA [*sitting down beside him*]: And this is the Kingdom of love. *The three embrace with interlaced arms and vanish in black darkness.*

[1]

Shaw of course is not exploiting the polygamy theme solely for its humor; he long had advocated experimental marital arrangements as well as eugenics. But especially in view of such advocacy it is surprising to see him fail twice to body forth any superior progeny from a mixture of eastern and western blood, and also fail twice to present a successful utopian community.

The play's other subject now emerges in the short remainder of Act II, and it is nothing less than the staging of a literal Day of Judgment, with an angel arriving on the scene to separate the damned from the saved. And he is only one of a host of angels throughout the world who will, in the next year, weed out those who do not deserve to live. Lengthy newspaper and telephone reports describe the liquidation taking place in England, where "the useless people, the mischievous people, the selfish somebodies and the noisy nobodies are dissolving into space." Typical of such reports is the following news item which Pra receives by telephone:

Extraordinary disappearances. Indescribable panic. Stock Exchange closes: only two members left. House of Commons decimated: only fourteen members to be found: none of Cabinet rank. . . . Mayfair a desert: six hotels left without a single guest. Fresh disappearances. Crowded intercession service at Westminster Abbey brought to a close by disappearance of the congregation at such a rate that the rest fled leaving the dean preaching to the choir. . . . Noted Cambridge professor suggests that what is happening is a weeding-out of the nonentities. He has been deprived of his Chair; and The Times, in a leading article, points out that the extreme gravity of the situation lies in the fact that not only is it our most important people who are vanishing, but that it is the most unquestionably useful and popular professions that are most heavily attacked, the medical profession having disappeared almost en bloc. . . . Happy husbands and fathers disappear from the family dinner with the soup.

Several popular leaders of fashion and famous beauties, after ringing their bells for their maids, have been found non-existent when the bells were answered. More than a million persons have disappeared in the act of reading novels.

|11|

On the island itself the four young people are suddenly dissolved; and Iddy then heads back to England, the other Westerners go back to work to prove that they are useful, and the two Indians plan new commonwealths.

The play can thus be seen to have two very different, and in fact incompatible, subjects. It is as if Shaw could look away from England for only part of a play before his bitterness returned with increased force, and then in his impatience to discharge his feelings he scarcely meets the challenge of dramatizing them, for the lengthy reports of the extermination suspend all stage action and are decidedly crude in their humor. Shaw releases his anger at the expense of the play.

Yet this explanation, adequate as far as it goes, is still too general. It does not account for Shaw's inability to sustain the mood and the utopian subject of the earlier part of the play or for his evident indifference to consistency of plot and characterization. (Indeed he frequently treats his characters as if they were purely abstractions. In the prologue, the emigration officer and a young woman tourist are referred to merely as E. O. and Y. W., and Shaw does not even follow his usual practice of describing his personae in stage directions, relying instead on tag lines for characterization, as in the young woman's tiresomely reiterated "Let life come to you.") To attribute all these flaws simply to a deterioration in Shaw's powers is misleading since those powers could still create the thematically unified and vigorous next work, *The Millionairess*. Hence we are obliged to probe further into the play to locate the deeper sources of its failure and the conflicts in Shaw himself from which that failure derived.

II

I have said that the play separates into two parts, the first seeking to portray a good and beautiful future world, the second releasing destructive impulses against the repellent world of the present. But looking more closely we see that Shaw gives vent in comic guise to destructive impulses even in the prologue, in which a clerk at the customs desk abruptly commits suicide, the emigration officer tries to kill himself soon afterward, and the young

30

woman is shoved off a cliff into the water in a kind of mock murder. Thus *The Simpleton* really has a tripartite division of the light-hearted killing and near killing of particular individuals, followed by the utopian section, and then by the mass killings of the Judgment Day. One might conjecture, in terms of Shaw's own feelings, that the beneficent or utopian impulse came into play to block the destructive one and that the latter then returned with increased intensity. But however that may be, the utopian impulse is itself peculiarly feeble in this work. Only for a few moments is Shaw able to devote himself to the four offspring of the eugenic experiment, and it was after all for the sake of creating superior children that the community was established. These offspring have developed powers of imagination that enable them to enter vicariously into another person's being, and at least the two girls have a gift of love. Yet, oddly, Pra is made to utter the following criticism of the children: "Our four wonderful children have all sorts of talents, all sorts of accomplishments, all sorts of charms. And we are heartily tired of all their attractions because, though they have artistic consciences, and would rather die than do anything ugly or vulgar or common, they have not between the whole four of them a scrap of moral conscience." Even apart from the question of why the parents should not be held somewhat responsible for this deficiency, it is startling to find no moral value whatever being ascribed to love and imagination. Yet Shaw removes even these qualities from the youngsters in the latter part of the play and turns them into fools shouting vulgar slogans and ugly jingoisms. He creates the very opposite of acceptable human types, to say nothing of superior types.

This shift in characterization and the refusal to allow the eugenic experiment any success—even though Shaw himself had long favored such experiments—suggest that undercurrents of emotion were pushing strongly against the movement visible on the play's surface. For one thing, there seems to be an urge to disparage youth. Shaw's letters of this period indicate that his advanced age weighed heavily on him, and apparently one way of lightening his burden was to heap contempt on the young. This technique he had in fact used for many years, beginning in his early fifties in plays like *Misalliance*, continuing in his sixties in *Back to Methuselah*, and persisting even in his most recent play, *On the Rocks*. His now septuagenarian envy of youth doubtless helped weaken his desire to create ideal results for the eugenic experiment. Since this envy was also to some extent sexual, we can see why he belittles particularly the young people's talent for feeling love.

More is involved, however, than a disparagement of sex, or what decades earlier Shaw himself wittily described (while referring to someone else) as a soured old man's regret for the virtues of his youth. It seems that human potency itself is under attack. To see how this is done, let us consider the character who gives the work half of its title—Iddy the Simpleton. When we are shown that Iddy is a man with a highly developed moral sense, who loves to give long speeches and who differs from other people because he was raised on a special vegetarian diet, then we begin to suspect an oblique caricature of Shaw himself. Our suspicions are strengthened when Iddy complains of the burdens of being idolized despite his weak-mindedness, for the idolized Shaw also complained of such burdens and of now being in weak-minded old age. Shaw's practice in many of his works of introducing a character who bore some resemblance to himself is familiar enough (Robert Smith and Sidney Trefusis in the novels, Leonard Charteris and John Tanner in the plays being perhaps the most obvious instances) and Iddy may well be another in this line of partial self-portraits, all drawn with derisive exaggeration. It should also be kept in mind that Shaw in these later years had had some serious bouts of sickness and may well have regarded every new play as possibly his last one; and had this indeed been his final work, critics might have already wondered at the possible degree of self-reference in the title, since the Unexpected Isles are the whole world and the simpleton's words are often identical to Shaw's own. But certainly beyond speculation is that Iddy and Shaw are both childless men, and it is on this similarity that the plot turns. Iddy's young wives, largely because of his sterility, have come to loathe him. Yet on the Judgment Day, Shaw does not allow the Angel to vaporize this socially useless creature, an indulgence that should be contrasted with the harsh fate accorded to Maya. She is a ravishing blonde who represents the principle of love, and her failure to have children with Iddy seems entirely his fault. However she, not he, is killed by the Angel; in fact her death alone is described to us, while we are merely left to infer the dissolution of her sister and brothers. In thus making certain that the beautiful girl is killed, Shaw attacks with a new deadliness not only his old enemies romantic love and sexual desire but in effect those who can produce the children of the future. Youth and potency are destroyed, and Shaw thereby betrays his animus against the human race itself, an animus that we will soon see emerging elsewhere as well. Only the impotent and the old are left alive at the end of the play; and although the elderly priest and his wife talk of creating new commonwealths, they plan to do so by making war. "We shall make wars," declares the priestess, smugly sure of her own survival, "because only under the strain of war are we capable of changing the world; but the changes our wars will make will never be the changes we intended them to make."

These elders, Pra and Prola, appear gradually to drift toward a partial overlapping with Shaw and his wife Charlotte, for if the playwright in some respects seems to identify with Iddy, in others he merges with Pra. The same depreciation of the importance of children, which was just noticed in the contrasting fates of Iddy and Maya, appears again in a calloused exchange between the two elders soon after their children are killed.

PRA: [The children] grew up to bore me more intensely than I have ever been bored by any other set of human creatures. Come, confess, did they not bore you?

PROLA: Have I denied it? Of course they bored me. They must have bored one another terribly. [II]

Again one has a taste of sour grapes as Shaw may be indirectly rationalizing his own childless state. But a still more painful matter than his failure to have had children seems to be plaguing him behind the fragile fantasy, and it suggests a final reason for his destroying the principle of love in the play—namely, an uncertainty whether he had had a marriage really based on love even apart from its not having been sexually consummated. Let us first listen to Iddy's speech on love:

IDDY: I love you all here intensely; and I enjoy loving you. I love Vashti; I love Maya, and I adore Prola with a passion that grows and deepens from year to year.

PROLA: Dolt! I am too old.

IDDY: You were never young and you will never be old. You are the way and the light for me. But you have never loved me and never will love me. You have never loved anything human. . . . But every decent creature has some capacity for loving. [II]

There is a half-hidden note of querulousness in the final sentence, and Iddy's praise of Prola as the way and the light is contradicted by his denial of her human decency—she apparently lacks any capacity for loving. To see how Iddy muffles the complaint, let us now restore the omitted words:

33

But you have never loved me and never will love me. You have never loved anything human: why should you? Nothing human is good enough to be loved. But every decent creature has some capacity for loving. Look at me! What a little worm I am! My sermons are wretched stuff, except these last two, which I think really have something in them. I cannot bear being loved, because I know that I am a worm, and that nobody could love me unless they were completely deluded as to my merits.

[11]

Though of course we cannot equate these sentiments with Shaw's own, some personal element seems to be involved, for the character is incongruously addressing these remarks to the older woman rather than to his wives. The pattern is to complain of lovelessness, to remove the sting of personal rejection by declaring that no one deserves to be loved anyway, and to fluctuate between grievance and self-belittlement.

To explore further the possibility that this fluctuation of feelings is Shaw's and not just Iddy's, let us turn to a section of the last dialogue in the play, the one between Prola and her husband. It should be remarked before presenting this passage as an excerpt, however, that any reader of the entire play would be unprepared for its abrupt movement into an entirely new key. The leaders of the colony have been presented as mysteriously hieratic and self-assured. Suddenly they are transformed into an old self-doubting husband and his elderly wife. They are given lines which bear so little relationship to the plot or to their earlier personalities that it almost appears as if Shaw is musing about Charlotte and himself and is writing after the end of the play's action a courtly private message to the first reader of his script. Here is the passage, spoken as soon as the couple is alone:

PRA: Tell me the truth, Prola. Are you waiting for me to disappear? Do you feel that you can do better without me? Have you always felt that you could do better without me?

PROLA: That is a murderer's thought. Have you ever let yourself think it? How often have you said to yourself "I could do better alone, or with another woman"?

PRA: Fairly often, my dear, when we were younger. But I did not murder you. That's the answer. And you?

PROLA: All that stuff belongs to the past: to the childhood of our marriage. We have now grown together until we are each of us a part of the other. I no longer think of you as a separate possibility.

PRA: I know. I am part of the furniture of your house. I am a matter of course. But was I always that? Was I that in the childhood of our marriage?

PROLA: You are still young enough and manlike enough to ask mischievous questions.

34

PRA: No matter: we shall both disappear presently; and I have still some curiosity left. Did you ever really care for me? I know I began as a passion and have ended as a habit, like all husbands; but outside that routine there is a life of the intellect that is quite independent of it. What have I been to you in that life? A help or a hindrance?

PROLA: Pra: I always knew from the very beginning that you were an extraordinarily clever fool.

PRA: Good. That is exactly what I am.

PROLA: But I knew also that nobody but a fool would be frivolous enough to join me in doing all the mad things I wanted to do. And no ordinary fool would have been subtle enough to understand me, nor clever enough to keep off the rocks of social ruin. Ive grown fond enough of you for all practical purposes;—

PRA: Thank you.

PROLA: —but Ive never allowed you or any other man to cut me off my own stem and make me a parasite on his. That sort of love and sacrifice is not the consummation of a capable woman's existence: it is the temptation she must resist at all costs.

PRA: That temptation lies in the man's path too. The worst sacrifices I have seen have been those of men's highest careers to woman's vulgarities and follies.

PROLA: Well, we two have no reproaches and no regrets on that score.

PRA: No. We are awaiting judgment here quite simply as a union of a madwoman with a fool.

[II]

Now the shifts in this discussion are more complicated than those in Iddy's speech, but a similar pattern is evident. The old man must accept in answer to his sad question of whether his wife ever really cared for him the patronizing reply that she grew fond enough of him for practical purposes; Pra must accept himself as a fool even as Iddy belittles himself as a worm. And he must also accept as a sensible and shared resolve the woman's past decision (presented in vaguely sexual terms) to withhold their beings from one another. Yet at the end, even as the man declares himself to be a fool, he gives the gentle thrust of calling his wife a madwoman. There is, in short, just as in Iddy's speech, an undertone of complaint and melancholy both for having missed a woman's full love and for having to join her in rationalizing its absence.

This note of unhappiness, muffled by self-mockery, can be heard throughout the play, and it is related to Shaw's personal disappointments in the present and the past. But a final source of his frustration lies in his professional life as a dramatist. If, as Iddy says, "nothing human is good enough to be loved," if even the best people in the play are madwomen or fools, then human creatures are scarcely worth bothering about, and the effort of imagin-

35

ing their inner beings—surely one of the playwright's essential activities—is meaningless. When Shaw denigrates the imaginative powers of the young people in the play, he may also be denigrating his own activity as a writer. He may feel that art in the exigent modern world is not merely irrelevant but obstructive, giving pleasure at a time when people should be making themselves useful. As one of the characters says toward the end of the play: "Look here, I have an uneasy feeling that we'd better get back to our work. I feel pretty sure that we shant disappear as long as we're doing something useful; but if we only sit here talking, either we shall disappear or the people who are listening to us will." These last few words, twitting the play's audience, hint at Shaw's disaffection with the whole enterprise of playmaking and playgoing. Such disaffection is not, to be sure, unheralded in our author's work: it appears in an extended way as early as *Man and Superman*. But here Shaw goes further by finding no use whatsoever in imagination and by destroying its possessors, and since he too possessed imagination, he is in effect seeking to destroy it in himself as well.

These, in sum, appear to be the sources of emotional resistance that disabled Shaw's initial impulse to set forth a utopia; and the resentments against youth, sexuality, and potency were aroused precisely by his effort to create ideal young people, their very characters threatening his equilibrium and his egotism, reminding him of what he had lost or never had, stirring up a sense of lovelessness and a misanthropy which made even playwriting seem pointless. It is this multiple frustration that makes Shaw himself play the role of destroying angel toward his own utopia.

III

Yet the collapse of the utopia need not have led to a Judgment Day and to the innumerable killings of the last part of the play. That Shaw drove the work to this conclusion suggests that he finally longed to contemplate killings more than life in an ideal community and that this very longing joined the aforementioned resistances in blocking his will to create a utopia. Such homicidal longing seems of course preposterous to ascribe to Bernard Shaw— the Shaw that everybody knows, at least; and it would be helpful if facts were available to buttress the implications in the play. Fortunately they are to some extent available in Shaw's latter-day

political opinions, those that he held both before and after writing
The Simpleton. Hence to lend support to the present interpretation, and to increase our awareness of a central strain in Shaw's
other work, let us glance for a moment at his late political views
and then at a revealing essay he wrote just before beginning the
play.

The 1920's marked the decade in which Shaw increasingly
abandoned his belief in democracy. He turned savagely against
Britain's parliamentary system as well as Britain itself, and for
the next thirty years he sought to discredit them on almost every
possible occasion. The British Parliament, he was saying in 1933,
was "the most effective engine for preventing progress of any kind
that has ever been devised by the wit of man." In 1935 he declared
himself in hearty agreement "with Signor Mussolini that liberty
under Parliamentary government of the British type is a sham; that
Oppositions as such cannot be tolerated in modern public business any more than they would be in private business." In 1938
he announced: "I don't really want to see a Hitler in this country,
but I am not sure that it would be a bad thing. It might be an improvement on a so-called democracy that is not really a democracy at all." After Hitler and Stalin carved up Poland in 1939,
Shaw informed the world that England had committed ten times
the atrocities of Hitler and Stalin combined, and he attacked "the
present complete despotism of Mr. Chamberlain's War Cabinet
and its innumerable Gestapos." He thought that "Churchillism"
was as bad as Hitlerism, and he complained that power had been
granted to democratic leaders that no "Fascist dictator would
dream of claiming." While the Second World War was proceeding,
Shaw announced that "Western democracy is, as Hitler says, a lie,
and Western liberty, as Mussolini says, a stinking corpse." As the
war moved toward its climax, Shaw declared that "the British
Party system should be scrapped ruthlessly," and he thought unanswerable Hitler's allegation "that British democracy is nothing
but Anglo-Semitic plutocracy." Soon after the war, and despite its
outcome, Shaw still maintained that the British parliamentary
system was "a sham," and that "Hitler was right when he called
Adult Suffrage sham democracy."

Hitler was right for him in other ways as well. Though Shaw
took exception to the dictator's antisemitism, and particularly
his persecution of Einstein, he declared himself favorably impressed by *Mein Kampf* and also by Hitler's facial expression of

37

"intense resentment." In 1934 he excused Hitler's violence and brutality. In 1935 he demanded that his friends give him the Fascist salute, and he ended articles in defense of Nazism with a "Heil Hitler." Concurrently, throughout the thirties, he vigorously opposed all efforts at disarmament and favored the rearming of Germany, saying for example that he would not at all want to prevent Germany from building a thousand planes and twenty new battleships; and he seemed to be looking forward to the next war when "all the most diabolical means of spreading death and destruction will be ready for use." When Hitler's troops marched into Austria in 1938, Shaw, having recommended the move for several years, acclaimed it as "a highly desirable event." When Germany and Russia signed their friendship pact in 1939, Shaw regarded it as "joyful news" and was amazed that everyone else was "frightened out of his or her wits." When Nazi battalions attacked Poland in September, Shaw was ready to announce on the BBC that "Mr. Hitler did not begin this war; we did"; and he maintained elsewhere that "we are not the terrified victims of Mr. Hitler's aggression: quite the reverse." After Britain had entered the war, Shaw still eulogized the German dictator for "moral courage" and "diplomatic sagacity." "I was a National Socialist before Mr. Hitler was born," he declared. "I hope we shall emulate and surpass his great achievements in that direction. I have no prejudice against him personally: much that he has written and spoken echoes what I myself have written and said."

Shaw admired Mussolini even more than Hitler, and for him the Italian dictator could apparently do no wrong. High Fascist officials, well aware of the Irish playwright's vanity, courted him royally when he paid a tourist's visit to Stresa in 1927, and Shaw came home with his enthusiasm for the new regime at fever pitch. "Europe has begun to clamor for political disciplinarians to save her," he announced, adding with approval that Italy had "knocked its parliament down and handed the whip to Signor Mussolini to thrash Italian democracy and bureaucracy into some sort of order and efficiency." Words like "whip," "thrash," "knocked down," "disciplinarians" lead one to suspect that Shaw's devotion to Il Duce's Italy may not have come solely from the efficiencies achieved but also from the means employed; and these suspicions are strengthened when Shaw defends both Mussolini's torturing of political prisoners with overdoses of castor oil and the bombings in 1935 of defenseless Abyssinians. In Italy's African war, he favored "the necessary intimidation" of the Abyssinian natives to the point of necessary "extermination," and he objected to the efforts to have the League of Nations impose sanctions on Italy even though Italy had violated League principles to which it had subscribed. Shaw refused to sign the protests against the arrest of the philosopher Unamuno, or the protests against the murder of the Socialist leader Giacomo Matteotti, or to help support victims of Fascism including Matteotti's widow and children. He reserved his moral outrage for what he called Britain's failure at the end of the war to protest when Mussolini's "star was eclipsed and he was scandalously lynched in Milan."

But the brightest star in Shaw's firmament of dictators was Stalin, whom he modestly acknowledged in 1948 to be the greatest man alive after having eagerly defended him for two decades past. Shaw apparently likened the Kremlin's inner circle to his own band of Fabians, and he ignored all the differences he had once emphasized between Fabianism and Communism, alternately terming himself a Communist and Stalin "a good Fabian." He took credit for many Soviet policies that he claimed had been first advanced by the Fabians, yet in un-Fabian fashion he came to long for a revolution and civil war in England which would Bolshevize the country. "I do not want the catastrophe to be deferred," he wrote in 1932 while praising Guy Fawkes. "I am impatient for the catastrophe. I should be jolly glad if the catastrophe occurred tomorrow." He informally placed his pen at the service of the Soviet government, in 1939 championing its attack on Finland and the bombing of Helsinki, and in 1945 declaring that "there are no democracies in the West. . . . England is in fact at present the leading Fascist power in Europe." A couple of years earlier he had said that the Russians were "the freest civilized people in the world" and a few years later that "the only country in the world where you can get real freedom is Russia." By real freedom he did not mean free elections or the rights of assembly or speech or information or privacy, but solely a decrease in working hours. He professed to disbelieve that "men are so constituted that they will work twelve hours a day, and pay monstrous rents out of their sweated wages if only they may think and say what they like in the rest of their time, rather than work eight hours a day for higher wages under complete State regulation of their lives and thoughts."

This last phrase points to a certain bluntness in Shaw's communist apologetics which must have caused embarrassment in Moscow's propaganda ministry, always alert to the publicity value of praise by distinguished Westerners. Shaw was unlike those fellow travelers who denied or extenuated the coerciveness of the Russian regime. To him "the dictatorship of the proletariat" meant that "the proletariat is much more effectively dictated to for its own good than under our system." And he welcomed excluding the following groups of Russian citizens from the franchise:

the ignorant, the incompetent, the indifferent, the corrupt, and the pugnacious and politically incapable masses who, though they revel in a party fight or any other sort of fight, can make no intelligent use of their votes. . . . The political machinery is built for immediate positive use; and it is powerful enough to break people who stick ramrods into it. In short, it is much more democratic than Parliament and party.

The Pickwickian meanings that Shaw now ascribed to "democratic"—*now* because he once knew its signification quite well, having for instance defined it in 1911 as the right of the majority to "elect and remove their lawgivers according to their favorable or unfavorable judgments of them and their work"—these meanings would be comical if not for the sinister reference to the state's power to break its opponents. It is here that we hit the hard common ground beneath the dictatorships of the left and the right that Shaw supported. Undoubtedly in his later years he grew impatient with Britain's slowness in introducing socialist remedies for a sick economy and turned with hope to energetic foreign leaders who seemed from a distance to be helping their people even while ignoring the niceties of democracy. But there can be no doubt either that the draconian measures of totalitarian regimes pleased him and made him especially willing to defend those regimes. His destructive passion, encompassing both sadistic and homicidal urges, was more gratified by dictatorships than by parliamentary systems, whose laws and habits of debate impeded the use of terror. In his comments on dictatorships Shaw clearly identified himself, not with the citizenry, but with the rulers who broke people, poured quarts of castor oil into them, exterminated them. He felt that Hitler should have given him credit for introducing the idea of gas chambers, and he congratulated himself for instilling in the Russian leaders the idea of liquidation. He thoroughly sympathized with Stalin's extermination of five million peasants by starvation, and he looked forward to in-

troducing extermination procedures into England. According to
his secretary, Blanche Patch, he startled a group of simple Lan-
cashire chapel-goers with his remedy for idlers: "I would like to
take everyone before a tribunal, and, if it were found that they
were not doing as much for the community as the community
was doing for them, I would give them a few days to make their
peace and then put them in the lethal chamber." Miss Patch insists on her employer's perfect sincerity in advancing this proposal, and it is of course an extension of his frequently pro-
pounded belief that all incorrigible criminals should be killed.
That he nonetheless took pleasure in imagining the work of the
lethal chambers can be demonstrated by an important inconsistency in his reasoning. Whenever he upheld another of his favorite proposals, equal pay for everyone, he argued that the social
value of different types of work was far too elusive to measure. Yet
he ignores this crucial argument when advocating extermination
tribunals. Such tribunals, he seems eager to convince himself,
could exactly measure every individual's social contribution and
kill all who fell one jot short of the mark. In fact, impatient even
with the pretense of concern for the individual, Shaw baldly announced in 1945 that he favored "ruthlessly exterminating the
poor in spite of their amiable jollity and charity, and burying the
rich along with them." (Since he also hated the middle class, it is
hard to say who besides Shaw himself would be left in his uto
pia.)* He held that Britain could imitate Russia's "ultra-democratic system" by liquidating all slackers and all people "who
want to be free all the time." He urged that "what the Russians
can do we can do," and he confided that "a great part of the secret
of the success of Russian Communism is that every Russian
knows that unless he makes his life a paying proposition for his
country he will probably lose it." The same man who once exposed loose political language, and the euphemisms with which
capitalism cloaked its barbarities and science hid its errors, now
became the man who redefined democracy to mean its negation

---

*Even in the "Peroration" to *The Intelligent Woman's Guide to Socialism and
Capitalism* (London, 1928), Shaw wrote, "For my part I hate the poor and look forward eagerly to their extermination. I pity the rich a little, but am equally bent on
their extermination. The working classes, the business classes, the professional
classes, the propertied classes, the ruling classes, are each more odious than the
other: they have no right to live; I should despair if I did not know that they will
all die presently, and that there is no need on earth why they should be replaced by
people like themselves" (p. 456).

and dubbed himself "a Totalitarian Democrat," who used euphemisms like "weeding the garden" and "cleansing the community" to justify communist murders, and who sought to make extermination respectable by saying it would be done "scientifically" and "put on a scientific basis."

IV

This, then, is the sad general context of political opinion in which *The Simpleton* must be placed, and it leads us to the immediate context of an essay published just before the play was begun. This essay is attached as a preface to *On the Rocks*, Shaw's preceding play, though it bears hardly any relationship to that work. Instead, it clarifies the inner impulses of *The Simpleton* far more than does the play's official preface, which was merely an angry response to the New York critics' unfavorable reception of that play's premiere in February 1935. The official preface instructs those critics on the supposed moral of the play, but it actually narrows the meanings of the work and conveys an authorial certainty belied by the work itself. Shaw here ignores the three-quarters of the play that did not at all deal with a Judgment Day, declaring that he wished to present "an up-to-date Vision of Judgment" and in effect to justify "the special inquisitionary work of the Tcheka [the Soviet Secret Police]," and the right of their tribunals to determine whether "people were public spirited enough to live in a Communist society, and, if not, to blow their brains out as public nuisances." As he converts the preface into an occasion for Soviet apologetics, he neglects the play's prominent polygamy motif, and then finally notices and dismisses it in a concluding paragraph.

In contrast to this subsequently written preface, which simply compounds *The Simpleton*'s confusions, the earlier essay reveals the emotional conflict that was then carried over into the play. The essay begins by reflecting one of the elements of that conflict in an enthusiasm for Russia's policy of exterminating people:

The planners of the Soviet State have no time to bother about moribund questions; for they are confronted with the new and overwhelming necessity for exterminating the peasants, who still exist in formidable numbers. The notion that a civilized State can be made out of any sort of human material is one of our old Radical delusions. As to building Communism with such trash as the Capitalist system produces it is out of the question.

42

Shaw rejects "the notion that persons should be safe from extermination as long as they do not commit wilful murder" or other specified crimes:

But the most elaborate code of this sort would still have left unspecified a hundred ways in which wreckers of Communism could have sidetracked it without ever having to face the essential questions: are you pulling your weight in the social boat? are you giving more trouble than you are worth? have you earned the privilege of living in a civilized community? That is why the Russians were forced to set up an Inquisition or Star Chamber, called at first the Cheka and now the Gay Pay Oo (Ogpu), to go into these questions and "liquidate" persons who could not answer them satisfactorily.

It seems that Shaw would have all citizens considered guilty until they proved themselves innocent, and would have all Russian prisons practically empty. He scorns the principle of legal restraint on those who wield power:

It may be quite impossible to convict a forestaller or regrator under a criminal code of having taken a single illegal step, but quite easy to convince any reasonable body of judges that he is what the people call "a wrong one." In Russia such a conviction would lead to his disappearance and the receipt by his family of a letter to say that they need not wait up for him, as he would not return home any more.

At this point, eager to advise and protect the gentlemen who run the secret police, Shaw adds this egregious footnote: "Note, however, that a sentence of extermination should never be so certain as to make it worth the delinquent's while to avoid arrest by murdering his or her pursuers."

The quiet gloating over all these prospective exterminations is as unmistakable as it is repellent, and it accounts for Shaw's strange worry that killings may cease once private property is completely abolished and every able-bodied person has an equal share in the national dividend. Would then, he anxiously inquires, "the practice of extermination thereupon disappear?" And immediately he reassures himself that the killings "might continue much more openly and intelligently and scientifically than at present" and hopes further that extermination will someday "become a humane science."

Shaw seeks to distinguish between extermination and cruelty, but he overlooks his own cruelty of tone and the ways in which the police will have their own cruel impulses abetted by being allowed to eliminate anyone they deem unfit. Shaw refuses to imagine the pain of the victims and their families, the terror of waiting for the knock on the door. (His only word of sympathy is for the "unfortunate Commissar" who "with his own hand [had to] shoot stationmasters who had thrown his telegrams into the dustbin instead of attending to them," and Shaw kept on his mantelpiece a picture of that efficient commissar and later organizer of the secret police, the "gentle Djerjinsky" as he called him elsewhere.) By exposing this very need to crush imagination and to do away with all thoughts of human love, the essay clarifies what is happening in *The Simpleton*, since there too Shaw had to destroy love and imagination, and there too we hear the grunts of delight as he vicariously wipes out vast numbers of Englishmen.

But if this essay illuminates the Judgment Day episode in *The Simpleton*, it also casts light on the utopian episode as well. For there comes a remarkable moment in the essay when, after having appeased his bloodlust in defending exterminations, Shaw finally begins to think again and to undercut everything he has just said. His egotism struggles to rescue him from the folly of his position as he realizes that he would not even have been born in a country that exterminated such socially useless individuals as his own father. The polemicist who had been calling for a "weeding of the garden" suddenly offers opposite horticultural advice:

It is true that in the generations of men continuous high cultivation is not expedient: there must be fallows, or at least light croppings, between the intense cultivations; for we cannot expect the very energetic and vital Napoleon to be the son of an equally energetic father or the father of an equally vital son. Nobody has yet calculated how many lazy ancestors it takes to produce an indefatigable prodigy. . . . There may be as good biological reasons for the existence of the workshy as of the workmad. Even one and the same person may have spells of intense activity and slackness varying from weeks to years.

With such comments everyone can readily agree, though we may wonder how this tolerance can be reconciled with the demand that one must always pull one's weight in the boat. The positions are in fact irreconcilable, a truth Shaw clearly senses. For after shuffling back and forth in the argument, glibly misstating the case for tolerance put forward by Socrates and John Stuart Mill, absurdly declaring that he himself is not "free to say and write" what he pleases, he finally stops trying to solve the problem he has created and transposes the question to a higher level in an imagined conversation between Jesus and Pilate, which at last gives him the opportunity to use his mind unrestrictedly, to identify with opposite positions, and to state the advantages of toleration. "Terror drives men mad," Jesus declares, and "you must not judge me lest you be yourself judged."

Without sedition and blasphemy the world would stand still and the kingdom of God never be a stage nearer. The Roman Empire began with a wolf suckling two human infants. If these infants had not been wiser than their fostermother your empire would be a pack of wolves. It is by children who are wiser than their fathers, subjects who are wiser than their emperors, beggars and vagrants who are wiser than their priests, that men rise from being beasts of prey.

When Pilate insists that governments must rule with "a salutary severity," Jesus quickly interrupts: "Oh please! You must excuse me, noble Governor; but I am so made by God that official phrases make me violently sick. Salutary severity is ipecacuanha to me." Regrettably, Shaw himself overcame this sensitivity to euphemisms when he resorted to such phrases as "weeding the garden." And here he also acknowledges that mere reason will not decide the behavior of those in authority:

If it is your will to crucify me [Jesus continues], I can find you a dozen reasons for doing so; and your police can supply you with a hundred facts to support the reasons. If it is your will to spare me I can find you just as many reasons for that; and my disciples will supply you with more facts than you will have time or patience to listen to. That is why your lawyers can plead as well for one side as another.

In these too few pages of interpolated debate Shaw breaks loose from the constraints of his communist apologetics and from the cruel impulses they sanctioned, recaptures the libertarianism of his earlier years, and dramatically projects his own divided will— or at least admonishes himself against his own destructive will. Yet by giving the victory to Jesus and the cause of toleration, he of course realizes that he has contradicted his earlier argument in favor of governmentally enforced orthodoxy. In the essay's concluding paragraphs he tries unsuccessfully to harmonize the two positions, and then at the very end he overrides his self-admonition and justifies once again governmental rule by terror.

V

Now exactly this same oscillation is duplicated in *The Simpleton*, although there the underlying sequence of thought and feeling appears in reverse order. Whereas the essay first justifies mass extermination, then moves into a defense of humaneness, and ends with a bland reaffirmation of the need for killing, the play starts with bland acts of killing, moves toward a humane utopia, and ends with supposedly justified deeds of mass extermination. The totality of essay and play thus completes a circle and Shaw arrives back at his starting point, arrives back where his destructive impulses had been carrying him—impulses no doubt intensified by the chaotic world of the early 1930's. At one point in the essay he tries to turn away from that world into the past, and the resulting debate between Jesus and Pilate is the best part of the essay because it gives scope to a variety of feelings. In the play he turns away from the contemporary world into the future, and the utopian section is best because again the subject permitted the exercise of varied feelings. The destructiveness could be kept under control and counterbalanced by life-affirming impulses. But as we have seen earlier, the strength of Shaw's desire to fashion a utopia was weakened even as he created it—he had to fortify his own old age by attacking youth and its capacities—and this so loosened the restraints on the destructiveness that the latter part of *The Simpleton* is turned into an execution chamber, with the giggles of its architect rebounding from the walls. It may have been a healthy desire to keep his destructive impulses at arm's length that made Shaw begin the play many years away from the final action, so far away in fact that one wonders whether he began with a Vision of Judgment in mind at all. In any case he seems to have been seeking to delay the point of attack, dramaturgically and emotionally. And then of course when the Judgment Day does come, it comes without sufficient preparation, and he has not allowed himself enough theatrical time to remedy the defect. The technical confusions of the play, in short, ultimately derive from Shaw's immense and understandable uneasiness over the particular emotions pressing for release. This uneasiness is also responsible for the curious disjointedness in many of the shorter passages of the play, miniature versions of the larger structural disunity, and for a kind of hovering effect as Shaw seems doubtful on which side of an issue to take his stand— the fluctuation over the wisdom of "letting life come to you" being only the most conspicuous instance.

But Shaw's anxiety over his destructive impulses stimulated other and more positive responses as well, not least of all his humor. We may notice in the following passage, when Iddy rushes in to inform the collective parents of Maya's death, how both direct statement and humor have the same end of annulling the significance of murder:

IDDY: Heaven and earth shall pass away; but I shall not pass away. That is what she said. And then there was nothing in my arms. Nothing. Nothing in my arms. Heaven and earth would pass away; but the love of Maya would never pass away. And there was nothing.

PRA: Do you mean that she died in your arms?

IDDY: Died? No. I tell you there was nothing. Dont you understand? Where she had just been there was nothing. There never had been anything.

PROLA: And the others? Quick, Pra: go and find the others.

PRA: What others?

PROLA: The other three: our children. I forget their names.

IDDY: They said "Our names shall live forever." What were their names?

HYERING: They have gone clean out of my head.

SIR CHARLES: Most extraordinary. I cant for the life of me remember. How many of them did you say there were, Prola?

PROLA: Four. Or was it four hundred?

[11]

The feebleness of the humor should not obscure its aim of minimizing both the cruelty and the importance of the murders. The humor tries to bribe us to forgo a moral judgment on the events. Shaw clearly enjoys the callousness of the joking, as he enjoyed the extermination reports from England that we sampled a few pages back; but such open displays of enjoyment (though inadvertently confirming the presence of Shaw's sadism) mark the decline of his humor. Still, the wonderful humor of Shaw's prime, though less self-indulgent, was equally intent on either blocking his destructive impulses or else rendering them acceptable.

Similarly, the energy behind the wonderful talk in the major plays was often heightened by the same need to block the destructiveness or to justify it. In *The Simpleton* the talk, like the humor, is attenuated by the general weakening of Shaw's powers, but this very decline in brilliance exposes the lurking predisposition to violence within the dialogue. Thus Shaw prepares us to tolerate the forthcoming murders by having Iddy sermonize against love. At times, however, the talk gravitates to the absolute center of Shaw's destructive urge, and then a curious phenomenon occurs. Notice in this exchange the implicit condemnation of the homicidal impulse:

IDDY: We must believe that to establish that beautiful and good world on earth is the best thing we can do, and the only sort of religion and politics that is worth bothering about.

PROLA: What about the people who have no original ideas, Iddy?

PRA: The great majority of mankind?

IDDY: Theyll be only too glad to do what you tell them, Prola, if you can make them feel that it's right.

47

PROLA: And if they are incapable of feeling it?
JANGA: Kill.
KANCHIN: Kill.
VASHTI: Kill.
MAYA: Kill.
PROLA: They can do that as easily as I. Any fool can. And there are
more of them.   [11]

No matter that in this passage the youngsters' characterization
has been altered, or that the supposedly high-minded priestess rejects mass murder on grounds of expediency rather than morality.
Of greater importance is Shaw's recognition of the thirst for blood
and his condemnation of it. Yet shortly afterwards he brings on
the Angel to begin the killing! It is as if his conscience blazons
a warning against the oncoming destructiveness and is then ignored. We have seen a few moments ago this same procedure in the
Jesus/Pilate debate when Shaw in effect cautions himself against
his destructive will and then dismisses the admonition. Since the
presence as well as the wide-ranging significance of this mechanism in Shaw's work has never been recognized, I shall take the
liberty of naming it for future referral the Unattended Admonition. In the above passage we have the mechanism in its barest
and least interesting form, but underneath the elaborate variations in other plays lies a similar warning against the upsurging
destructive impulse and then a rejection of that warning. Contrastingly, on many other occasions he attends to the admonition
and maneuvers against his destructiveness.

Besides arousing the humor and the talk into activity, Shaw's
anxiety over his destructive impulses also stimulated his fantasizing power. It is not accidental that *The Simpleton* contains the
most numerous killings in all of Shaw's work and at the same time
the most fanciful of all his stage characters, an angel. The parti-
colored garb of fantasy is stitched together to disguise the destructive yearnings, exactly as had been done in that earlier life-hating
fantasy *Back to Methuselah*. Superficially, Shaw's imagination
seems intensely at work, yet in truth it is fancy serving as a substitute for imagination, at least that imagination of reality displayed in his better plays. The power of imagining other people's
feelings, which Maya and Vashti are credited with, is deliberately
curbed in the play, and the girls are destroyed, quite as if their
imagination and compassion threatened Shaw and the venting of
his destructiveness. Still, his conscience did require the reassurance that all this was unreal, mere fancy; and as if to be doubly

reassuring he attempted to remove the work even further from reality by fitfully making it allegorical. Thus the Indian names of some of the characters have obvious mythological overtones, the sexually irresistible male priest Pra, for example, probably deriving his name from Prajâpati, the familiar potency figure of Buddhist legend and the protector of those who beget children. Similarly the name of the girl Maya, meaning literally "illusion," is the name of the famous queen mother of Buddha. But these and other possible mythological references are not worth dwelling on since the allegory is hardly sustained and is at best decorative. It is part of the protective fancifulness of the play as a whole, a bromide to Shaw's conscience, allowing him to hide his pleasure in killing off the ravishing blonde and to say that she was never real anyway, a Maya, or, as he declared afterward, a "phantasm."

VI

The one thing that the destructive impulses did not stimulate, however, was thought. In finally turning *The Simpleton* into an execution chamber, and in claiming its "moral" to be the need to set up tribunals "from which worthless people will not come out alive," Bernard Shaw the thinker discloses his intellectual bankruptcy. And with this added to those other sources of septuagenarian futility we have already examined, it is not surprising that in the early 1930's thoughts of suicide seem to have been moving through Shaw's mind. "I feel apologetic for my existence," he had written to Mrs. Campbell two years before completing the present play, "now that all decent men of my age are committing suicide. . . . But I can still write to some purpose, and so I must brazen it out until some assassin saves me the trouble of shooting myself." In the penultimate sentence of the preface to *On the Rocks*, he oddly remarks that "people with any tenderness of conscience will feel the deepest misgivings as to whether they are really worth keeping alive in a highly civilized community"; in the prologue of *The Simpleton* he shows us two attempted suicides, one of which is successful; in the beginning of the next work, *The Millionairess*, he introduces a heroine who intends to commit suicide. That all these suicides are treated comically indicates only Shaw's characteristic way of dealing with threatening emotions. But being Shaw he also had to find some rationale for staying alive, and in a sense he provides it in the last scene of *The Simpleton*, in that undesignated epilogue whose earlier passages on love we have already considered. Now, at the end, the woman tries to cheer up her husband with a new resolve:

We shall plan commonwealths when our empires have brought us to the brink of destruction; but our plans will still lead us to the Unexpected Isles. We shall make wars because only under the strain of war are we capable of changing the world; but the changes our wars will make will never be the changes we intended them to make. We shall clamor for security like frightened children; but in the Unexpected Isles there is no security; and the future is to those who prefer surprise and wonder to security. I, Prola, shall live and grow because surprise and wonder are the very breath of my being, and routine is death to me. Let every day be a day of wonder for me and I shall not fear the Day of Judgment.

[11]

Perhaps these lines should not be given too much weight. Even for a death-filled fantasy, Shaw liked to provide an upbeat ending. But if the words are to have any serious import, then clearly he has no social advice to offer here except the making of wars for the sake of change, wars that will cost the two old people nothing. Their callousness and unearned sense of superiority go unnoticed by Shaw's satiric eye. Instead he recommends, as consolation for the vanity of social causes, a welcoming attitude toward experience— irreproachable advice, certainly, but akin to the bravado of Robert Browning's "Greet the unseen with a cheer!" It would be unfair to discredit Shaw's advice that people should ignore security by recalling that it is being offered by a rich man traveling on a luxury liner. It is enough to mention its limited value and its irrelevance to the social reforms that Shaw had advocated for decades. One may respect the personal resolve of a disillusioned old man to meet the future with a modicum of energy and wonder. One is saddened at how very little the sage has left to say.

Thus *The Simpleton*'s misanthropy is partially deflected at the end toward a mild acceptance of life. The contempt for mankind remains, however, and only the old couple are immune from that contempt. Although Shaw may be lightly caricaturing himself in the figure of Iddy, he does not come to grips with his own illogicality, for if man is monstrous then no member of the species is exempt. It may be that to keep himself alive at the age of seventy-eight, to avoid the discouragement unto death that afflicts the old gentleman in *Back to Methuselah*, Shaw could not allow himself to remember either that great moment when Swift's Gulliver realizes that he too is a Yahoo and detests the sight of himself reflected in a lake, or the tragic absurdity of Molière's misanthrope, who forgives himself for the very follies he derides in others. Shaw may come close to depicting his own current condition when he has Pra remark to Prola that they are "a union of a madwoman with a fool"; but since this is said teasingly and is then ignored as the old couple plan new commonwealths, the self-criticism in no way penetrates the play. The unpleasant taste we carry away from a reading of *The Simpleton*, apart from its many confusions and its many killings, its advocacy of execution chambers and wars, is finally caused by the self-pampering dishonesty at its core, by the writer's refusal to include himself in the wide sweep of his misanthropy. Evidently Shaw forgot, when the angels were weeding out "the useless people, the mischievous people, the selfish somebodies and the noisy nobodies," that he too had once been a noisy nobody, had long been regarded as a mischievous person, and was now writing like a selfish somebody.

For all its inadequacies as a play, then, *The Simpleton* provides a magnified view of basic Shavian impulses and conflicts, and of some of his ways of dealing with them. The benign utopian section of the play on the one side, and the harsh Judgment Day section on the other, reflect two halves of the writer himself—the one idealistic, humane, and altruistic, the other destructive, misanthropic, and self-admiring. It is unnecessary to attribute primacy to either set of impulses though obviously the destructive ones often took the lead and then evoked their countering impulses, Shaw's social conscience rousing itself to fight against his destructive yearnings. It is also at present unnecessary to distinguish other than by name between the sadistic and homicidal components of the destructiveness, or to remind ourselves that a marked sadistic streak can coexist with beneficent impulses—de Sade himself having been tenderhearted toward his wife and his children, and Shaw himself notably generous toward scores of people throughout his long lifetime. What is truly essential to grasp is that the conflict between the two halves of Shaw's temperament lies at the heart of his writings and that the very methods he used to mediate the conflict—the humor, the talk, the fancy, the intellectuality—have hitherto camouflaged its existence. But having now perceived this fundamental conflict in a late play, we may look for it in earlier works also; and we will immediately do so by turning back some fifty years to the first work in which he himself dealt with his antisocial impulses, the aptly entitled novel *An Unsocial Socialist*.

3

An Unsocial Socialist

THE BARBED PLEA

For the fox not only declares that the grapes he cannot get are sour: he also insists that the sloes he *can* get are sweet.

Shaw, *The Quintessence of Ibsenism*

Yet each man kills the thing he loves,
By each let this be heard,
Some do it with a bitter look,
Some with a flattering word.

Oscar Wilde, "The Ballad of Reading Gaol"

Overleaf: Alice Lockett.

I

 SHAW was aware of his powerful antisocial impulses as early as his twenties, when he methodically completed five unpublished novels, the last of which, obliquely autobiographical, he entitled *An Unsocial Socialist*. This work, originally called "The Heartless Man," has the unevenness of the other novels but is of particular interest in throwing light on its author's ways of dealing with his supposed heartlessness and also with a severe personal crisis, for it was written during Shaw's love affair with a nursing student named Alice Lockett. The strains of this relationship, in which his emotions appear to have been more intensely involved than Miss Lockett's, spurred him to seek relief in writing about her and to her, and the novel is at once a self-justifying attack on the young woman and possibly a plea for her hand in marriage.*

But before considering the romantic aspect of the book, which is its emotional center, it will be useful to glance at its pretensions as a socialist novel. Shaw himself chose to emphasize only this facet when he commented on the book several decades later. He said he had intended it to be the first chapters of a vast work "depicting capitalist society in dissolution," but found after finishing the present text that he had nothing more to say. A Shaw without words on political matters seems improbable, and perhaps this indirectly confirms that he was not mainly concerned with politics in the novel at all, even though he wrote the book in the same year he converted to Marxism. In any case it was fortunate that he abandoned the exposure of capitalist society since the passages devoted to it are awkwardly handled. In one incident, for example, a shepherd seeks shelter in the girls' college which is the setting for most of the first half of the novel. The shepherd's house has just been wrecked in a storm, and he remarks to the headmistress on the cruelty of the gentry toward their tenants, noting that "the poor gets poorer and the rich richer

---

*The work appeared in the Socialist monthly *Today* from Mar. to Dec., 1884, and Shaw sent copies to Alice through her older sister Jane.

every day." Shaw, having made his Marxian point, then drops the shepherd from a plot in which he had so abruptly appeared. In the second half of the novel, which takes place at the country home of Sir Charles Brandon, Shaw again introduces some workers, this time marching in protest against the baronet for walling off a road on his estate. After this short intrusive scene, little more is heard about the road, the workers, or the cruelties of the parasitic aristocracy. Nor is much heard about the ruthlessness of capitalism even though Shaw makes available to himself a representative of the capitalists in the person of the banker John Jansenius, who functions in the plot as the supposedly inadequate father of the hero's wife, Henrietta. In fact the only rich businessman present is that hero himself, Sidney Trefusis, a self-appointed socialist leader.

Neither through character nor incident, then, is Shaw able to meet his supposed goal of depicting capitalist society in dissolution. Instead he resorts to the outright lecture, as Trefusis offers monologues on labor-value theory, the evils of enclosure, the self-destructiveness of free trade, and so forth—tiresome lectures despite Shaw's attempt to enliven them with wit. In effect Shaw the novelist rests his pen to listen to Shaw the Marxist preach the new gospel. These speeches in no way serve as generalized comment on the story, which moves in other directions. And perhaps it is even because the story turns far more on the conflict between the sexes than between the classes that Shaw's social conscience impels him to insert the lectures, which are intended to show that both he and his surrogate Trefusis are men of feeling concerned with the plight of the poor.

Trefusis himself preoccupies Shaw, and if the work has little value as a political novel or as a critique of capitalism, it is largely because Shaw is busy fashioning for himself a new model hero, the superman as socialist. Trefusis dominates the novel, and not always to its advantage, for the early scenes at the college before he appears are the most delightful in the book, enlivened by the pranks of the clever Agatha Wylie, leader of the fifth-form girls. Trefusis later appears at the college disguised as a laborer named Smilash in order to hide from his wife, a clinging woman who soon conveniently dies. Trefusis claims that his alias Smilash is compounded of *smile* and *eyelash*, but this derivation is received with justified doubt since he in fact enjoys applying the lash of irony and mockery with a smile. He also enjoys flattering the young women, especially Agatha and her friends Gertrude and

Jane; and Agatha actually falls in love with him. In the second part of the novel, several years later, Trefusis reappears in his own person as a neighbor of Sir Charles and of Lady Jane, who has invited her old schoolmates Agatha and Gertrude down for a stay at Brandon Manor. Trefusis soon reawakens Agatha's love for him and captures Gertrude's as well. He dominates everyone by his forcefulness, assurance, and verbal skill. He exposes the aesthetic pretensions of Sir Charles and provisionally converts him to socialism, cures Gertrude of her snobbery and makes her promise to marry the lovelorn poet Erskine, and at the end persuades Agatha to accept his own marriage proposal. A vigorous and decisive man, forthright in declaring his convictions, indifferent both to social forms and to lying if it achieves his ends, Trefusis is more convincing as a superior being than were Shaw's earlier novelistic heroes Owen Jack and Conolly, for whereas their genius as composer and inventor had to be taken for granted, Trefusis's brilliance as a speaker is almost too amply demonstrated.

Shaw is of course creating in Trefusis a model for himself, an alter ego, as Gordon Ray has observed, which allowed him vicariously to play out "that grand public rejection of the Victorian social order which his narrow circumstances gave him no opportunity of making in his own person." He boldly exhibits, not a saintly socialist, but one with many of the faults usually ascribed to socialists—irreverence and impiety, contempt for accepted norms, disregard for the sanctity of marriage—and he wants to show that even in these respects Trefusis is a worthy man. Yet at the same time Shaw is attempting something more challenging, the portrayal of his very own self magnified; he is exploring certain aspects of himself and is intermixing self criticism and self-justification in ways that make it amusingly difficult to distinguish between them. Trefusis for example acknowledges his "selfish nature" and the likelihood that he is deficient in the average man's share of "natural affection." He finds himself at times possessed of an impulse to cut cruelly into people in order to test their reactions, "the curiosity of the vivisector," as he calls it. His self-righteousness and his presumption in instructing others he condemns in a double-edged comment: "With my egotism, my charlatanry, my tongue, and my habit of having my own way, I am fit for no calling but that of saviour of mankind—just of the sort they like." Shaw devotes an entire chapter to Trefusis's response to the death of his nineteen-year-old wife, Henrietta, and as we encounter the following passage from that chapter we cannot be sure exactly how much of Trefusis's callousness Shaw wishes to expose and how much he simply does not see.

Death seemed to have cancelled her marriage and womanhood; he had never seen her look so young. A minute passed, and then a tear dropped on the coverlet. He started; shook another tear on his hand, and stared at it incredulously.

"This is a fraud of which I have never even dreamed," he said. "Tears and no sorrow! Here am I crying! growing maudlin! whilst I am glad that she is gone and I free. I have the mechanism of grief in me somewhere; it begins to turn at sight of her, though I have no sorrow; just as she used to start the mechanism of passion when I had no love. And that made no difference to her; whilst the wheels went round she was satisfied. I hope the mechanism of grief will flag and stop in its spinning as soon as the other used to. It is stopping already, I think. What a mockery! Whilst it lasts I suppose I am really sorry. And yet, would I restore her to life if I could? Perhaps so; I am therefore thankful that I cannot." He folded his arms on the rai! and gravely addressed the dead figure, which still affected him so strongly that he had to exert his will to face it with composure. "If you really loved me, it is well for you that you are dead—idiot that I was to believe that the passion you could inspire, you poor child, would last. We are both lucky; I have escaped from you, and you have escaped from yourself." . . .

He touched the cheek with a faint attempt at roughness, to feel how cold it was. Then he touched his own, and remarked:

"This is what I am hastening toward at the express speed of sixty minutes an hour!" He stood looking down at the face and tasting this sombre reflection for a long time. When it palled on him, he roused himself, and exclaimed more cheerfully:

"After all, she is not dead. Every word she uttered, every idea she formed and expressed, was an inexhaustible and indestructible impulse." He paused, considered a little further, and relapsed into gloom, adding: "And the dozen others whose names will be with hers in the Times tomorrow? Their words too are still in the air, to endure there to all eternity. Hm! How the air must be crammed with nonsense! Two sounds sometimes produce a silence; perhaps ideas neutralize one another in some analogous way. No, my dear; you are dead and gone and done with, and I shall be dead and gone and done with too soon to leave me leisure to fool myself with hopes of immortality. Poor Hetty! Well, good-bye my darling. Let us pretend for a moment that you can hear that; I know it will please you."

All this was in a half-articulate whisper. When he ceased he still bent over the body, gazing intently at it. Even when he had exhausted the subject, and turned to go, he changed his mind, and looked again for a while. Then he stood erect, apparently nerved and refreshed, and left the room with a firm step.

It would appear that Shaw wants the honesty of Trefusis's reactions to serve as a decent substitute for their insensitivity. Yet we cannot decide whether even the novelist himself would reject the notion that Hetty's death was a lucky one. Shaw certainly seems to find no fault, either, in Trefusis's characteristic method of insisting on the miseries of the masses as a means of distracting attention from his own personal culpability and his want of feeling. His running away from his wife had been the basic cause of the events leading to her death, and his flirtation with Agatha had been the more proximate cause, yet he shows no remorse for his behavior. Instead, he freely questions the genuineness of other people's feelings about Hetty's death. "Jansenius," he declares, "can bear death and misery with perfect fortitude when it is on a large scale and hidden in a back slum. But when it breaks into his own house, and attacks his property—his daughter was his property until very recently—he is just the man to lose his head and quarrel with me for keeping mine." He soon damns the parents' feelings and curses them for not sparing "their feelings for the living, on whose behalf I have often appealed to them in vain"— though he himself has egregiously ignored Hetty's feelings! And just before he leaves the house he lashes out at the bereaved father, accusing him of loving only his own respectability. Trefusis's virtue, in sum, is supposedly established by his attack on the sincerity of other people and by his dedication to the cause of socialism.

That dedication itself, however, is less high-minded than Trefusis and Shaw would have us believe. Trefusis has found that "socialism is often misunderstood by its least intelligent supporters and opponents to mean simply unrestrained indulgence of our natural propensity to heave bricks at respectable persons." Yet his own socialist activities give him a more refined form of the same pleasure. He has for instance made a collection of contrasting photographs of the wretched tenements of the poor and the luxurious stables of the rich, and he intends to "harrow" the feelings of the rich until they join him in removing the evil. When he shows his collection to Sir Charles Brandon and the poet Erskine, he is pleased by their distress. His own concern for the poor seems more self-enhancing than disinterested. For the most part he regards the poor as slaves needing to be freed by enlightened leaders such as himself. The apparent goodness of the working class springs from lack of opportunity to be as corrupt as their capitalist masters. (As soon as a young mason makes some money with Trefusis's help, he sets up shop as a small capitalist and exploits his own workers.) Trefusis knows that socialism will improve the material condition of the poor, but he has less faith that it will improve their character. Self-made capitalists like his own father, whatever their morality, are men of intelligence and energy, whereas the poor show little of either quality. Indeed Trefusis wonders whether he is not foolishly working to create "an international association of creatures only fit for destruction." Later when the workers accuse him of profiteering in their cause, and actually mob and stone him, he occupies himself only in planning the reorganization of industry and in attacking his own class. It may be concluded that socialism appeals to Trefusis—and perhaps to his creator as well—because he is a rebel looking for a cause, an intellectual seeking a coherent system of thought, a practical man struck by the inefficiencies and waste of capitalism, and a moral man outraged by its injustices; but socialism also gives him the pleasure of heaving verbal bricks at respectable persons and of proving to himself and to others that he is a humane man, a need all the greater because his feelings toward the poor are tinged with contempt and an occasional desire to wipe them out altogether.

Shaw's delight in Trefusis exceeds what a reader is likely to feel, and he is treated more leniently than any other figure in the novel. Shaw admires Trefusis's trick of getting Sir Charles to sign a petition that in effect calls all employers felons. He also admires his talent for flattering women and turning their heads. Trefusis may at one point admonish the school's headmistress against coercing the students into sharing her own convictions, but throughout the book he ignores the admonition himself, freely manipulating people for their own supposed good, and with his creator's approval. For Shaw, all is finally forgiven Trefusis because his heartlessness is only apparent and he ministers to the socialist ideal. For us, on the other hand, despite a saving degree of self-criticism and realism, Trefusis seems a dangerous man to entrust with political power; and the young author's admiration for him is ominous in view of his later regard for dictators.

Shaw's enthusiasm for his hero also seems to blind him to Trefusis's inconsistent pronouncements on love. Love, the hero insists, "is not to be despised when it comes from a fine nature." Erskine the poet, in love with Gertrude, apparently has such a nature, and Trefusis spends most of the last third of the book pleading with Gertrude to marry "the poor man who loves you," finally winning her promise to do so. He himself will marry again, this time Agatha Wylie, and though he views this union as a prosaic arrangement, in which he will acquire "a genial partner for domestic business" and a mother for his future children, he knows that Agatha loves him and that he is charmed with her, which therefore insures what he calls "a consoling dash of romance in the transaction." Yet despite his busy activities as matchmaker for Erskine and himself, despite too his flirtatiousness, he affects to be quite superior to the need for love and cynical toward its manifestations. Here for instance is how he accounts for his early conduct with Agatha:

"I amuse myself by paying a few compliments to a schoolgirl for whom I do not care two straws more than for any agreeable and passably clever woman I meet. Nevertheless, I occasionally feel a pang of remorse because I think that she may love me seriously, although I am only playing with her. I pity the poor heart I have wantonly ensnared. And, all the time, she is pitying me for exactly the same reason! She is conscience-stricken because she is only indulging in the luxury of being adored by 'by far the cleverest man she has ever met,' [as Agatha called him] and is as heart-whole as I am! Ha, ha! That is the basis of the religion of love of which poets are the high-priests. Each worshipper knows that his own love is either a transient passion or a sham copied from his favorite poem; but he believes honestly in the love of others for him."

And further along he declares that "love is an overrated passion; it would be irremediably discredited but that young people, and the romancers who live upon their follies, have a perpetual interest in rehabilitating it." But, with additional inconsistency, Trefusis elsewhere implies that he personally finds it impossible to control himself with a woman. "The first condition of work with me is your absence," he tells Henrietta. "When you are with me, I can do nothing but make love to you. You bewitch me." In another place, again, we are told that lovemaking for Trefusis was "only a pleasant sort of trifling, enhanced by a dash of sadness in the reflection that it meant so little." Yet, in further contradiction, he comes to keep his dead wife's portrait constantly before him in his study to correct his "natural amativeness." "A glance at my lost Hetty has cured me of the slightest inclination to marry," he cruelly boasts—though soon afterwards he is arranging his marriage to Agatha—and this despite his claim that he "was not made for domestic bliss." Trefusis, in short, is ludicrously confused in his pronouncements on love and in his behavior toward women, though Shaw himself seems hardly aware of it.

The reason for the hero's inconsistencies can be discerned if we now move on to relate the book to Shaw's own life, a procedure which also will enable us to see the first appearance of a pattern that will repeat itself in his later work.

II

An Unsocial Socialist, written in just under four months of 1883, was the most rapidly composed of Shaw's novels. It was written at the height of his relationship with Alice Lockett, a nursing student who took music lessons from Shaw's mother. The surviving correspondence indicates that the young woman was drawn to Shaw but unable to adapt herself to his seriocomic manner. He was also a political radical, an upstart, and a hand-to-mouth writer without definite prospects—not at all a likely candidate for marriage. For his part, Shaw was totally in love, but he was still able to criticize what he considered to be Alice's snobbery and her thirst for respectability. There is no outright evidence that he proposed to her, yet the letters contain enough hints to suggest that he contemplated marriage and may have discussed it with her. The first extant letter, written two years after he and Alice had met, and while he was working on the present novel, shows that they had been quarreling:

Forgive me. I dont know why, on my honor; but in playing on my own thoughts for the entertainment of the most charming of companions last night, I unskilfully struck a note that pained her—unless she greatly deceived me. I have felt remorseful ever since. . . . I cannot (or perhaps will not) resist the impulse to write to you. Believe nothing that I say—and I have a wicked tongue, a deadly pen, and a cold heart—I shall be angry with myself tomorrow for sending you this, and yet, when I next meet you, I shall plunge headlong into fresh cause for anger.

Alice replied the next day:

May I ask what was the object of your letter to me? Did you think it necessary to revive the pain caused by your words of last evening? All people are not machines: some are capable of genuine feelings. You know very well you have the power of paining me, and you are not very careful in exercising it. You have done it over and over again. As I cannot accuse you of want of discrimination, I presume you enjoy the power you possess. Your letter proves what I have many times told you—that you are one of the weakest men I have ever met; and in spite of your cleverness I cannot help despising you.

And a month later, a note from her read: "That is right, put your own construction on what people say, be wilfully blunt. How dense you are! You [don't] even give me the benefit of a serious mood. If you did, perhaps I might understand you."

Shaw responded in a variety of ways to these attacks. Occasionally he allowed his vexation to show through: "Am I a dancing bear or a learned pig that I should be insulted thus?" Or again:

I will be your slave no longer: you used me vilely when we met before, and you disappointed me horribly tonight. I recant every word I have ever said to you, and plead temporary insanity as my excuse for having uttered them. I am exceedingly glad that I had not to wait another half hour at that waiting room. I detest the entire universe. I did nothing all the time but tell you monstrous lies –I wonder you can be so credulous as to believe my transparent flatteries. I say the same things to everybody. . . . Must I eternally flatter flatter flatter flatter flatter?

At other times he almost abased himself:

I am sorry that I offend you by not being serious. I am sorrier that I please you still less when I am serious, . . . Granted that I am a buffoon—one whose profession it is to bribe people to listen to me by literary antics such as silly tales of lovemaking and so forth. But has anyone been more serious with you than I? . . . I am, as I have private reasons for knowing, opinionated, vain, weak, ignorant, lazy and so forth. . . . You must not expect perfection from me.

He continued to flatter, to proclaim himself ill-treated, to rhapsodize his love and his need for her. One night he dashed off the following letter about his delight in sitting earlier in the evening at the piano with her; he quotes eight lines of music and then declares:

You are dancing through my head to this tune and I cannot refrain from telling you so. Forgive me. . . . Oh the infinite mischief that a woman may do by stooping forward to turn over a sheet of music! I am alone, and yet there is a detestable, hardheaded, heartless, cynical, cool devil seated in my chair telling me that all this is insincere lying affection. But I defy him—it is he who lies. I have sold only my working hours to him. Hate and mistrust him as much as you will; but believe me too, and help me to snatch a few moments from his withering power. . . . One more goodnight, fatal one. I protest that it is all your fault, Alice Alice Alice Alice Alice Alice Alice Alice Alice Alice Alice Alice Alice Alice Alice Alice undeservedly beloved Alice.
Am I not a wretched fool?
GBS

Intensely in love, Shaw warded off many of Alice's attacks by ascribing to her a double personality, one of which he labeled Miss Lockett, the other Alice. The letter in which this device is presented is worth quoting at length as we prepare to return to the novel. It is a reply to the letter in which Alice called him "one of the weakest men I have ever met."

Let Miss Lockett beware, for she is the dragon that preys upon Alice, and I will rescue Alice from her. I hate her with a mortal hatred. Already I have shaken her. I have (as she admits) power to pain her, and I have (as she presumes) the will to use that power. I do not respect her, do not admire her, know her for one of those to whom it was said that the first shall be last, and that she that loveth her life shall lose it. I will shew Alice what she is, and Alice will abandon her for ever. Miss Lockett says she cannot help despising me. It is false; Miss Lockett fears me, and is piqued when I dispraise her. . . . But there is only one Alice, and her sayings are her own, and therefore memorable. She is the sweetest of companions, and for her sake I have sworn war against foolish Miss Lockett, who is ashamed of her and suppresses and snubs her as the false and artificial always suppresses, snubs, and is ashamed of the natural, simple, humble, and truthful. But Miss Lockett, proud as she is of her strength, is a weakling; and her complaints, her pains, her bitter letters beginning with that vile phrase "May I ask," and going on to ask without waiting for the permission that she was not sincere in begging, are the throes of her dissolution. She has no patience and no faith: I, her enemy, have patience and knowledge, and care nothing for her opinion, knowing that I must win that of Alice. I hear Miss Lockett protest: she is always ready to answer for Alice. But I know better. . . .

Farewell, dear Alice—do not shew this letter to Miss Lockett; it will only enrage her. Do not let her write to me again—write yourself.

In *An Unsocial Socialist* the character who bears this double self is Gertrude Lindsay. We note how close the resemblance is in the following exchange between Gertrude and Trefusis:

"The expanse of stars above us is not more illimitable than my contempt for Miss Lindsay, nor brighter than my hopes of Gertrude."

"Miss Lindsay always to you, if you please, Mr. Trefusis."

"Miss Lindsay never to me, but only to those who cannot see through her to the soul within, which is Gertrude. There are a thousand Miss Lindsays in the world, formal and false. There is but one Gertrude."

"I am an unprotected girl, Mr. Trefusis, and you can call me what you please." . . .

"Unprotected!" said Trefusis. "Why, you are fenced round and barred in with conventions, laws, and lies that would frighten the truth from the lips of any man whose faith in Gertrude was less strong than mine. Go to Sir Charles and tell him what I have said to Miss Lindsay, and within ten minutes I shall have passed these gates with a warning never to approach them again. I am in your power, and were I in Miss Lindsay's power alone, my shrift would be short. Happily, Gertrude, though she sees as yet but darkly, feels that Miss Lindsay is her bitterest foe."

"It is ridiculous. I am not two persons; I am only one. . . . I cannot tell whether you are in earnest or not."

Shaw in 1880.

Gertrude is obviously a close portrait of Alice Lockett, and Shaw took pains to notify her that her "dual entity" had been "made the foundation of the most sentimental part of my new book." Presumably the most sentimental part should have been the romance between Trefusis and Agatha, and Shaw's remark explains why Agatha fades into the background in the second half of the story, much to its loss, since she had been skillfully animated in the earlier half whereas Gertrude had been given scant appeal. The novel in fact is pulled awry by Shaw's determination to write in the first instance for Alice Lockett's eyes rather than for the general reader's.

Throughout the book Shaw chastises and punishes Alice for her ill treatment of him as he was apparently unable to do in his own person. One can imagine Alice's mortification when she read that the woman modeled on herself had not been taught "to express her feelings as well as . . . to dissemble them"; or that "hopeless discontent was her normal state and enjoyment but a rare accident"; or that she was "cold, mistrustful, cruel to nervous or clumsy people, and more afraid of the criticisms of those with whom you dance and dine than of your own conscience"; or that she was "contemptuous by nature" and "too proper to be pleasant"; that she "plumed herself on her condescension to her inferiors" and "was resolved to die an old maid sooner than marry an upstart." It was a portrait etched in acid, a revenge for all those times Shaw felt he had been compelled to flatter Alice, though in his eagerness to vent his anger he makes Gertrude so repellent that we can hardly accept the reality of Erskine's love for her.

Alice Lockett might also have been less than amused by actual incidents involving Gertrude Lindsay. The latter will allow Erskine to propose to her not because she intends to accept him but because "she counted the proposals of marriage she received as a Red Indian counts the scalps he takes"; and when a dog took a fancy to her she "encouraged him with more kindness than she had ever shown to any human being." (The dog is a St. Bernard, and Shaw probably intended Alice to understand that she was treating the human Bernard worse than a dog.) Gertrude Lindsay is also nearly killed in the book. She goes off to pick hemlock leaves and faints from the poisonous fumes before Trefusis rescues her. A psychologically inclined reader might conjecture that Shaw was half-screening an impulse to destroy Alice Lockett when he nearly killed off her surrogate Gertrude, and that the gratuitous lingering over Hetty's dead body, and Trefusis's hardheartedness when viewing it, were displaced expressions of Shaw's own anger toward Alice. Indeed Shaw himself knew about such impulses, for when Hetty was still alive and received an infuriating letter from Agatha bragging of Trefusis's love for her, she stabbed the air with a pair of scissors before she became conscious "of her murderous impulse, and she shuddered at it." But then when her jealousy swept back upon her she cried out, "I dont care; I should like to kill her!"

Precisely this murderous impulse toward Alice Lockett, I believe, enters powerfully into the novel, accounting at one extreme for Hetty's death, more mildly for Gertrude's hemlock poisoning, and then for the general hostility toward women throughout the book. It accounts for the peculiar question Trefusis asks himself early in the work when he sees the girls skating boisterously on the ice and wonders whether he would laugh if the ice were to burst and they were to drown. (When it does begin to burst and the girls scatter, he finds himself startled and notes "that wishes for the destruction of the human race, however rational and sincere, are contrary to nature.") Shaw's destructive impulse toward women also enters into his characterization of Sir Charles's spoiled wife, Jane. She is said by Agatha to need "an occasional slapping" and even "a sound thrashing." Agatha tells Jane that if she were Sir Charles, she would "get a big stick; beat you black and blue, and then lock you up on bread and water for a week." Shaw himself, directly in his authorial voice or through his surrogate Trefusis, figuratively beats all the women in the novel black and blue except Agatha, and his immediate animus against the female sex was probably caused by Alice's rejection.

The same cause had another consequence: the disparagement of marriage throughout the book. Shaw seeks to console himself for Alice's rejection by discrediting marital happiness. The novel opens with Trefusis running away from his marriage because its very felicities oppress him; and the second half opens with the even more disastrous marriage of Sir Charles, who in the author's view foolishly married for love and now cannot escape from his cold and disrespectful wife. True, these two failed marriages are in a sense balanced out by the forging of alliances between Erskine and Gertrude and between Trefusis and Agatha, but these come almost in mocking deference to the conventions of the popular novel; and except for Erskine's marriage, which we shall attend to in a moment, Shaw seems on the whole determined to reassure himself for being forced to remain a bachelor.

This generalization is peculiarly confirmed by the very marriage between Trefusis and Agatha at the end of the book. Agatha is the only favorably regarded woman on the scene, but she appears to have been created primarily as a foil to Gertrude and thus as a model against whom Alice Lockett could measure herself disadvantageously. Agatha has a ready smile, a playful temperament, and a frank and sensible manner; she has "quickness of wit, dexterity of hand, audacity, aptness of resource, capacity for forming or following intricate associations of ideas, and consequent power to dazzle others"—in all these particulars the opposite of Gertrude Lindsay. Yet upon further reflection we see that Agatha is more than just a personified sermon to Alice on the sort of woman she should try to become. Agatha is strikingly similar to the young Shaw himself, and every one of the above traits could apply to the author too. The similarity is heightened even more when we add some of Agatha's other characteristics: her "flippancy" and her "half cajoling, half mocking air," her talent for mimicry and for making other people laugh, her spirit of "insubordination" and her firm control over her temper. Like Shaw, she could be "as serious and friendly with a single companion as she was mischievous and satirical before a larger audience." And like Shaw even in her supposed faults, she is accused by some characters of selfishness and self-love, and of having no heart. When she thinks that she is not up to loving Trefusis recklessly and wholly, as she presumes he loves her, and when she says, "I am selfish, cold, calculating, worldly, and have doubted until now whether such a thing as love really existed," she directly echoes the words that Shaw himself would later write to Alice Lockett: "We are too cautious, too calculating, too selfish, too heartless, to venture head over heels in love." (Yet of course both Agatha and Shaw were totally in love despite their pretense of calculation.) Shaw later said that the character of Agatha had been suggested by the sight of a woman who sat nearby in the British Museum while he was working on the novel, a woman he never addressed. There is no reason to doubt the accuracy of his statement, yet he well could have noticed qualities in the woman that mirrored his own, or could have filled out her image with projections of his own character. At least to some extent he was aware of the resemblance between Agatha and himself, for he has Gertrude recognize that many of Agatha's qualities were "much nearer akin than her own to those of Trefusis," and Trefusis, as we have seen, was consciously intended to have character affinities to the author himself. Hence the air of contrivance in the hero's prospective marriage to Agatha, the repellent coldness of the transaction, derives from its being not a felt reality for Shaw but another and subtler form of fantasized revenge against Alice Lockett. The simple revenge was the mere reversal of the actual relationship as Trefusis teases, torments, and then rejects an infatuated Gertrude. Then, by having him marry someone superior to her, Shaw rubs salt in Gertrude's wound and enhances his own fantasy satisfactions. But, significantly, his is not the rejected man's typical dream of a substitute and complaisant beloved; rather, it is a withdrawal into the ego, an attempt to reestablish self-sufficiency, a renewal of primitive narcissism. In fantasy, and as it were therapeutically, Shaw turns away from the tormenting Alice figure and marries his own self again in the person of Agatha. Most of Trefusis's inconsistencies disappear once we regard Agatha less as a separate woman than as himself in female form, and regard his marriage to her as a marriage to himself, a renunciation of the real world of womankind variously embodied in those pain-producing creatures Hetty, Jane, and above all Gertrude Lindsay.

III

Yet intermittently, though now returned to his shell, the young novelist reaches out a hand for Alice to take and pull him back into romance. Counterbalancing his desire to attack her and withdraw into self-dependency is a desire for union with her, and Shaw apparently refuses to relinquish the hope that Alice will at last marry him. No matter that the portrait of Gertrude might exasperate Alice and turn her permanently against him, no matter that he disparages love and marriage and women: he still believes that she will finally attend more to his message of love than to his missives of denunciation. Trefusis keeps urging Gertrude to marry the poor young writer who loves her, Chichester Erskine, and Shaw transparently uses this means to urge his own case to Alice. Here for example is one of Trefusis's many pleas to Gertrude, touching in its effort to use leftist social criticism and even the young suitor's poverty to augment his desirability as a mate:

"Erskine is a poor man, and in his comfortable poverty—save the mark—lies your salvation from the baseness of marrying for wealth and position; a baseness of which women of your class stand in constant peril. They court it; you must shun it. The man is honorable and loves you; he is young, healthy, and suitable. What more do you think the world has to offer you?"

"Much more, I hope. Very much more."

"I fear the names I give things are not romantic enough. He is a poet. Perhaps he would be a hero if it were possible for a man to be a hero in this nineteenth century, which will be infamous in history as a time when the greatest advances in the power of man over nature only served to sharpen his greed and make famine its avowed minister. Erskine is at least neither a gambler nor a slave-driver at first hand; if he lives upon plundered labor he can no more help himself than I. Do not say that you hope for much more; but tell me, if you can, what more you have any chance of getting? Mind, I do not ask what more you desire; we all desire unutterable things. I ask you what more you can obtain!"

"I have not found Mr Erskine such a wonderful person as you seem to think him."

"He is only a man. Do you know anybody more wonderful?"

"Besides, my family might not approve."

"They most certainly will not. If you wish to please them, you must sell yourself to some rich vampire of the factories or great landlord. If you give yourself away to a poor poet who loves you, their disgust will be unbounded. If a woman wishes to honor her father and mother to their own satisfaction nowadays she must dishonor herself. . . . If you do not marry betimes from choice, you will be driven to do so later on by the importunity of your suitors and of your family, and by weariness of the suspense that precedes a definite settlement of oneself. Marry generously. Do not throw yourself away or sell yourself; give yourself away. Erskine has as much at stake as you; and yet he offers himself fearlessly."

Gertrude raised her head proudly.

"It is true," continued Trefusis, observing the gesture with some anger, "that he thinks more highly of you than you deserve; but you, on the other hand, think too lowly of him. When you marry him you must save him from a cruel disenchantment by raising yourself to the level he fancies you have attained. This will cost you an effort, and the effort will do you good, whether it fail or succeed. As for him, he will find his just level in your estimation if your thoughts reach high enough to comprehend him at that level."

The lecture continues for another few hundred words, and coming at the very close of the novel it may fairly indicate the extent to which Alice Lockett preoccupied Shaw during the writing. It may also indicate the true course of the relationship between Shaw and Alice, with his possible offers of marriage being refused because of his poverty and the opposition of her family.

Yet even this serious lecture is partly undermined by other phrases Trefusis concurrently employs, as when he tells Gertrude to "sacrifice" herself by marrying Erskine, or when out of her earshot he observes with contempt that "you sometimes have to answer a woman according to her womanishness, just as you have to answer a fool according to his folly." Such phrases may indicate more than the puzzling seriocomic manner which Alice Lockett complained about in one of her letters: they may point to a greater ambivalence of feeling toward Alice and toward marriage than Shaw was willing to admit. This same ambivalence seems to be reflected in the characterization of young Erskine. Shaw makes little effort to build up Erskine's appeal. He permits Agatha to think Erskine "a very nice fellow indeed, thoroughly good and gentlemanly," but yet one who "realized her conception of the human ass most completely." She pitied him because he was a mere minor poet "and therefore a pronounced ass." Shaw himself makes considerable sport of Erskine's shyness and awkwardness, and of his inadequacy in dealing with Trefusis. Erskine is not allowed to show much promise either as a man or a writer, and from the evidence provided he is likely to remain obscure. Only his poverty and his love for Gertrude seem to be in his favor, and given the sagging chain of faults that Shaw hangs around Gertrude's neck, Erskine's devotion to her bespeaks a conspicuous want of judgment. Shaw may be trying to talk Alice Lockett into marrying him when he arranges lectures for Gertrude, yet in the half-mocking portrait of the infatuated young writer he also seems to be trying to talk himself out of wanting to marry at all.

As we now see, Shaw divides himself into Erskine and Trefusis, each one possessing some of his own present traits, but the former representing the self he would like to disown and the latter the self he would like to become. Erskine as a shy, unsuccessful young author in love with a recalcitrant woman clearly resembles Shaw, and he writes weak sonnets to Gertrude just as Shaw wrote little poems to Alice. Trefusis, in contrast, is the self-possessed intellectual man of action, a socialist leader and commanding talker, irresistible to women, heart-whole even if liable to the charge of heartlessness, a man not at the mercy, as Shaw may have felt himself to be, of the whims of a mere girl. And in so far as Shaw identifies himself with Trefusis, he is expressing a desire to be free of Alice Lockett and of the agonies she forced him to endure.*

IV

An Unsocial Socialist is thus a work which has, quite apart from its modest literary interest, a considerable value in illuminating the psychological processes of its author. He uses his writing (as we shall further see in our later chapters) to relieve the pressures of personal stress and not, as his subsequent comments on his works would have it, solely to examine this or that social or human issue. He explores and attempts to work through his own most intimate problems, including that of self-definition, always exacting for a writer since he risks dissolving his inner being in the study or creation of other people's characters. Shaw criticizes and justifies himself; he hits out under appropriate disguise at individuals who have hurt him; he includes in his work special pleading intended for the eyes of nameable readers. In this novel

---

*That the agonies of a love relationship form the true burden of the book seems confirmed by the epigraph that Shaw jotted down on the cover of his first draft—the closing couplet of Shakespeare's plaint against lust in Sonnet 129: "All this the world well knows; yet none knows well / To shun the heaven that leads men to this hell" (Brit. Mus. Add. MS. 50656).

there are doubtless dozens of references which Shaw designed mainly for Alice Lockett's recognition, and which extended beyond her own similarities to Gertrude. (For instance Agatha Wylie is a nursing student, Hetty shares the author's own birthday, Chichester Erskine bears the first name of one friend of Shaw's and Sidney Trefusis bears that of another—Sidney Webb—and Jane has the name of Alice's sister.) More important, the novel shows how our author responds to emotional disturbances caused by women. He launches a counterattack which arouses and channels his powerful destructive impulses but cannot wholly contain them. His attack on Alice's surrogate Gertrude spills over into misogyny and a disparagement of love and marriage. "When all the love has gone out of me I am remorseless: I hurl the truth about like destroying lightning," he once wrote to Alice. The truth he hurls in his loveless state tends to be cynical rather than profound, but the destructiveness hits deep, resulting here in the death and near death of two of the principal women, and in occasional reflections on the rationality of destroying the working class and even the human race itself. And when he is not counterattacking, he seeks to withdraw into himself and nurse his grievances with a willed accession of self-love.

Shaw is especially concerned over the common denominator of his counterattacking and withdrawing, namely, the indifference to others, the heartlessness. It distresses him because it may have been as responsible as his poverty for the breakdown of the romance with Alice, who had after all charged him with deliberately paining her over and over again, of being a machine, of lacking genuine feelings. And to her he admits his coldness of heart and pleads for help. We have heard him say to her, after expressing his love, "There is a detestable, hardheaded, heartless, cynical, cool devil seated in my chair telling me that all this is insincere lying affection. But I defy him—it is he who lies. I have sold only my working hours to him. Hate and mistrust him as much as you will; but believe me too, and help me to snatch a few moments from his withering power." These are more than rhetorical flourishes, as Shaw truly feared his destructive impulses, which were fierce enough to drive him to contemplate, even in his twenties, the destruction of the human race. Indeed if we keep in mind the hideous appetite for killing in Shaw's later life, as recorded in our last chapter, it should not now be surprising to see a homicidal longing as one component of his destructiveness. Shaw's portrayal of Hetty when she met with keen frustration was probably drawn from his own response to Alice's frequent rebuffs: "Henrietta looked around for something sharp. She grasped a pair of scissors greedily, and stabbed the air with them. Then she became conscious of her murderous impulse, and she shuddered at it." Much of the initial impetus of the novel may lie in these very lines—the reaching for something sharp to use against Alice (though he could bring only his words to the cutting point), the veiled expression of the murderous impulse, and the shudder.

For the shudder at his murderous, destructive, or at the least "heartless" impulses led Shaw to cultivate countermeasures which would demonstrate that he had plenty of heart. His conversion to Marxism during the very years of his tormenting relationship with Alice may not have been prompted solely by the logic of *Das Kapital*. Conversions to religions and ideologies are often grounded in emotional needs, and Marxism is a quasi-religious ideology allowing the faithful to transcend pain and personal drift by joining the god named History in defeating the capitalist devil and ushering in heaven on earth. A true Marxist, in his own eyes, cannot be primarily concerned with self. His concern with society and the toiling masses is self evident in his commitment. He cannot be accused of lack of heart. And any pain caused to others—as when Trefusis hurts Jansenius and Sir Charles—is to better them or to force them to swallow unpalatable social facts. Because Shaw's manhood was under assault during the affair with Alice, and he was still adrift professionally, he was especially susceptible to the appeal of Karl Marx, who, as he said, "made a man of me." He now could turn from the frustrations of an unsuccessful love affair to the satisfactions of working for a distant utopia, and he could thereby reassure himself, and perhaps Alice too, that his heart was really immense.*

Other countermeasures took an opposite tack. For one thing,

---

*Other emotional gratifications of course entered into Shaw's conversion. He himself would later call attention to "the real secret of Marx's fascination," the appeal to "the passion of hatred in the more generous souls among the respectable and educated sections for the accursed middle-class institutions that had starved, thwarted, misled, and corrupted them from their cradles" ("Who I Am, and What I Think," 1901, reprinted in Laurence, ed., *Selected Non-Dramatic Writings*, p. 446). By sanctioning hatred, and by placing the enemy entirely outside the self in middle-class institutions, Marxism offered an opiate guaranteed to dull conscience and to promote self-righteousness and destructiveness; and Shaw's own destructive impulses as well as his humane ones were offered an outlet when he turned Marxist. Indeed, Fabianism may in part have later appealed to Shaw precisly because it tried to curb the destructive passions which Marxism had dangerously aroused in him, and which enter this particular novel here and there, as when he speaks of stock owners as "dividend-consuming vermin" (p. 207).

what the world called heart was often what Agatha Wylie terms "drivelling sentimentality" and romantic illusion, involving deception of others and the self. Trefusis is, as Shaw later said, an unusual hero because he violates canons of sentiment and not just of propriety; yet at bottom he punctures hollow sentiments which thwart the growth of true ones, and it is to promote honest feelings that Trefusis (and Shaw) must resort to methods that strike conventional individuals (like Alice) as heartless and cold. For another thing, attacks on other people are made more tolerable by attacks on the self, and Shaw ridicules many aspects of himself in the persons of Trefusis and Erskine and, more generally, ridicules artists and writers, clever novels in which the characters talk too much, and even socialism itself. Lastly, the manner of the book, its spirited lightness and humor, which at times, as with Smilash, grows strained, is nonetheless meant to temper the destructive impulses and render them acceptable. Agatha threatens to kill Gertrude for her sulkiness and snobbery—to kill her by relentlessly tickling her ribs and the soles of her feet—and Shaw chooses the same means to chasten Alice, hoping through the writing of the book to tickle her into recognizing her faults, perhaps his virtues, and certainly the wisdom of marrying him.

Under its controlled lightness of texture, then, and under its apparent self-assurance, Shaw's last novel discloses a talented young writer variously responding to the frustrations of unrequited love, as well as a still unprofitable career and some burdensome traits of character. He fluctuates between self-love and self-criticism, between desiring women and denouncing them, between cynicism and idealism. As a man in conflict, full of ambivalent feelings and resourceful in dispersing them among diverse characters, he has not yet discovered that drama rather than fiction is to be for him a more congenial medium, one which also, as the most objectifying of literary modes, would simultaneously curb his self-absorption and his long-windedness. In 1885 he would give up his hopes of success as a novelist and begin to make a name for himself as a music and drama critic, and in the 1890's he would begin to devote himself seriously to writing plays. Yet these were often to echo situations and themes, characters and scenes from the novels, and also to reflect their author's same fundamental conflicts.

As we turn now to the best of these early plays and leave *An Unsocial Socialist* behind us, courtesy as well as completeness requires a final word about the young woman in Shaw's life who inspired this novel. She did not, as we know, become the writer's wife. Had she done so he might immediately have sought remunerative work and never embarked on the underpaid job of critic or, later, the uncertain path of dramatist. Certainly his plays and his outlook would have been different since both were further shaped by his later experiences with women. As it is, Alice probably did influence his interpretation of socialism, for he came to believe that only his poverty had prevented their marriage, and as a political theorist he then came to advocate equality of income as the basic tenet of socialism, much to the surprise of his fellow Fabians. He seemed determined that no future Shaw would lose his beloved merely because of poverty. In later years he saw Alice now and then after her marriage to Dr. William Sharpe in 1890. Thoughts of her recur in at least one of his plays, *The Doctor's Dilemma*, and he kept her letters bound in a colored ribbon for the rest of his life.

But given the evidence of the novel, it is hard to conceive that Shaw did not know he was alienating Alice more than he was persuading her to marry him. The urge to punish her predominated over the desire to capture her, and Sidney Trefusis despite his flirtatiousness runs away from women and exhibits sexual timidity and apprehension. Shaw when he wrote the book was still a virgin. It was only on his twenty-ninth birthday, two years later, that the widow Jenny Patterson gave him his first carnal knowledge of women. It is clearly possible that sexual anxieties entered into the relationship with Alice and helped to undermine it. Perhaps there was something in Shaw that feared Alice and feared the happiness he might have had with her. Perhaps he even needed to punish himself by driving her away with the very book he consciously thought would win her. Let us see if *Candida* cannot throw some light on these possibilities.

4

Candida

HOME TRUTHS

We make out of the quarrel with others, rhetoric, but of the quarrel with ourselves, poetry.

W. B. Yeats, *Mythologies*

Overleaf: William Butler Yeats in 1894.

$\mathcal{W}$ITH THE WRITING of *Candida* in 1894 Shaw came into his full estate as a dramatist. However large the promise and the merits of his four earlier plays, it was only now that he conclusively showed the mark of the born dramatist: the ability to throw forth characters who breathe by themselves and talk to each other so naturally that we forget they are on stage. Shaw's controlling hand, clearly felt in his earlier work, here seems absent, and the resulting air of spontaneity and verisimilitude lends plausibility even to the famous ending, when the heroine is made to choose between the two men who love her, the young poet Eugene Marchbanks and her husband the Reverend Morell. So skillful is Shaw in letting his story tell itself and letting his characters assert their separate claims that critics have come to disagree sharply over his intentions. Despite Joseph Wood Krutch's pronouncement in 1946 that it was unnecessary "at this late date to point out that the author's own sympathies are principally on the side of the clergyman husband," more recent commentators have argued that Marchbanks is the author's favorite; and despite the opinion of many that Candida is an admirably competent and emotionally mature woman, others have damned her as a cruel and domineering philistine. That the characters are complex enough to sustain such varying interpretations compliments the dramatist's powers even as it gives the work the right to be known as the *Hamlet* of Shaw criticism. And perhaps the author anticipated the future puzzlement over his meanings when he finally subtitled the work "A Mystery."

Yet skill alone cannot account for the play's independent life. If Shaw's presence is less directly felt in *Candida* than in his earlier plays, it is paradoxically because he has now found both a subject and characters through which he can express more of himself—including his unconscious self. No doubt he was right to claim that the play was "a counterblast to Ibsen's *Doll's House*, showing that in the real typical doll's house it is the man who is the doll"; and he may also have been influenced, as some have suggested, by *The Wild Duck* and *The Lady from the Sea*. It would have been hard for a man steeped in Ibsen, who had recently championed him in print, not to call to mind occasionally this or that work by the Norwegian while writing a play of his own on the theme of domesticity; and in fact we shall soon see that Shaw had other plays in mind also. It is nevertheless not incompatible with his calculated intentions to allow for the presence of un-deliberated and unconscious elements. He himself implied in a letter in 1904 that he had not known "the whole truth" about particular scenes when he wrote them down; and it is this less conscious material, this tapping of some of his own buried conflicts, that helps to vitalize the work and indeed generates the widely divergent responses to it, his conflicts being human enough to speak to ours.

Conflict and a seemingly un-Shavian charge of emotion strike us immediately as we enter the play. The atmosphere is thick with disputes and accusations, thrust and counterthrust. The characters fight each other and often themselves. Listen at the outset to the bickering between the pert secretary Proserpine Garnett and the young curate Lexy Mill:

PROSERPINE [*impatiently, pulling the letter she has been working at off the typewriter and folding it*]: Oh, a man ought to be able to be fond of his wife without making a fool of himself about her.

LEXY [*shocked*]: Oh, Miss Prossy!

PROSERPINE [*snatching at the stationery case for an envelope, in which she encloses the letter as she speaks*]: Candida here, and Candida there, and Candida everywhere! [*She licks the envelope*]. It's enough to drive anyone out of their senses [*thumping the envelope to make it stick*] to hear a woman raved about in that absurd manner merely because she's got good hair and a tolerable figure.

LEXY [*with reproachful gravity*]: I think her extremely beautiful, Miss Garnett. [*He takes the photograph up; looks at it; and adds, with even greater impressiveness*] *extremely* beautiful. How fine her eyes are!

PROSERPINE: Her eyes are not a bit better than mine: now! [*He puts down the photograph and stares austerely at her*]. And you know very well you think me dowdy and second rate enough.

LEXY [*rising majestically*]: Heaven forbid that I should think of any of God's creatures in such a way! [*He moves stiffly away from her across the room to the neighborhood of the bookcase*].

PROSERPINE [*sarcastically*]: Thank you. Thats very nice and comforting.

[1]

A moment later Morell quarrels with his father-in-law Burgess:

BURGESS: . . . James: three years ago, you done me a hil turn. You done me hout of a contrac; and when I gev you arsh words in my natral disappointment, you turned my daughrter again me. Well, Ive come to hact the part of a Kerischin. [*Offering his hand*] I forgive you, James.

MORELL [*starting up*]: Confound your impudence!

BURGESS [*retreating, with almost lachrymose deprecation of this treatment*]: Is that becomin language for a clorgyman, James? And you so particlar, too!

MORELL [*hotly*]: No, sir: it is not becoming language for a clergyman. I used the wrong word. I should have said damn your impudence: thats what St Paul or any honest priest would have said to you. Do you think I have forgotten that tender of yours for the contract to supply clothing to the workhouse?

BURGESS [*in a paroxysm of public spirit*]: I hacted in the hinterest of the ratepayers, James. It was the lowest tender: you carnt deny that

MORELL: Yes, the lowest, because you paid worse wages than any other employer—starvation wages—aye, worse than starvation wages—to the women who made the clothing. Your wages would have driven them to the streets to keep body and soul together. [*Getting angrier and angrier*] Those women were my parishioners. I shamed the Guardians out of accepting your tender; I shamed the ratepayers out of letting them do it: I shamed everybody but you. [*Boiling over*] How dare you, sir, come here and offer to forgive me, and talk about your daughter.

[I]

A while afterward Marchbanks tells Morell he loves Candida and then counters the older man's patronizing tone:

MARCHBANKS: . . . You are very calm and sensible and moderate with me because you can see that I am a fool about your wife; just as no doubt that old man who was here just now is very wise over your Socialism, because he sees that you are a fool about it. [*Morell's perplexity deepens markedly. Eugene follows up his advantage, plying him fiercely with questions*] Does that prove you wrong? Does your complacent superiority to me prove that I am wrong?

MORELL: Marchbanks: some devil is putting these words into your mouth. It is easy—terribly easy—to shake a man's faith in himself. To take advantage of that to break a man's spirit is devil's work Take care of what you are doing. Take care.

MARCHBANKS [*ruthlessly*]: I know. I'm doing it on purpose. I told you I should stagger you.

They confront one another threateningly for a moment. Then Morell recovers his dignity.

[I]

And after Morell speechifies at him, the poet replies:

MARCHBANKS [*looking round wildly*]: Is it like this for her here always? A woman, with a great soul, craving for reality, truth, freedom; and being fed on metaphors, sermons, stale perorations, mere rhetoric. Do you think a woman's soul can live on your talent for preaching?

MORELL [*stung*]: Marchbanks: you make it hard for me to control myself. My talent is like yours insofar as it has any real worth at all. It is the gift of finding words for divine truth.

MARCHBANKS [*impetuously*]: It's the gift of the gab, nothing more and nothing less. What has your knack of fine talking to do with the truth, any more than playing the organ has? Ive never been in your church; but Ive been to your political meetings; and Ive seen you do whats called rousing the meeting to enthusiasm: that is, you excited them until they behaved exactly as if they were drunk. And their wives looked on and saw what fools they were. Oh, it's an old story: youll find it in the Bible. I imagine King David, in his fits of enthusiasm, was very like you. [*Stabbing him with the words*] "But his wife despised him in her heart."

MORELL [*wrathfully*]: Leave my house. Do you hear? [*He advances on him threateningly*].

MARCHBANKS [*shrinking back against the couch*]: Let me alone. Dont touch me. [*Morell grasps him powerfully by the lappell of his coat: he cowers down on the sofa and screams passionately*] Stop, Morell: if you strike me, I'll kill myself: I wont bear it. [*Almost in hysterics*] Let me go. Take your hand away.

MORELL [*with slow emphatic scorn*]: You little snivelling cowardly whelp. [*He releases him*]. Go, before you frighten yourself into a fit.

[I]

And we are not yet out of Act I! The very directions for the way characters are to say their lines read like a Wagnerian opera's expression marks: Burgess replies "trembling with rage"; Proserpine "highly incensed"; Marchbanks "passionately," "desperately," "piteously"; Morell "in a suffocated voice," "almost fiercely," "grimly"; and Candida herself ranges from "gaily" to "remorsefully." Critics who say that Shaw's theater is too intellectual have surely not read this play.

The emotional quality of the work is further intensified by a whole series of small climaxes before the major one of the last act, and Shaw achieves these climaxes mainly by the device of multiple revelation. The play is built on the uncovering of secrets; the conflicts most often spring from one individual defending a secret that another individual is determined to expose. We have already seen Proserpine being provoked by Lexy into exposing her jealousy of Candida, and a moment later he is forced to acknowledge his slavish adulation of Morell. Old Burgess is compelled to agree that he is a scoundrel under Morell's demand that truth be faced, and then Morell himself begins to show self-doubt under Marchbanks's withering directness. And the revelations continue until the play's end when, with marvelous counterpointing, Shaw makes the poet, who had been eager to reveal his secret love for Candida, acquire a special secret of his own as he flies out into the night.

Another counterpointing device, this time set against the episodes of hostility, is the unusual degree of physical contacting. In none of Shaw's other plays is there so much actual touching. For instance, when Candida returns home she is kissed by her husband and by her father, and at the end of the play the husband and wife again embrace. In the erotically laden scene by the fireplace, Marchbanks rests his head and then his arms in Candida's lap. Morell at one point puts his arm affectionately on the poet's shoulder, and the poet himself, at the very moment when the men are about to ask Candida to choose between them, places his hand on Morell's forearm as if to draw courage from him. Marchbanks twice suffers rough handling from an enraged Morell, and his knee is tapped and then gripped by Burgess when he confides in him. Candida above all displays a very active pair of comforting hands, whether she is caressing her husband, or sitting at his feet and embracing his knees, or arranging the poet's hair and adjusting his collar. It is as if the playwright, responding to some obscure personal impulse but directing it with consummate control, has allowed the human body itself to become the chief theatrical prop.

Still another estimable feature of the play, one which invisibly contributes to its air of reality, is the fullness with which the offstage world is detailed. The sheer length of the opening description of Morell's East End suburb and his parsonage, at least twice as long as the opening descriptions in any of the earlier plays, indicates the sureness that comes only with an author's being on home ground. Shaw never lets himself or his characters forget that outer world. To take again only Act I, we start in Morell's drawing room, whose front windows look out on a large park. The minister's bookshelves are lined with contemporary works by Morris and Browning and Marx and even Shaw himself. Morell is seen sifting through the morning delivery of newspapers and letters, scheduling his week's appearances in town. Lexy Mill is soon sent forth on the parish rounds, armed by Morell against the cold October wind. Before leaving, he reports having earlier passed Burgess coming through the park to visit his daughter but stopping to argue with someone. A few minutes later Burgess arrives and is soon arguing with Morell; and with his entrance Shaw is able to introduce another segment of the offstage world, that of factories, county council politics, and the struggles of working women. Soon Candida arrives in traveling clothes and asks her husband to go outside to pay the cab and bring in the luggage. We learn about her children who are still in the country and about how Morell found Marchbanks sleeping on the Embankment five months ago and took him under his wing. Presently Burgess has to leave to catch a train, and Marchbanks resists going for a stroll in the park in order to stay for dinner. These and other seemingly casual details throughout the play are the spatial equivalent of the background of past events. They show the outer world inter-penetrating the world on stage and help to give the visible scene the density of life itself. One may contrast *Candida* in this re-spect with a play written earlier in the same year, *Arms and the Man*, where the exotic Bulgarian landscape and interiors seem somewhat artificial, in want of that assured circumstantiality of the later play.

II

This difference between the two plays does not extend to any cru-cial contrast in their themes. In fact much of the misunderstand-ing of *Candida* is dispelled when we view it as another effort by Shaw to propound the philosophy that had animated the earlier play. In essence that philosophy regarded the human creature as good, his natural appetites worthy of cultivation rather than re-pression, his brain an instrument for satisfying his emotions and his will. The material world and the people in it, though no doubt in need of betterment, were precious for what they already were and not for what they might yet become. "I demand respect, in-terest, affection for human nature as it is, and life as we must still live it even when we have bettered it and ourselves to the ut-most," Shaw declared in the same year that he wrote the two plays. "I am tired to utter disgust of imaginary life, imaginary law, imaginary ethics, science, peace, war, love, virtue, villainy, and imaginary everything else, both on the stage and off it." This idealism of cherishing the real had to struggle against a more fa-miliar idealism, rooted in Platonism and Christianity, which measured man against a standard of spiritual perfection and inev-itably found him defective. The conflict between these idealisms, the one for Shaw desirable, the other pernicious, became the bur-den of the two plays written in 1894; and once we move beyond the differences between the plays we can easily perceive this identity in their outlook.

Captain Bluntschli and Candida Morell, each of them blunt and candid, are twin idealists of the real—or, to follow Shaw's usage, simply "realists"—who are confronted by old-style idealists. Raina and Sergius in the one play, Morell and Marchbanks in the other, attitudinize in a noble vein, the former pair quite consciously and the latter by second nature. Raina and Sergius dupe themselves into viewing war heroically, just as Marchbanks views marriage and as Morell views his mission to preach divine truth. Raina's horror when told the facts of war is equalled by Marchbanks's when told of the scrubbing brushes and sliced onions that mark the prosaic domestic world. Practical, earthy, and independent-minded, Bluntschli and Candida (the hotelkeeper's son and the factory owner's daughter) manage the overgrown children among whom they find themselves, even as they nurture in them a sense of reality. When Bluntschli has prodded Raina into dropping her assumed idealism, she wonders whether he will now despise her and is delighted to find that his admiration remains undiminished. When Candida drives the truth home to her husband that his dependence on her is far greater than hers on him, he is delighted to find that she still loves him. Both Raina and Morell discover, once they stop claiming impossible virtues, "that the affections of their friends, wives and sweethearts for them is not a reasoned tribute to their virtues but a human impulse towards their very selves," as Shaw generalized elsewhere. It is Candida's occasional impatience at her husband's self-delusion that prompts her to tell him the truth roundly, just as Bluntschli is impelled to call Raina a liar to her face. Both realists share with their creator the desire to implant a truer faith, and a cherishing of life as it is, in the minds of the misled idealists around them.

Candida is not merely a Bluntschli in skirts, yet the two of them have more in common with each other than with any of the other characters in the plays—with one exception. A subsidiary figure in *Arms and the Man* is Mrs. Petkoff, Raina's mother, whose dominant trait is her maternal protectiveness. Raina even rebukes her for it by saying that Mrs. Petkoff would pet and spoil Sergius if she could. It is common enough for a background figure in a writer's work to become a foreground figure in one of his later works, and if we were to blend Mrs. Petkoff's motherliness with Bluntschli's practicality we would be coming close to the essential Candida.

The similarities between the two plays extend also to some of their general plot lines as well as to bits of dialogue. An outsider in each instance threatens a supposedly secure couple, and the romantic triangle of two men and a woman forms the base of the respective stories. The leading characters in both plays are a mature sensible adult and an idealistic youth (the later play simply reversing the sex of the two parties), and the age difference in both cases figures significantly in the outcome. The near sword duel between the two men in the first play is transformed into the fierce verbal duels between Marchbanks and Morell. In dialogue, too, some striking resemblances occur. Raina's protest, "I am not here to be sold to the highest bidder," is later echoed in Candida's sarcastic remark, "I am up for auction, it seems." Bluntschli's statement, "I appealed to you as a fugitive, a beggar," has its echo in Marchbanks's line, "I could only go to her as a beggar." Sergius's declaration to Raina, "All my [death-defying] deeds have been yours. You inspired them," is extended in Marchbanks's chivalric boast to Candida, "I would die ten times over sooner than give you a moment's pain." And Bluntschli's proposal toward the end of the play, "Let's be pleasant and talk it over in a friendly way," is nearly duplicated in Candida's line in the final act, "Let us sit and talk comfortably over it like three friends."

So many remarkable similarities exist between the two plays that it may be understandable why Shaw chose not to call attention to them in his comments on *Candida* but referred instead to Ibsen. Yet we may still wonder why he decided merely to rearrange many of the same counters when writing the later play. The answer, which also throws further light on *Candida*, is fortunately available in two events that occurred after the opening of *Arms and the Man*.

III

The first event was the play's success, the only theatrical success in fact that Shaw had enjoyed up to that time. But he found himself being praised for what he regarded as the wrong reasons—as a whimsical funny man, a new paradoxer of the Gilbertian variety, a dealer in fantastical and thoroughly entertaining nonsense. "I had the curious experience," he confided in a letter recounting the play's premiere, "of witnessing an apparently insane success, with the actors and actresses almost losing their heads with the intoxication of laugh after laugh, and of going before the curtain to tremendous applause, the only person in the theatre who knew that the whole affair was a ghastly failure." (He was not quite the only person, for when he went before the curtain someone in the audience shouted a dissenting boo and Shaw made his famous reply—"My dear fellow, I quite agree with you, but what are we two against so many?"—which is always taken as an instance of his ready wit but in truth reflected something of what he really felt.) He was, in his own opinion, a serious man with a serious and positive message for serious people, a philosopher who had gone beyond what he termed "the old categories of good and evil"; and now, as if Savonarola were to be praised for the rakish cut of his tonsure, he found himself acclaimed "as a monstrously clever sparkler in the cynical line," as he half-ruefully summed it up. He quickly moved to correct his mistaken admirers. Within a few weeks after the reviews appeared he had completed an essay entitled "A Dramatic Realist to His Critics," in which he defends at some length the literal accuracy of the military matters his play dealt with, citing parliamentary debates and soldiers' accounts in his support. He insists that drama critics so completely derive their knowledge of life from the stage that when a realistic playwright presents true life they term it false. "The stage world," he argues, "is for people who cannot bear to look facts in the face" and who therefore take refuge in exactly that idealized view of the world which his play had satirized. "I created nothing," he contends; "I invented nothing; I imagined nothing; I perverted nothing; I simply discovered drama in real life."

It was a bold counterattack, and not without its incidental truths. Who for instance would wish to argue with Shaw's contention that "no class is more idiotically confident of the reality of its own unreal knowledge than the literary class in general and dramatic critics in particular"? But the knife cuts both ways since Shaw himself was a member of the literary class and a dramatic critic too. And when he undertook to write a play about warfare and social life in Bulgaria he drew on a knowledge of Bulgarian affairs that was somewhat less than encyclopedic. In truth, as he elsewhere admitted, he fortified himself when finishing the first draft with facts gleaned from conversations with a couple of Slavs based in London. Though his characters are plausible enough for the stage, and their psychology is often acutely perceived, the play as a whole cannot be placed in that tradition of realistic drama that Shaw curiously demanded for it. To satirize operatic plays in the interests of reality is not to create that reality; and *Arms and the Man* lent itself well to the light opera treatment it duly received because in his parody Shaw had exploited rather than abandoned many of the conventions of operatic melodrama, and had created stage Bulgarians who seem to have just hurried back from a long residence in England. It was probably because Shaw's reply to his critics protested too much that he undertook to reuse many of the components of the play in a new work, as if to down the talk of extravaganza by now writing of the world he really knew—the world of London, of socialist agitation and meetings, of factory owners and progressive clerics and busy wives and possessive secretaries, the world, in short, of contemporary life.

The second event that prompted Shaw to reaffirm the philosophy of *Arms and the Man* in another play was the coincidence of having William Butler Yeats's *The Land of Heart's Desire*, a one-act romantic fantasy of rural Ireland, serve as a curtain raiser to his own satire of the romantic fantasies of some contemporary Bulgarians. The two Irish expatriates had known each other casually for six years and shared a wary mutual respect. Shaw by 1894 was a reputable critic of music and drama, a busy socialist speaker and theorist, a man of cosmopolitan interests; Yeats, his junior by nine years, was a promising poet and Irish nationalist who hid his shyness behind flowing ties and sweeping black capes. They had in common, besides their accents, a devotion to Shelley and the still-living William Morris; but they differed contentiously in their theories of art, Shaw holding that all art is didactic at its fountainhead and serves vital social functions, Yeats at this time regarding art as a beautiful island refuge from reality. Shaw had good reason to feel that in theater matters he knew vastly more than his compatriot; yet as a dramatist his reputation was still about as insignificant as Yeats's. None of the older man's three earlier plays had had any success or had even received productions beyond the makeshift ones required to secure copyright. Yeats was luckier, for *The Land of Heart's Desire* was only the second play he had written and was to enjoy a run of over fifty performances. What may have particularly irritated Shaw about his young rival's early success was that their hopes for modern drama were as adverse as their attitudes toward art in general. Shaw wanted contemporary life brought to the stage and he revered Ibsen for having done so. Yeats hated Ibsen's naturalism, his supposed lack of music and style, and his failure to adhere to Yeats's own credo that "art is art because it is not nature." And the differences between the two Irish writers were clearly manifested in their respective plays.

Candida

Yeats's little verse drama tells of a young wife, Mary Bruin, who loves her husband but yearns to escape from her household chores and the scoldings of her mother-in-law. We first see Mary lost in reverie over a book of ancient fairy legends while near her swirls the conversation of her husband and his parents and an old priest, Father Hart. Presently a wandering child is heard singing outside and is invited into the house. It quickly ingratiates itself by virtue of its pretty face and strange, dreamy talk. But when it catches sight of a crucifix on the wall it shrieks and insists that "the ugly thing on the black cross" be taken away, a request Father Hart complies with, foolishly, because the child then reveals itself as one of the fairy people whose evil power the disarmed priest can no longer thwart. The fairy soon urges Mary to come away and live a life free from drudgery and old age, to "ride the winds, run on the waves, / And dance upon the mountains." Forced to decide between her husband and the poetic child, the entranced wife chooses the latter and suddenly dies, perhaps liberated now in spirit to dance upon the mountains with the fairy people.

Yeats keeps a decent dramatic balance in his charming play between the claims of the real world and the lures of a fantasy world. Yet the choice before Mary Bruin is fairly bleak: on the one side the dreary round of domesticity, as life "moves out of a red flare of dreams / Into a common light of common hours," and on the other side the perilous delights of an escapist world of dance and song, which may fulfill her secret desires but at the cost of premature death. Nevertheless, since death itself comes so painlessly for Mary at the end of the play, and since before that moment the play's brightest glow had been provided by the alluring poetry of the fairy child, the delights of the escapist world, as Yeats makes us feel them, outweigh its perils.

The contrast between the implicitly romantic viewpoint in this work and the explicitly antiromantic one in *Arms and the Man* could hardly have been lost on the two Irish geniuses who prowled the theater during many a night of the run, suffering through each other's productions and the actors' occasional mismanagement of the lines. Yeats's antipathy toward Shaw's work can be sensed even in his comments nearly thirty years later, when the constraints of both men's fame probably made him try to present a more balanced judgment than he had originally formed.

I listened to *Arms and the Man* with admiration and hatred [he wrote in his *Autobiography*]. It seemed to me inorganic, logical straightness and not the crooked road of life, yet I stood aghast before its energy as to-day before that of the Stone Drill by Mr. Epstein or of some design by Mr. Wyndham Lewis. . . . Presently I had a nightmare that I was haunted by a sewing machine, that clicked and shone, but the incredible thing was that the machine smiled, smiled perpetually. Yet I delighted in Shaw the formidable man. He could hit my enemies and the enemies of all I loved, as I could never hit, as no living author that was dear to me could ever hit.

The supposed dream of the smiling machine was most likely told to Florence Farr, the manageress of the theater with whom Yeats often discussed Shaw, and it is reasonable to assume that she, as an intimate friend of Shaw's, lost little time in relaying the dream to Shaw himself. He took it in good spirit, no doubt, as he usually took most personal criticism; but such composure would not preclude a willingness to hit back in his own formidable way at Yeats the dreamer. Although his opinion at the time of *The Land of Heart's Desire* was not put into print, through *Candida* it can be indirectly perceived; and even in advance we might imagine that the man who at Yeats's age had been busy ripping the veil from the face of capitalism in *Widowers' Houses*, and had continued the attack in *Mrs. Warren's Profession*, was not likely to have much tolerance for sentimental purveyors of Hibernian superstitions.

Indeed from the evidence of *Candida* we can almost see Shaw resolving to answer those critics who had accused him of writing fantastic extravaganzas by bringing his so-called extravaganza home to English ground, and to answer too that young aesthete Yeats by showing not only the true behavior of a contemporary wife but also the probable fate of a rural fairy adrift in London. Which is to say that up to a point *Candida* can be usefully regarded as an amalgam of components of both *Arms and the Man* and Yeats's play, though the latter is often parodied. Marchbanks, for instance, is described as a strange shy youth, slight, effeminate, and almost unearthly, with a delicate childish voice and a shrinking apprehensive manner—a modern embodiment of Yeats's fairy child. His odd-looking outfit, in which "he has apparently lain in the heather and waded through the waters," suggests his countryside haunts. As the fairy was thought to be high-born, so Marchbanks is made a scion of aristocracy. As the fairy sings its verses to Mary in front of one fireplace, so Eugene recites his verses to Candida in front of another. The crucifix that must be removed before the frightened child can put its arms around Mary is now replaced by a secular means of protection, the brass poker in Candida's hand that makes Marchbanks "horribly uneasy" and must be put down before he will rest his arms in her lap. His cryptic boast to her, "I'm ever so much older than you, if you only knew," is somewhat clarified when we recall that Yeats's fairy child admits that it is actually very old. Just as the fairy offers to take Mary to see "the ruler of the Western Host," so Eugene offers to go to the West to find an archangel for Candida. Just as the fairy warns Mary that she will become like other prosaic wives who must "bear children, cook, be mindful of the churn, / And wrangle over butter, fowl, and eggs," so too Marchbanks, dismayed that Candida soils her hands with cooking, scrubbing brushes, and paraffin oil for the lamps, implies that she may become like "all the dreadful people who live in these hideous rows of houses." The fairy tempts Mary with the prospect of dancing on the mountains, and Eugene tells Candida that her feet will be beautiful on the mountains. Almost directly using Yeats's language, Shaw has Marchbanks announce that his heart "is crying out bitterly in its hunger." And more generally mimicking Yeats's descriptions of fairyland and his early poetry, Shaw has Marchbanks offer Candida a tiny shallop,

a tiny shallop to sail away in, far from the world, where the marble floors are washed by the rain and dried by the sun; where the south wind dusts the beautiful green and purple carpets. Or a chariot! to carry us up into the sky, where the lamps are stars. [II]

Candida, however, who must also decide between a husband and an alluring youth, does not at all make Mary's choice. She enjoys Eugene's presence and his poetic effusions, but she recognizes that the fairy stories her father told her as a child cannot be translated into adult life. She seeks ways to make Eugene grow up, even by having him learn to slice onions and to cook. And through her and the play as a whole Shaw is, as it were, telling his younger compatriot Yeats to grow up too, telling him that by the age of twenty-eight even poets should say farewell to fairyland and should recognize that real wives do not die from domesticity but survive and thrive, fulfilling themselves through love of their children and husbands and homes.

As a parodist of Yeats's play, Shaw thus reverses the ending to make it more realistic. Where Yeats has his priest fear for Mary's life, Shaw has his parson finally fear for Marchbanks's life. Not people but fairies had best watch out when they stray from their woodland haunts into the city. A fairy figure who falls in love with a human woman and wants to marry her will find itself threatened by destruction from within, as if controlled by an ancient curse; it can never gain the land of its heart's desire but must remain out in the night, doing only what it is fit to do, and forever renounce the pleasures of a normal human marriage.

On the fairy-tale level this is the meaning of Shaw's revised version of Yeats's play. The renunciatory demand may be part of the secret in Marchbanks's heart as he flies out into the night, and the hidden origin of that demand may be part of what Shaw meant when he subtitled his play "A Mystery." He may well have intended that subtitle too as a bantering reply to Yeats, who liked to regard his own early dramas as miracle plays, having in mind those medieval dramas which dealt with religious and supernatural events. To Shaw, as a self-declared dramatic realist, the strand of fairy tale was only part of the tapestry of his play, yet in Marchbanks he deftly interweaves a modernized fairy with a real poet and self-evidently enjoys satirizing Yeats's little play.

Perhaps he even enjoyed it too much. For while scoring points against Yeats he forgot that poets and fairies usually manage to win in the end and had best not be trifled with at all. Poets get beneath the skin, and fairies put wires across one's path which cause accidents. We shall presently see that Shaw was more affected by Yeats's play than he realized, and that surefooted as he was in the first two acts, in the last one he tripped over a hidden wire and nearly fell flat on his face.

Yeats's play was valuable to Shaw not only because it prompted a rejoinder. Ironically, it also supplied him with what would turn out to be one of his best plots, the very sort of plot that Desmond MacCarthy, a wise critic of Shaw, regretted he abandoned for the looser constructions of many of his later works. Shaw expands the plot frame to three acts but uses the same number of actors as had Yeats. He coalesces Mary Bruin's in-laws into one parent, Burgess, and even more cleverly coalesces Yeats's two characters of a husband and a priest into the Reverend James Morell. This economizing allows him to create Proserpine Garnett and Lexy Mill, those amusing figures whose admiration for Morell counterbalances Eugene's contempt. If Mary Bruin as wife is nominally transformed into Candida (whose competence and directness of character were borrowed, as we saw, largely from Bluntschli), Mary's name may have suggested the picture of the Virgin hanging over the mantelpiece and also the name of the offstage cook Maria.*

Because Shaw's personal familiarity with fairies was limited (he now having been away from Ireland for many years), he had to flesh out his stage creature Marchbanks with traits borrowed from real poets: a touch of early De Quincey perhaps, more than a touch of the popular view of Shelley—a view Shaw had publicly corrected just two years earlier—combined with something of Shelley's anticlericalism, and several touches of early Yeats, such as a proneness to despondency and sentimentality, a timidity sometimes overborne by anger, a trained taste in painting, a preference in poetry for Pre-Raphaelite exoticism, and a vague religiosity and worshipful posture toward women. Even that part of Eugene's stage description which does not relate to his fairy aspect might be construed as applicable to young Yeats: "The very intensity with which he feels a perfectly commonplace position comes from excessive nervous force; and his nostrils, mouth, and eyes betray a fiercely petulant wilfulness, as to the bent of which his brow, already lined with pity, is reassuring." Yet Marchbanks's portrayal also benefited from earlier studies Shaw as a novelist had made of artists and aesthetes, like the young Chichester Erskine we met in the last chapter, that shy young poet whose only article of belief was that fine art is "the sole refiner of human nature." And as we saw in considering Erskine, he represented something in Shaw himself that he was trying to transcend. Marchbanks, too, reflected some of Shaw's own early experiences and traits; for instance, Eugene's near overpayment of a cab fare was based on Shaw's own actual overpayment when he first arrived in London, Eugene's haunting of the Embankment was similar to George's early frequenting of the same place, Eugene's shyness and gaucherie were very reminiscent of young Shaw's. In Marchbanks we have a worldly and more confident Shaw presenting to some extent a mockingly exaggerated version of his earlier self, the self he saw partly reincarnated in the younger and less

*The parodistic aspects of Shaw's play would of course best be appreciated in performance if Yeats's work served as a curtain raiser, a reasonable combination since *Candida* is not a long play. One obvious set of castings would have Father Hart reappear as Morell, Bridget as Candida, Mary as Proserpine, Maureen as Burgess, Shawn as Lexy. Having the fairy play Eugene would make demands on the actor but still might be done; though Yeats wrote the fairy role for a girl, and so far as I know it is always performed by one, there is no reason why a boy could not serve equally well. Needless to say, performance parallels between the two works—in gestures, movements, and tableaux—would have to be presented with restraint.

experienced Yeats. And in Marchbanks's development in the course of the play, his movement toward manliness and an acceptance of his arduous vocation even at the expense of his heart's desire, the older Irishman was perhaps seeking to guide his brother writer toward his own conception of what a poet should be: a Shelley who puts his art at the service of mankind. It was probably this development that Shaw had in mind when he later remarked in the preface that he intended his play to "distil the quintessential drama from pre-Raphaelitism" by showing it "at its best in conflict with the first broken, nervous, stumbling attempts to formulate its own revolt against itself as it develops into something higher." And we may wonder whether Shaw would not have felt vindicated had he known that Yeats did in fact a decade later repudiate the mood that had produced his Irish fantasy. "In my 'Land of Heart's Desire,' and in some of my lyric verse of that time, there is an exaggeration of sentiment & sentimental beauty which I have come to think unmanly," Yeats wrote to his friend AE in 1904. "The [play's] popularity," he continued, "seems to me to come not from its merits but because of this weakness. I have been fighting the prevalent decadence for years, & have just got it under foot in my own heart—it is sentiment & sentimental sadness, a womanish introspection."

Shaw's ridicule does not of course depend for its effect on our knowing that its most immediate target was probably William Butler Yeats. But such knowledge tends to confirm that Shaw was satirizing excesses of the poetic temperament and was not simply unable to create a convincing poet, as has often been claimed. Especially in the first half of the play Shaw seems to be repaying Yeats's compliment of calling him a smiling sewing machine by smiling back at him with mockery—Shaw as Smilash again. At least here is one playwright, he is in effect saying, who may be a machine but will nevertheless attack bosses who make working girls slave over real sewing machines, and who will create a heroine who is interested not in fairies but in tutoring sewing machine girls in her home. Indeed at the amusing opening of Act II Shaw may even be turning the very image of the machine against Yeats (who never learned to type and was always intimidated by machines) when he shows Eugene's hapless encounter with a typewriter. And a moment afterwards the poet is off dramatizing his emotions before the bewildered Proserpine:

> MARCHBANKS: Really! Oh, then you are shy like me.
> PROSERPINE: Certainly I am not shy. What do you mean?

MARCHBANKS [*secretly*]: You must be: that is the reason there are so few love affairs in the world. We all go about longing for love: it is the first need of our natures, the first prayer of our hearts; but we dare not utter our longing: we are too shy. [*Very earnestly*] Oh, Miss Garnett, what would you not give to be without fear, without shame—

PROSERPINE [*scandalized*]: Well, upon my word!

MARCHBANKS [*with petulant impatience*]: Ah, dont say those stupid things to me: they dont deceive me: what use are they? Why are you afraid to be your real self with me? I am just like you.

PROSERPINE: Like me! Pray are you flattering me or flattering yourself? I dont feel quite sure which. [*She again tries to get back to her work*].

MARCHBANKS [*stopping her mysteriously*]: Hush! I go about in search of love; and I find it in unmeasured stores in the bosoms of others. But when I try to ask for it, this horrible shyness strangles me; and I stand dumb, or worse than dumb, saying meaningless things: foolish lies. And I see the affection I am longing for given to dogs and cats and pet birds, because they come and ask for it. [*Almost whispering*] It must be asked for; it is like a ghost: it cannot speak unless it is spoken to. [*At his usual pitch, but with deep melancholy*] All the love in the world is longing to speak; only it dare not, because it is shy! shy! shy! That is the world's tragedy. [*With a deep sigh he sits in the visitor's chair and buries his face in his hands*]

[11]

Shaw is clearly making merry with his moody young man and is writing in the same vein that gave rise to Gilbert's teasing of Wilde in *Patience* or, earlier, Peacock's teasing of the romantic poets in *Nightmare Abbey*. Satirically, Shaw emphasizes Eugene's gaucherie and his frequent difficulty in understanding people. Eugene cannot fathom why Morell—the commanding, virile, generous, eloquent Morell—appeals to women; nor can he see through Burgess's cynical bonhomie. For all of his quivering sensibility he is still something of a fool, and what is remarkable is Shaw's ability to carry Marchbanks to the edge of farce without going over it. He still keeps him strong enough to make Morell fear him; and he allows him to reap the benefits of his ingenuousness, for Proserpine a moment after we left her does break down and confess her love for Morell, and the Reverend also breaks down when alone with Eugene. The plot itself, Shaw proved, could tolerate a good deal of ridicule of the young poet since his inexperience had to be established before his growth could be shown.

Shaw does not neglect, in creating Marchbanks, a final aspect of Yeats's fairy child—its cruelty. The innocence of Yeats's fairy is entirely feigned. Father Hart declared that fairy people were "spirits of evil," and his confrontation with the fairy child matches the power of the church against a demon power. Marchbanks, too, is not quite so innocent as he appears to be, and he is demon-like in his confrontations with the churchman Morell, who tells him that "to break a man's spirit is devil's work." Yet March-banks "ruthlessly" persists, "plying him fiercely with questions" and "stabbing him" with words. "Remorseless," he rubs in his victory at the end of Act I, and then in Act III he prolongs Morell's agony by not directly telling him what happened when he was alone with Candida. While Morell is "suffering deeply," March-banks crows over him, calling him "a pig-headed parson," and then a fool. That he takes pleasure throughout in torturing his rival, downright sadistic pleasure, is beyond question even though this has been curiously ignored by critics who react quickly enough to Candida's supposed cruelties.

In any case Shaw's own view of Marchbanks is neither simple nor unequivocal, and it reflects the complexities of the play as a whole. Earlier I set up an easy contrast between Yeats and Shaw, which may now be usefully modified. *The Land of Heart's Desire* can indeed for convenience be labeled a romantic fantasy; yet there is nothing really romantic about Mary's death, and the fairy child for all its charm is deceitful and evil. This is why Yeats keeps in dramatic suspension at the end any complete resolution of feeling; he himself is not without ambivalences toward the romantic view even in 1894, ten years before he would condemn the play's "decadence," its unmanly "exaggeration of sentiment and sentimental beauty." Correspondingly, Shaw is not simply antiromantic, either in *Arms and the Man* or in *Candida*. The earlier play has a notable reversal at the end as the practical Bluntschli insists that he is a romantic, and at the close of *Candida* the romantic poet apparently has the final victory as he strides out into the night. In short, the opposition between Yeats and Shaw is far less extreme than it seems to be at first blush and than they themselves thought it was. In their dispute they were at bottom struggling against that element of the other reflected in themselves (Shaw battling the residual aesthete, Yeats the incipient moralist), and it was precisely out of that quarrel with themselves that they were able to give strength to the various positions and feelings in their respective plays.

IV

The negative or ridiculed side of Marchbanks produces a current of sympathy for his antagonist Morell, which is strengthened when Eugene and Candida verbally assault him. He also wins our respect by his kindliness to his secretary and his curate, by his firmness with Burgess, his forbearance toward his exasperating young rival, and his courage in leaving that rival alone in the house with Candida. In other words Shaw here again, as with Marchbanks, strikes the difficult balance between creating a purely satiric character and an admirable one, and he makes the clergyman a worthy opponent for the more inherently romantic figure of the poet. Some of Morell's traits, particularly those relating to his personal appearance, were drawn from contemporary Christian Socialist ministers; Shaw said he had Stopford Brooke chiefly in mind, but other names have been put forth also. No doubt the portrait is a composite one, as it was with Marchbanks also. Yet just as with Marchbanks, Shaw may have found the creative process facilitated by being able to identify with Morell. The Reverend is a forty-year-old Christian Socialist who lives by words and is highly dependent on the maternal care of his wife. Shaw is a thirty-eight-year-old Fabian Socialist who lives by words, resides at his mother's house in London, and is still to a large extent financially and emotionally dependent on her. Both men preach their varieties of socialism to entranced audiences and are attractive to women. As Shaw in one of his letters noted Morell's "readiness to boss people spiritually," his "certainty that his own ideas, being the right ideas, must be good for them," so too did various people note these qualities in Shaw himself; and the description of Morell in his public role as "facile, cheery, spontaneous, fluent, emphatic, unhesitating and bumptious" could on the whole be applied as well to the public Shaw. If in Marchbanks Shaw partly mocks aspects of his past self, in Morell he partly mocks aspects of his present self.

Seen in this light, some of the play's criticism of Morell can be viewed as Shaw's self-criticism. At a later time, when famous and rich, Shaw would quip that he did not throw himself into the struggle for existence, he threw his mother into it; but his guilt over this still continuing dependency can perhaps be seen behind Marchbanks's thrust at Morell: "It horrifies me when I think of the doses of [cant] she has had to endure in all the weary years during which you have selfishly and blindly sacrificed her to minister to your self-sufficiency." At a later time, too, Shaw openly doubted the value of his Fabian lecturing to audiences determined to be entertained rather than enlightened, a doubt perhaps reflected in Candida's remark on her husband's rhetoric: "Of course what you say is all very true; but it does no good: [the listeners] dont mind what you say to them one little bit. . . . you preach so splendidly that it's as good as a play for them." And after she tells him that the women especially are attracted by his person rather than his doctrines, she goes further and asserts that he too is deluded, that he is not so much in love with truth as "in love with preaching because you do it so beautifully." Even more bluntly, Marchbanks calls Morell a windbag. And when the minister boasts that his chief gift is "the gift of finding words for divine truth," Marchbanks retorts: "It's the gift of the gab, nothing more and nothing less. What has your knack of fine talking to do with the truth? . . . Ive been to your political meetings; and Ive seen you do whats called rousing the meeting to enthusiasm: that is, you excited them until they behaved exactly as if they were drunk. And their wives looked on and saw what fools they were." Morell finally comes to accept the derogation of his gift though he rejects the notion that he is not a man but a mere "talking machine to be turned on for their pleasure every night of my life." This last image of course recalls Yeats's nightmare vision of Shaw as a smiling sewing machine, and Morell's protestations may to some degree reflect Shaw's fear that Yeats may have been right. Throughout the play it is almost as if talkativeness itself is the central target; both Marchbanks and Morell are men of words, each with his own kind of rhetoric, and both are belittled in their dealings with Candida, the woman of deeds. Through Morell especially, but also through Marchbanks, Shaw masochistically attacks the mere talker.

In fact so intent is Shaw in his self-criticism that at times it results in small inconsistencies, as when Marchbanks implies that the women at the meetings remain unaffected by Morell's eloquence whereas Candida had said that the women in particular were affected by it. Perhaps Shaw ignores this shift because in both instances he has fulfilled his intention of ridiculing Morell's vanity as a speechmaker and of indirectly ridiculing himself as well. Such self-criticism may also be at the root of another small inconsistency, this time of characterization. Very early in the play, long before events have shaken Morell's confidence in himself and his complacency as husband and provider, he abruptly wilts under Marchbanks's confession of love for Candida and half pleads for the younger man to help him: "There are so many things to make us doubt, if once we let our understanding be troubled. Even at home, we sit as if in camp, encompassed by a hostile army of doubts. Will you play the traitor and let them in on me?" Nothing up to that point had at all prepared us for this outburst, and even allowing for the oratorical heightening to which the Reverend is addicted, it does seem out of character for him to intimate such susceptibility to self-doubt. He sounds suddenly like the diffident Eugene, and this momentary lapse in characterization suggests that the dividing line was not as firm as Shaw would have liked between that past self represented by Marchbanks and the present self represented by Morell. For all of Shaw's conspicuous self-assurance at the time he wrote *Candida*, he still possessed vestiges of that shy young man who had wandered the streets of London eighteen years earlier; and it was probably not Morell but Shaw himself who occasionally sat at home assailed by doubts—about his ability to provide for himself materially, to be successful as a dramatist or as a Don Juan or as anything other than a mere talking machine—and this mood of doubt was momentarily foisted on James Mavor Morell.

Candida Morell, the third member of the triangle, is obviously the most complex figure in the play and the one toward whom our feelings are apt to be the most complex, as were Shaw's as well. A beautiful woman, radiating maternal warmth and physical desirability, a woman whose poise and competence are softened but not weakened by her ready tenderness, Candida evokes in audiences feelings reaching back to childhood and forward to the latest ideals of feminine excellence. Because these ideals have changed in the decades since Shaw wrote, and the primacy of marriage and motherhood and the home has lost much of its traditional sanction, our attitude toward Candida will differ somewhat from that of late-Victorians whose very security in patriarchal patterns made it possible for them to relish Shaw's exposure of the strong man's dependence on the woman he thought he was protecting. That the play is less frequently performed today than in the earlier decades of the century, and that actresses now find more satisfaction in roles as career women than as heroines of the hearth, suggest that judgments of Candida are peculiarly implicated in the changing outlook on women's position in society. The "liberated" women may no longer find Candida a model and the insecure men no longer admire her domestic supremacy. Hence it might be well to emphasize for a moment how emancipated a woman she actually is and how firmly she recognizes her own worth. Her mettle is best seen in her response to Morell's demand that she choose between him and Marchbanks:

CANDIDA: Oh! I am to choose, am I? I suppose it is quite settled that I must belong to one or the other.

MORELL [*firmly*]: Quite. You must choose definitely.

MARCHBANKS [*anxiously*]: Morell: you dont understand. She means that she belongs to herself.

CANDIDA [*turning on him*]: I mean that, and a good deal more, Master Eugene, as you will both find out presently. And pray, my lords and masters, what have you to offer for my choice?   [III]

And though she chooses the weaker of the two men, her husband, she has played his foolish game in a way that exposes and punishes his folly. Then, driving the lesson home, she explains to Marchbanks that her husband has always unwittingly relied on the support of women:

Ask James's mother and his three sisters what it cost to save James the trouble of doing anything but be strong and clever and happy. Ask me what it costs to be James's mother and three sisters and wife and mother to his children all in one. Ask Prossy and Maria how troublesome the house is even when we have no visitors to help us to slice the onions. Ask the tradesmen who want to worry James and spoil his beautiful sermons who it is that puts them off. When there is money to give, he gives it: when there is money to refuse, I refuse it. I build a castle of comfort and indulgence and love for him, and stand sentinel always to keep little vulgar cares out. I make him master here, though he does not know it, and could not tell you a moment ago how it came to be so. [*With sweet irony*] And when he thought I might go away with you, his only anxiety was—what should become of me!   [III]

And then she finishes off the lesson by deftly complimenting the loser on his superior strength and reminding him that he has been spared an alliance with a woman too old for him. Throughout, her mastery of the situation has been unmistakable.

But she has been guided, we must remember, by good sense and love rather than by any obligation to fulfill marital duties or social expectations. Indeed the degree of her freedom from conventions is daringly indicated in an earlier conversation with Morell on whether Marchbanks will someday forgive her for not teaching him about love:

MORELL: . . . I dont know what you mean.

CANDIDA [*explaining*]: If he learns it from a good woman, then it will be all right: he will forgive me.

MORELL: Forgive? . . .

CANDIDA [*realizing how stupid he is, and a little disappointed, though quite tenderly so*]: Dont you understand? [*He shakes his head. She turns to him again, so as to explain with the fondest intimacy*]. I mean, will he forgive me for not teaching him myself? For abandoning him to the bad women for the sake of my goodness, of my purity, as you call it? Ah, James, how little you understand me, to talk of your confidence in my goodness and purity! I would give them both to poor Eugene as willingly as I would give my shawl to a beggar dying of cold, if there were nothing else to restrain me. Put your trust in my love for you, James; for if that went, I should care very little for your sermons: mere phrases that you cheat yourself and others with every day.

|11|

This woman clearly follows her own moral code rather than law or custom. She obeys not the dictates of an externally imposed ideal of duty but the promptings of her heart, which impose their own restraints. She exemplifies the recommendation Shaw had given a few years earlier that women should "repudiate duty altogether" in order to gain their freedom. Or, as he summed it up a decade later, "[Candida] is straight for natural reasons, not for conventional ethical ones." Conventionally she might be considered "a very immoral female," but in truth her "brains and strength of mind" are her salvation. Motherly wife as she undoubtedly is, Candida is shown to be an independent-minded woman as well.

It does honor to Shaw's powers as a dramatist that he was able to show the woman as well as the mother since Candida's motherliness constituted for him her primary appeal. "I have written THE Mother Play," he assured the actress Ellen Terry; Candida "is the Virgin Mother and nobody else." That this claim was figuratively true for him is confirmed by the picture he chose to have displayed above Morell's fireplace, "a large autotype of the chief figure in Titian's Assumption of the Virgin" which Marchbanks presented to Candida "because he fancied some spiritual resemblance between them." Given Shaw's powerful feelings toward his own mother, it is not surprising to find the work suffused with a greater warmth of feeling than his earlier plays. In fact, his first two plays had dealt solely with fathers and daughters (as if the mother figure were being deliberately avoided), and Shaw had not even mentioned the existence of the mothers of his first three male protagonists—Dr. Trench, Leonard Charteris, and Captain Bluntschli. It was only with *Mrs. Warren's Profession*, written the year before *Candida*, that he finally gave a mother full attention, and, significantly, that lady is a whore, the direct antithesis of a virgin mother. Indeed Shaw's deep ambivalence toward his mother, his fears and hopes for her, are perhaps evidenced when we momentarily consider the two plays together, written as they were so close to each other in time. His fears that his mother Lucinda might have been George Vandeleur Lee's mistress, and that Lee's gift to her of a house overlooking Galway Bay might have been a repayment for her being more than a musical assistant, and that that very George Lee might actually have been his father—these fears may have covertly entered into *Mrs. Warren's Profession*, where Vivie's prostitute mother has been set up in houses on the Continent by the same George Crofts who might actually have been Vivie's father. Correspondingly, Shaw's ancient hopes that his mother had really been pure, and had loved him as much as he had worshiped her, may have guided his hand in drawing Candida's portrait. The earlier play expressed one side of his ambivalence, with an exaggeration both protective and cathartic, and the later play expressed the other side, as one extreme begot another. Yet despite the contrasting natures of the two mothers, it should be observed that the endings of the plays are remarkably similar: the Shavian young woman Vivie Warren rejects her mother quite as decisively as Marchbanks rejects Candida. It is as if something is impelling our dramatist, now that he has directly confronted the mother figure in two nearby works, to reject her in all guises, madonna as well as whore. What that something was will presently become clear, but even at this point it seems reasonable to conclude that the emotional strength in both works derived in some measure from their author's lifelong emotional involvement with his own mother.*

*Farfetched as it may seem, the name Candida may have had its unconscious significance for Shaw. Consciously he used it, as I implied earlier, as a companion name to Bluntschli. He knew it could be used as a woman's name because he had heard of "an Italian lady named Candida Bartolucci, afterwards a British marchioness," as he recounted. But only the name was borrowed. "I had no models for Candida," he insisted; she was "entirely imagined" (Mander and Mitcheson, *Theatrical Companion to Shaw*, p. 43). Yet we may wonder whether it is possible for any writer to deal so prominently with a mother figure and not have his inspiration fed by feelings associated with the foremost mother in his life. Perhaps beyond the primary meaning of the word *candid*—honest and open—there was some aspect of the name that made it especially appealing to Shaw, some part of its sound or its length or its collocation of letters, or perhaps all of these together. If we compare the name of Shaw's own mother with the fictive one, we see that Lucinda and Candida are three-syllable words of exactly the same length, that they both end in the same two letters, and that three of the remaining five letters in each name are identical. The coincidence is a little unusual; yet it is heightened even more when we reflect that not only do the two words form a slightly modi-

A "pure" mother in any event is what Candida represents to
both Marchbanks and Shaw himself. She is made to regard the
rival males as mere boys and to comfort and pet them as if they
were her children. (In an early draft of the play Candida's actual
children were not even mentioned until the last act, and even in
the final version they are such distant presences that the parents
never once mention them to each other.) That Shaw continued to
conceive of Candida's relationship to Morell in predominantly
maternal terms is revealed in a letter he wrote in 1920 to some
boys at Rugby who had speculated about the secret in Marchbanks's heart at the end of the play:

The secret is very obvious after all—provided you know what a poet is.
What business has a man with the great destiny of a poet with the small
beer of domestic comfort and cuddling and petting at the apron-string of
some dear nice woman? Morell cannot do without it: it is the making of
him; without it he would be utterly miserable and perhaps go to the
devil. To Eugene, the stronger of the two, the daily routine of it is nursery
slavery swaddling clothes, mere happiness instead of exaltation—an atmosphere in which great poetry dies. To choose it would be like Swinburne choosing Putney. When Candida brings him squarely face to face
with it, his heaven rolls up like a scroll; and he goes out proudly into the
majestic and beautiful kingdom of the starry night.

Thus it was the wife as mother, whether mothering a Morell or a
Marchbanks, that the playwright had at the forefront of his mind
when creating Candida, and he ignores the sexual and procreative
aspects of marriage almost entirely. The only time his control
wavers in the play is when that sexual aspect must be dealt with,
when the inherent contradiction of a pure virgin mother could
not be avoided. This is not to say that he completely shies away
from sexuality since in an attenuated way it does pervade the
play, whether in all the talk of Prossy's infatuation with Morell,

---

fied anagram but their etymological roots show a striking similarity if we take
lucid as the closest English word to Lucinda, for *candid* derives from *candere*, to
gleam, and *lucid* from *lucere*, to shine. Furthermore both words carry within
them the idea of purity, *lucid* by connotation, and *candid* in one of its older de-
notations. Shaw may have been right in insisting that he had no models for Candida, but perhaps only because the model was engraved too deep in his memory to
bring easily to consciousness.

It is consistent with this speculation to assume that had Shaw, after he hit upon
the name, checked it in a reference book of Christian names (at least later he did
possess such a book in his library), he would have found that St. Candida was the
name of a 1st-century saint often identified with Blanche and possibly called in
England St. Whyte (Morgan, *Shavian Playground*, p. 70). The white color association would naturally have suited Shaw's conception of his heroine as a virgin
mother.

or in all the kissing and touching mentioned earlier. Yet Shaw, like Eugene, seems to grow uneasy when Candida's physical appeal becomes too prominent and the male animal gives signs of becoming aroused.

V

The source of this uneasiness lies within the core of the play, for fundamentally the work is not the traditional romantic triangle which generations of critics have assumed it to be but rather the familial triangle of a son, a mother, and a father. Incredibly condensing into a single day an archetypical pattern of human development that normally takes years, Shaw has Eugene enter the play as all but a child and leave it as a man, just turned eighteen, and seemingly freed of his involvement with a parental couple. More specifically, the play recapitulates under slight disguise the classical Oedipal situation of a boy vying with a man old enough to be his father for the possession of a motherly woman. Physically cringing before the older male, whose recurrent impulse is to throttle him for his impudence, the boy continually wounds his rival with sharp-edged words and reduces him at the end to a sobbing wreck seated in a child's chair. Eugene triumphs over the bigger and stronger Morell, emasculates him, and has the joy of hearing Candida confirm that her husband is "the weaker of the two." Yet in his encounters with Candida, Eugene is passive and feeble, embarrassed to reveal his love for her and remorseful for having humiliated her husband:

> CANDIDA [*to Eugene*]: What have you been saying?
> MARCHBANKS [*appalled*]: Nothing. I—
> CANDIDA: Eugene! Nothing?
> MARCHBANKS [*piteously*]: I mean—I—I'm very sorry. I wont do it again: indeed I wont. I'll let him alone. [III]

It is this altering of an adult romantic triangle into an Oedipal one that constitutes the primary difference between *Candida* and the Ibsen plays to which it bears an occasional resemblance. In none of the three Ibsen plays suggested as prototypes, nor in the Yeats play, is the conflict centered in the competition between an older and a younger man for the hand of a maternal woman. Shaw's creative fantasizing, at its profoundest levels stirred by his own incestuous urges, moves the play through all the stages of a typical Oedipal pattern.

Candida

The standard Oedipal fantasy may be said to have three stages at its outset: the boy tries to stop the father from possessing the mother, tries to slay him, and then tries to replace him. Since the slaying looks back to past resentments and forward to future rewards, it has the double purpose of hurting the father and of removing him from the scene so that the son can possess the mother exclusively. In the private fantasy satisfactions of writing *Candida*, Shaw has no difficulty with the earlier phases but encounters problems as he drives toward the goal of possessing the mother. He has Marchbanks at the beginning of the play prevent any lovemaking between Morell and Candida though the husband had emphatically wanted to be alone with his wife after their three weeks of separation. Morell urges the young man to "take a turn in the park and write poetry" for an hour and then return to lunch, but Marchbanks manages to avoid going away and immediately starts to ridicule and hurt the older man, accusing him of being afraid to let him see Candida again and of wanting to get rid of him "because you daren't let her choose between your ideas and mine." Then when Morell finally takes up the poet's challenge and leaves Candida alone with the young man, the naked moment of incest has arrived—and must at once be clothed. The poet nervously delays the announcement of his love by reading poetry aloud for two hours; and Candida, seated at the fireside with gathering boredom, drifts off into "a waking dream" while "looking intently at the point" of a poker held "upright in her hand." The poker, Marchbanks tells her, makes him horribly uneasy. He says it signifies for him a sword to ward him off. (What it signifies for her we are not told though doubtless Shaw wanted it to serve as a phallic reminder of her absent husband.)* Once the intimidating poker is put down, Marchbanks can declare his feelings to Candida as he lies with his arms in her lap:

CANDIDA: Now say whatever you want to.

MARCHBANKS [*the eager expression vanishing utterly from his lips and nostrils as his eyes light up with pathetic spirituality*]: Oh, now I cant say anything: all the words I know belong to some attitude or other—all except one.

---

*The draft of the play indicates that Shaw's first thought was to have Candida hold Marchbanks's manuscript. He then cancelled this and gave her the poker to hold "in her hand" (Brit. Mus. Add. MS. 50603C, f. 2). To make the point sharper, he later added "upright in her hand." Again, he later changed the original draft's "looking up at the point of it curiously" to the intensified "looking intently at the point of it." Margery Morgan also regards Candida's fascination with the phallic poker as suggestive of "subconscious preoccupations" (*Shavian Playground*, p. 75).

CANDIDA: What one is that?

MARCHBANKS [*softly, losing himself in the music of the name*]: Candida, Candida, Candida, Candida, Candida. I must say that now, because you have put me on my honor and truth; and I never think or feel Mrs Morell: it is always Candida.

CANDIDA: Of course. And what have you to say to Candida?

MARCHBANKS: Nothing but to repeat your name a thousand times. Dont you feel that every time is a prayer to you?

CANDIDA: Doesnt it make you happy to be able to pray?

MARCHBANKS: Yes, very happy.

CANDIDA: Well, that happiness is the answer to your prayer. Do you want anything more?

MARCHBANKS: No: I have come into heaven, where want is unknown.

|III|

But we notice that he has not even begun to express any desire for her physically or, more consequentially, to hint in any way that he wants her to live with him. The dramatist could easily have delayed Morell's return for at least another line to allow Marchbanks to broach these matters, but perhaps Shaw did not do so because the safe part of his own fantasizing was now fulfilled and its dangerous part had to be handled obliquely. The danger did not lie chiefly in the oncoming confrontation with the husband, since Marchbanks handles this with ease, but rather in the possibility that Marchbanks may actually win in the competition for Candida's love; and for certain psychic reasons Shaw had to ensure that the poet rejected Candida *before* she rejected him. Thus after Morell's return and for the first time in the play, the poet is given remarks which indicate a surprising reduction in his desire for the woman. He suddenly exclaims to the distressed husband, when Candida is out of the room, that his own love is now entirely selfless and his yearnings are completely fulfilled:

I am the happiest of men. I desire nothing now but her happiness. [*In a passion of sentiment*] Oh, Morell, let us both give her up. Why should she have to choose between a wretched little nervous disease like me, and a pig-headed parson like you? Let us go on a pilgrimage, you to the east and I to the west, in search of a worthy lover for her: some beautiful archangel with purple wings— |III|

This moment of renunciation, in which Marchbanks upholds his desexualized image of Candida by wishing her beyond the reach of earthly male lovers, has been preceded by another of the poet's claims that all he really wants is the pleasure of loving Candida platonically. When Morell anxiously asks if she repulsed his advances, Eugene replies that "she offered me all I chose to ask for:

her shawl, her wings, the wreath of stars on her head, the lilies in her hand, the crescent moon beneath her feet." All he chose to ask for, in other words, was that she perpetuate for him Titian's Virgin Mother, and he could not allow himself to think of her as a fleshly human woman. "I loved her so exquisitely," he tells Morell, "that I wanted nothing more than the happiness of being in such love. And before I had time to come down from the highest summits, you came in." To descend from the summits, apparently, would be to descend to the body and its demands, and to the desires and responsibilities of mundane existence. As Morell tells the boy:

MORELL: Man can climb to the highest summits; but he cannot dwell there long.

MARCHBANKS [*springing up*]: It's false: there can he dwell for ever, and there only. It's in the other moments that he can find no rest, no sense of the silent glory of life. Where would you have me spend my moments, if not on the summits?

MORELL: In the scullery, slicing onions and filling lamps.

[III]

Marchbanks's ethereal sentiments run counter to his supposed desire to marry Candida and live an earthbound life with her, "to give her children to protect, to help and to work for," as he subsequently asserts. He soon shows a desperate eagerness to leave the house even though up to that point he had insisted on staying. He also tries to avoid having Candida make a decision even though earlier he had wanted her to do so. It is only after she bars him from leaving, and only after Morell insists that she make a choice, that Marchbanks puts in his bid for her. By his statements and his actions in Act III, he belies his occasional claims that he still wants Candida for himself. And these inconsistencies of his, the most striking of which we have yet to notice, are of a kind that no competent dramatist, building toward the suspense of Candida's decision, would have allowed. If it is Candida's play, she needs to have both men maintain the pitch of their desire for her until she makes her choice; if it is Marchbanks's play then he needs to have his hesitancies and retreats explored. But the play cannot successfully move in opposite directions in its last act. Perhaps the fairy demon in Marchbanks, so deft in tripping up Morell, had put a hidden wire across Shaw's path too and caused him to stumble badly. Or less figuratively put, the tension between the demands of the plot and the Oedipal pattern of Marchbanks's love probably lay in Shaw himself, in a conflict between the playwright and the man: the playwright struggling to meet the dramatic imperatives of his material, and the man struggling to vent a buried incestuous fantasy and to complete its painful final stages.

For of course the penalty for incestuous behavior would be castration, and the fear of this is what renders Marchbanks unable to declare a physical passion for the motherly woman. Candida's "purity" had to be maintained in his imagination; to attempt to violate it would bring down on him a terrible vengeance. Indeed, he refers metaphorically to the threat of castration as soon as Morell returns home:

MORELL: Have you anything to tell me?

MARCHBANKS: Only that I have been making a fool of myself here in private whilst you have been making a fool of yourself in public.

MORELL: Hardly in the same way, I think.

MARCHBANKS [*eagerly, scrambling up*]: The very, very *very* same way. I have been playing the Good Man. Just like you. When you began your heroics about leaving me here with Candida—

MORELL [*involuntarily*]: Candida!

MARCHBANKS: Oh yes: Ive got that far. But dont be afraid. Heroics are infectious: I caught the disease from you. I swore not to say a word in your absence that I would not have said a month ago in your presence.

MORELL: Did you keep your oath?

MARCHBANKS [*suddenly perching himself on the back of the easy chair*]: It kept itself somehow until about ten minutes ago. Up to that moment I went on desperately reading to her—reading my own poems— anybody's poems—to stave off a conversation. I was standing outside the gate of Heaven, and refusing to go in. Oh, you cant think how heroic it was, and how uncomfortable! Then—

MORELL [*steadily controlling his suspense*]: Then?

MARCHBANKS [*prosaically slipping down into a quite ordinary attitude on the seat of the chair*]: Then she couldnt bear being read to any longer.

MORELL: And you approached the gate of Heaven at last?

MARCHBANKS: Yes.

MORELL: Well? [*Fiercely*] Speak, man: have you no feeling for me?

MARCHBANKS [*softly and musically*]: Then she became an angel; and there was a flaming sword that turned every way, so that I couldnt go in; for I saw that that gate was really the gate of Hell.

[III]

The castrating instrument, the castration threat which disables him from going in, and the infernal torment awaiting him if the incest craving is maintained—these could hardly be more economically expressed. And insofar as the poet indicates that he has now recoiled from the possibility of a physical relationship with

Candida, he renders her choice superfluous, though her over-wrought husband does not realize this.

But Marchbanks knows that he has already transgressed, partly in deed by having injured the fatherly Morell and partly in imagination by having wanted the motherly Candida for himself. For these transgressions he must atone through self-imposed punishment, as severe as his own serious nature and the serious nature of his sins demand, yet bleakly glorious in its very severity. He announces his punishment the moment after Candida chooses Morell and says she has served her husband as mother, sister, and wife all in one:

MORELL [*quite overcome, kneeling beside her chair and embracing her with boyish ingenuousness*]: It's all true, every word. What I am you have made me with the labor of your hands and the love of your heart. You are my wife, my mother, my sisters: you are the sum of all loving care to me.

CANDIDA [*in his arms, smiling, to Eugene*]: Am I your mother and sisters to you, Eugene?

MARCHBANKS [*rising with a fierce gesture of disgust*]: Ah, never. Out, then, into the night with me!

CANDIDA [*rising quickly*]: You are not going like that, Eugene?

MARCHBANKS [*with the ring of a man's voice—no longer a boy's—in the words*]: I know the hour when it strikes. I am impatient to do what must be done.

MORELL [*who has also risen*]: Candida: dont let him do anything rash.

CANDIDA [*confident, smiling at Eugene*]: Oh, there is no fear. He has learnt to live without happiness.

MARCHBANKS: I no longer desire happiness: life is nobler than that. Parson James: I give you my happiness with both hands: I love you because you have filled the heart of the woman I loved. Goodbye.

[III]

The strangeness of Marchbanks's farewell has generally been overlooked. He might have been expected to say something else, to say in effect that he is not renouncing future happiness, that if Candida prefers her snug home there will nevertheless be other women willing to share with him the joys of the mountains and the night. Obviously Candida herself intends something along these lines when she compliments Eugene for having learned to live without happiness, meaning to live if necessary without women, in devotion to his high calling but still available for happiness should he fall in love with a woman nearer his own age. But Marchbanks is saying something more: he is renouncing sexuality itself. And our sense that this is his meaning is affirmed by a letter Shaw wrote to the actress Janet Achurch soon after completing the play, a letter in which he makes explicit the conjunction between sex and happiness on the one side and some sort of exaltation on the other.

Everybody is quoting Stevenson's dictum about the height of happiness being attained when you live in the open air with the woman you love. Convinced as I am that love is hopelessly vulgar and happiness insufferably tedious to those who have once gained the heights, I nevertheless find that these material heights—these windswept cliffs [of Folkstone]— make me robustly vulgar, greedy and ambitious. If you by any chance tumble off the heights yourself ever, you will understand how vigorously despicable I am under these circumstances. The ozone offers an immense opportunity to any thoroughly abandoned female who would like to become the heroine of a play as black as "Candida" is white.*

Shaw himself is not quite ready yet to sacrifice women and happiness, but he is in a sense testing it out through Marchbanks, who atones for wanting to possess the motherly Candida and to destroy the fatherly Morell by pledging chastity, voluntarily emasculating himself in order to ward off the primitive fear of an imposed punishment by castration. He offers this sacrifice of his own sexuality, his own happiness, to the father, and then finally offers him his love even as he withdraws it from Candida, the woman he lov*ed*. His only consolations are that now, through renunciation, he may lead a nobler life and fulfill his destiny as a poet.

It was artful of Shaw not to dwell on the self-sacrificial masochistic ending but rather to bring the incest fantasy to completion implicitly, and even to allow Eugene the small triumph of having a secret to take with him. But the secret of the play's power to move us lies finally in its disguised presentation of that most universal of love triangles, the one involving a father and a mother and a child. And this familial pattern explains, too, the widely varied estimates of the play's central figures, who pluck at buried memories of our own experiences as children and as adults.

VI

Candida provides a more subtle instance than *An Unsocial Socialist* of the interrelationship between Shaw's work and his life, and since this play emanated from deeper regions of his psyche, it

---

*Perhaps further evidence for Shaw's conjoining of sex and happiness can be seen in his reputed remark to a friend, after the Shaws had begun their unconsummated marriage: "On the day we married we both renounced happiness" (in Stephen Winsten, *Jesting Apostle* [Philadelphia, 1957], p. 125).

can tell us much about his inner being and therefore about the tendencies and tensions of his thought. Let us speculate for a few last moments on these matters, recapitulating some of our earlier discussion and keeping in mind that in 1894 Shaw was only a few years away from embarking upon his unusual marriage, which was to remain sexually unconsummated.

We saw earlier that Shaw reversed the ending of Yeats's *Land of Heart's Desire* to make it more realistic, showing that a fairy figure who falls in love with a human woman and wants to marry her will find itself threatened by destruction from within, as if controlled by an ancient curse. We may now begin to perceive that Shaw's realism was grounded in psychological insights which preeminently applied to himself. Yeats's fairy tale of old Ireland aroused more than Shaw's ire at escapism in the modern theater. It also aroused memories of Shaw's own life in Ireland and precipitated an attempt to deal with them. The story of a discontented wife tempted by a romantic outsider to leave her husband and her home was after all the basic story of George's own adolescence, during which his mother broke up the Dublin household and followed the romantic outsider Vandeleur Lee to London, abandoning her husband and her sixteen-year-old son. Moreover these events of George's late childhood duplicated experiences he had had at a still earlier time, when his mother first made Lee the central figure in her life, neglecting her drunkard of a husband and her children too. Night after night, during several spring months of 1894, Shaw could come to the Avenue Theatre at Charing Cross and hear, before his own play went on, Yeats's fantasy delicately hammering at realities in Shaw's own past life.

It also hammered, just as eerily, at his present life. For Shaw at times fancied himself a sprite, a close relation to a fairy, and was even regarded as such by his friend Beatrice Webb. And then again, just like Yeats's fairy, the sprightly Shaw enjoyed acting the role of intruder in the marriages of his friends and acquaintances, not seducing the wife but nevertheless disturbing her relationship with her husband. It was as if as an adult he were now reenacting the part of Lee but modifying it to gratify longings still alive from his childhood. By scrupulously avoiding direct sexual overtures to his friends' wives, he could perhaps fulfill the hope that Lee, too, had avoided any sexual intimacy with Lucinda Shaw; his mother's chastity, if Shaw could come to believe in it, would reassure him of the legitimacy of his own birth and even allow him to feel that she might still have loved him best of all the males in the household. Alternately, and satisfying a related longing, he now could prove that he was Lee's superior, an individual who could resist the temptations of a ménage à trois. Both longings, as we realize, he was able to satisfy in the writing of *Candida*, for when he revised Yeats's ending so as to keep the intruder from winning the wife, he was showing to himself a chaste wife fully in control of a delicate situation and also showing a male who was able to resist the temptations of a ménage à trois; and to the extent that Shaw identified with Marchbanks at the end of the work, he was thereby gaining a long-delayed, vicarious triumph over Lee. He was also demonstrating to that maternal presence which he carried within his being (as everyone does) that he would have been more worthy of her love than Lee, more self-sacrificing and adept at "playing the Good Man," as Marchbanks half boasts he behaved with Candida. And further, as if Shaw were making a secret pact with that maternal presence, he would in his mind allow the story of Candida to be the true version of his mother's behavior decades earlier; while as his part of the pact, matching in its way his ideal of his mother's chastity, there would be his own future chastity, his own striving to convince himself that love for another woman was "hopelessly vulgar" and sexual happiness "insufferably tedious."

These probably were the more important fantasy satisfactions Shaw could derive from *Candida*, and they indicate some of the ways in which his parents' association with Lee created for him a complicated variant on the standard Oedipal situation. Yet whether or not we allow Shaw these special satisfactions, it is difficult to deny him the pains of his Oedipus complex. The sexual desires provoked by the motherly figure of Candida, even the dangerous little fantasy of having Candida think of instructing the young man in making love, prompted Shaw to exact from Marchbanks the penalty of renouncing women altogether, and later exact from himself precisely the same penalty. For, as we now may see, the pattern of *Candida* not only drew on memories of Shaw's past life and made him refurbish it to bring it closer to his heart's desire, but it also provided a blueprint of his future life. He himself would be the fairy figure renouncing the pleasures of a normal human marriage and being controlled from within by an ancient curse, a curse as old as Jocasta's son.

None of this accounts in biographical terms, however, for Marchbanks's pacifying of Morell at the end of the play and his near declaration of love to him. It may be, of course, that Shaw is simply having Marchbanks make amends for all the earlier cruelties to Morell. Yet this atoning impulse may also have been reinforced for Shaw by three curious facts. He was, to begin with, writing the play at the age of thirty-eight, and his father at exactly the same age was partaking of the first year of his marriage to Lucinda. In a psychological sense, Shaw through Marchbanks was pitting himself against the husband for the possession of the mother, and not just as he may have done as a child in fantasy but now as a fully grown fantasizing man, exactly equal to his father in years; this adult recapitulation of the Oedipal conflict would encompass guilt and the need to make amends. Again, in the play he had written a few months earlier, *Arms and the Man*, he had allowed himself to kill, offstage, the first person to be killed until then in any of his plays, a father, the innocent old father of Captain Bluntschli, the hero with whom he had been identifying himself; and it is through old Bluntschli's death that the ending could be such a happy one, as the son thereby inherited enough wealth to marry the beautiful heroine. Fictional killing of fathers is likely to leave a writer with traces of guilt, especially in Shaw's case in view of his hatred of his own father. And then lastly Shaw's fate after he completed *Arms and the Man* paralleled to a certain extent Bluntschli's fate, because he made money for the first time in his career as a dramatist and actually opened his first bank account. (Though the run of the play lost money, Shaw was able to realize a profit of £341 from royalties.) In a sense Shaw discovered that killing off a father could be profitable—a possibly upsetting discovery and apt to create its own fund of guilt. At any rate these facts from the dramatist's own life, when taken together, may help to account for Marchbanks's wide oscillation of feeling toward Morell, his swinging from savage attacks to demonstrative compassion. It is as if Shaw is now including in a single play those extremes of feeling toward the male parent that he had displayed toward the female parent in two separate works, *Mrs. Warren's Profession* and *Candida*.

Yet beyond this, the guilt feelings toward the father, and more especially the masochistic renunciation of women, cast their shadows on the sunny philosophy that Shaw held at the time he wrote *Candida*. Ostensibly he held, as we noted earlier, that man's natural appetites were worthy of cultivation rather than repression; he demanded "respect, interest, affection for human nature as it is," a cherishing of the real as over against the ideal; he favored the freer expression of human impulses and championed Shelley and Ibsen as preachers of such freedom; he denounced restraints imposed in the name of traditional morality and duty and self-sacrificing nobility. Yet from the evidence of *Candida*, this was what Shaw wanted to believe rather than what he wholly felt. The Reverend Morell may be the weaker of the two men in the play, and yet Morell's traditional morality is made to triumph over Marchbanks's ideals of free expression, as the poet acts the role of the good man when alone with Candida and then finally rejects even human happiness in favor of self-denying nobility. Marchbanks is as it were a shy Eros figure converted by the Super-ego personified in the aptly named Morell. And that conversion foreshadows Shaw's own in a few more years from a relatively hedonistic to an ascetic outlook. The play thus tells us more about the conflicts within Shaw than does his avowed philosophy, and considered in conjunction with the other plays of this period it clearly exhibits his mixed feelings toward love. In *Mrs. Warren's Profession* Vivie rejects love to pursue her career, in *Arms and the Man* love is celebrated in a prospective marriage, and then in *Candida* both impulses are presented as the married couple embrace even while Marchbanks turns his back on love to follow his calling. But since Shaw at the end is more on Eugene's side than on Morell's, this may be taken to signify the growth of a latent tendency in Shaw toward renunciation of the body, with all of the grim pleasures of such a renunciation, including a temporarily lightened anxiety over his attachment to his mother. Marchbanks thought he was rejecting the motherly wife when he proudly strode out into the night, and perhaps he was, yet Shaw would find that he himself could not so easily turn away from the mother. One of the saddest sentences he ever wrote came toward the end of that letter of 1920 to the Rugby boys in which, as we recall, he had boldly declared: "What business has a man with the great destiny of a poet with the small beer of domestic comfort and cuddling and petting at the apron-string of some dear nice woman? Morell cannot do without it. . . . To Eugene, the stronger of the two, the daily routine of it is nursery slavery swaddling clothes, mere happiness instead of exaltation—an atmosphere in which great poetry dies." But then he seemed to remember something, which ran counter to everything he had just said: "Mind, I have no doubt that Eugene found that though his head was in the stars he had to keep his feet on the ground as much as Morell, and that some enterprising woman married him and made him dress himself properly and take regular meals." The self-identification with Marchbanks is apparent, and however the poet may have fared, his creator two years after completing the play did meet the enterprising woman who became a new mother to him in a sexless marriage lasting forty-five years, a marriage in which Shaw had to accept the small beer of domestic comfort and was not even to have "mere happiness" instead of exaltation. And it was also a marriage, as we shall see in our next chapter, which was to have fateful effects on his work and his thought.

5

Man and Superman

ERECTING A CREED

You are like the bird that presses its breast against the
sharp thorn to make itself sing.

Ann Whitefield in *Man and Superman*

One of the laws of the phenomenon called a human being
is that, hurt this being mortally at its sexual root,
and it will recoil ultimately into some form of killing.

D. H. Lawrence, *Phoenix*

Overleaf: Shaw in 1900.

$\mathcal{B}$ERNARD SHAW's sizable tenth play, like an imposing fortress, invites the viewer's curiosity even while it intimidates him. Emblazoned with the formidable title *Man and Superman: A Comedy and a Philosophy*, moated by an "Epistle Dedicatory" at the front and a "Revolutionist's Handbook" at the back, the work has somehow resisted the efforts of critics to guide us into its interior. The play's most famous critic, Shaw himself, set forth in a prefatory essay the terms in which the work should be approached, and there he introduces the names of a score of people who presumably bear some relation to the play's ideas, including Diderot, Meredith, Burke, Turgenev, Stendhal, Gounod, Goethe, Wells, Tolstoy, Conan Doyle, Westermarck, Turner, Dickens, Byron, Micah and W. S. Gilbert, Copernicus and Cecil Rhodes. Later critics have followed Shaw's lead and added their own roster of supposedly helpful names. Thus Maurice Valency in his recent study invokes the names of Maeterlinck, Strindberg, Ibsen, Hauptmann, Hofmannsthal, Yeats, Synge, Barrie, Swedenborg, Schopenhauer, Kant, Hegel, Fichte, Schilling, Comte, Mill, Bergson, and a dozen more. Thus Louis Crompton, in another recent volume, invokes the names of Shelley, Arnold, Plato, Ricardo, Marx, Havelock Ellis, Darwin, Schiller, Nietzsche, Montaigne, Wagner, Molière, Bizet, Swinburne, Merimée, Tennyson, and a dozen and a half more. Yet despite this barrage of erudition, the work still smiles at us, enigmatic and impregnable, and one begins to wonder whether Shaw had not deliberately misdirected the attention of his readers and commentators. Perhaps more truly than for Eugene Marchbanks, there are secrets in Shaw's heart, and the philosophic sections of *Man and Superman* might be defensive barriers which are only strengthened by erudite discussion. At any rate, since it seems doubtful that the gates of the play will now suddenly unlock if only we could conjure up the name of some omitted luminary, let us try an altogether different approach and see how far it will take us.

119

Man and Superman

In its formal structure and as an experiment in playwriting, *Man and Superman* is clearly one of Shaw's most unusual works. The experiment was, in its conception, audacious and yet simple: to include in a romantic comedy a philosophic interlude of dramatic interest which would also elucidate events in the play. Perhaps challenged by the complaint that his comedies were slowed down by too much discussion, Shaw may have determined to extend the discussion beyond all earlier limits, make it as lively as the physical action, and yet blend it within a traditional play—even at the risk of excessive length. He further intended the dream interlude to provide not only philosophic implications but also musical and literary references, for the strains of Mozart's *Don Giovanni* heralding the interlude, and the legendary names of the participants, set the dialogue against a background of other versions of Don Juan's story.

Despite the ambitiousness of its conception, however, the work has failed to win the unanimous acclaim of the critics. Some regard it as one of Shaw's masterpieces, others as one of his most tedious plays. My own view lies somewhere between these positions. I find it a period piece whose parts are considerably greater than the whole, and which has many delightful moments scattered throughout—more of them in Act I than in Act II, more in the Devil's speeches than in Don Juan's. But since the work's virtues have received adequate attention from earlier commentators, it will perhaps be of greater use here to examine first what I take to be some of its flaws.

The unusual length, it should immediately be settled, is not at all a fault. Long plays can be staged quite successfully—witness Ibsen's *Peer Gynt*, for example, or O'Neill's *A Long Day's Journey Into Night*. Yet the length of Shaw's dream interlude, by itself, does do damage because it suspends interest in the surrounding play for too great a time. Interludes as used by earlier dramatists (whether in the form of masques, pantomimes, or ballets) are kept short so as not to halt completely the achieved momentum of the play. Furthermore the mood of such interludes is never so intense as to make the return to the plot seem anticlimactic. The ninety-minute dream sequence, both by its length and its intellectual intensity, distracts attention from the play, and even Shaw's best efforts in writing the final act, inventive and fast-paced as that act is, can never quite recapture our full interest or the necessary theatrical illusion.

Yet this defect might have been more apparent than real if the dream actually did illuminate the surrounding comedy. In fact it does not, because the ideas relating to the play have already been explicitly presented and are now mostly redundant. For instance Tanner, the revolutionary propagandist, talks at great length of the general conflict of the sexes, of the particular conflict between the artist-man and the mother-woman, of the irresistible Life Force; Don Juan then simply restates these notions, often in the same terms. As for the other ideas in the interlude, most are either irrelevant to the play or actually contradict it. In sum, Shaw has really written two plays, very different in mode and only superficially integrated.

He himself recognized what had happened, for in his afterthoughts in the preface he remarks that the dream interlude is "totally extraneous" and implies that he had intended it to be so. Whether or not he was merely being defensive (for it seems inconceivable that he would deliberately write an extraneous interlude), his opinion has certainly been shared by most directors even if not by his academic defenders: the work has been tacitly recognized as two plays by the frequent omission of the Hell sequence in production and, conversely, by its occasional presentation as an independent dramatic unit. But when the sequence is omitted, the play's title is misleading; Tanner is scarcely a Superman and all the talk of the Superman is in the omitted section. If the play were more justly entitled, say, "The Taming of Tanner," then it would be judged for what it is   a fairly standard Shavian comedy, very much akin to such earlier works as *The Philanderer* and *You Never Can Tell*, and by no means superior to them.

But of course it is the Hell sequence that gives renown to the work and has earned the deference of critics. As the longest set debate in English drama—thrice the length of the fifteenth-century *Everyman*, with which it bears some affinities—it can provide an exhilarating experience when presented by skilled actors. Yet for all the wit and eloquence in the expression of its wide-ranging ideas, it does require such actors, not so much to meet the demands of the lengthy speeches as to divert attention from its theatrical and intellectual limitations. For theatrically the Hell sequence is static and its conflicts, even when intense, are mostly cerebral; it curbs the emotional range of drama and converts the stage into a platform of costumed debaters. Shaw declared that he was writing for "a pit of philosophers," but such an intention deliberately thwarts the expectations of the intelligent layman as much as it misconceives the reasons why the philosopher himself might go to the theater. And if the latter does go only in his professional capacity rather than as a man, then he may find himself smiling for reasons Shaw never intended, smiling at the meretriciousness of many of the ideas for all their verbal dazzle, at the confusion, the inconsistencies, and the evasions.

The philosophic confusions in the dream sequence will be laid bare at a later point in our discussion. But why, we may first wonder, did Shaw allow the play to fall into two detachable segments? Was he truly unequal to the technical challenge of his experiment? I think not. Rather, I believe that the form was created as a way of dealing with some extremely intimate experiences and that the conflicting nature of these experiences, the raw content of the work, required two separate plays. The disunity of the play's structure reflects a disunity in Shaw himself and not merely an unsolved technical difficulty. Hence in pursuing our new approach to the play we must concentrate, not on the ideas he picked up here and there from earlier writers, but on the root experiences that made him responsive to those ideas. And we must address ourselves to such questions as the following: What was the experiential material that made it difficult for Shaw to write a unified work? What are the virtues and the faults of the romantic comedy and how might we account for them? Why did Shaw allow the dream sequence to run on at such length? What is the nature and source of its confusions? What is the dream's true relationship to the surrounding play? Fortunately the answers to these questions are tightly linked, and all signify that *Man and Superman*, whatever its artistic inadequacies, marks a critical change in Shaw's outlook even as it deals with the most significant experience of his adult life.

The nub of this experience, to anticipate, may be suggested by a remark of the play's heroine to the poet Octavius: "You are like the bird that presses its breast against the sharp thorn to make itself sing." Similarly, I believe, the energies Shaw poured into his play were aroused by pressing himself against the sharp thorn of his recent marriage to Charlotte Payne-Townshend. The song was a prolonged one, with intricate variations on a plaintive yet hidden theme; but I think that if we listen closely we can come to hear the muffled cry from the heart sounding in the very depths of the work.

II

We may take as our point of departure the conventional view of the work as a fairly standard romantic comedy. As Maurice Valency has ably summarized the matter:

The pattern of the action is conventionally Scribean. There are four acts, and, as usual in plays of this sort, two plots which converge toward the climax and are simultaneously resolved in the final scenes. The main plot is of the A loves B loves C variety. . . . As between the two candidates for the hand of Ann it becomes evident that it is Tanner who is predestined to be the husband. . . . This comes as a surprise to nobody except the men most nearly involved. When the situation is made clear to Tanner, however, he is terrified and makes off in his high-powered car, with Ann in hot pursuit. The chase takes them all halfway across Europe, to the Sierra Nevada in Spain. . . . The action could not be simpler. It is a love chase, the originality of which consists in the reversal of traditional roles. In this case, the lady is aggressive; the gentleman is coy; what gives the play its comic tone is that in this unconventional situation everyone tries to preserve appearances. The lady plays the coy maiden; and the gentleman, as the seemingly aggressive male, finds himself engaged in a rearguard action against impossible odds. . . . The result is a well-made play of conventional shape, founded upon a *méprise*, centered upon a love chase, embellished with melodramatic incidents involving brigands and rescuers, and resolved, in accordance with the usual tenets of romantic comedy, in the happy union of young lovers.

To this description of the play according to its general type, we now need to add those features that distinguish it from other romantic comedies and Shaw's own earlier plays in the genre. And we must also amend the view that the play's comic tone derives from an attempt to preserve appearances. Oddly enough, Tanner and Ann contribute little to the comic tone in their scenes alone together. The subplot is more amusingly and inventively developed than the main plot; and the rest of the humor derives from the secondary characters—the antiquated liberal, Roebuck Ramsden; the cockney chauffeur, Henry Straker; the lovelorn chief of the revolutionary brigands, Mendoza; the rich Irish Americans, Hector Malone and his son. In presenting these men, Shaw resorts to a technique he had never before employed so systematically, that of introducing a new character in each act, a technique not in itself praiseworthy, as some critics hold, since it is often used by hack playwrights simply to revive flagging attention. And pleasant as these new characters undoubtedly are, drawn with a deftness beyond the range of any hack writer, their almost mechanical inclusion one after the other may indicate Shaw's apprehension that his central characters were not sufficiently magnetic. Yet though these secondary figures are distinctive comic types, in another respect they are remarkably alike. To perceive this likeness, let us first examine the comic technique that Shaw employs throughout the play, both in dialogue and in action.

Its essence can be seen in the device used by Mendoza's mountain brigands to stop the tourist cars which pass through their territory: they fill the roadway with nails to puncture the tires. And this device of physical deflation has its equivalent in the puncturing of any pretentiousness of rhetoric or viewpoint. A one-line example is Mendoza's ringing cry to his heroic gang as a car is sighted: "To arms! Who has the gun?" Another short instance is Straker's dry response when the poet Octavius Robinson earnestly declares his belief in the dignity of labor—"Thats because you never done any, Mr Robinson." A more extended example can be seen in Act I, as the discussion turns to the unknown man who has made Violet pregnant, and Tanner defends her before old Ramsden.

TANNER: What on earth does it matter who he is? He's done his part; and Violet must do the rest.

RAMSDEN [*beside himself*]: Stuff! lunacy! There is a rascal in our midst, a libertine, a villain worse than a murderer; and we are not to learn who he is! In our ignorance we are to shake him by the hand; to introduce him into our homes; to trust our daughters with him; to— to—

ANN [*coaxingly*]: There, Granny, dont talk so loud. It's most shocking: we must all admit that; but if Violet wont tell us, what can we do? Nothing. Simply nothing.

RAMSDEN: Hmph! I'm not so sure of that. If any man has paid Violet any special attention, we can easily find that out. If there is any man of notoriously loose principles among us—

TANNER: Ahem!

RAMSDEN [*raising his voice*]: Yes sir, I repeat, if there is any man of notoriously loose principles among us—

TANNER: Or any man notoriously lacking in self-control.

RAMSDEN [*aghast*]: Do you dare to suggest that *I* am capable of such an act?

TANNER: My dear Ramsden, this is an act of which every man is capable. That is what comes of getting at cross purposes with Nature. The suspicion you have just flung at me clings to us all. It's a sort of mud that sticks to the judge's ermine or the cardinal's robe as fast as to the rags of the tramp. Come, Tavy! dont look so bewildered: it might have been me: it might have been Ramsden; just as it might have been anybody. If it had, what could we do but lie and protest—as Ramsden is going to protest.

RAMSDEN [*choking*]: I—I—I—

TANNER: Guilt itself could not stammer more confusedly.

[I]

Now Shaw ingeniously exploits this traditional comic device of undercutting, but a more typical use of the technique is seen in the following exchange, undoubtedly the best comic moment in Act I, when Tanner as advocate of enlightened morality is himself deflated after he has congratulated Violet for being pregnant.

TANNER: Oh, they know it in their hearts [that you are in the right], though they think themselves bound to blame you by their silly superstitions about morality and propriety and so forth. But I know, and the whole world really knows, though it dare not say so, that you were right to follow your instinct, that vitality and bravery are the greatest qualities a woman can have, and motherhood her solemn initiation into womanhood; and that the fact of your not being legally married matters not one scrap either to your own worth or to our real regard for you.

VIOLET [*flushing with indignation*]: Oh! You think me a wicked woman, like the rest. You think I have not only been vile, but that I share your abominable opinions. Miss Ramsden: I have borne your hard words because I knew you would be sorry for them when you found out the truth. But I wont bear such a horrible insult as to be complimented by Jack on being one of the wretches of whom he approves. I have kept my marriage a secret for my husband's sake. But now I claim my right as a married woman not to be insulted.

OCTAVIUS [*raising his head with inexpressible relief*]: You are married!

VIOLET: Yes; and I think you might have guessed it. What business had you all to take it for granted that I had no right to wear my wedding ring? Not one of you even asked me: I cannot forget that.

TANNER [*in ruins*]: I am utterly crushed. I meant well. I apologize—abjectly apologize.

VIOLET: I hope you will be more careful in future about the things you say. Of course one does not take them seriously; but they are very disagreeable, and rather in bad taste, I think.

TANNER [*bowing to the storm*]: I have no defence: I shall know better in future than to take any woman's part.

[I]

This exchange is more characteristic than any of the earlier examples because the undercutting is performed by a woman, and every male in the play is in fact deflated by a female. Tanner is the most frequent victim of this procedure, and Shaw strangely overuses the joke of having Ann puncture Tanner's flights of rhetoric by some casual reference to mere talking. After her first retort, for instance, we read that "he collapses like a pricked bladder." The overt imagery associated with women is of spiders, bees, hungry lions, and tigers, with the male regarded as "the marked-down quarry, the destined prey." But the implicit and more functional metaphor is of woman as undercutter of the male, as castrater. (The dominant image relating to Ann is the boa constrictor, which neatly links both the overt and the implied image clusters.) All the men, however different in type, share the fate of being humiliated by women: Violet deals with the two Malones, Ann with Ramsden and Octavius, and both ladies take a turn at humbling Tanner. Even a woman offstage achieves this effect: Mendoza has been reduced to his outcast existence by the absent Louisa Straker, to whom he writes maudlin doggerel verses, and her brother Henry Straker's sole defeat in the play—his inability to stand up to Mendoza—is secured when he is required to think of his sister's honor. Thus while the puncturing device is repeatedly used for comic effects, it also is responsible for the vague sense of defeat that afflicts all the men in the play. Masculine embarrassment as caused by women is in fact the underlying theme of the work; and although Tanner in an early speech boasts of his shamelessness, he too is frequently embarrassed and indeed is finally shamed into accepting Ann as his wife.

But Tanner's capture, the prime instance of the deflation device, supplies less of the play's comedy than at first appears. Robert Brustein is quite right when he summarizes what should be the central joke of the play: "The joke on Tanner, of course, is that all the time he is theorizing about the Life Force, he is being ensnared by it, until he is finally enmeshed in that machinery whose cogs and screws he has so accurately described. Thus, Shaw demonstrates how the self-conscious theoretician is caught up, against his will, by an unconscious, irrational force." Yet the demonstration is considerably overdone. Shaw so heavily emphasizes Tanner's obtuseness, and so repeatedly exposes him as a windbag, that it becomes difficult to accept him as a worthy object of Ann's regard. He shines as a potential husband only in comparison to the feeble flicker of his rival Octavius. Shaw seems to want us to share his own astonishment at his hero's fate, but he diminishes our interest in that fate by making Tanner too much of a fool. And this in turn diminishes our interest in Tanner's theory of the universal conflict between the creative man and the woman who wants to capture him as a superior mate. Although Shaw wishes us to believe in the reality of that conflict, he does not provide Tanner with the superiority needed to serve as a compelling instance of the theory; and this deficiency in characterization partly explains why critics are incorrect in grouping Tanner and Ann with those other famous pairs of reluctant lovers, Shakespeare's Beatrice and Benedict, and Congreve's Millamant and Mirabell, whose secret delight in each other's charm and wit we can share from their very first encounters. In contrast, on the two occasions when Ann and Tanner are left alone together before their brief final scene, the play markedly sags.*

Ann, too, contributes to the unpersuasiveness of the relationship. Shaw gives her a certain amount of appeal but considerably less than he had bestowed upon several young women of his earlier plays. In fact, he displays a good deal of hostility toward her and is more intent upon exposing her trickery than in enhancing her attractiveness even as a siren. He provides her with an uncongenial imagistic atmosphere by the repeated references to destructive animals and her repeated acts of puncturing the male. He describes her as a liar even before she appears on stage, and then arranges incidents to substantiate that trait. He amply shows her up as a coquette and a hypocrite, self-indulgent and sometimes cruel. He creates in Violet a woman whose greater independence of character makes Ann's deviousness more repugnant. He portrays Ann's admirer Octavius as a pathetically deluded young lover and thereby renders it difficult for us to succumb to the one who arouses his infatuation.

Shaw is now and then aware that he is treating Ann too harshly. He has Tanner talk at length about the Life Force she supposedly embodies, and also has Tanner remind her of their love compact as children; but these statements merely assert a theoretical tie which their present behavior scarcely makes credible. Shaw's damaging ambivalence toward his heroine is clearly indicated in the half-mocking description with which he first introduces her: "Whether Ann is good-looking or not depends on your taste; also and perhaps chiefly on your age and sex. To Octavius she is an enchantingly beautiful woman, in whose presence the world becomes transfigured. . . . To her mother she is, to put it as moder-

---

*Shaw, too late, may have been prompted to create a respect for Tanner's intelligence (not especially earned in the play itself) by writing Tanner's "Revolutionist's Handbook" as an appendix.

ately as possible, nothing whatever of the kind." Yet in truth the question of Ann's appearance really does not depend on one's taste, age, or sex, for we are immediately told that "Ann is a well formed creature, . . . perfectly ladylike, graceful, and comely, with ensnaring eyes and hair." Unable to say unequivocally whether she is physically attractive or not, Shaw then seeks to make the issue irrelevant by declaring that however she looked, "Ann would still make men dream." Vitality, we are suddenly assured, is the true source of her charm: "Vitality is as common as humanity; but, like humanity, it sometimes rises to genius; and Ann is one of the vital geniuses." But even this generous statement is immediately cancelled when she is said to be simply "what the weaker of her own sex sometimes calls a cat." Thus the opening stage directions confirm Shaw's confused feelings toward his heroine, feelings that pervade the entire play. In consequence, despite his insistence that Ann's physical appearance has nothing to do with her appeal, it is absolutely necessary to assume that she is beautiful, for only her beauty and not her supposed vitality could counteract the unsympathetic traits with which he burdens her; and in no other Shaw play is the principal actress so fully required to lend her own charms to a role designed to discredit her. Ann's putative appeal is of course meant to be the bait covering the hook of her will, but Shaw has such unwonted difficulty in making her alluring that long before she finally captures Tanner the hook is practically bare, and all that remains visible is her sharp will to conquer and her readiness in devising stratagems.

Ann's will is not simply a personal characteristic. She is an agent of the Life Force which drives women to seek out the best fathers for their children. The males may be caught without much struggle or may try to run away, but the sexual initiative rests with the females. And this introduces into Shaw's work a new view of the relationship of the sexes. He had given a somewhat different version of the Life Force in earlier plays, though without using that capitalized term. In *You Never Can Tell*, for example, in the delightful second-act encounter between Gloria and Valentine, we have the following exchange:

GLORIA: I wonder what is the scientific explanation of those fancies that cross us occasionally!
VALENTINE: Ah, I wonder! It's a curiously helpless sensation: isnt it?
GLORIA [*rebelling against the word*]: Helpless?
VALENTINE: Yes helpless. As if Nature, after letting us belong to ourselves and do what we judged right and reasonable for all these years,

were suddenly lifting her great hand to take us—her two little children—
by the scruffs of our little necks, and use us, in spite of ourselves, for her
own purposes, in her own way.

GLORIA: Isnt that rather fanciful?

VALENTINE [*with a new and startling transition to a tone of utter reck-
lessness*]: I dont know. I dont care. [*Bursting out reproachfully*] Oh, Miss
Clandon, Miss Clandon: how could you?

GLORIA: What have I done?

VALENTINE: Thrown this enchantment on me. I'm honestly trying to be
sensible and scientific and everything that you wish me to be. But—
but—oh, dont you see what you have set to work in my imagination?

GLORIA: I hope you are not going to be so foolish—so vulgar—as to say
love.

VALENTINE: No, no, no, no, no. Not love: we know better than that.
Let's call it chemistry. You cant deny that there is such a thing as chemical action, chemical affinity, chemical combination: the most irresistible
of all natural forces. Well, you're attracting me irresistibly. Chemically.

|II|

What distinguishes this dialogue from anything in *Man and Superman* is simply Valentine's initiative, and although Valentine
and Gloria alternate in being aggressive, they each share some responsibility for the final marital outcome. In *Man and Superman*,
on the other hand, the woman is entirely the aggressor, controlling the man against his will. He bears no responsibility for his relations with women up to marriage and, by implication, after
marriage as well. If the woman decides on motherhood, as presumably the domineering Violet decided, the man must accommodate her. If she chooses not to be a mother, that choice also is
hers, imposed on her by the Life Force. Ann Whitefield, we may
imagine, will take the initiative on the honeymoon as she has
throughout the courtship, for the Life Force, acting through the
woman, will determine what sort of erotic activity will occur.

Shaw's notion of the aggressiveness of the woman and the passivity of the man is of course a comic reversal of the usual formula of the duel of the sexes. As a theatrical conceit it had most
recently been exploited by W. S. Gilbert, whose contraltos throb
with menacing lust. Shaw domesticates the lust, makes its pos-
sessor more youthful, and turns her into a central figure. To some
extent he follows Gilbert in using the reversal solely for comic
purposes, but he also seeks to establish it as the real truth about
the relationship between the sexes. And his failure to take his
idea comically enough, his insistent attempt to convert its partial
truth into the total truth, contributes to the implausibility of the
main romance and to the play's frequent sense of strain.

Why was he so insistent? Why, furthermore, was he so hostile to Ann as to reduce her appeal as the embodiment of the Life Force? I believe that the answer in the most general terms is that Shaw's hidden feelings toward his wife entered into the portrait of Ann Whitefield. To substantiate this, we must first remind ourselves of Shaw's close personal identification with Tanner and his counterpart Don Juan of the dream sequence. That identification was made visible in the first London staging when the actor who played Tanner adopted Shaw's own style of dressing, on Shaw's orders, and thereby began a practice which is still current. Long before his marriage Shaw had fancied himself as "an Irish Don Juan" (as he confided in a letter in 1890), and he was called Don Giovanni by his Fabian friends in recognition of his love of Mozart's opera as well as his supposedly incorrigible philandering. In 1887 he had written a little story "Don Giovanni Explains," which draws on his own amatory adventures and pretends to lament the problems the Don faced from pursuing women. The portrait of Tanner, it is true, is based in some minor respects on the radical politician H. M. Hyndman, but in a fashion typical of many Shaw plays and novels, the central figure soon became a satirized self-portrait; and he finally made the matter explicit in 1919 when in one of his autobiographical sketches he admitted his personal degree of identification with Tanner and acknowledged that the last scene, "in which the hero revolts from marriage and struggles against it without any hope of escape, is a poignantly sincere utterance" which came "from personal experience."

In the same letter in which he mentioned being an Irish Don Juan, Shaw also admits that he has "an Irishman's habit of treating women with a certain gallantry." Perhaps it was this gallantry as well as his playwright's obligation to transmute any living models that prompted him to keep Ann from resembling his wife, Charlotte, too noticeably, and he introduces several calculated dissimilarities. Ann is considerably younger than Charlotte was when she met Shaw, and Ann unlike Charlotte knew her future husband from childhood. Ann, again unlike Charlotte, takes no interest in political matters. Yet on the other hand both women are heiresses. Both have a younger sister. Both revere the memory of their dead father. Both are women of strong will yet models of respectability. Both are attracted to intellectual men and are looking for husbands. Just as Shaw in his correspondence singled out

Charlotte's handsome eyes for especial comment, so too he singled out Ann's "ensnaring eyes" in the stage description of his heroine. In sum the playwright, self-admittedly identifying to a large extent with Tanner, creates in Ann a woman who has several key points of resemblance to Charlotte, and Shaw may have felt that his portrait of the relationship between the man and the woman was a fundamentally accurate version of his own courtship.

That he did believe this is evident from his latter-day comments on Charlotte's initiative in capturing him, which parallels the way Ann pursued Tanner into marriage. Whether Shaw was correct in his belief is not in itself important. Nor was he obliged in writing the work to duplicate in any respect his private life. But an acquaintance with the biographic matrix is nonetheless helpful in clarifying both the play and the dream sequence. Their strengths and shortcomings derived in part from Shaw's manner of using his private life. Let us consider then for a few moments the "personal experience" he claimed to be drawing on in creating the play.

III

Shaw's reasons for marrying Charlotte are of course amenable only to conjecture, yet we need not invoke a cosmic Life Force to explain some of them. Shaw in 1898 was overworked, emotionally unattached, and lonely. Physically he still lived in a small and dusty upstairs room in his mother's house. Psychologically he still lived on his ego, as he had since his arrival in London more than twenty years earlier, and the recognition he had received from the world was still vastly incommensurate with his own determined sense of his worth. He labored unstintingly and without pay as writer and lecturer for the small band of Fabians; he attended to his duties as vestryman of St. Pancras; he drudged at play reviews whose sparkle hid his weariness with the fashionable playwrights. As a playwright himself, he had scarcely established a foothold in the London theater: most of his seven full-length plays had received only makeshift copyright performances, and their published versions had a very limited sale. (Only in America had one of his plays, *The Devil's Disciple*, achieved a substantial success.) His professional income was still precarious, and he was beginning to feel his age. "I am old and breaking up," he had written to Charlotte in 1898, the same year in which he began to be weakened by a series of small illnesses. Charlotte had been informally serving as his unpaid secretary, but suddenly she went off to Italy, in part with hopes of seeing a man she had fallen in love with in 1894, the Swedish doctor Axel Munthe, still several years away from winning world fame as a writer. Feeling alone and deserted in London, Shaw wrote Charlotte a note which momentarily exposed a corner of his depression:

Wrote article. No secretary. Weary at the end. Slamming the typewriter is furious nervous work. No exercise. No digestion. All my body in active preservation below the waistband and above the diaphragm; but the intermediate zone weak—wont digest, wont carry me about. Neuralgic still rather. Lonely—no, by God, never—*not* lonely, but detestably deserted.

The loneliness was real enough, however. The Webbs were away on an overseas trip, and on Easter Monday, 1898, Shaw wrote to Sidney: "I have no news. I live the life of a dog—have not spoken to a soul except my mother and the vestry since you left. The change to spring has struck me down with feverishness and weakness." Then, a few days later, he was alarmed to discover a serious inflammation of his left foot, which would soon require surgery and would take several months to heal. Nine days before the operation, he limped from Charing Cross to Charlotte's home at Adelphi Terrace to greet her upon her return from Italy. "My troubles all over at last," he declared. "With a long gasp of relief, I lay my two-months burden down and ring the bell." These expressions from a letter he wrote to her recounting his visit, exasperated to find that she had not arrived at the scheduled time. But she arrived the next morning, dashing off the news to Shaw: "Yes, I *might* have telegraphed: it was horrid of me. I am a wreck, mental and physical. Such a journey as it was! . . . My dear—and your foot? Shall I go up to you, or will you come here, and when? Only tell me what you would prefer. Of course I am quite free."

Free she was, at least in the sense that she now realized the futility of pursuing Axel Munthe, whom she had not been able to see in Italy. The eagerness with which Shaw greeted her is unmistakable, as is the sense of a warm reunion. The actuality of their mutual fondness discredits the legend Shaw began to create after the marriage: that she had finally visited his room upon her return, viewed with alarm its woeful state and that of its crippled inhabitant, insisted that he be taken away with her for recuperation, and that to prevent a possible scandal he allowed her to marry him. Shaw may have been right in declaring that he had never formally proposed to Charlotte—had he gone down on bended knee in his physical condition, he might not have been able to rise again—but clearly marriage was now a foregone emotional conclusion, and the wedding took place within a month of her return, on the first day of June.

Shaw had known Charlotte for two and a half years before their marriage and had considered that possibility almost from the very beginning. Seven months after the first meeting, for instance, he had written the following words to his confidante Ellen Terry:

This time we have been joined by an Irish Millionairess who has cleverness and character enough to decline the station in life—"great catch for somebody"—to which it pleased God to call her, & whom we have incorporated into our Fabian family with great success. I am going to refresh my heart by falling in love with her—I love falling in love—but, mind, only with her, not with the million; so somebody else must marry her if she can stand him after me.

But two months later he is asking Ellen whether he himself should not "marry my Irish millionairess? . . . I think I could prevail on her; and then I should have ever so many hundreds a month for nothing." He thought he could prevail because from the outset he had taken the lead in the relationship and had sought to fascinate her, and once he had obtained success his struggle was mainly with himself. His letters indicate some uncertainty of the strength of his feelings and of the desirability of marrying at all, uncertainties common enough to middle-aged bachelors. Also, Charlotte's wealth made him doubt his motives: as he remarked in another communiqué to Ellen, "And must a woman who is nervous, and sensitive, and sleeps badly, and longs for healthy rest, be *honorably* charged for a very simple remedy the modest price of £5000 a year & her hand in marriage? What kind of a swindler and fortune hunter do you take me for?" To Charlotte herself he was often playfully frank about her wealth, and playfully flirtatious as well. If his letters to her do not sound the note of passion of his earlier ones to the nursing student Alice Lockett, or his later ones to Mrs. Campbell, they nevertheless reveal a liking for her and an interest in her physically. He threw out hints of desiring a full-fledged love affair, challenging her to "have the nerve to use me for your own development without losing yourself," or announcing elsewhere that he will leave to see the Webbs after an early evening visit to her "unless you deliberately and purposely practice enchantments to unman & prevent me." He notifies her in one letter that "there are two laps in which I could rest this fagged head of mine now—Nature's and yours," and less than a month before the actual marriage, he writes to her what is perhaps an inducement to hasten her return from Italy: "Curse this cycling & country air: it revives my brute strength & brings unrest. I want a woman & a sound sleep."

Yet the marriage was never consummated. Shaw's own unequivocal statement on the matter, in 1930, is as follows:

Not until I was past 40 did I earn enough to marry without seeming to marry for money, nor my wife at the same age without suspicion of being driven by sex starvation. As man and wife we found a new relation in which sex had no part. It ended the old gallantries, flirtations, and philanderings for both of us. Even of these it was the ones that were never consummated that left the longest and kindliest memories.

Do not forget that all marriages are different, and that marriages between young people, followed by parentage, must not be lumped in with childless partnerships between middleaged people who have passed the age at which the bride can safely bear a first child.

The accuracy of this seemingly matter-of-fact declaration has been rightly questioned in two respects by Shaw's biographers. R. J. Minney, echoing St. John Ervine, thinks that the remarks about Charlotte are "singularly unfair to her: The reference to her not being driven to marriage by sex starvation implies, and this is supported by a later phrase, that she too had given up 'her gallantries and philanderings,' that she had, like him, indulged in premarital sex relationships. It is unlikely that there is any truth in this." Secondly, "as for Shaw's abandoning his philanderings, this too is utterly untrue. The affair with Mrs. Patrick Campbell [in 1912], which many believe did have a sexual outlet, occurred after his marriage."

Now in examining a short passage containing what seem to be two self-serving untruths, it might have been appropriate for the biographers to have given some thought to the central sentence: "As man and wife we found a new relation in which sex had no part." There is no evidence that this statement is at all untrue, and there is no reason whatever why Shaw need have said any more. But in the context of a passage so fancifully reconstructing the past, the blandness of the statement has a certain tonal falsity. It implies a calm mutual decision to abstain from sex. Yet the reason Shaw gives for the decision is obviously inadequate. Charlotte may have "passed the age at which the bride can safely bear a first child," but this does not explain why she remained a virgin. Nor is it clear when that decision was made. The biographical tradition assumes that Charlotte insisted on sexual abstinence as a precondition of marriage. As Ervine puts it, without presenting any evidence in support of his assertion, "It is almost certain that the delay in their marriage was due to Charlotte's condition that there should not be consummation." Yet there is not the slightest hint in the premarital letters that this condition had ever been raised or that there was any resulting "delay." Ervine is quite right, I think, in claiming that the decision was Charlotte's. He asserts that Shaw "in his old age expressed regret that his marriage had been fruitless, and thought that he ought to have been firmer with Charlotte about sexual relations. But Charlotte's will was as firm as his." In this matter, surely, it was firmer than his, for according to the same biographer, Shaw "was a man who delighted in women and enjoyed carnal concurrence with them"—a formulation that for the moment may be accepted. There is no reason to believe that his desires or potency suddenly atrophied on the day he married at the age of forty-one. Nor is there any evidence, direct or indirect, that the conflict of wills occurred before marriage. Indeed, Shaw's own statement—"As man and wife we found a new relation in which sex had no part"— obviously suggests a postmarital decision. My belief is that Charlotte announced her decision very soon after the wedding, that Shaw was profoundly shocked by it, and that he lost the battle of wills which then ensued. The Irish Don Juan had been more than caught: he had been emasculated.

But it seems likely that Shaw lost the battle of wills because his own will was more divided than he may have realized. An ambivalence toward sexuality is clearly evident in his early writings. And equally evident in his private life is a sexual passivity, a need for a woman to take the lead, as did Jenny Patterson when she seduced him on his twenty-ninth birthday. Charlotte's fortune probably put him at a further disadvantage in insisting on his marital prerogatives, especially since he was unsure of the extent to which that fortune had influenced his feelings toward her. The wedding itself took place when he was still recovering from his foot operation;* and the honeymoon in Surrey, with the rented house and the two nurses paid for by Charlotte, had the character of a convalescence which he seemed determined to prolong. Sixteen days after the marriage, while hobbling about in the house on his crutches, he suddenly tumbled down a flight of stairs and broke his left arm. Within a month he had to have another operation on his foot. Shortly thereafter he sprained an ankle. It was as if by staying incapacitated, he had less obligation to prove his capacities, as if abstinence might justify itself merely by becoming habitual. In any case it was almost a year before the married couple resumed their life in London.

Unascertainable causes doubtless shaped the pattern of this strange marriage. Yet, allowing ourselves to speculate on some of the less conscious pressures of those critical early months, we might wonder whether Shaw had not transferred to Charlotte many of his past feelings toward his mother, including the powerful incestuous ones we have seen on display in *Candida*. Like Eugene Marchbanks, he may unconsciously have turned away from sex in order to avoid the crime of incest and its attendant punishment of castration. Moreover, in preserving Charlotte's virginity Shaw was perhaps still paying tribute to his mother and satisfying his ancient childhood longing to be the most favored male in her life: Charlotte's virginity within marriage proved, retroactively as it were, that Lucinda Shaw had been chaste in *her* marriage, was in a sense a virgin mother, not Lee's mistress, not disloyal therefore to the boy who had worshiped her. Self-denial could establish the principle that a man could live in nonphysical intimacy with a married woman. Yet of course that in itself did not prove that Vandeleur Lee had exemplified such a principle. Something more was needed to reinforce Shaw's hidden fantasy structure—a man like Lee was needed; and who knew Lee better or could impersonate him better than Shaw himself? Lee's most conspicuous physical trait was a deformed foot, which had once

---

*Shaw arranged to make a comedy out of the actual ceremony. As he recounted to his biographer Henderson: "I was very ill when I was married, altogether a wreck on crutches and in an old jacket which the crutches had worn to rags. I had asked my friends, Mr. Graham Wallas . . . and Mr. Henry Salt . . . to act as witnesses, and, of course, in honour of the occasion they were dressed in their best clothes. The registrar never imagined I could possibly be the bridegroom; he took me for the inevitable beggar who completes all wedding processions. Wallas, who is considerably over six feet high, seemed to him to be the hero of the occasion, and he was proceeding to marry him calmly to my betrothed, when Wallas, thinking the formula rather strong for a mere witness, hesitated at the last moment and left the prize to me" (*Shaw: Man of the Century*, p. 418).

Charlotte Shaw in 1905.

received surgery and imposed upon him a distinctive limp; and we notice now that Shaw's neglect of his own slightly injured foot a few months before his marriage results in surgery and then requires him to limp to his wedding. Lee's foot had been originally injured in a fall down a flight of stairs; and we notice now that Shaw falls down a flight of stairs a few weeks after his wedding and again injures a limb. Recall, too, that George's childhood in his parents' ménage à trois had been haunted by confusion about his mother's true mate; and notice now that Shaw at his own nuptials recreates confusion surrounding the identity of the bride's true mate and converts past pain into present laughter. Recall also that Lee is forty-three when he is joined in London by Mrs. Shaw, who leaves her husband and her son behind in Dublin; and now notice that Shaw habitually gave the age at which he was joined in wedlock as forty-three though in fact he was still only forty-one. Recall finally that Lee was a music commentator and opera conductor who had composed his own version of *Don Giovanni*, in which Lucinda Shaw played the role of Doña Ana; and notice now that Shaw's first book after marriage is a commentary on Wagner and his first new theater work is his own version of *Don Giovanni*, in which Ann is made to possess many of Charlotte's traits. In sum, it seems reasonable to suspect that Shaw at the outset of his marriage displayed an increased identification with that very individual who had been his mother's most intimate male companion, and that he now showed how a man like Lee could live with a married woman without damaging her chastity.

Yet even had there not been these secret satisfactions undermining Shaw's will to insist on his marital prerogatives, it must be recognized that overcoming Charlotte's resistance would have proven difficult. Her childhood years, as described by her biographer Janet Dunbar, were marked by an unusual closeness to her father (whom she helped in several of his business and humanitarian enterprises) and by a hatred of her domineering mother. Later, as an adult, she always retreated from the marriage proposals she half courted. Charlotte was resolved never to be "the mother of a child who might suffer as she had suffered," and she came to loathe babies and to dislike all physical contact. With Shaw she appears to have sought an alliance that would duplicate the one between her friends Beatrice and Sidney Webb; but it is likely that behind the Webbs she dimly sensed the many times she had worked with her father and that she yearned to recapture in marriage the same affectionate relationship with an intellectual man that had provided her with the happiest days of her girlhood.

Let us now conclude our digression from the play by glancing at two passages that illustrate the two extremes of Shaw's attitude toward sexuality in marriage. The first is from the 1914 preface to *Misalliance*. In the midst of a section dealing with the need to educate schoolchildren fully on sexual matters, we suddenly encounter a strongly worded shift to the sexual ignorance of adult women:

The dogmatic objection, the sheer instinctive taboo which rules the subject out altogether as indecent, has no age limit. It means that at no matter what age a woman consents to a proposal of marriage, she should do so in ignorance of the relation she is undertaking. When this actually happens (and apparently it does happen oftener than would seem possible) a horrible fraud is being practised on both the man and the woman. He is led to believe that she knows what she is promising, and that he is in no danger of finding himself bound to a woman to whom he is eugenically antipathetic. She contemplates nothing but such affectionate relations as may exist between her and her nearest kinsmen, and has no knowledge of the condition which, if not foreseen, must come as an amazing revelation and a dangerous shock, ending possibly in the discovery that the marriage has been an irreparable mistake. Nothing can justify such a risk. There may be people incapable of understanding that the right to know all there is to know about oneself is a natural human right that sweeps away all the pretences of others to tamper with one's consciousness in order to produce what they choose to consider a good character. But they must here bow to the plain mischievousness of entrapping people into contracts on which the happiness of their whole lives depends without letting them know what they are undertaking.

The emotional ring of this passage contrasts with the neutral tone of his statement of seventeen years later: "As man and wife we found a new relation in which sex had no part." And although the passage contains an evasive phrase which negates part of the argument, the insistent use of the words of outrage seems to indicate a strong personal grievance.*

*The evasion is twofold and lies in the latter half of the following sentence: "He is led to believe that she knows what she is promising, and that he is in no danger of finding himself bound to a woman to whom he is eugenically antipathetic." The point of the entire paragraph is obviously that a woman kept in ignorance of her sexual obligations will contentedly expect only such affectionate asexual relations as she had known with her nearest kinsmen. Yet according to the logic of

The words of outrage relate to several remarks in *Man and Superman* and to the entrapment of Tanner, who declares early in the play: "We live in an atmosphere of shame. We are ashamed of everything that is real about us. . . . we are ashamed of our naked skins." There is, of course, no way of proving that the passage bears upon Shaw's own marriage. Undoubtedly the situation he describes did occur in Victorian England and even afterward. Yet Shaw's parenthetical claim to this supporting evidence—"it does happen oftener than would seem possible"—is very dubious in view of the sad ignorance of married life he reveals in the 1910 preface to *Getting Married*. In this contrary argument, Shaw mocks the happiness of people who are not "eugenically antipathetic" and declares that "the licentiousness of marriage" is destroying the race. He upholds what he terms St. Paul's and the Catholic priesthood's belief that marriage is incompatible "with the higher life." He confidently states that "every thoughtful and observant minister of religion is troubled by the determination of his flock to regard marriage as a sanctuary for pleasure." And then he offers his observations on a married men's conference he once attended which gave the sociologists present, "of whom I was one, an authentic notion of what a picked audience of respectable men understood by married life."

It was certainly a staggering revelation. . . . Peter the Great would have been shocked; Byron would have been horrified; Don Juan would have

---

this sentence, she should be able to fulfill her promise despite her sexual ignorance if she finds her husband eugenically congenial. In trying to make his own marital arrangements not altogether uncommon, Shaw blurs two entirely different situations, one in which the woman marries while knowing nothing of her sexual obligations, and the other in which she knows the sexual nature of most marriages but denies that sex need be a part of her own marriage. The "horrible fraud" being practiced on the male in the latter instance lies in the wife's failure to have told him before accepting a marriage proposal that she found him "eugenically antipathetic" and did not intend to have sexual relations with him.

The second evasion is in the somewhat inflated phrase "eugenically antipathetic." If we free it of its scientific sound, which is meant to keep the idea emotionally neutral, and if we also free the idea of the exclusively procreative function in which Shaw binds it, then the term would be something like "physically unattractive," and the latter part of the sentence would read: "he is in no danger of finding himself bound to a woman to whom he is physically unattractive" or "bound to a woman who does not find him sexually desirable." But the pain of putting it in the more direct way was apparently intolerable for Shaw, even after fifteen years of marriage. That Charlotte, who knew the facts of sexual relations, should not have found him physically attractive enough to allow the marriage to be consummated was simply too tormenting to contemplate or admit. Hence Shaw's sudden recourse, in an otherwise forcefully worded paragraph, to the depersonalizing evasion of "eugenically antipathetic."

fled from the conference into a monastery. The respectable men all regarded the marriage ceremony as a rite which absolved them from the laws of health and temperance; inaugurated a lifelong honeymoon; and placed their pleasures on exactly the same footing as their prayers. It seemed entirely proper and natural to them that out of every twenty-four hours of their lives they should pass eight shut up in one room with their wives alone, and this, not birdlike, for the mating season, but all the year round and every year. How they settled even such minor questions as to which party should decide whether and how much the windows should be open and how many blankets should be on the bed, and at what hour they should go to bed and get up so as to avoid disturbing one another's sleep, seemed insoluble questions to me.

The revelation may indeed be somewhat staggering as well as melancholy; though well into his fifties when he wrote this passage, Shaw the self-proclaimed sociologist and expert on the relations between the sexes had apparently never actually spent an entire night with a woman. Although he finds the minor question of bedroom arrangements insoluble, he presumes to know "the laws of health and temperance." Wallowing in the puritan's orgiastic imaginings, he inevitably moves toward the puritan's spiteful condemnation of pleasures which are denied to him:

Please remember, too, that there was nothing in their circumstances to check intemperance. They were men of business; that is, men for the most part engaged in routine work which exercised neither their minds nor their bodies to the full pitch of their capacities. Compared with statesmen, first-rate professional men, artists, and even with laborers and artisans as far as muscular exertion goes, they were underworked, and could spare the fine edge of their faculties and the last few inches of their chests without being any the less fit for their daily routine. If I had adopted their habits, a startling deterioration would have appeared in my writing before the end of a fortnight, and frightened me back to what they would have considered an impossible asceticism. But they paid no penalty of which they were conscious. They had as much health as they wanted: that is, they did not feel the need of a doctor. They enjoyed their smokes, their meals, their respectable clothes, their affectionate games with their children, their prospects of larger profits or higher salaries, their Saturday half holidays and Sunday walks, and the rest of it. They did less than two hours work a day and took from seven to nine office hours to do it in. And they were no good for any mortal purpose except to go on doing it.

And he goes on with spiraling extravagance to ascribe all the faults of civilization to conjugal intemperance, concluding that "marriage will have to go, or else the nation will have to go." The taste of sour grapes in the entire passage is acrid.

The contrasting sentiments in these two passages appear elsewhere in Shaw's postmarital writings and indicate his troubled and vacillating attitude toward sexuality and also his lifelong effort to reconcile himself to his strange marriage. His most considerable single effort was in the play he began to work on soon after the marriage, and we may now return to that play more adequately prepared to see how it reflects his private difficulties, especially the difficulty in facing the truth.

IV

It will now be realized that Shaw not only half disguises the similarities between Ann and Charlotte, and between Tanner and himself. He also distorts his courtship experiences, and precisely these distortions lessen the persuasiveness of the play's romance. Shaw had sought to fascinate Charlotte and to fulfill his role as an Irish Don Juan. Tanner, by contrast, even though absurdly claiming to be a modern Don Juan, is completely passive with Ann. At the cost of credibility, Shaw has now to insist—in plot, characterization, and preachment—on the woman as ruthless aggressor and the man as helpless victim. Male passivity has to be made a general truth so as to minimize the particular truth of his own postmarital passivity. A cosmic Life Force has to be invoked to explain marriage and to obscure thereby the individual's own responsibility for his marital fate. Shaw has to annul retroactively his personal initiative *before* marriage in order to reduce anxiety over his insufficient sexual initiative *after* marriage. Perhaps his outrage at what he may have regarded as Charlotte's trickery is being vented in Tanner's contempt for Ann's trickery, but this makes it hard to understand why Tanner would succumb to her. In sum, it was Shaw's exigent postmarital adjustments as a man that curbed his ability as a playwright to capture the truth of his early relationship to Charlotte, to make the heroine unequivocally appealing and the romance wholly convincing.

His need to fantasize the past in ways that would diminish his accountability for the present also prompted him to omit from the play certain embarrassing motives which seem to have entered into his courtship of Charlotte, namely, an eye for her money and apprehension over a rival male. The most conspicuous difference between Tanner and Shaw is the former's financial independence. Ann is an heiress, but since Tanner is also rich the question of money never enters into their relationship. Shaw on the other hand was from the outset aware of Charlotte's wealth and always took what he termed a "reasonable" interest in it. At the time of writing *Man and Superman*, 1900 to 1902, he was for the most part financially dependent on his wife. (During the year after his marriage he earned merely £473, and in 1902 a scant £90.) By conveniently avoiding the issue of money in the play's central romance, Shaw keeps uncontaminated the theory of the woman as the pursuer and keeps himself from probing into his own motives for pursuing Charlotte. The desire to avoid this discomfiting issue may have dictated his choice of Tanner's initial prototype, the *rich* radical Hyndman. Yet what Shaw may have found too unsettling to deal with directly in the characters who most resembled Charlotte and himself, he indirectly considers in the subplot of the play: Violet is determined that her marriage will not be ruined for lack of money, and her callow husband is ridiculed chiefly for his indifference to money.

Shaw also avoids the element of rivalry, which in all likelihood entered into his own readiness to marry immediately after Charlotte's return from Italy. Charlotte's reasons for visiting Rome in 1898 are not fully known. Apparently she had been advised by friends to stay away from Shaw for a while because he had begun to take her companionship and secretarial assistance for granted. The declared reason for her trip was to study municipal services in Rome, but Axel Munthe lived there also. Shaw quite understandably had his suspicions, including uncertainty whether Charlotte's "broken heart" (as he called it in a letter to Ellen Terry) had really mended. Dr. Munthe was a rival formidable enough to make Shaw apprehensive of losing Charlotte entirely. After not having heard from her for several days, for example, he wrote to her: "All this time, no letter from Rome. Some Italian doctor, no doubt, at the bottom of it." Moreover, Shaw's apprehension may have been heightened by the coincidence of having his infected foot attended to by Dr. William Sharpe, Alice Lockett's husband. There is evidence that Shaw still felt love for Alice and still believed that his early poverty had been the prime obstacle to their marriage. Now his memories of that abortive love affair may have been reawakened, intensifying the fear of losing another woman in his life to a doctor. That the fear was groundless he was not in a position to know, but the imagined threat of Charlotte's leaving him permanently for Dr. Munthe may have contributed to Shaw's "long gasp of relief" when she finally returned. Shaw, however, was too proud to admit jealousy, too insistent on his self-reliance to admit fears of rejection. It was flattering to come to think that he had been the pursued one, not the pursuer. In the consolatory fantasy of the play, Shaw omits the rivalry motive completely even though such a motive would have made Tanner's interest in Ann more comprehensible. Ricky, the other man in the triangle, is hardly allowed to be a man at all; and far from showing any jealousy toward him, Tanner behaves magnanimously; he wins out over Ricky with ease and believes that Ann pursues him because he is a superior man, a bold political thinker. This altering of the past may have been soothing to Shaw, but in now limiting the range of emotions he had actually experienced, he diminished Tanner's emotional range and credibility as well.

If the complicating elements of financial self-interest and jealousy were too threatening for Shaw to include, their omission nevertheless allowed him to keep intact the principle of the woman as the aggressor and necessary victor in the duel of sex. The superior man, however, could still rescue his masculinity by claiming an inviolate realm of his own—his work. This idea is developed in the course of the longest private conversation in the play, as Tanner and Ann recount their childhood friendship. As remarked earlier, Shaw may have felt compelled to emphasize a history of affection between his protagonists for dramatic reasons. But precisely this dissimilarity to his own past with Charlotte seems to have allowed him to relieve some confessional pressure safely. We can readily sense a personal note in the sober tone of the conversation and in the way Shaw now treats his surrogate Tanner more seriously than anywhere else in the play. Here, despite the earlier brag that his fairy godmother had not burdened him with a sense of shame, Tanner admits to Ann something of his childhood humiliations: "A sensitive boy's humiliations may be very good fun for ordinary thickskinned grown-ups; but to the boy himself they are so acute, so ignominious, that he cannot confess them—cannot but deny them passionately." He defines his arrival at manhood as the time when he acquired, not sexual capacity, but "moral passion; and I declare that according to my experience moral passion is the only real passion." When Ann tells him that there are other, very strong passions, Tanner grows inconsistent and evasive—though Shaw himself may not have been aware of it. Tanner acknowledges what he had just denied, that there are other real passions; yet he insists that "all the other passions were in me before; but they were idle and aimless—mere childish greedinesses and cruelties, curiosities and fancies, habits and superstitions, grotesque and ri-

Granville Barker as Tanner and Lillah McCarthy as Ann Whitefield in Man and Superman, *Royal Court Theatre, 1905.*

diculous to the mature intelligence." He recognizes that the beginning of manhood may mean, to most people, the beginning of love, but he asserts that "love began long before that for me. Love played its part in the earliest dreams and follies and romances I can remember." Shaw seems to be shying away from any acknowledgment of the distinctive sexual awakening that marks the biological passage into manhood. One wonders if it is the sensitive man as well as the sensitive boy who cannot confess his acute and ignominious humiliations. But in any event an odd shift now occurs in the conversation, as Tanner needlessly elaborates upon the connection between his moral sense and his destructiveness. "You were a dreadfully destructive boy," Ann reminds him.

TANNER: Destructive! Stuff! I was only mischievous.
ANN: Oh Jack, you were very destructive. You ruined all the young fir

trees by chopping off their leaders with a wooden sword. You broke all the cucumber frames with your catapult. You set fire to the common: the police arrested Tavy for it because he ran away when he couldnt stop you. You—

TANNER: Pooh! pooh! pooh! these were battles, bombardments, stratagems to save our scalps from the red Indians. You have no imagination, Ann. I am ten times more destructive now than I was then. The moral passion has taken my destructiveness in hand and directed it to moral ends. I have become a reformer, and, like all reformers, an iconoclast. I no longer break cucumber frames and burn gorse bushes: I shatter creeds and demolish idols.

ANN [*bored*]: I am afraid I am too feminine to see any sense in destruction. Destruction can only destroy.

TANNER: Yes. That is why it is so useful. Construction cumbers the ground with institutions made by busybodies. Destruction clears it and gives us breathing space and liberty.

ANN: It's no use, Jack. No woman will agree with you there.

TANNER: Thats because you confuse construction and destruction with creation and murder. Theyre quite different: I adore creation and abhor murder. Yes: I adore it in tree and flower, in bird and beast, even in you. [*A flush of interest and delight suddenly chases the growing perplexity and boredom from her face*]. [1]

Shaw seems to reveal some defensiveness in mentioning Ann's perplexity and boredom, for in fact the passage adds nothing to the play's themes and the colloquy of which this is only a small part is already the longest in the play. It is almost as if Shaw himself is speaking in this passage and gravitating, as soon as he denies the importance of love, toward a concern with destructive impulses, returning to the play's action only when he reaches the problem of distinguishing between destruction and murder. He justifies the destructiveness because it is yoked to moral ends, and we note that he regards it as distinctively masculine. Love and sex are the woman's realm; the superior man is defined in relation to the moral passion, "the only real passion" for him. Thus the hero's ego and even his masculinity can remain intact, his work as a reformer expressing his truest self, his sexual passivity insignificant.

It is a consoling position for Shaw to adopt as part of his attempt to adjust to a sexless marriage, but it is fraught with psychological and philosophical consequences. The man may concede the realm of love and sex to the woman, curbing his sexual appetites if she demands it and serving the Life Force in his own way through his moral passion as a reformer. But this complicity in his own castration will obviously affect his work, as it affects

Shaw's own work in this play with damaging bitterness toward women and a fruitful bitterness toward men; for as we have seen earlier, the pervasive comic technique of puncturing the male, and the underlying theme of masculine embarrassment as caused by women, delineate the play's primary successes even while they limit the plausibility of the romance between Tanner and Ann. In emasculating all the men in the play, in a central respect making all of them over in his own present image, Shaw indicates the difficulty of keeping his life compartmentalized, of keeping the supposedly inviolate realm of his work unaffected by his bodily renunciations. And he indicates also a treacherous philosophical position, as we shall presently examine, for to separate the passion of love from the moral passion is almost to annihilate the meaning of morality.

The dialogue between Tanner and Ann that we have just examined is one of several passages in which the "discussion" bears very little relationship to the play, and it is this lack of pertinence rather than the mere length of Tanner's speeches that contributes to the sense of strain in the play. All of the irrelevant passages can be understood as Shaw's further efforts to rationalize his present, postmarital situation. The need to do this was far more pressing than the need to reshape the past, though such reshaping was itself part of the total rationalization. However Shaw might overlay the courtship between Tanner and Ann with his present feelings, and thereby distort the reality he had lived, the story of a woman capturing a man could not resolve in imagination his immediate situation. The mortifying personal events following upon that supposed capture required another play, and really another form than any play he could then allow himself to imagine. For the unconsummated marriage was too painful and without action to be suitable for a comic drama; and the traditional form of a play, even as he had modified it in his own earlier work to accommodate discussion, was too restrictive in that he would have to attend to plot and characters and action. The essence of his postmarital adjustment was to talk himself into accepting the situation, and talk was all there was. Hence to give adequate space to the inner debate, he boldly adopted the ancient form of the philosophic dialogue, in which ideas had more reality than characters and in which issues could be fully explored. He wrote, that is to say, the famous Don Juan in Hell sequence, whose intensity is so much greater than the romantic play surrounding it precisely because it grapples with his imperative present problem. Moreover its dialogue form, inviting comparisons to Plato and Diderot and Hume, was part of his attempt to cancel his body's defeat by a triumph of mind. We have seen Tanner dismiss the importance of all passions other than that moral seriousness through which he defines his manhood; similarly, Shaw now has to define his own manhood by emphasizing his moral seriousness, by regarding himself as more than an entertainer, a writer of romantic comedies, a "pander, buffoon, beauty monger, sentimentalizer," which "rich people" would force the artist to be. He must regard himself as a serious thinker, "no mere artist, but an artist philosopher," and to make his claim unmistakable he subtitles the play "a Comedy *and a Philosophy*." The comedy is almost a concession to public taste and theatrical requirements, merely "a trumpery story of modern London life," as he calls it in the same preface from which the above quotations are drawn. Thus the philosophic dialogue, though he recognizes it as "totally extraneous" to the play, reflects his now urgent need to establish his credentials as a thinker.

Indeed he began writing the philosophic section before writing the play; and keeping this fact in mind enables us to avoid much of the usual critical confusion about the work as a whole. Because Tanner is referred to in the play as a descendant of Don Juan, and because the Hell sequence in Act III is ostensibly Tanner's dream of his ancestor, commentators have assumed that Shaw was giving his own version of the legendary Don Juan, and Shaw himself tried to make it appear so in the interests of connecting the two parts of the work. Yet the integration of the parts is superficial because on a psychic level Shaw was recreating Don Juan as Tanner's successor, not his ancestor. Tanner is the earlier Shaw, the one who supposedly capitulated to marriage; Don Juan, turning contemptuously away from women, is the present Shaw, the Irish Don Juan with a virginal wife, struggling to renounce a desire for women. In short, the best way to comprehend the inner drama of *Man and Superman* is to view the romantic play section as Shaw's attempt to incorporate into his art the events leading up to his marriage to Charlotte—though those events are infiltrated by his later feelings and distorted to suit his present needs—and to view the dream sequence as his attempt to incorporate and expand the rationalizations that he developed after his marriage.

Let us turn then to a consideration of this celebrated debate, with the possibility of uncovering new meanings if we attend to its roots in the playwright's life and also treat it seriously as a statement of Shaw's creed.*

V

The Don Juan in Hell debate, with its four participants, is leavened by reasonable amounts of Shavian comedy—provided mainly by the secondary characters Doña Ana and her father, the Commander—and Shavian nimbleness in treating ideas in a lively fashion. Of the two primary debaters, the Devil is conceived with more originality and presented with more artistic control. He should in fact be recognized as one of Shaw's most remarkable creations, especially if we take into account both the constraining form of the philosophic dialogue (in which action is minimal and the personae must come alive solely through their speeches) and the weight of assumptions about the Mephistophelean character. Shaw's unique Devil is never malevolent or terrifying, is scarcely hypocritical or truly cynical, is not responsible for man's destructive impulses; but as a catalyst who brings out man's innate wickedness, he is more cunning than perhaps even his creator realized. Don Juan, in contrast, is a curiously one-dimensional character, at least if we accept Shaw's way of perceiving him and the way he is invariably perceived by actors. He obviously serves as the author's mouthpiece, and Shaw's excessive identification with the Don impairs his ability to give the character the benefit of some detached contemplation. This does not mean that we need share the adoring way Shaw regards his protagonist, and I shall presently suggest an alternate view. But first we must look at the general philosophic difference between the two men be-

*For instance in 1909 he told a young Fabian that "the third act of *Man and Superman* will remain on record as a statement of my creed" (Collected Letters, II, p. 873); and as late as 1947 he said that "there is a studied theory of Creative Evolution behind all my work; and its first statement is the third act of *Man and Superman*" (*Self Sketches*, p. 160).

It should perhaps be made explicit that the following interpretation of the dream sequence, and indeed of the play proper, does not hinge on whether Shaw agreed before the wedding day or afterward not to have sexual relations with his wife. The only critical biographical assumption I am making, based mainly on the evidence of the play itself, is that Shaw became to some extent unhappy with the arrangement and resented Charlotte's unwillingness to consummate the marriage. This does not exclude the possibility that at times he may have assured himself that he was content with the arrangement and that he could have overcome Charlotte's resistance had he really wanted to do so.

cause they are principally characterized by their respective ideas.

The difference, in an initial formulation, is clear enough. The so-called Devil, in a world in which all progress is illusory, favors self-cultivation and epicureanism. He wants humanity "to sympathize with joy, with love, with happiness, with beauty." Espousing a semi-Paterian credo, which distrusts abstractions and recognizes man's capacity for self-deception and destructiveness, he asserts that he would rather be his own master than the tool of any blundering Life Force. "I know," he declares, "that beauty is good to look at; that music is good to hear; that love is good to feel; and that they are all good to think about and talk about. I know that to be well exercised in these sensations, emotions, and studies is to be a refined and cultivated being." In adjuring Don Juan not to be the sort of "fool who pursues the better before he has secured the good," the Devil shows himself to be both a realist and an idealist. His ideals are earthbound, present-minded, sensuous, contingent, aesthetic. He offers a honeyed version of Ecclesiastes and embraces the pleasure principle in a social way. He would be at ease in Bloomsbury.

Don Juan, in contrast, believes that evolution is unconsciously purposeful and that through the philosopher's brain it seeks to bring that purpose to consciousness. As an idealistic servant of the Life Force he believes it his duty to help "Life in its struggle upward," to work "for human perfection." He rejects the present as unsatisfactory and the search for happiness as futile. He exists for the future and willingly sacrifices himself and his personal contentment. "I tell you," he declares, "that as long as I can conceive something better than myself, I cannot be easy unless I am striving to bring it into existence or clearing the way for it." Through the labors of his brain he intends to become one of the "masters of reality," a goal made easier because the pleasures favored by the Devil are either overrated or distracting. Aestheticism he has found to be of limited value since the cultivation of his sense of beauty through the arts finally led him to the worship of women, and women interfere with his responsibilities as a philosopher.

It may seem at first glance that we have here an irreconcilable conflict between two opposing ideals and temperaments, and in the development of these contrasting positions Shaw for the most part succeeds in giving equal strength to the Devil's side even though his own sympathies are clearly with Don Juan. The Devil makes several telling speeches, and one magnificent one on mankind's destructiveness, but the Don's refutations always seem adequate, especially as they are voiced with total self-assurance. Throughout the debate the Don maintains an authoritative manner, suavely winning small verbal victories over Ana and the Commander, and earning respectful attention during his confident analysis of the psychology of love. In physical appearance as well as in manner he is the Devil's superior: the Don is handsome and aristocratic looking whereas the Devil, we are told, is "a disagreeably self-indulgent looking person," whose sentimentality and effeminacy Shaw tries to indicate by an exaggerated mode of expression. Thus even though the playwright does not allow the Don's victory in the debate to be conclusive, he predisposes us to believe that it is conclusive by making him far more attractive than his antagonist. And much of the peripheral uneasiness we may experience in watching the debate derives from the Don's physical attractiveness and intimidating fluency, which may incline us to acquiesce in his position for extrinsic reasons, may make us sense that our minds are being seduced— an appropriate enough activity for a Don Juan, but not for a would-be philosopher. Shaw did not, I believe, intend this effect but wanted us to be genuinely persuaded. Yet he found himself forced to resort to various devices apart from the Don's actual arguments in order to make that persuasion certain, above all to himself. However, if we free ourselves of the Don's physical presence in the theater by studying the debate, then we can come to see that the philosophical conflict, though real enough when stated in summary fashion, is tangential to the actual conflict in the encounter, which is simply between the clear-headed consistency of the Devil and the muddle-headedness of the handsome Don, who completely discredits his own case by his method of defending it and whose desire to help the Life Force achieve understanding would first require that he achieve it for himself. For whatever the Don says—beyond the implied banality that exclusive pursuit of pleasure is self-defeating—betrays a grievously confused mind.

In one place, for instance, the Don is attacking man's civilization: "All his civilization is founded on his cowardice, on his abject tameness, which he calls his respectability." In another place the Don praises man for being "too imaginative and mentally vigorous to be content with mere self-reproduction. He has created civilization without consulting [Woman], taking her domestic labor for granted as the foundation of it." Again, in one speech he declares with contempt that "the earth is a nursery in which men and women play at being heroes and heroines," and he further announces that he sings "not arms and the hero, but the philosophic man." Elsewhere, however, he announces admiringly that man "will fight for an idea like a hero," and he praises the "fanatic": "[Man] can only be enslaved whilst he is spiritually weak enough to listen to reason." Yet again, at one point the Don mocks Hell as "the home of honor, duty, justice, and the rest of the seven deadly virtues." At another point, in a glibly rhetorical attack on man, the Don declares that men are "not moral: they are only conventional. They are not virtuous: they are only cowardly . . . , not dutiful, only sheepish . . . not just, only vindictive"—all of which contradicts his earlier jibes at virtue, duty, and justice. Still again, we find that Juan advocates careful "breeding [of] the race, ay, breeding it to heights now deemed superhuman"; yet elsewhere he maintains with blithe inconsistency that it is useless to impose "careful selection" on "the irresistible force of Life."

Qualified in his own estimation to use his intellect to become a "master of reality," Don Juan actually displays an awesome talent for self-contradiction, for holding mutually exclusive positions with equal assurance. Even in defending his supposed asceticism the Don is inconsistent. He condemns Hell as the home of "the seekers for happiness"; he rejects the "vulgar pursuit of happiness." Yet elsewhere he boasts that the philosopher is the one "sort of man [who] has ever been happy," and his conflict with the Devil turns on different methods of obtaining enjoyment. "Even as you enjoy the contemplation of such romantic mirages as beauty and pleasure, so too would I enjoy the contemplation of that which interests me above all things: namely, Life." When Ana asks him if there is nothing in heaven but contemplation, he replies, "In the heaven I seek, no other joy."

Other and more consequential instances of the Don's delightful talent will be examined in due course, but perhaps enough has been presented to indicate that Shaw's Don Juan is really a comic figure of rare distinction, a worthy cousin of Molière's self-righteous and inconsistent reasoner Alceste. In the theater Don Juan should be played, as has not yet been done, as a desperately voluble intellectual bully, self-deceiving but pathetic—a Sergius aping the manner of Socrates—with the Devil sardonically appreciative of his opponent's pretensions. And the comedy is heightened because Shaw was only fitfully aware of what he had achieved: although he allows the Devil to rebuke the "wrigglings, and evasions and sophistries" in one of the Don's flights, the playwright is so urgently using the Don to expound his own positions that he cannot afford to expose the sophistries; and on the whole we must regard the Don's confusions as Shaw's own, and as symptomatic of powerful emotional conflicts in the playwright himself.* Unable however to resolve these conflicts, he often resorts to mere bursts of petulance, assaulting targets that shift from moment to moment. As we have seen, he sneers at civilization and then upholds it in order to denigrate women, sneers at mindless heroics and then praises the fanatic, sneers at happiness and then seeks it for himself. So powerful is Shaw's exasperation that he cannot allow himself to assess Juan at all critically, and only when the debate is finally completed and Juan has left the scene, only when Shaw has fully appeased his craving to attack, does he put into the Devil's mouth a warning against Don Juan's position: "Beware of the pursuit of the Superhuman: it leads to an indiscriminate contempt for the Human." These are the wisest words in the entire play, but the truth of this afterthought, assuaging Shaw's social conscience, is not allowed to temper the vexation of spirit underlying the Don's earlier attacks.

The root of this vexation, I submit, was Shaw's defeat in his battle with Charlotte over sexual relations. If the jeering indicates some of the frustration created by this defeat, the Don's actual arguments indicate Shaw's attempts to accommodate himself to it, and his immense stake in these arguments accounts for the weaknesses as well as the strengths of the entire Hell sequence. It blinds our author to the speciousness of the reasoning and makes him indifferent to the lengthiness of the debate, but it also draws forth a more vehement mental effort than was required in the surrounding play, whose greater humor and ease were attainable precisely because there he was dealing with the more distant event of his getting married. The wit in the dream sequence often collapses into mere abuse, its satiric anger often discharges itself indiscriminately, but it often has a redeeming forcefulness born of despair. Far more than his surrogate, Tanner,

*Further evidence of the similarities between Shaw and his protagonist is presented in the Appendix.

Bernard Shaw was in a private hell—and we must now briefly consider some of his proposed strategies for escape.

The initial strategy, as has been noted, is to wrap himself in the philosopher's cloak and to glorify contemplation as man's highest activity. From this lofty ideal, Shaw can now deprecate mere bodily pleasures and such mundane concerns as love, beauty, and happiness. In thus rejecting those satisfactions no longer easily available to him, and in elevating the importance of intellect, Shaw remains in control of his existence; but to relieve the possible bleakness of such an existence he has Juan inconsistently claim for the thinker that very possibility of happiness which had been previously rejected. The philosopher, in fact, has the best of both worlds: he is the only truly happy man and is additionally serving mankind and the Life Force.

Now in our discussion of *Candida* we saw that the playwright considered sexual fulfillment to be a large component of happiness, and that Marchbanks's boast, "I no longer desire happiness," is really a renunciation of sex. At the time when Shaw wrote the play, in 1894, he was having affairs with women despite his ambivalent feelings about sex. Any renunciations he made then were voluntary or, as in *Candida* itself, merely fantasized. But now, with the renunciations imposed upon him by his wife, he could no longer so airily reject happiness, even if he had to redefine it so as to sever its connection with sex. Hence he now claims that the philosopher is the only truly happy man and, conversely, he now belittles the happiness offered by sex.

But as he further seeks to regard himself as an exemplary servant of the Life Force, Shaw must overcome an awkward difficulty in his argument. The philosopher should not be a married man, since "the Life Force respects marriage only because marriage is a contrivance of its own to secure the greatest number of children," and Shaw's marriage was obviously going to be childless. Marriage for someone like the Don, who seeks to be a philosopher, limits his experience:

That unless the lady's character and intellect were equal to or superior to my own, her conversation must degrade and her counsel mislead me; that her constant companionship might, for all I know, become intolerably tedious to me; that I could not answer for my feelings for a week in advance, much less to the end of my life; that to cut me off from all natural and unconstrained intercourse with half my fellowcreatures would narrow and warp me if I submitted to it, and if not, would bring me under the curse of clandestinity.

Yet here was Shaw married to a woman whose intellect he never regarded as remotely equal to his own, who cut him off from unconstrained intercourse with half his fellow creatures, and who refused him sexual relations. Could *he* have made such a double blunder—of getting married in the first place and then to the wrong woman? Could *he* have trapped himself into a relationship that lesser men avoided? Might not these errors disqualify him for his self-appointed role as artist-philosopher and master of reality? Whatever logic might dictate, only one self-respecting conclusion was possible: No, he had not made a mistake—the Life Force had made a mistake! "The Life Force is stupid," Don Juan insists. But Shaw, having personally suffered the consequences of its stupidity, would undertake to correct it. In fact the Life Force, in its blind will for survival, had really chosen him as its agent—along with a choice band of other (unnamed) philosophers—to bring it greater self-awareness and self-understanding so that it would stop its blundering. Thus what might have been viewed unsympathetically as a personal failure and a sign of unfitness to be a master of reality, Shaw converts into a cosmic justification. "My brain is the organ by which Nature strives to understand itself," the Don modestly declares. Nature had him in its unconscious mind from the beginning and would allow him to assist it. Rightly viewed, the bandages on Shaw's battered ego were really medals for services to be rendered.

But this initial strategy for transcending his marital difficulties does not satisfy Shaw. Although he would have liked to accept this dignified renunciation of his sexual being, allowing the Irish Don Juan to be transformed into an ascetic philosopher, he could not fully do so. The Life Force had given him a body as well as a mind, and it had forced him into marriage with an adamantly virginal wife. The Life Force may wish the philosopher to develop for it an "intenser self-consciousness and clearer self-understanding," as Shaw keeps reiterating, but the only consciousness readily available is that of the self, and whatever purposes the self attributes to "blind" Nature are of course extensions of its own purposes, a reading back into Nature of the self's own will and desires. Hence the only goal Shaw now perceives for the Life Force is, not surprisingly, what he wants for himself; for if we seek some inkling of what high thoughts are actually being thought by this particular philosopher, what profound consciousness this philosopher is bringing to the Life Force, then we find Shaw putting into Juan's mouth, and later into the "Revolutionist's Handbook," nothing other than various schemes for extramarital sex!

This second strategy commences with the Don's prediction that man will find a completely effective means of birth control which will enable him to have "romantic delights" without any of the consequences.

> Do you not know [he tells Ana] that where there is a will there is a way? that whatever Man really wishes to do he will finally discover a means of doing? Well, you have done your best, you virtuous ladies, and others of your way of thinking, to bend Man's mind wholly towards honorable love as the highest good, and to understand by honorable love romance and beauty and happiness in the possession of beautiful, refined, delicate, affectionate women. You have taught women to value their own youth, health, shapeliness, and refinement above all things. Well, what place have squalling babies and household cares in this exquisite paradise of the senses and emotions? Is it not the inevitable end of it all that the human will shall say to the human brain: invent me a means by which I can have love, beauty, romance, emotion, passion, without their wretched penalties . . . ?   [III]

It was of course an accurate prediction, as the variety of twentieth-century contraceptive devices indicates, but if we allow ourselves to speculate on the reason for the appearance of this idea at this particular moment in Shaw's life, not long after his marriage, then we can perhaps regard it as a response to Charlotte's most telling argument for avoiding coitus—her fear of pregnancy. The language of Shaw's prediction suggests that reliable methods of birth control will be invented almost as a form of revenge on those scornfully addressed "virtuous ladies," those "refined" and "delicate" ladies who want to avoid the biological function of marriage and to substitute "unbearable frivolities" for Nature's purposes. Nature respects marriage, we have been told, "only because marriage is a contrivance of its own to secure the greatest number of children," but if the virtuous ladies disregard this fact they had better be prepared for consequences that ultimately will undermine women's "virtue."

That the refined lady whom Shaw had most in mind was probably Charlotte seems confirmed by an adjacent passage which offers the absurd generalization that the procreative purpose of marriage, "which is now hidden in a mephitic cloud of love and romance and prudery and fastidiousness, will [someday] break through into clear sunlight . . . [and] the real purpose of marriage will be honored and accepted, whilst their romantic vowings and pledgings and until-death-do-us-partings and the like will be expunged as unbearable frivolities." Given the size of Victorian families, it seems odd of Shaw to suppose that most people did not honor its procreative function, but we must remember that there was one such person living with Shaw at the time.

To recommend sexual gratification as an end in itself, and thereby support the pleasure principle too openly, was of course uncongenial to Shaw, and he quickly moves on to an alternate proposal that would subordinate sexual gratification to high social goals, namely, the selective breeding of the race "to heights now deemed superhuman." This proposal of eugenics is the most positive one that the Don advances, and Shaw himself provisionally entertained the idea with great seriousness since it reappears in the preface and is elaborately developed in Tanner's "Handbook," some of whose arguments can be conveniently referred to at this time in conjunction with the development of the idea by Don Juan.

Shaw hedges in the dream sequence on whether the breeding of the Superman is to be within marriage or not, for his objectives shift as he looks back on his experience with Charlotte and then forward to his possible relations with other women. When doing the former, as we have just seen, he will attack the virtuous ladies who do not honor and accept "the real purpose of marriage," who cloud that purpose in "prudery and fastidiousness." When looking forward to other women, however, Shaw has the Don describe marriage in the hardly favorable image of a policeman and his prisoner, or of felons chained together on a galley. And further weakening the argument that genetic improvement of the species should occur within marriage is Shaw's presently useful contention that the sexual relationship is completely impersonal. Thus the Don, presuming to speak for all men, urges Ana to "do my sex the justice to admit, Señora, that we have always recognized that the sex relation is not a personal or friendly relation at all."

But these contradictory attitudes toward the role of marriage in a program of eugenics are completely resolved by the time Shaw came to write the "Handbook." There we read that those chosen for breeding should not be man and wife—"mating such couples must clearly not involve marrying them." In fact, "marriage, whilst it is made an indispensable condition of mating, will delay the advent of the Superman." Will marriage, then, disappear as an institution? Not at all, Shaw argues, for marriage has traditionally had two functions: "regulating conjugation and supplying a form of domesticity." But conjugation is, he now asserts, a "purely accidental and incidental condition of marriage." The institution may in the future be allowed to continue, he generously maintains, only if there is "the complete extrication of conjugation from it." The true purpose of marriage will then be fulfilled, since it is basically an "economical, convenient, and comfortable" arrangement to allow two people to live together.

Having thus demonstrated how the philosopher engages in disinterested contemplation, Shaw finally arrives at a position which justifies his own peculiar marital state, would force every husband and wife to live in like manner, and would allow only superior people to have sexual relations—not of course for personal enjoyment but for the good of the State. And Shaw would wish us to believe that it is urgent for superior people to begin their activities, for the human race is doomed unless it can breed better human material. No political or economic or social reform can ensure survival—only eugenics. The eugenics program might involve setting up private companies "for the improvement of human live stock," a "human stud farm." Or it might mean establishing a "State Department of Evolution, with a seat in the Cabinet for its chief, and a revenue to defray the cost of direct State experiments and provide inducements to private persons to achieve successful results."

Now whatever the merits of Shaw's proposal—and the Nazis were to demonstrate how a kindred program could be carried through—it is not unlikely that our author is indulging in an elaborate private fantasy. We can easily imagine Shaw graciously volunteering to put in an appearance now and then at the stud farm, taking no pleasure in it, of course—Tanner condemns the man "in whom the instinct of fertility has faded into the mere itch for pleasure"—but still, society must be saved and men with first-class brains must do their duty. Thus Bernard Shaw, socially conscious even in his sexual fantasies, or allowing himself to indulge them only on condition that he will not find them too obviously pleasurable, envisions ways of solving his present matrimonial difficulties. And he would even be willing, if the matter were dealt with discreetly, to have other people assist him to a solution. At the very end of the "Handbook"'s discussion of the absolute need for eugenics, we learn that "a conference on the subject is the next step needed. It will be attended by men and women who, no longer believing that they can live for ever, are seeking for some immortal work into which they can build the best of themselves before their refuse is thrown into that arch dust destructor, the cremation furnace." It is not clear from this description whether the conference would be devoted solely to scholarly purposes or to an immediate fulfillment of the conferees' desire to build the best of themselves into some immortal work; nor is it clear what genetic qualifications the participants would possess. All that is relatively certain is that Shaw would be there, and available to any of the women delegates seeking a father for the Superman. And all that is absolutely certain is that Shaw, who usually was a one-man conference issuing directives, is here calling for the assistance of others. Indeed, if one reads the half-serious proposal with any sense of its melancholy autobio graphical undertones, remembering that Shaw had now spent well over a thousand and one platonic nights with Charlotte, had been living off her wealth, had yet to find success in London as a playwright and was feeling old, then perhaps we can hear within the proposal that embarrassed *cri de coeur* which reverberates in the depths of the entire work.

This culmination of the second strategy, with its endorsement of sexual activity, of course differs completely from Don Juan's earlier goal of sexual renunciation. Hence in a crucial respect the Don's conflict is within himself rather than with the Devil. The discursiveness of the discussion as well as Juan's aplomb hide that inner debate from all the participants, including Juan himself. Put somewhat differently, in relation to Don Juan's creator, we may say that Shaw's first impulse was to solve his marital problem by being "philosophical" about it and by glorifying the life of the ascetic philosopher. But though this ideal of enduring his pain with noble strength might satisfy his pride, his frustrated lust prompted him to devise another solution, one which would justify his obtaining women outside of marriage. The physical pleasure to be derived from enacting such a solution had to be kept from full consciousness if Shaw were to respect himself as a social thinker. Therefore the language in which he frames the proposal for selective breeding is invariably impersonal and high-minded. It was apparently not until he came to write the preface that he finally saw through the rationalization and then had to struggle with the significance of his perception. In the Hell scene he seems unaware of the conflict between the two strategies.

Yet neither of them could be taken very seriously. The contemplative life could not satisfy him temperamentally, and the program of eugenics was remote in time and likelihood. He therefore devised a final and more immediately enjoyable strategy, that of discharging his pain in a resentful destructiveness against the human race. Instead of fantasizing additional ways of escaping from his private hell, he would now seek to extend the boundaries of hell so as to draw into it the rest of mankind. This life-hating strategy, it should be recognized, is not strictly the "final" one Shaw offers while presenting Don Juan's various positions, for these are not marked out in the sequence in which we have been examining them. The contemplative ideal, for instance, appears intermittently throughout the dialogue and is never overtly repudiated. Even our use of the term *strategy* is apt to be misleading if it is taken to imply Shaw's calculated presentation of alternatives. The dialogue is fairly unsystematic, with sudden shifts in its topics. And it is particularly necessary to recognize this in considering the "final strategy," which is far more subtly developed than the other two and is more obedient to urgent emotions which Shaw could not fully permit himself to recognize, ugly emotions that lurk within prestigious abstractions and cause the reasoning to stumble into error. From one viewpoint, the final life-denying strategy is simply the combined neglected halves of the other two; from another, it is what we have noted earlier to be an impulse to sneer now seeking a theory to justify itself. But let us quickly piece together Shaw's scattered development of this argument, which is to be the most consequential of them all in his future work.

The misogynistic component is readily apparent. Just before he leaves Hell, Don Juan asks the Commander whether there are any beautiful women in Heaven, and when he receives a negative reply—"Absolutely none. All dowdies. . . . They might be men of fifty"—he declares his impatience to get there. Heaven, it seems, far beyond anything else, is the state of freedom from the intolerable problems created by women. And since on this side of heaven such a monastic escape was impossible for Shaw, he resorts instead to a campaign of disparagement: dismissing romantic love, depersonalizing sex, denying women a role in creating civilization, mocking all ideals of delicacy, refinement, and beauty, seeking almost to tear apart woman's physical being. "When I stood face to face with Woman," Juan declares,

my eye, exercised on a thousand paintings, tore her voice, her features, her color to shreds. I caught all those tell-tale resemblances to her father and mother by which I knew what she would be like in thirty years' time. I noted the gleam of gold from a dead tooth in the laughing mouth: I made curious observations of the strange odors of the chemistry of the nerves.

[III]

There are echoes here both of Shakespeare's 130th sonnet and of some remarks in Shaw's letters which help to clarify that elusive phrase about the strange odors of the chemistry of the nerves. Writing to William Archer in 1901, Shaw condemns the emphasis on romance in the contemporary theater, the ways in which particular playwrights are under the influence of the actress Mrs. Patrick Campbell and her "overpowering *odor di femmina*." He wants Archer to join him in protesting "against the *odor di femmina*" and defending the "unvoluptuous." In the passage cited above there is a Swiftian revulsion at the physicality of the female animal, suggestive of a Swiftian attempt to ward off the female's attractiveness by magnifying parts of her body to the point of grotesqueness.

The palpable misogyny of the dream scene is apt to make us overlook the less openly expressed but quite pervasive destructive misanthropy. Both kinds of animus have been noted earlier in the play section, where Shaw meanly characterizes the heroine and emasculates all of the men; however, in the dream the misanthropy is harder to detect because it is not vented on single characters but couched within Don Juan's apparently noble generalizations. He upholds civilization, as we have seen, in order to disparage women's contribution to it, yet when he speaks directly of civilization he betrays his hostility against the human race itself. This might be apparent enough when Shaw puts into Juan's mouth the array of more than two dozen embarrassingly mechanical antitheses about men, for example, "They are not loyal, they are only servile; not dutiful, only sheepish; not public spirited, only patriotic; not courageous, only quarrelsome; not determined, only obstinate." But this passage despite its tedium might still be regarded as the indictment of an idealist rhetorically aggrieved that mankind has let him down. For the more distinctive and sinister note in Shaw's brand of misanthropy we must turn to a different passage, seemingly in praise of man, a passage that contains the most egregious of the Don's lapses in reasoning:

DON JUAN: Why, that you can make any of these cowards [human beings] brave by simply putting an idea into his head.

THE STATUE: Stuff! As an old soldier I admit the cowardice: it's as universal as sea sickness, and matters just as little. But that about putting an idea into a man's head is stuff and nonsense. In a battle all you need to make you fight is a little hot blood and the knowledge that it's more dangerous to lose than to win.

DON JUAN: That is perhaps why battles are so useless. But men never really overcome fear until they imagine they are fighting to further a universal purpose—fighting for an idea, as they call it. Why was the Crusader braver than the pirate? Because he fought, not for himself, but for the Cross. What force was it that met him with a valor as reckless as his own? The force of men who fought, not for themselves, but for Islam. They took Spain from us, though we were fighting for our very hearths and homes; but when we, too, fought for that mighty idea, a Catholic Church, we swept them back to Africa. . . . Every idea for which Man will die will be a Catholic idea. When the Spaniard learns at last that he is no better than the Saracen, and his prophet no better than Mahomet, he will arise, more Catholic than ever, and die on a barricade across the filthy slum he starves in, for universal liberty and equality.

THE STATUE: Bosh!

DON JUAN: What you call bosh is the only thing men dare die for. Later on, Liberty will not be Catholic enough: men will die for human perfection, to which they will sacrifice all their liberty gladly.

THE DEVIL: Ay: they will never be at a loss for an excuse for killing one another.

DON JUAN: What of that? It is not death that matters, but the fear of death. It is not killing and dying that degrades us, but base living, and accepting the wages and profits of degradation. Better ten dead men than one live slave or his master. Men shall yet rise up, father against son and brother against brother, and kill one another for the great Catholic idea of abolishing slavery.

THE DEVIL: Yes, when the Liberty and Equality of which you prate shall have made free white Christians cheaper in the labor market than black heathen slaves sold by auction at the block.

DON JUAN: Never fear! the white laborer shall have his turn too. But I am not now defending the illusory forms the great ideas take. I am giving you examples of the fact that this creature Man, who in his own selfish affairs is a coward to the backbone, will fight for an idea like a hero. He may be abject as a citizen; but he is dangerous as a fanatic. He can only be enslaved whilst he is spiritually weak enough to listen to reason.

[III]

There is much in this extraordinary passage that might well be paused over—its half-truths, its misreadings of history, its weird logic (for example, the strange assumption that the ideal of human perfection does not include human liberty and then the contradicting justification of war because it promotes human liberty). For our present purposes, however, it is enough to observe that this passage praises man when he is least humane, when he has given up being a citizen and has become a bellicose fanatic, when father and son, brother and brother are engaged in killing one another. We grasp at the possibility that Shaw is trying to have his protagonist unintentionally mock himself, but we grasp in vain, for we know from Shaw's later work that Don Juan's lust for killing is Shaw's very own, that increasingly over the next three decades and as late as *The Simpleton of the Unexpected Isles* Shaw will call for tribunals "from which worthless people will not come out alive," for wars which will be fought for the sake of making war. Indeed, if we had to choose in all of Shaw's work the pivotal words that distinguish the nineteenth- from the twentieth-century playwright, we find them here in Juan's response to the Devil's accusation that men will always find an excuse for killing each other: "What of that?" *What of that!* Death does not matter and killing does not degrade. And this from the supposed reasoner who had initially condemned the high-sounding abstractions that provide man with an excuse for perpetrating "all the wickedness on earth." It is a momentous contradiction, standing midway between Caesar's condemnation of violence in 1898 and Undershaft's diabolical urging to "make war on war" in the 1905 *Major Barbara*. It marks the distance Shaw has traveled since 1883 when he made Hetty in *An Unsocial Socialist* respond to her murderous impulses with a revulsive shudder.

Now this easy dismissal of the value of life, the presumed desirability of giving man an idea that will make him fanatically reckless enough to kill and be killed, may enable us to perceive another satisfaction that Shaw temporarily found in the idea of eugenics. For if this supposed panacea were introduced it would not only provide him with select women to engender upon but also restrain other men from having intercourse and producing descendants. The children of the average man in a modern democracy, we learn from the "Handbook," are "riff-raff," and no amount of environmental improvement can overcome their hereditary inadequacies. They will still be "riff-raff; and to hand the country over to riff-raff is national suicide, since riff-raff can neither govern nor will let anyone else govern except the highest bidder of bread and circuses." Under the idealistic guise of creating the Superman, the program of eugenics would in effect sterilize huge numbers of the population and deny existence to as yet unborn generations. Thus each of the three prospects for the future that Don Juan puts forth actually involves death: the reduction of the population through perfected methods of birth control, the finding of an idea "for which Man will die," and eugenics. The last of these, we realize, embraces the other two, because the pursuit of the Superman gives man an idea to die for and in its method wipes out the production of "riff-raff." Advocating the pursuit of the Superman, even while it appeases Shaw's fantasy of a high-minded way of obtaining women, simultaneously gratifies his destructive misanthropy.

That these gratifications were in fact hidden within the seemingly impersonal and idealistic proposal of eugenics can perhaps be further indicated by the fate of this proposal in Shaw's later work. Oddly, it is scarcely advocated again. And this is because its two disguised components, parting company, were soon to reappear in new formulations. The sexual fantasizing came to express itself in Shaw's frequent playing with the idea of polygamy; and his destructive misanthropy led him to advocate the prompt elimination of the "unfit." Indeed, even while he was writing *Man and Superman*, and expressing his homicidal impulses in the publicly acceptable and even altruistic form of a eugenics program, he was privately beginning to frame justifications for eliminating the unfit, for "weeding the garden" as he would later call it. Thus in a letter written in 1900 we find the following declaration: "I should make each citizen appear before a Board once in seven years, and defend his claim to live. If he could not, then he should be put into a lethal chamber. He could, of course, be represented by counsel; and Death would be represented by an Attorney General." It would take some time for this proposal to move from private correspondence to publicly advocated policy, but the homicidal impulse here seeking to justify itself would be filtered into many subsequent writings. And its first distillate can be seen to lie at the bottom of the proposal for eugenics.

The condemnation and rejection of the human race, the general hope that man will find an idea worth dying for, and the particular hope that the pursuit of the Superman is one such idea—this constitutes the final strategy of the Hell sequence. Although Don Juan is an inconsistent reasoner, he is diabolically clever in concealing his malevolence within an altruistic guise and his hostility to life within that glittering abstraction called the Life Force—clever enough, too, to hide even from himself an awareness that he is a minister of death. Shaw has this awareness at times, but far more frequently he is simply blind to the depravity of his protagonist's doctrines and of their underlying emotions. The deepest irony of the Hell scene is that Shaw unwittingly makes Don Juan far more evil than the Devil himself.

Having now tracked out the three strategies, we have carried ourselves to the point at which we can relinquish our initial formulation of the differences between Don Juan and his antagonist and can attempt to grasp the deeper opposition between them, an opposition no less critical than that between the principles of Life and of Death. And we can deal with this issue most directly by considering Shaw's position on good and evil.

What, then, in his philosophical dialogue, is Shaw's conception of ultimate good? It is to serve Nature's purpose, which is no less than to transform man into a god.

Are we agreed [asks Juan] that Life is a force which has made innumerable experiments in organizing itself; that the mammoth and the man, the mouse and the megatherium, the flies and the fleas and the Fathers of the Church, are all more or less successful attempts to build up that raw force into higher and higher individuals, the ideal individual being omnipotent, omniscient, infallible, and withal completely, unilludedly self-conscious: in short, a god? |III|

The little joke about the Church Fathers should not distract us from noticing an error that would have amused them. The attributes of Shaw's deified individual are presented in the familiar triadic form of theology, but infallibility is substituted for benevolence even though logically it is redundant, being inherent in the joint attributes of omnipotence and omniscience. Shaw seemed more determined to avoid including benevolence than to find a substitute which would at least not be superfluous—"just" or "holy" might have been adequate. He is so urgently trying to dismiss the importance of romantic love that he wants to banish the very principle of love from the universe, and he seems not to realize that he is thereby creating a morally neutral godhead and is prescribing a Superman who need not have any ethical sense whatsoever.

This omission of benevolence is not a mere slip of the pen, for Shaw has Don Juan immediately proceed to buttress the argument by citing the supposed course of evolution.

Will you not agree with me further that Life has not measured the success of its attempts at godhead by the beauty or bodily perfection of the result, since in both these respects the birds, as our friend Aristophanes long ago pointed out, are so extraordinarily superior, with their power of flight and their lovely plumage, and, may I add, the touching poetry of their loves and nestings, that it is inconceivable that Life, having once produced them, should, if love and beauty were her object, start off on another line and labor at the clumsy elephant and the hideous ape, whose grandchildren we are? |III|

Beneath the seemingly plausible contention that Life, having produced the birds, is no longer interested in producing beauty—a contention that might nonetheless surprise an observer of ga-

165

zelles and vultures—Juan smuggles in the claim that Life is equally indifferent to creating love, and he adduces as evidence the ugliness of elephant and ape. The reasoning is of course doubly faulty, since the birds no more incarnate the principle of love than do the mammals, and the mammals' supposed ugliness is irrelevant to their capacity to love. Elephants find each other beautiful, and worms find birds repulsive.

But however faultily arrived at and defended, Shaw's conception of the ultimate good is clear. A person is good to the extent to which he helps to promote the purpose of Nature, which is to transform man into an omnipotent and omniscient god. Conversely, the evil person is simply one who fails to work for that purpose and thwarts it "by setting up shortsighted personal aims." Shaw's Devil is evil because he does not share Juan's desire to "conceive something better than myself" and to be always "striving to bring it into existence or clearing the way for it." The Devil, in short, lacks the instinct to help life surpass itself.

It is the absence of this instinct in you [Don Juan asserts] that makes you that strange monster called a Devil. It is the success with which you have diverted the attention of men from their real purpose, which in one degree or another is the same as mine, to yours, that has earned you the name of The Tempter. It is the fact that they are doing your will, or rather drifting with your want of will, instead of doing their own, that makes them the uncomfortable, false, restless, artificial, petulant, wretched creatures they are. [III]

Demonstrably this is not simply Don Juan's position but Shaw's own, for its essential part is repeated in the preface, where we read that man has the (question-begging) choice of being either "a feverish selfish little clod of ailments and grievances complaining that the world will not devote itself to making you happy," or else "a force of Nature . . . used for a purpose recognized by yourself as a mighty one." Evil, in so far as it is an active principle, is thus the pursuit of personal happiness, in its elementary form what we have come to call since Freud the pleasure principle. But Shaw senses the difficulty of making the pleasure principle an active one, a will-to-pleasure, for then the self-renunciatory definition of good would be threatened by a more immediately attractive alternative. He tries to discredit the pleasure principle by pointing to the futility of embracing it—an individual thereby ends up as "a feverish selfish little clod of ailments and grievances" as he declares in his own voice, or as an "uncomfortable, false, restless, artificial, petulant, wretched creature" as he declares in Juan's voice. More fundamentally, Shaw tries to disallow the autonomy of the pleasure principle. The Devil is not permitted to have a will of his own: "It is the fact that they are doing your will, or rather *drifting with your want of will.*" The modification (in the phrase I have italicized) is important because "drifting" became one of Shaw's favorite words of abuse and was, in fact, the chief charge leveled against Western civilization in *Heartbreak House.* We drift into pleasure, without volition, and the only real will is "the inner will of the world" striving to create a race of Supermen. Whatever will we possess apparently comes from yoking ourselves to that world will.

There is, in brief, only a single active principle, the Will-to-the-Superman, and a shadowy negation of that principle, the Drift-to-Pleasure. Unconsciously caricaturing the ancient philosophical position that evil has no independent existence but is merely the absence of good, Shaw makes the drive toward a morally neutral man-god constitute the ultimate good, and he makes the pleasure principle, because it is a distractive illusion, constitute the ultimate evil.

It is obviously a dangerous position. If the goal is a morally neutral godhead, then the means can be morally neutral as well. But moral neutrality of either means or ends is impossible. Moral codes can differ radically, but every act or failure to act is susceptible to judgment within a given code. If Shaw reduces evil to the pleasure principle, then he leaves no criteria for determining evils as traditionally conceived. More significantly, he actually converts those evils into good. Destructiveness, for example, cannot be evil for Shaw if it helps to fulfill Nature's supposed purpose of turning man into a god. When Don Juan declares that he cannot be easy unless he is striving to bring something better than himself into existence "or clearing the way for it," he is sanctioning destructiveness, as Tanner does also when he asserts that his destructiveness is acceptable because it is directed "to moral ends." Any means are appropriate if they secure the ends. Human destructiveness is thus not an evil in itself—and with perfect consistency Shaw will later hold to this principle in his fantasized acceptance of the destroying angels in *The Simpleton of the Unexpected Isles* and in his political acceptance of the butcheries of Hitler, Stalin, and Mussolini. However, it is impossible for the end, and not only the means, to be morally neutral. Even leaving aside the familiar fact that ends are in practice simply the sum of their means, we recognize that Shaw's Superman, denied the attribute of benevolence, cannot be anything other than malevolent; and when Shaw comes to create his race of Supermen Ancients in *Back to Methuselah* he is therefore blind to their monstrousness because it falls outside his narrow criterion for evil.

Further, by making the Will-to-the-Superman constitute the ultimate good, Shaw turns life itself—the life of the present human race—into a necessarily expendable means to an end. The Life Force may be the name Shaw gives to the "inner will of the world" striving to create a race of Supermen, but since present man must be eliminated, the Life Force from any immediate perspective really signifies the opposite, and Shaw's ultimate good thus turns into the Death Force. It must quite literally seek to wipe out people—if not the entire human race then at least those who are thwarting the inner will of the world by embracing the pleasure principle. For even though Shaw may wish to regard that principle as illusory, the people who hold such illusions are real. "Riff-raff" perhaps, as Shaw might term them, but flesh-and-blood creatures nonetheless. And so again, with perfect consistency, Shaw would communicate to a friend, even while writing *Man and Superman*, that each citizen should be able to defend his claim to live or else "should be put into a lethal chamber." Presumably we would be destined for the chamber if we were finding joy in life and not helping the will of the world fulfill itself—in the manner prescribed by Shaw.

At the bedrock of the argument, then, Shaw's position is extraordinarily consistent, and many of Don Juan's inconsistencies spring precisely from Shaw's reluctance to bar the pleasure principle from his own future life by converting it into ultimate evil. Shaw's double-mindedness on this issue is of course additionally revealed by the strength of the countering arguments provided for the Devil. Nevertheless, insofar as Shaw wants both us and himself to believe that Juan makes the better case, he has arrived at an undeniably consistent yet completely inhuman position. To repudiate the pleasure principle as it applies to oneself may perhaps be socially immaterial, but to regard it as the very essence of evil because it obstructs progress toward the Superman is to set the self into conflict with the human race. The average man will suppress his instinct for pleasure only under coercion, and then only with the promise of future rewards, but Shaw wishes him to renounce present and future satisfactions entirely, except for the satisfaction of replacing himself by a supposedly superior species. To achieve that goal, Don Juan will gladly embrace pain and seek to destroy himself, yet he insists that the rest of mankind should be equally self-destructive. And the surest immediate way to begin is to wipe out anyone who is too preoccupied with enjoying his own life and is thereby ignoring the claims of the remote Superman.

It is at bottom, as we can now see, a sadomasochistic and homicidal fantasy, born of deprivation and hidden with cunning beneath a seemingly resplendent idealism and a seemingly ineluctable law of evolution. Love is merely vestigial, and in the Superman it will be totally absent. Sex is impersonal and is tolerated as a remnant of the banished pleasure principle only because it serves the Will-to-the-Superman. Thus Don Juan, though from one angle merely an amusingly inconsistent thinker, is from another angle a moral monster. "An indiscriminate contempt for the Human"—to repeat the Devil's words—is as neat a catchall definition as any for the principle of evil, and it epitomizes Juan's doctrines. The precise extent to which Shaw agrees with all of these doctrines cannot be fully ascertained, although evidence in the preface, and in many of his latter-day opinions, establishes that several of Juan's doctrines are indeed Shaw's own. Nevertheless, in an important sense Shaw in the Hell sequence is still exploring certain ideas without yet being ready to embrace them; and in fact the really fierce debate in the sequence reflects more of the ideational conflict within Shaw, more of the range and intensity of the emotions beneath the ideas, than does the one-sided restatement of several of the doctrines in the ostensibly assured preface. That Shaw comprehends, even if only intermittently, something of the perniciousness of Juan's ideas is clearly indicated by those moments in the debate when the Devil is allowed to be more than a ridiculed figure or one whose arguments are designed to make Juan impressive in rebuttal. Paradoxically, it is when Shaw permits the so-called Devil to utter cogent rejoinders that he saves himself from complete identification with the truly diabolical positions espoused by Don Juan. Even Shaw's mockery of the Devil is often a covert form of self-mockery, part of the playwright's continuing battle against the aesthete in himself. More crucially, Shaw is in the toils of a struggle with his Christian heritage. For the Devil—and here Shaw's unintended ironies become rather intricate—is in fact the most nearly Christian figure in the debate. Whereas Don Juan advocates impersonal sex, the Devil upholds spiritual love. Whereas Don Juan is eager to start "clearing the way" for the Superman through various death-producing schemes, the Devil warns against the arrogance and inhumanity of such a pursuit. Whereas Juan, after he abandons his contemplative ideal, shows that he has respect for intellect only as it subordinates itself to action, the Devil believes in the Word and would like to spend eternity in conversation. Above all else, the Devil may be considered a Christian in his attitude toward man, since his magnificent speech on humanity's destructiveness is not a cynic's view so much as it is testimony to the presence of evil in man, and its echoes of the King of Brobdingnag's speech in *Gulliver's Travels* should remind us that the Devil simply shares the Christian view of man asserted by Dean Swift.*

The recognition of man's appetite for violence is not of course exclusively Christian; and although in biographical terms it may be momentarily useful to regard Shaw's struggle as an attempt to destroy the residual Christian in himself, in a larger perspective he is struggling against the reality principle and against that large element of Christian thought which in its knowledge of the darker recesses of the human heart is necessarily a part of the reality principle. Hence we may regard the Devil in the broadest sense as a spokesman for both the reality *and* the pleasure principle, the life principle in fact, as he brings his arguments to bear upon the lethal proposals of Don Juan. The passion and the very length of the Devil's speech on the destructiveness of man— nearly the longest speech in all the plays—provide a measure of the intensity of the conflict within Shaw himself, the most

---

*The Devil's speech, twice as long as any other in the scene, is far too lengthy to cite here in its entirety, but the following extract conveys its central import: "And is Man any the less destroying himself for all this boasted brain of his? Have you walked up and down upon the earth lately? I have; and I have examined Man's wonderful inventions. And I tell you that in the arts of life man invents nothing; but in the arts of death he outdoes Nature herself, and produces by chemistry and machinery all the slaughter of plague, pestilence, and famine. . . . There is nothing in Man's industrial machinery but his greed and sloth: his heart is in his weapons. This marvellous force of Life of which you boast is a force of Death: Man measures his strength by his destructiveness. . . . Their imagination glows, their energies rise up at the idea of death, these people: they love it; and the more horrible it is the more they enjoy it. . . . I could give you a thousand instances; but they all come to the same thing: the power that governs the earth is not the power of Life but of Death; and the inner need that has nerved Life to the effort of organizing itself into the human being is not the need for higher life but for a more efficient engine of destruction" (III).

deeply rooted of all of Shaw's conflicts, and it should be recognized that this battle against his own destructiveness would continue to vitalize his drama for another twenty years. Thus the Devil's speech, considered in relation to the playwright, may be viewed as Shaw's warning to himself of his own motives for craving the Superman. Yet he curiously prevents Don Juan from learning anything at all from that speech, and when Juan immediately thereafter calls for ideals for which man should be willing to die, he unintentionally demonstrates how human energies rise up at the idea of death. Shaw thereby manifests what I have elsewhere identified as the Unattended Admonition—that moment when he states the case against killing and then simply ignores it, quite as if the mere statement in itself were sufficient to placate his conscience. It is a striking instance of Shaw's ability to dissociate his intelligence from his destructive emotions, the intelligence first cautioning the emotions and then the latter justifying themselves without any regard to the recent objections. This willed dismissal of the evil in Juan's position, with its attendant rage to destroy mankind, were prompted, as I have argued, by the trauma of Shaw's unconsummated marriage; and it may be useful to conclude our discussion by restating from our present vantage point the relationship of the Hell scene to the playwright's life.

The Don Juan in Hell scene purports to be Tanner's "dream" as he dozes in the Sierra Nevada, and certainly never in dramatic literature have we had a dream like this one, in substance so talkative and argumentative, and with such an appearance of rational control. Yet our analysis shows that however undreamlike it may seem to be, and however out of character for Tanner ever to have had such a dream, in relation to Shaw himself the sequence is pervaded by the same fundamental urges as lie within actual dreams, and that these urges—sexual and aggressive—emerge just as they do in actual dreams, with disguises imposed by a censor, meanings turned inside out, logic suspended, and time distinctions nullified. Indeed the very talkativeness of the dream, as well as its apparent rationality and impersonality, are the chief disguises beneath which Shaw permits himself to express his sexual and aggressive urges. The Hell scene, in a word, is Shaw's own therapeutic daydream as "an Irish Don Juan," newly emasculated. Its resolutely cerebral form seeks to place the dreamer as far as possible from his wounded psyche and to establish himself as a philosopher, superior to mere bodily appetites. Fearing in the depths of his being that he might be less than a man, he fantasizes himself as a Superman, enlisting his humor in a task somewhat beyond its resources and selecting whatever he finds suitable from Nietzsche's doctrines even while avoiding Nietzsche's disconcerting theory of *ressentiment*. As a Superman, he assures himself, his brain is the culminating achievement of the evolutionary process and the very tool for Nature to bring its further purposes to consciousness. But since such grave responsibilities would render mere human pleasure frivolous, Shaw summons up an alternate fantasy in which Nature's most immediately discernible purpose is for him to transmit his mental superiority to a succeeding generation. Admittedly, to advocate eugenics as a means of creating the Superman lessens his claim to Superman status in the present, but it does rescue the possibility of having sexual relations with women: far better to be a near-Superman if women will still be available than to be a full-fledged abstinent one, though of course such relations will be undertaken only as a solemn social obligation and not for brute pleasure.

Yet alongside these improbable fantasies Shaw cannot refrain from venting his resentment toward all males who happen to have less forbidding wives. Hence the proposal to eliminate sex from marriage (establishing his own marriage as the model for all others) and to confine sex to an elite (conspicuously including himself) who could improve the race through selective breeding, both proposals reflecting the same malice that had prompted him to emasculate all the men in the play. Shaw's resentment further led him to call for civil carnage, when men would "rise up, father against son, and brother against brother, and kill one another." In fact he yearned for the extinction of the whole human race, though he hid this yearning within the folds of a handsome idealism, a putative Life Force driving toward a race of Supermen to replace the present race of men. The Superman's transcendence of ordinary moral codes enhanced his appeal for Shaw, nagged as he was by a social conscience which cautioned him that the Superman would regard men and women as indifferently as he would a collection of cats. The Superman's omnipotence also exerted a particularly strong appeal to a man in Shaw's state of enforced continence, and it embodied the classic compensatory longing of the impotent. The deliberate omission of benevolence from among the Superman's attributes further points to the more sinister attraction Shaw found in the Superman's limitless power—the power to kill with impunity and a clear conscience.

Since the yearning to kill more fortunate men and to possess omnipotence drew its strength from envy, it was accompanied by a self-hatred which even a determined narcissism could not truly hide, and this made Shaw perfectly ready to destroy himself along with the rest of mankind. His surrogate Tanner reveals this impulse to Ann at the climactic moment in the final act: "If we two stood now on the edge of a precipice, I would hold you tight and jump." This desire to coalesce murder and suicide, though it carries the dual components of sadomasochism to their ultimate ecstasy, simultaneously destroys the peculiar pleasures they afford, and Shaw therefore usually contents himself with expressing his sadomasochistic impulses well on the near side of fantasized death. Both impulses are present throughout *Man and Superman*, the sadism more prominently in the dream sequence as Don Juan lashes men and women for every fault he can name, and the masochism in the romantic comedy as Shaw endlessly embarrasses Tanner, that protagonist who was even clothed to look like himself. From this psychological angle we can also see why making Tanner credible as a superior man received so little of Shaw's attention, busy as he was enjoying Tanner's humiliations.

In several ways, then, *Man and Superman: A Comedy and a Philosophy* validates the warning that Shaw had once uttered to Alice Lockett: "Beware. When all the love has gone out of me, I am remorseless: I hurl the truth about like destroying lightning." Certainly the remorselessness and the destructiveness underlie the entire work, and the truth that Shaw unintentionally offers is that the frustrations of his unconsummated marriage aroused his malevolent impulses and corrupted his idealism. Celebrating the Superman was a high-minded pretext for consigning present man to Nature's scrap heap and for belittling programs designed to improve present man's social condition. Before 1900 Shaw held as a paramount ethical tenet that life should be regarded as an end rather than a means. But now, with his increased need to mock the average sensual man, he begins to view the lives of others as means to achieve a supposedly higher form of life, with of course the imagined joys of coercing those present beings necessarily more vivid than the joys of contemplating the distant Superman. This new position, it should be understood, did not simply replace the older one but rather existed alongside it, adding a powerful ideational and emotional conflict to many of Shaw's later plays even while it undermined his Fabianism and prepared him to welcome dictators who would emasculate the average man's will and impose forced marches toward would-be utopias. When the political world finally caught up with the destructive fantasies Shaw elaborated in *Man and Superman*, he would be more than ready to surrender himself to it.

Philosophically, then, the ideas in the dream sequence enunciated by Don Juan constitute a radical shift in Shaw's outlook, and though the ideas in one sense belong to the character rather than to the playwright, and in another sense are often only exploratory, Shaw would champion these same ideas in later life and would claim that the play incorporated his own credo. In relation to his career as a dramatist, too, *Man and Superman* has an importance beyond its intrinsic qualities as a theatrical work and marks a change in his development; once we perceive the grimmer tendencies of its philosophical position, hostile to love and sex and life itself, then we can also see that these tendencies demolish the very values on which romantic comedies are built. The story of Ann and Tanner, though at times astringent in tone, has affiliations with such earlier love comedies as *The Philanderer*, *Arms and the Man*, and *You Never Can Tell*. The ideas in the dream sequence, in contrast, lead directly to the darker, more satiric, and often more cynical dramas of the following decade, such as *John Bull's Other Island*, *Major Barbara*, and *The Doctor's Dilemma*. The work in its totality is thus visibly transitional, one of its parts looking backward, the other ahead. This double aspect, however, creates discords when the work is viewed as an aesthetic entity—the "Man" and the "Superman" sections pulling in opposite directions, the "Comedy" and the "Philosophy" of the subtitle fundamentally at odds with each other—and these discords are only partially hidden beneath the wit and the humor and the desperately clever talk Shaw lavished on the work. For when looked at finally in biographical terms, the play had its roots in personal desperation; and just as Goethe relieved the pains of a broken romance by writing of Werther's sorrows, so too did Shaw relieve the pains of a frustrating marriage by writing of Tanner's griefs. The play was a many-sided effort to recapture a lost equilibrium, and both its substance and its form reflect the same quest. Disequilibrium itself becomes almost the prime enemy in Don Juan's discourse, which is why "drift" is the chief sin ascribed to the Devil; and to achieve personal equilibrium Shaw was willing to distort the nature of his past experience with Charlotte Townshend and to disguise the singularity of his present re-

lationship to her, thereby imposing on the play's principal characters and its philosophical passages burdens of persuasion that
they could hardly bear. Correspondingly, in the form too Shaw
would strive to regain his equilibrium, since even beyond the
claim implicit in the philosophic interlude that he now be taken
seriously as a thinker, there is the very lengthiness of the entire
work, which allows him to turn his secret defeat as a lover into a
public victory as a writer, answering the threat to his masculinity
by erecting his biggest single dramatic structure to date, seeking
almost to humiliate the men in his audiences by his brilliance
and to make the women half fantasize whether such a formidable
man as this dramatist might not father for them a Superman.
True, there was one woman who knew of this Don Juan's secret
defeat as a lover, the dramatist's wife, but Shaw's private message
to her was clear enough. She could if she wished see unflattering
bits of herself mirrored in the play's heroine, and could perhaps
be even more insulted by the primary difference between Ann
and herself: Ann's willingness to accept the noble role of motherhood after her bird, as Don Juan phrases it, had been caught in her
net. Charlotte could also see that if Shaw was a captured bird he
would be a defiant one, boldly pressing itself against the sharp
thorn of its wound to make itself sing, and warbling with such
range and power as to triumph over her forever. If not to her a
superman, he would prove he was at least a superbird, and one
whose song could distress her mightily.

And, it seems, Mrs. Shaw was less than pleased by her husband's new play.

6

Pygmalion

THE TWO GIFTS OF LOVE

He, too, had a private vision of reform, but the first principle of it was to reform the reformers.

Henry James, The Bostonians

For each, though he cannot govern
His inner self, would only too gladly govern
His neighbor's will as his own proud mind dictates.

Goethe, Faust

When in revulsion I detest myself
Thus heartily, myself with myself appal,
And in this mortal rubbish delve and delve,
A dustman damned. . . .
So may I yet recover by this bad
Research that good I scarcely dreamt I had.

Edwin Muir, "Comfort in Self-Despite"

Overleaf: Mrs. Patrick Campbell on stage in 1900.

$\mathcal{P}$YGMALION's enduring popularity has somewhat embarrassed Shaw's critics. Its fairy-tale atmosphere, traditional form, and romantic undertones, as well as its apparent absence of philosophic weight and social significance, have made it seem rather an anomaly in the dramatist's output, and its very fame in several stage and screen versions has further encouraged the critics to dismiss it as merely a superior piece of commercial theater. Shaw himself abetted this snobbery by calling the play a "shameless potboiler" and by allowing it only a scanty preface, which reduced its meaning to little more than a plea for alphabetical reform. Yet despite the opinion of Shaw the critic and his more deferential followers, the public has been right to esteem this work, which is in fact one of his richest creations not only in its obvious charms but precisely in the depth of its psychological insights, the range of its philosophical implications, and the wit of its many literary allusions; and its apparent lack of the Big Issues in the other major plays only indicates Shaw's achievement here in weaving those issues so finely into the fabric of characterization and structure that one can scarcely talk about the ideas without talking about the people, who happily transcend anything that can be said about them. Moreover like other true works of art, the play affects us in hidden ways and came from hidden recesses in the writer's own being. It was drawn from depths Shaw had never before reached and was incubated longer than any other play he wrote. His later belittling of the play arose in part from a desire to deflect attention from the ways it incorporated essential aspects of himself. In short, *Pygmalion* is neither the "lucky" hit that one critic has called it, nor yet again the oddly atypical work that others have considered it to be, but rather the one play of them all that Shaw was born to write.

It is a remarkable work in another respect as well. It shows even more conclusively than does *Man and Superman* the intimate relationship between the dramatist's life and his art. It lays to rest the notion, which Shaw himself so much encouraged, that his plays were products solely of his busy brain rather than of his feelings, his hopes, and his fantasies. Because of the fortunate availability of the letters between Shaw and Stella Campbell, we can now see the often amusing ways in which that famous romance of Shaw's maturity was intertwined with the creation of *Pygmalion* and substantiates certain of its meanings. Hence if one goal of our journey through the play is to notice its neglected riches, another is to explore the reasons for Shaw's readiness to create, at this particular moment in his long career, his most fabulous work.*

PART ONE

I

The signs of the playwright's exuberant mastery over his material can be seen wherever we look. The dialogue, for instance, is rapid but never rushed, supple enough to allow each character not only individualizing rhythms but also a variety within those rhythms of mood and emotional intensity. Take as illustration Eliza's lines when she first arrives at Professor Higgins's house, starting with her defensively proud declaration,

I'm come to have lessons, I am. And to pay for em too: make no mistake.

moving on to her momentary collapse,

HIGGINS: Pickering: shall we ask this baggage to sit down, or shall we throw her out of the window?
LIZA: . . . Ah-ah-oh-ow-ow-ow-oo! [*Wounded and whimpering*] I wont be called a baggage when Ive offered to pay like any lady.

next to her sudden strength when Higgins finally asks her how much she is ready to pay,

Now youre talking! I thought youd come off it when you saw a chance of getting back a bit of what you chucked at me last night. [*Confidentially*] You had a drop in, hadnt you?

---

*The subsequent analysis is based on the original *Pygmalion* written in 1912 and reprinted in the Odham's Press one-volume *Complete Plays*.

The Constable Standard Edition and all current ones include much of the material Shaw added for the 1938 filmscript. The major additions—which will be examined in the next chapter—are the Embassy Ball at the end of Act III and Eliza's meeting with Freddy at the end of Act IV. In the original text the visit to Mrs. Higgins's home is immediately followed by the midnight scene in the laboratory, and Eliza at the end of that act does not go off with Freddy, but thinks of drowning herself. The text considered here is superior in all respects to the later version.

and then to her outraged reply to Higgins's continued badgering,

I'm going away. He's off his chump, he is. I dont want no balmies teaching me.

[11]

Shaw is clearly hearing the very lilt of his character's voice and is
running her easily up and down the scale of emotional responses.
His ear for speech was never more sensitively displayed than in
this work, perhaps because its ostensible subject was the importance of the spoken word. And when the words and rhythms are
so unerringly chosen, the characterization is well advanced; and
Higgins, Eliza, and her father, Doolittle, are decidedly among
Shaw's most memorable creations, while even such lesser figures
as Mrs. Higgins, Colonel Pickering, and the housekeeper, Mrs.
Pearce, are drawn with distinction. Similarly, Shaw deftly inte-
grates imagery into the work's meanings. Sculpturing of course is
the dominant image, determining action as well as names like
Pearce and *Pick*ering; but also prominent are the paired opposites
of dirt and flowers as Eliza the flower girl, "horrible dirty" at the
outset, is herself transformed into a beautiful flower, even as her
father the dirt collector is transformed into a gentleman sporting
a buttonhole flower. These two main image clusters (and a subsidiary one relating to rain and the sun) are mutually supportive,
since Higgins may be said to mold his human flower out of the
mud and dirt that mark the original Eliza. Again, Shaw's mastery
as a playwright is evident in his animated use of a large number of
stage props and in the varied patterns he creates for his cast, en-
sembles alternating with duos and trios, with entrances and exits
smoothly dovetailed into the movement of the story, and even the
different ways doors are closed in each act carrying significance.
Shaw's mastery over the play's structure, too, is apparent in the
development of tensions and climaxes within each of the five
acts, as well as along the rising slope of the entire action, which
attains its summit in the marvelous fourth act, when Eliza returns from her triumph at the party, and then descends to the
final confrontation between the professor and his pupil and the
uncertain vistas of their future relationship.

That famous unresolved ending of the play, teasing us forever
with the question of whether Eliza will come back to Higgins
after she has walked out on him, is of course far more than an
effective theatrical finale. It reflects, as do the finest plots, aspects
of character and theme. The ambiguity of the ending transposes
into structure the ambiguities of feeling between Higgins and

Eliza which date from their first encounter, and several of the themes are kept open-ended as well. For example, the play is among other things a comedy of manners, the word *manners* itself being sounded as a keynote and appearing more often than elsewhere in Shaw's work. He is fully aware that *manners* is an elastic term, stretching at once from the way an individual eats to the way he behaves toward others. Thus Mrs. Pearce scolds Higgins not only for ignoring table etiquette and polite speech but also for his manner of treating another human being, Eliza, with indifference to her future. Thus Mrs. Higgins scolds her son for a social crudeness that inflicts pain. Higgins's manners blend indivisibly into his morals, and indeed the fundamental social issue of the play is the degree of relatedness of manners to morals and of both to class. To what extent do an individual's manners determine his social class? Do they reveal or mask his intrinsic class? Is Higgins, for all his wealth and learning, a gentleman? Is Eliza ever a lady? Do their respective manners totally define their appeal for us? Such are a few of the questions Shaw plays with, swiftly yet keenly, allowing no one to have the last word, including himself.

This inconclusiveness, as we know, irritates people who want to be sure of the playwright's meaning and the extent of his seriousness. Critics then rush forward with assurances that the serious meaning is evident enough if only we would recall the playwright's views from other writings. Since Shaw was a socialist, *Pygmalion* must therefore be "a socialist parable," implying that the "characteristics of different social classes can be eliminated," as Bernard Dukore put it in an interesting recent volume. Yet we must be careful not to rescue Shaw's standing as a good Fabian at the cost of his greatness as a dramatist, and instead must be prepared to recognize that in his best plays, such as *Pygmalion*, he is less concerned with illustrating his political beliefs than in exploring them, either reopening issues as a dramatist that may have been settled for him as a socialist, or else testing out the theoretical validity of his beliefs against imagined actualities. Consider, for example, in regard to the play's supposed socialism, the response of Higgins and Pickering after Eliza is finally accepted as a lady at the society party. They gloat over the ease with which the deception has been practiced and the manners of the aristocracy mimicked. Yet the two men may be more deceived than anyone else (just as Mrs. Higgins had shown them to be deceived in the preceding act), and Eliza may now really be a lady, not because she can mimic the well-bred but because her natural aristocratic distinction is no longer encrusted by a cockney accent and the habits of a flower girl. Except for the mere lack of a title she is every inch a duchess in the last two acts, and the people at the party, rather than having been duped, may simply have recognized her true nature far more intelligently than did Higgins. We know that she has an extraordinary quickness of ear, an aptitude for learning, a talent for music which Pickering declares amounts to genius. Higgins and Pickering clearly take far more credit than they should for her success, and Shaw clearly intends Higgins's repeated boast to Eliza, "I made you," to be yet another indication of his obtuseness. Perhaps his experiment proved far less about the value of phonetics as a dissolvent of class distinctions than he imagined. Perhaps the implication of the experiment is quite antisocialistic, or at least antiegalitarian, since Eliza triumphs precisely because she was never a typical flower girl at all. Perhaps the implication is that the talented poor should receive money for their education so that they can rise to their proper class in a capitalistic society which benefits from social mobility. The issue in sum remains open, and it is this playful inconclusiveness that helps to keep *Pygmalion* provocative and fresh.

Similarly, we cannot safely isolate single lines or speeches and judge them at face value apart from their dramatic context. Eliza's famous remark that "the difference between a lady and a flower girl is not how she behaves but how she's treated" may have its truth, but that truth is qualified both by her motive for saying it at the time—to rebuke Higgins while complimenting Pickering—and by other events in the play; at Mrs. Higgins's home, for instance, everyone treats Eliza like a lady although Mrs. Higgins herself still finds her quite far from being one. Again, Professor Higgins's famous formula, "The great secret, Eliza, is not having bad manners or good manners or any other particular set of manners, but having the same manner for all human souls," obviously contains its ounce of self-justification along with its bit of truth.

Yet to insist that the mercurial quality of the work prevents our pinning labels on it is not to imply that all its themes are equally open-ended, nor to underrate its wealth of social observation. Higgins's skill in relating accents to geographic origin is a minor accomplishment compared to Shaw's quick precision in locating his characters on the social scale. Each bears the mark of his respective class, and without laboring it Shaw makes apparent the connections between money and status. More acutely, he shows that snobbery is born of insecurity and is as powerful among the poor as among the middle class. Clara Eynsford Hill and Eliza Doolittle, however different they may be at the beginning in dress, speech, and way of life, are sisters in snobbery, equally priggish and concerned with appearances. Eliza's retort to Higgins at the outset, "I'm a respectable girl, I am," expresses Clara's thought when she first snubs Higgins for addressing her casually. Further, the snobbery of both girls is associated with language: Eliza wants to speak like a saleslady in a flower shop, and Clara, a few turns higher on the same spiral, wants to speak like a member of the most fashionable set. Since Clara's aspirations to gentility are unsupported by wealth or self-assurance, she rivals Eliza herself in mimicry, as we see later in the play. But by then Eliza has been outwardly transformed and appears to Clara to be above her on the social scale. With Higgins's encouragement, Clara imitates Eliza, unaware that she is picking up only Eliza's regressions into slang, which Clara mistakes for the smart new style of speech:

HIGGINS: . . . Goodbye. Be sure you try on that small talk at the three at-homes. Dont be nervous about it. Pitch it in strong.
CLARA [*all smiles*]: I will. Goodbye. Such nonsense, all this early Victorian prudery!
HIGGINS [*tempting her*]: Such damned nonsense!
CLARA: Such bloody nonsense!
MRS. EYNSFORD HILL [*convulsively*]: Clara!
CLARA: Ha! ha! [*She goes out radiant, conscious of being thoroughly up to date, and is heard descending the stairs in a stream of silvery laughter*].

[III]

Clara, then, though in several respects Eliza's "double," differs from her in remaining a sadly synthetic creature, victimized by her own snobbery, and this difference sharpens our sense of Eliza's growth. Eliza's early snobbery is discarded only as she develops her independence, the discarding made visible when she peels off the jewels in Act IV and practically flings them in Higgins's face, and then immediately thereafter disowns all the clothes he has bought her, the clothes of the doll he was training, the clothes she once had coveted along with the taxi rides, the expensive candy, and the other indulgences of wealth. Secure in what she is, she now can dispense with these tokens of a borrowed identity and thereby complete the journey, as the play-wright beautifully shows, from snobbery to selfhood.

Shaw could sympathetically speed her on this journey because in certain important respects Eliza's fairy-tale career paralleled his own. For once upon a time, as we recall, an impoverished young man wandered the streets of London, too shabbily dressed even to be accosted by flower girls. His Dublin accent marked him as an outsider, and his manners were so gauche that he spent hours poring over books of etiquette. Behind him, in Ireland, he had left a humorously inclined father who was able to do little besides wage a perpetual battle against drunkenness. The young man, eager to rise in the world, knew that he could count among his qualifications an aptitude for learning, an extraordinary quickness of ear, a talent for music, and, above all, an ability to manipulate words. But until his accomplishments matched his ambitions, he clung to his self-respect to the point of priggishness and possessed a snobbery born of insecurity. He would have you know that he was not what he appeared to be, that in fact his cousin was a baronet and his family traced itself back to Shakespeare's Macduff. But somehow the young man's aristocratic distinction did not shine through at cultured London houses, and he gave himself away quite as thoroughly as Eliza did at the home of Mrs. Higgins. And like Eliza too, Shaw as a young man in London studied hard to change his accent and to eliminate his provincialisms of appearance and manner, studied in fact with a voice teacher who improved his way of pronouncing vowels as well as of wearing his hair.

Thus Eliza's growth in self-confidence through mastery of language could be zestfully portrayed because it recapitulated the writer's own early development. Higgins, on the other hand, bears some obvious character traits of the mature Shaw—the egocentricity, the puritanism, the immodesty—and these are quite unsympathetically treated. Yet to appreciate the points of similarity between Higgins and his creator, we must first consider the various roles that Higgins plays and the many sides of his relationship to Eliza.

II

Higgins is of course quite unlike Shaw in regarding himself first as a scientist. His drawing room has been partly converted into a laboratory fitted out with a laryngoscope, burners, tuning forks, charts, and a phonograph with a supply of wax cylinders for recording accents. He is a man described as "violently interested in everything that can be studied as a scientific subject," and his scientific achievements have made him arrogant and overbearing.* Though quick to notice any slights to his own vanity, he is careless of the feelings of others; indeed his preoccupation with his subject is at times used as a pretext for ignoring the pain he inflicts on others:

> HIGGINS: . . . She'll only drink if you give her money.
> LIZA [*turning on him*]: Oh you are a brute. It's a lie: nobody ever saw the sign of liquor on me. [*To Pickering*] Oh, sir: youre a gentleman: dont let him speak to me like that.
> PICKERING [*in good-humored remonstrance*]: Does it occur to you, Higgins, that the girl has some feelings?
> HIGGINS [*looking critically at her*]: Oh no, I dont think so. Not any feelings that we need bother about. [*Cheerily*] Have you, Eliza?
> LIZA: I got my feeling same as anyone else.
> HIGGINS [*to Pickering, reflectively*]: You see the difficulty?
> PICKERING: Eh? What difficulty?
> HIGGINS: To get her to talk grammar. The mere pronunciation is easy enough.   [11]

This insensitivity, to put it mildly for the moment, gives Professor Higgins a family resemblance to some of Shaw's other scientist figures such as Dr. Paramore and Dr. Ridgeon; and Higgins's indifference to Eliza's fate after his "experiment" is concluded may be taken as part of Shaw's indictment of science's vaunted pursuit of truth without regard to consequences.

Higgins as a scientist will require some further comment after we broaden our knowledge of his character, but now we must note some of the ways in which he is, not professionally different from Shaw, but surprisingly like him. As the play's title intimates, Higgins is something of an artist, a role compatible with his scientific pursuits since the experiment with Eliza will supposedly confirm his theories even as it provides him with a creative way of displaying his skills. But what type of artist is he? Here the sculptural reference in the title is suggestive rather than definitive, for Higgins as an artist most clearly resembles none

---

*Since our visual image of Higgins has been shaped by the glamorous film stars who played the role, Leslie Howard and Rex Harrison, it will be a useful corrective to know that Shaw would have favored "a heavy man like Charles Laughton" in the part (1947, Brit. Mus. Add. MS. 56631, f. 194).

other than a playwright-director. He creates a role for Eliza, supplies her with lines and polishes her delivery, plots for her a climactic scene, and then tests her out beforehand in a dress rehearsal at his mother's house; but ironically he treats her throughout as if she were a slab of stone.

In thus making the protagonist into a sort of playwright-director tempted by a sculptor's attitude toward his material, Shaw offers a profounder consideration of his own art than can be found anywhere else in his dramatic writings, and this underlying professional similarity undoubtedly accounts for his greater sureness of touch with Higgins than with such other artists as the painter Dubedat or the poet Marchbanks.* The struggle between Higgins and Eliza, as he prepares her for her debut, duplicates the struggle for ascendancy between the director and his leading lady, as Shaw himself knew from having directed many of his own plays; and as much as Higgins would like to credit himself with Eliza's achievement, hers is clearly the greater contribution. This struggle represents as well the initial one between the writer and the creatures of his imagination, who may guide his pen in ways he neither anticipated nor even desired, and who somehow take on independent lives. Shaw in the prefaces often claimed that this or that character had been consciously designed to prove some particular point, and as the world came to accept these claims it drew the reasonable inference that the author's characters were merely his talkative dolls. But in *Pygmalion*, to the very degree that it satirizes a would-be dollmaker, Shaw honors those unconscious forces within himself that gave the soul of life to his more successful creations. And Shaw's muse, returning the compliment, gave this play's doll and its dollmaker their immortal souls.

This mystery of the creative process seems to have been on Shaw's mind even as he wrote the play, or perhaps as the play wrote itself, since it appears to propel itself forward with the rapid inevitability of a happy dream. Shaw acknowledged not long after finishing the work that actors often stimulated his imagination: "If Forbes Robertson had not been there to play Caesar, I should

---

*It will of course be understood that the phrase "sculptor's attitude toward his material" is used with deliberate looseness in order to emphasize the title's implied irony that this modern Pygmalion, unlike his legendary prototype, is a fatally flawed artist. True sculptors, in contrast to Henry Higgins, cherish their material and seek to awaken the form that lies sleeping in the stone, as Rodin once put it.

not have written Caesar and Cleopatra. If Ellen Terry had never been born, Captain Brassbound's conversion would never have been effected." And of course, had Mrs. Patrick Campbell not lived, *Pygmalion* would never have been written, for the part of Eliza was written expressly for her and had been directly inspired by her. Fifteen years earlier, in 1897, even while Shaw was in the midst of conceiving *Caesar and Cleopatra*, he informed a friend that the historical play had been nearly driven out of his mind by another one he had hit upon after watching Mrs. Campbell and Forbes Robertson working together. It was to be the story of a flower girl and a West End gentleman. This is the only remark available on the play before its actual composition in 1912, but it indicates that the gestation period had been unusually lengthy; and when Shaw finally came to write the play he no doubt found his control facilitated by a prior unconscious integration of the material. The question of who had really created Eliza, Mrs. Campbell or himself, is in the play transposed into the question of who created the independent Eliza of the last two acts, Higgins or Eliza herself? The obvious answer in both cases is that the creation was collaborative, though Higgins resists acknowledging it. "*You* won my bet! You! Presumptuous insect! *I* won it." "I said I'd make a woman of you, and I have," he still boasts to Eliza, and Shaw smiles and would have us smile too at this misplaced assertion of artistic vanity.

Yet the vanity is not always humorous. Higgins as an artist is at one with Higgins as a scientist in dehumanizing people so as to augment the importance of his own activity. People's lives beyond the reach of the artist's or scientist's specialty limit its significance and thereby diminish the specialist's ego. Higgins wants to deny Eliza's feelings partly in order to reduce her to what he knows best and can best control—a machine for making sounds. The more he can regard her as a dead stone that he alone can bring to life and keep alive—"She will relapse into the gutter in three weeks without me at her elbow," he brags—the more he can play god and feel alive himself. One may reasonably detect some self-rebuke or at least self-warning in Shaw's ridicule of Higgins's pretensions as a creator, for Shaw well knew what it was like to play god with his own stage creatures and knew also the temptations of regarding people as playthings, mere objects for study and use in future dramas. Higgins's arrogance thus expresses a dehumanizing impulse within the very heart of the artist-creator, who may deny the claims of real life at the behest of a manufactured life.

That these considerations on the creative process were in Shaw's mind when he wrote *Pygmalion* is perhaps further confirmed by noticing the one Shakespeare work that he also had in mind and delicately alluded to here and there, namely, *The Tempest*, which of course contains Shakespeare's profoundest reflections on the artist-creator. The potent imagination of Prospero's art, made visible through Ariel, has its equivalent in the stimulus to Higgins's imagination provided by Eliza, who at one point is accused of having too much imagination; and in both romances the stimulating agent departs at the end, with a consequent loss to the artist-protagonist. Higgins needed his Eliza as Prospero needed the powers represented by Ariel, and as Shaw himself needed actors and actresses to spur his creativity. Shaw probably intended Prospero to serve as an implicit standard in judging Higgins. When Prospero asks Ariel, "Hast thou, which are but air, a touch, a feeling / Of their afflictions, and shall not myself / . . . be kindlier mov'd than thou art," he is preparing to subordinate his ego to the moral claims urged on him by his imagination; and this contrasts decisively with Higgins's aggrandizement of his ego at the expense of his imagination and his related indifference to the lives of others.*

Higgins in his own eyes is not, to be sure, really an artist but rather an expert in phonetics and a teacher. Yet just as it is useful to regard him as a sort of playwright-director tempted by a sculp-

*On the resemblances between the two plays, we might notice that heavy rain is falling at the beginning of each work, and at the end Eliza wins "independence" and Ariel "freedom." Both plays deal with fathers and daughters, with manners, and with the mixed blessings of language. The names of Clara and brother Freddy may have been adapted from *The Tempest*'s Claribel and brother Ferdinand. Beyond this, though the drawing of strict parallels between the two works is unwarranted, one may see in Eliza distinct touches of Miranda as well as of Ariel; and in Doolittle, albeit a Dickensian type, touches of Trinculo and Stephano, and seemingly of Caliban. (The character with a deeper kinship to Caliban will be identified further along.) Shaw's thoughts may have slid over into *The Tempest* after first landing on *The Winter's Tale*, for no one knowing Shakespeare could undertake to write a play about a legendary statue coming to life without thinking of Hermione. Indeed *The Winter's Tale*, and possible conversations with his friend Granville Barker about it, may have initially reminded Shaw of his old notion of a "statue" play of his own, which had first crossed his mind back in 1897. That *The Winter's Tale* was certainly on Barker's mind is indicated by his production of the play at the Savoy Theatre in September 1912—that is, later in the same year in which Shaw finished *Pygmalion* (C. B. Purdom, ed., *Bernard Shaw's Letters to Granville Barker* [New York, 1957], p. 184).

tor's attitude toward his material, so too as a teacher he may be seen as one who is tempted to play the sculptor with his pupils. *Pygmalion*, this is to say, deals among other things with education and is in fact the most original of Shaw's several explorations of a subject to which he, as an inveterate teacher himself, had devoted much thought. He had conceived the play even while he was in the midst of writing another one which showed how Caesar taught a naive girl to pass herself off as a true queen; and not longer after finishing *Pygmalion* he set forth his ideas on education in a long treatise entitled "On Parents and Children," which spells out the same pedagogic position embodied in the play.

As a teacher, then, Higgins holds to a sculptural or somewhat Lockean view of a pupil's mind. (Locke, as we recall, supposed the mind to be originally like "white paper, void of all characters" and passively "imprinted by external things.") True, Eliza is not the unmarked paper or piece of fresh wax Higgins would ideally prefer; even more than his other pupils, the American millionairesses, she comes to him with an accent and defects in grammar that he must first expunge; and even as Eliza is at first bathed to scrub away the grime of the streets, so she must also allow Higgins to clean off her deposits of cockney pronunciation. Submissiveness is the one quality he insists upon. The limitations of this method are shown in Eliza's debut at Mrs. Higgins's home, and Mrs. Higgins declares her son's "experiment" a failure:

You silly boy, of course she's not presentable. She's a triumph of your art and of her dressmaker's; but if you suppose for a moment that she doesn't give herself away in every sentence she utters, you must be perfectly cracked about her.

[III]

Eliza's final transformation is admittedly as mysterious as is any other successful venture in education, but she herself contributed the main components, including her innate capabilities, a strong will to learn and to work hard, and a desire to please teachers toward whom she felt both affection and respect. More nearly a palimpsest than a blank paper, Eliza may not be a wholly adequate example of Plato's theory that knowledge is based on recollection, but like Meno's slave boy she knew more than she thought she knew, the lady she was to become as much folded within her as were once the petals within the flowers she sold. "It was from you that I learnt really nice manners," she tells Colonel Pickering, whose human warmth helped her to blossom despite the chill severity of Higgins's methods. Eliza rightly declares that she will be

a far better teacher than Higgins because she "can be civil and
kind to people." She knows, as Higgins does not, the difference
between drawing forth the understanding of living creatures and
treating them like clay.

In thus showing the importance of will and desire and feeling in
the prospective student, Shaw is illustrating the theories he advanced in "On Parents and Children." There he inveighs against
the "violation of children's souls" and declares it essential "that
submissiveness should no longer be inculcated." Higgins's self-
declared delight in his ability "to take a human being and change
her into a quite different human being" stands rebuked by the essay's claim that every new human creature is nature's experiment, which will be vitiated "if you make the slightest attempt to
abort it into some fancy figure of your own." And Mrs. Pearce's
protests against her employer's callousness,

> You cant take a girl up like that as if you were picking up a pebble on the
> beach. . . . And what is to become of her when youve finished your teach-
> ing? You must look ahead a little.
>   HIGGINS [*impatiently*]: Whats to become of her if I leave her in the gut-
> ter? Tell me that, Mrs. Pearce.
>   MRS. PEARCE: Thats her own business, not yours, Mr. Higgins.
>
> [II]

are directly echoed in the essay's pronouncement,

> If you once allow yourself to regard a child as so much material for you to
> manufacture into any shape that happens to suit your fancy you are de-
> feating the experiment of the Life Force. You are assuming that the child
> does not know its own business, and that you do.

Both in the essay and the play, then, Shaw clearly sides with those
educational reformers who sought to alter the entrenched theory
that a student is a mere receptacle to be stuffed with learning.
Shaw's distinctive contribution lay in his exposure of a particular,
but not entirely unrepresentative, teacher's character and inadequacies.

Higgins lacks knowledge of people, ultimately because he lacks
knowledge of self. He is seemingly not cruel but blind, and he
amuses us by the contrast between his brash assurance and his
displays of ignorance:

> MRS. PEARCE: . . . Mr. Higgins: will you please be very particular what
> you say before the girl?
>   HIGGINS [*sternly*]: Of course. I'm always particular about what I say.
> Why do you say this to me?
>   MRS. PEARCE [*unmoved*]: No, sir: youre not at all particular when

youve mislaid anything or when you get a little impatient. Now it doesn't matter before me: I'm used to it. But you really must not swear before the girl.

HIGGINS [*indignantly*]: I swear! [*Most emphatically*] I never swear. I detest the habit. What the devil do you mean?

MRS. PEARCE [*stolidly*]: Thats what I mean, sir. You swear a great deal too much. I dont mind your damning and blasting, and what the devil and where the devil and who the devil—

HIGGINS: Mrs. Pearce: this language from your lips! Really!

MRS. PEARCE [*not to be put off*]—but there is a certain word I must ask you not to use. The girl used it herself when she began to enjoy the bath. It begins with the same latter as bath. She knows no better: she learnt it at her mother's knee. But she must not hear it from your lips.

HIGGINS [*loftily*]: I cannot charge myself with having ever uttered it, Mrs. Pearce. [*She looks at him steadfastly. He adds, hiding an uneasy conscience with a judicial air*] Except perhaps in a moment of extreme and justifiable excitement.

MRS. PEARCE: Only this morning, sir, you applied it to your boots, to the butter, and to the brown bread.

HIGGINS: Oh, that! Mcrc alliteration, Mrs. Pearce, natural to a poet.

MRS. PEARCE: Well, sir, whatever you choose to call it, I beg you not let the girl hear you repeat it.

HIGGINS: Oh, very well, very well. Is that all?

MRS. PEARCE: No, sir. We shall have to be very particular with this girl as to personal cleanliness.

HIGGINS: Certainly. Quite right. Most important.

MRS. PEARCE: I mean not to be slovenly about her dress or untidy in leaving things about.

HIGGINS [*going to her solemnly*]: Just so, I intended to call your attention to that. [*He passes on to Pickering, who is enjoying the conversation immensely*]. It is these little things that matter, Pickering. Take care of the pence and the pounds will take care of themselves is as true of personal habits as of money. [*He comes to anchor on the hearthrug, with the air of a man in an unassailable position*].

MRS. PEARCE: Yes, sir. Then might I ask you not to come down to breakfast in your dressing-gown, or at any rate not to use it as a napkin to the extent you do, sir. And if you would be so good as not to eat everything off the same plate, and to remember not to put the porridge saucepan out of your hand on the clean tablecloth, it would be a better example to the girl. You know you nearly choked yourself with a fishbone in the jam only last week.

HIGGINS [*routed from the hearthrug and drifting back to the piano*]: I may do these things sometimes in absence of mind; but surely I dont do them habitually. [*Angrily*] By the way: my dressing-gown smells most damnably of benzine.

MRS. PEARCE: No doubt it does, Mr. Higgins. But if you will wipe your fingers—

HIGGINS [*yelling*]: Oh very well, very well: I'll wipe them in my hair in future.

MRS. PEARCE: I hope youre not offended, Mr. Higgins.

HIGGINS [*shocked at finding himself thought capable of an unamiable sentiment*]: Not at all, not at all. Youre quite right, Mrs. Pearce: I shall be particularly careful before the girl. |II|

In the light of such hilarious passages as these, it seems safe to conclude that Higgins's cruelties spring only from emotional immaturity, which would also account for his obliviousness of Eliza's future and his overvaluing of phonetics. Pickering tells him that he must learn to know himself, but he ignores this advice because his self-esteem requires him to remain unaware of his defects, and he resists the efforts of his mother and of Mrs. Pearce and of Eliza to make him grow up. Half the drama as well as the choicest humor of the play come from this effort to teach the teacher, to bring the sculptor himself to life. In a stray moment he acknowledges his lifelessness: "Ive taught scores of American millionairesses how to speak English: the best looking women in the world. I'm seasoned. They might as well be blocks of wood. *I* might as well be a block of wood." And later Eliza becomes the sculptor trying to bring this block of wood to life by showing him first of all the limitations of his own pedagogic methods. She teaches him that the sculptor's chisel should not be used on human beings, and she teaches him in the only way he seems able to learn: by cutting into him and making him feel pain.

LIZA: Before you go, sir—
HIGGINS [*dropping the slippers in his surprise at her calling him Sir*]: Eh?
LIZA: Do my clothes belong to me or to Colonel Pickering?
HIGGINS [*coming back into the room as if her question were the very climax of unreason*]: What the devil use would they be to Pickering?
LIZA: He might want them for the next girl you pick up to experiment on.
HIGGINS [*shocked and hurt*]: Is that the way you feel towards us? . . .
LIZA: I want to know what I may take away with me. I dont want to be accused of stealing.
HIGGINS [*now deeply wounded*]: Stealing! You shouldnt have said that, Eliza. That shews a want of feeling. |IV|

In the next act, after Eliza has chipped a little more at Higgins, he says with sudden humility, "I have learnt something from your idiotic notions: I confess that humbly and gratefully." He has learnt the error of equating Eliza's voice with her being. Her voice, as she pointedly remarks, is now easily available to him on his wax phonograph cylinders, and she makes him admit that he now wants her to be something more to him than a piece of human wax on which he has imprinted his verbal formulas. She has thus reduced to an absurdity the Higginsian theory of education and has forced the proud scientist to acknowledge that her immeasurable soul is far more important to him than her recordable voice and her photographable face.

Higgins may be able to learn that other human beings are not objects because he has become aware of his own vulnerability. "I shall miss you," he finally confesses to Eliza. "I have grown accustomed to your voice and appearance. I like them rather." Higgins's double lesson is now complete and he has the opportunity to perceive the connection between its two parts, to see that he treats people like stone because he himself has been a stone, and that even while he longs to be brought to emotional life he fears the risks of dependency and of losing the security of old habits. These fears seem victorious in the end (though the issue is not completely resolved) since Higgins lacks the desire to retain the lessons and quickly slides back into his defensively patronizing relationship to Eliza. Claiming at one moment that he would have contempt for her if she continued to fetch things for him, he orders her a moment later to fetch some things from a store. He is, as the stage directions at the very end indicate, still "self-satisfied" and "incorrigible." Yet even so, he has unintentionally exposed the flaw in his own educational theory, for he himself is no blank paper on which Eliza can imprint her lessons but a living creature with anxieties, passions, habits, and regrets, and unlike Eliza he is a bad pupil because his will to learn is far weaker than his will to deceive himself.

It is, however, a matter of will in either case, and Shaw as a proponent of vitalism thereby demonstrates the primacy of the will and infuses new philosophic meaning into the ancient comic formula of the uneducable teacher. Pedagogic theories and practices, Shaw confirms, are based on assumptions about human nature that often serve the psychological needs of the teacher rather than the pupil. The Lockean view of man errs in making the human mind too passive; yet Higgins adheres to this position because it justifies his will to dominate and enables him to avoid the dual embarrassments of self-knowledge and self-exposure. He can hide his emotional inadequacies behind his professional front and can correct Eliza's speaking style as a way of avoiding her meaning:

HIGGINS: How the devil do I know whats to become of you? What does it matter what becomes of you?

LIZA: You dont care. I know you dont care. You wouldnt care if I was dead. I'm nothing to you—not so much as them slippers.
HIGGINS [*thundering*]: *Those* slippers.
LIZA [*with bitter submission*]: Those slippers. |IV|

Or, again:

HIGGINS: . . . I'll adopt you as my daughter and settle money on you if you like. Or would you rather marry Pickering?
LIZA [*looking fiercely round at him*]: I wouldn't marry *you* if you asked me; and youre nearer my age than what he is.
HIGGINS [*gently*]: Than he is: not "than what he is."
LIZA [*losing her temper and rising*]: I'll talk as I like. Youre not my teacher now. |V|

Higgins prides himself on his sangfroid but these passages suggest, if not exactly an emotional coldness, a sexual nervousness which derives, as we shall soon see, from pronounced sexual perversities.

But before proceeding any further with our discussion, we have perhaps covered sufficient ground to conclude that Shaw has integrated into his comedy of manners, and his exploration of the creative process, a philosophical comedy on the nature of education, and that he treats this with a deceptive lightness of touch and great acumen. Several of his earlier works had dealt in effect with the relation between a "teacher" and a "pupil." Critics have rightly called attention to *Pygmalion*'s resemblance not only to *Caesar and Cleopatra* but also to Shaw's early novel *Love Among the Artists*, where the musical genius Owen Jack instructs a young woman in the art of acting. Other works might equally have been cited, for a teacher-pupil relationship appears in such plays as, say, *Major Barbara* and *Captain Brassbound's Conversion*, as well as in the novel we examined in an earlier chapter, *An Unsocial Socialist*. But what has hitherto gone unnoticed, and is of greater importance than the recurrence of the pedagogic situation, is *Pygmalion*'s originality in examining it. In all the earlier works the teacher is on the whole regarded simply and favorably, the lesson itself is stressed, and the pupil's degree of advancement is either admired (as with Barbara) or bemoaned (as with Cleopatra). But in *Pygmalion* the critical focus is on the teacher himself, and he is tested along with his pupil. Despite the play's fairy-tale mood, Shaw treats its pedagogic theme more realistically here than elsewhere in his work. Higgins is more human-sized than Caesar, Lady Cicely, Trefusis, Owen Jack, or Undershaft. His closest counterpart, in fact, is probably Jack Tanner, the self-declared bringer of enlightenment who is taught more than he wishes to learn by Ann Whitefield. But Tanner is an uncomplicated character compared to Higgins, who will remain Shaw's most compelling study of the would-be world-betterer, perhaps because it is his most elaborately mocking self-portrait, certainly because it is rendered so dramatically: not as a comedy with inserted philosophic passages but as a comedy whose ideas are entirely incorporated into character and story and plot.

Indeed from the perspective of the themes under review, it may now be seen how expertly the plot is integrated into the meaning of the play. Shaw refrained from writing the scene of Eliza's triumph at the party, seemingly the obligatory scene, because, as he said, it would have increased production costs and could better be left to the audience's imagination. The first reason is superficial since in earlier works Shaw had shown himself quite able to indicate the presence of large numbers of people without actually putting them on stage. The latter reason is more fundamental and suggests that artistic and emotional considerations were more decisive than technical or financial ones. Shaw was far more interested in the relationship between Higgins and Eliza than in the masquerade of her public triumph; and since he was embodying ideas on the imagination and the will, he sensed the fitness of appealing directly to the audience's imagination and will, as if to draw it into the play in a special way and to have its reactions confirm his meanings. In deliberately shaping the plot so as to make the audience conceive for itself the omitted party scene and, at the end, Eliza's future relationship with Higgins, the dramatist impelled the audience into an obligatory act of collaboration with him, which parallels the collaboration in the play between the director and the actor, the artist and his imagination, and the teacher and his pupil. The audience thereby confirms, by being forced to will its imagination into action, the play's vitalistic position.

Further, the creative urge itself is transmitted to the audience. As Shaw builds our feelings of identification with the two principal characters, he makes us wish for more than strictly romantic reasons that the two will remain together. An act of creation is being left unfinished, and we share the frustrations of both the creator and the incompleted object: Eliza being the creator and Higgins the object. For we know by the end of the play that Eliza can now look after herself; we want her to stay with Higgins more for his sake than her own, so that she can continue to instruct her first pupil and mold him toward emotional maturity. Eliza, in the role reversal that occurs during the play, becomes the teacher and sculptor, and we want her to finish the job by bringing her wooden man to life. We want this particularly because the phonetics professor contains bits of ourselves, for who has not at times been more wooden than he would wish to admit? More childish and petulant, more inconsiderate and self-important, more as it were *Higginsian*? Identifying thus with Eliza and Higgins, we enter the psychological crosscurrents of the myth of Pygmalion, the sculptor who had to create in order to complete himself, whose creation had to complete him even as Eliza tries to complete Higgins. The play's unresolved ending leaves us with a threatening sense of personal incompleteness and the creative urge to relieve it. Shaw turns us, in a word, into Pygmalion.

Needless to say, he succeeds only too well, for the history of the play from its opening night onward is a series of attempts to change its ending. Starting with Beerbohm Tree's production in 1914, through Gabriel Pascal's film version in 1938, to the stage and film versions of *My Fair Lady*, the prospective marriage of Higgins and Eliza has always been sharply implied. Shaw continually objected, but despite all of the creator's injunctions that no man should join together what he had kept asunder, everyone defied him, spurred on by forces within the work itself to create a more satisfying conclusion. And finally Shaw himself could not resist tinkering with the ending, as if the old master sculptor would now teach all the little Pygmalions he had created how to do the job right—and of course he bungled it completely.

III

Yet Shaw was not being at all arbitrary in insisting on the unresolved ending: he was being faithful to the work's inherent constraints. He knew that in longing for the union between Eliza and Higgins we ignore the secret appeal of the Pygmalion legend, which he himself fully recognized and exploited. For after all the sculptor would be committing incest in marrying the woman he had fathered parthenogenetically. And if the obvious appeal of the Pygmalion story lies in its adolescent fantasizing of the ideal woman, its hidden and concomitant appeal lies in incest, initially between father and daughter, but also between son and mother. For deep within the male fantasy of the ideal woman are memories of the most fulfilling of ideal women, the mother. Galatea is thus daughter and mother simultaneously, as Pygmalion is father and son. The play's ending frustrates us, beyond all else, because the specific, illicit, and powerful completion we had been led to expect is withheld. Indications of a marriage between Eliza and Higgins would have allowed us to fulfill the incest fantasy, and fulfill it without guilt by seemingly turning the relationship into a romance with a socially acceptable conclusion. Shaw denies us that final satisfaction, or transfers to us alone the responsibility for imagining it, because he is aware of the incestuous appeal of the legend and repeatedly hints at that appeal within the play. That critics have overlooked these hints is a tribute to the subtlety and the hypnotic power of the work, which so innocently arouses buried longings and lets us unwittingly and at an enjoyable aesthetic distance transgress, almost to completion, the most primal of taboos.

Higgins—to illustrate—treats Eliza like a child from the moment she arrives in his house. He gleefully announces that "the girl doesn't belong to anybody," gives her candy, and tells her a fairy tale in which she is the heroine. Next she is commanded to take a bath, which literally and ritualistically washes away the dirt of her past life, and is then wrapped in one of Higgins's new blue kimonos. (To suggest that the flower girl is now herself turning into a flower, Shaw mentions that the bath soap has the fragrance of primroses and that jasmine blossoms decorate the kimono.) The idea of adopting Eliza is raised almost immediately though Higgins is not quite ready to recognize his own parental desires: right after declaring that Eliza is of "no use to anybody but me," he proposes that Mrs. Pearce adopt her, startling the housekeeper with the news that "a daughter would be a great amusement to you." Eliza herself seems to sense what is happening and rebukes Higgins when he bullies her by saying, "One would think you was my father." To which he replies, "If I decide to teach you, I'll be worse than two fathers to you."

Yet two fathers is exactly what Eliza has throughout the play, and Higgins struggles to assert his primacy over her natural father, Doolittle, whom he actually resembles in a curious way, for if Doolittle is a collector of dirt, so too is Higgins in his perception of Eliza: he has picked her up "out of the gutter," as he says, "out of the mud," and, according to Eliza, he treats her "as if I was dirt." Higgins's most impressive moments, apart from his demonstration of professional skill in the opening scene, are reserved for his first encounter with Doolittle, a male struggle for dominance in which Higgins wins what he feels is the ownership of Eliza. Doolittle accepts five pounds to seal the arrangement, declaring that he cannot be expected "to let her go for nothing." Thereafter Higgins acts as if Eliza belonged to him—training her with paternal firmness, showing her off with paternal pride, scolding her paternally to "get up and come home and dont be a fool" when he finds her hiding in his mother's house. Eliza then acknowledges herself to be in some ways "a child" in Higgins's world, and she declares again that he is much like her own father. The very real feelings she has for Higgins, the very fact that she has become "attached" to him, as his mother informs him, indicate the countering strength she must find to break away from her filial dependency and to accept the burdens of adulthood. In the great confrontation scene of Act IV, Eliza realizes that she has simply substituted one father for another and must once more gain control of her fate. With marvelous appropriateness she hurls the domestic-daddyish slippers at Higgins's head after he has acted condescendingly toward her, and then returns the jewels and the necklace chain he had provided for her:

HIGGINS [*furious*]: Hand them over. [*She puts them into his hands.*] If these belonged to me instead of to the jeweler, I'd ram them down your ungrateful throat. [*He perfunctorily thrusts them into his pockets, unconsciously decorating himself with the protruding ends of the chains.*]

The umbilical cord has been cut. And Eliza Doolittle leaves the protective warmth of Higgins's house and, like a latter-day Marchbanks, rushes forth into the night, born into independence.

Shaw has deliberately created a father-daughter relationship, which parallels the one between Pygmalion and Galatea, and his awareness of the incestuous nature of the relationship influenced his avoidance of a nuptial ending. No doubt Shaw himself had been enjoying along with us the forbidden pleasures of an incest fantasy, but he could control its course, as he had not been able to do in *Candida*, because now he was more aware of the dangerous nature of the material he was tapping. Indeed at this point in the discussion I think it would be helpful for us to keep in mind *Candida*, since oddly enough the earlier play has much in common with *Pygmalion*, which is to say that Shaw was creating once again out of primal cravings and memories.

In Act V, when Higgins desperately seeks to retrieve Eliza, he suddenly makes explicit to her (and perhaps to himself) that he wants to be her father as much as is legally possible, asserting, "I'll adopt you as my daughter if you like." Eliza seems to have a vague sense of the strangeness of his feelings toward her, of the incestuous longings underlying his behavior. She tries to tell him that a normal relationship is possible—"You're nearer my age than [Pickering] is," she replies when he suggests that she might marry the Colonel—and she cannot help noticing his jealousy when she mentions Freddy Hill's love for her. But Higgins is incorrigible and lacks the will to change; he wants Eliza to return to his house so that "you and I and Pickering will be three old bachelors together." Against this stony indifference to her womanliness, Eliza must rebel. Eugene Marchbanks, at her age of eighteen, had rebelled also, but we saw that he was probably rejecting sexuality itself. Only in his youthfulness did he really have much in common with Eliza. In basic respects he was far more like Henry Higgins. Indeed we can easily imagine that now, two decades after Candida rejected him, he has perhaps settled down as a middle-aged bachelor and phonetics expert, writing poetry in his leisure "on Miltonic lines," and will soon again be asking another woman for whom he has incestuous longings to live with him. But that woman will turn the tables on him and demand that even as she has passed her test as a lady he must prove that he is a man. Henry Higgins—to call old Marchbanks by his present name—will fail the test; and Eliza, who first broke away from Higgins as a father figure, now breaks away from him as a man who has shown his inadequacy as a lover. If Marchbanks's secret was that he could do without happiness, Eliza's is that she refuses to do without it.

Marchbanks and Higgins seem to differ, it is true, in the object of their incestuous longing: the young poet wants Candida as a mother, the professor wants Eliza as a daughter. But this means only that Higgins seeks a mother indirectly, for as we noted earlier in terms of the myth, Galatea is both daughter and mother just as Pygmalion is father and son. What the sculptor ultimately seeks, as Shaw indicates in his modernized version, is to regain his boyhood with a new mother. The daughter is a substitute mother, the feeling for the daughter a deflected expression of the desire for the mother. Shaw thus shows Higgins behaving time after time like an adolescent, and we know how right his mother is when she calls him a "silly boy" and treats him as such, telling him to stop fidgeting in company and to take his hands out of his pockets; he himself admits that he has "never been able to feel really grown-up and tremendous like other chaps"; and the stage directions say that he reacts in "babylike" ways, that he is "rather like a very impetuous baby 'taking notice' eagerly and loudly, and requiring almost as much watching to keep him out of unintended mischief." Eliza is to be a combination mother-nurse-playmate, and Higgins is well on his way toward achieving his end in his increasing dependence on Eliza and in her apparent willingness to obey orders. "He coaxes women as a child coaxes its nurse," it is said of him at the beginning, and when at the end Eliza finally rejects the role he has cast for her, she declares that she "wont be coaxed round." She rejects the nursery world Higgins yearns to recreate and to inhabit with her, rejects his craving to turn her into a child-mother and to deny her the right to have an adult love with an adult man.

And with a man who is not cruel. For Eliza, we may imagine, would be surprised at our earlier statement that Higgins seems not cruel but blind and that his cruelties are caused by emotional immaturity alone. She might accuse us of accepting too readily the dramatist's words in his stage directions that Higgins is entirely "void of malice" and his mischief "unintended." The dramatist, she might assert, had simply not faced the fact, when he later came to write the stage directions, that Higgins's emotional immaturity is partly willed and is a convenient cloak for behavior that often goes quite beyond the malicious. And if we thought to ask Eliza for evidence, she might tell us to look again at Higgins's behavior throughout the play, starting in the first act when he terrifies her by seeming to be a police spy and then declares that she has "no right to live," moving into the second act when he disparages her and then threatens to have her head cut off if she does not obey him, advancing to the next act when he insults the Eynsford Hills collectively and individually and plays a nasty little trick on Clara, and arriving at the fourth act when, Eliza would insist, he is at his worst. Because no summary phrase can do justice to Higgins's behavior in this act, let us attend to it in more detail, the more willingly because this is one of Shaw's greatest dramatic scenes and most masterly in its psychological depth and grasp. Eliza may be right in feeling that Shaw hedged in describing Higgins's responsibility for his actions, but there is no doubt whatever that Shaw perceived the roots of those actions exceptionally well.

IV

The clock is striking midnight as we look in, at the opening of Act IV, on Higgins's empty laboratory. The preceding act had ended in his mother's drawing room, where Eliza had just completed a dress rehearsal, with ambiguous results. The amount of elapsed time between the two acts is not immediately clear. Only when Eliza finally enters in a brilliant evening dress may we begin to suspect that another and more formal rehearsal has taken place, or perhaps the society party itself. But why is her expression, as we are told, "almost tragic"? Why does she sit down on the piano bench "brooding and silent"? Perhaps her disguise has been detected or she has blundered in some way? Our speculations are interrupted by the arrival of Higgins and Pickering, and as they begin to talk we learn that the day was a complete success: at the garden party and the dinner party Eliza has easily passed as a duchess. Our curiosity is now appeased in one area but intensified in another, for why then is Eliza so unhappy? Silently she sits as Higgins and Pickering rattle on, Higgins professing boredom with the entire day once he saw that Eliza would succeed. He wonders where his slippers are, and she glides from the room and then returns to place them before his unseeing eyes. Gradually, as the two men continue talking, we realize the callousness of their behavior, realize as she sits again "stonily" on the bench that to them she is like a statue now brought back from an exhibition. "No more artificial duchesses," exclaims Higgins; "thank God it's over." The entire experiment, he tells the Colonel, had lost its interest for him months before, and now he "can go to bed without dreading tomorrow." As Pickering retires from the room, not quite willing to share Higgins's casual dismissal of the day's events, he tells his friend that "it's been a great occasion: a triumph for you." Higgins then leaves also, substituting for even the most perfunctory goodnight to Eliza the command that she put out the lights and arrange for his morning tea. These are the only words anyone has sent in her direction since the arrival home, and still she has not spoken a single word. Now she is left alone, and we have increasingly come to share her outrage at the men's indifference and her frustration at having absolutely no one to whom to express it. The atmosphere tingles with tension.

It is one of the great moments in Shaw, a superb use of the delayed-speech technique in which our suspense at what will finally be said becomes almost intolerable because we now share Eliza's need to break the silence and prove that she is alive. Yet since words cannot suffice, Shaw allows the dammed-up feelings to burst forth in words and actions simultaneously:

Eliza tries to control herself and feel indifferent as she rises and walks across to the hearth to switch off the lights. By the time she gets there she is on the point of screaming. She sits down in Higgins's chair and holds on hard to the arms. Finally she gives way and flings herself furiously on the floor, raging.

HIGGINS [*in despairing wrath outside*]: What the devil have I done with my slippers? [*He appears at the door*].

LIZA [*snatching up the slippers, and hurling them at him one after the other with all her force*]: There are your slippers. And there. Take your slippers; and may you never have a day's luck with them!

HIGGINS [*astounded*]: What on earth—! [*He comes to her*]. Whats the matter? Get up. [*He pulls her up*]. Anything wrong?

LIZA [*breathless*]· Nothing wrong   with you. Ive won your bet for you, havnt I? Thats enough for you. *I* dont matter, I suppose.

HIGGINS· You won my bet! You! Presumptuous insect! *I* won it. What did you throw those slippers at me for?

LIZA: Because I wanted to smash your face. I'd like to kill you, you self-ish brute. Why didnt you leave me where you picked me out of—in the gutter? You thank God it's all over, and that now you can throw me back again there, do you? [*She crisps her fingers frantically*].

HIGGINS [*looking at her in cool wonder*]: The creature is nervous, after all.

LIZA [*gives a suffocated scream of fury, and instinctively darts her nails at his face*]!!

HIGGINS [*catching her wrists*]: Ah! would you? Claws in, you cat. How dare you shew your temper to me? Sit down and be quiet. [*He throws her roughly into the easy-chair*].

LIZA [*crushed by superior strength and weight*]: Whats to become of me? Whats to become of me?

HIGGINS: How the devil do I know whats to become of you? What does it matter what becomes of you?

LIZA: You dont care. I know you dont care. You wouldnt care if I was dead. I'm nothing to you—not so much as them slippers.

HIGGINS [*thundering*]: Those slippers.

LIZA [*with bitter submission*]: Those slippers. I didnt think it made any difference now.

A pause. Eliza hopeless and crushed. . . . She suddenly rises and gets away from him by going to the piano bench, where she sits and hides her face. Oh God! I wish I was dead.

HIGGINS [*staring after her in sincere surprise*]: Why? In heaven's name, why? [*Reasonably, going to her*] Listen to me, Eliza. All this irritation is purely subjective.

LIZA: I dont understand. I'm too ignorant.

HIGGINS: It's only imagination. Low spirits and nothing else. Nobody's hurting you. Nothing's wrong. You go to bed like a good girl and sleep it off. Have a little cry and say your prayers: that will make you comfortable.

LIZA: I heard your prayers. "Thank God it's all over!"

HIGGINS [*impatiently*]: Well, dont you thank God it's all over? Now you are free and can do what you like.

LIZA [*pulling herself together in desperation*]: What am I fit for? What have you left me fit for? Where am I to go? What am I to do? Whats to become of me?

HIGGINS [*enlightened, but not at all impressed*]: Oh, thats whats worrying you, is it? [*He thrusts his hands into his pockets, and walks about in his usual manner, rattling the contents of his pockets, as if condescending to a trivial subject out of pure kindness*]. I shouldnt bother about it if I were you. I should imagine you wont have much difficulty in settling yourself somewhere or other, though I hadnt quite realized that you were going away. [*She looks quickly at him: he does not look at her, but examines the dessert stand on the piano and decides that he will eat an apple*]. You might marry, you know. [*He bites a large piece out of the apple and munches it noisily*]. You see, Eliza, all men are not confirmed old bachelors like me and the Colonel. Most men are the marrying sort (poor devils!); and youre not bad-looking: it's quite a pleasure to look at you sometimes—not now, of course, because youre crying and looking as ugly as the very devil; but when youre all right and quite yourself, youre what I should call attractive. That is, to the people in the marrying line, you understand. You go to bed and have a good nice rest; and then get up and look at yourself in the glass; and you wont feel so cheap.

Eliza again looks at him, speechless, and does not stir. The look is quite lost on him: he eats his apple with a dreamy expression of happiness, as it is quite a good one. [IV]

While he enjoys his apple, and before we return to the next significant conversation between them, let us make some quick observations on the scene we have just witnessed. That it happened at all should surprise us, for Pickering is right to regard the occasion as a triumph, and Eliza and Higgins should rejoice in their secret victory; almost any other playwright would have allowed the dramatic and psychological momentum to issue in some sort of verbal or gestural lovemaking. Shaw seemingly thwarts our expectations, not out of contrariousness but because he knows his man, knows that Higgins makes love in exactly this sadistic fashion. The play in fact has been driving toward this violent scene from the beginning, and all of the play's lines of force radiate outward from this emotional center. Higgins's very first words in Act I are these he addresses to Eliza: "There, there, there, there! who's hurting you, you silly girl?" And even as he torments her in the middle of Act IV he again reassures her, "Nobody's hurting you." He of course half means it, for although he would like to define hurt strictly as physical pain, he knows that mental pain can be just as effective in reducing Eliza to hopelessness. We might momentarily argue that this is not sadism but merely the least attractive side of Higgins's vanity: he ignores her presence now because she had always been a means to an end, her gulling of the public being the means of validating his theories. Yet Higgins's near disrelish for his victory indicates other motives controlling him, and this private scene gratifies him more than Eliza's triumph because now he is able to achieve with her an intense, though wounding, relationship; he has finally incited some bodily contact between them; and in thus directly venting his sadistic impulses he has offered her the only sort of love he is capable of offering.

Naturally Eliza neither understands this love nor desires it. It is enough for her to know that Higgins is, as she calls him, "a great bully." She would not be surprised to learn that his indifference to her after they arrived home was entirely calculated, he being perfectly aware of the presence of others when he chooses to be; but whether he ignores her intentionally or by oversight he is obviously denying her any existence as a human being. She believes that to him she is a presumptuous insect whose fate is of no consequence, and we feel that she is entirely justified in attacking him. Yet despite this compelling evidence of Higgins's cruelty, Eliza also knows that the full range of their feeling for each other is hidden during their bouts of shouting. She knows of her own fondness for the man, and she senses that she means more to him than he is yet willing to admit even to himself. Why then, she must wonder, does he torment her?

Shaw does not want us to share Eliza's puzzlement permanently. He presents several clues to the mystery of Higgins's behavior. He has shown how eagerly Higgins wishes to regard Eliza as a passive object, without feelings. We remember that when Pickering had reproved Higgins for insulting Eliza and had insisted that she had some feelings, Higgins had responded, "Oh, no, I dont think so. Not any feelings that we need bother about." This was said in front of Eliza and was meant to insult her further, but Higgins really would prefer not to bother about her feelings. He wants to release his cruel impulses guiltlessly, to inflict pain without being conscious of his enjoyment. He would agree with the grotesque opinion of a character in Shaw's next play that "cruelty would be delicious if one could only find some sort of cruelty that didnt really hurt." And the way Higgins hopes to find it is by turning Eliza into a statue, temptingly lifeless and completely malleable to his desires. When therefore he tries to ignore her and to deny her existence as a human being, we are meant to give Higgins some credit—scant consolation as it may be to his victim!—for at least in that way he attempts to keep himself unaware of the pain he is inflicting. But Higgins is nonetheless an uneasy sadist in the confrontation scene because until then his sadistic impulses, as Shaw demonstrates, have been fairly well sublimated and are well tolerated by society. As a celebrated scientist, he can allow himself the pleasure of hurting others through rudeness under the pretense of a concern with profounder things than mere manners. As a teacher of a subject that he believes valuable in uniting mankind, he can enjoy his pupils' slavish obedience. His subject, which is also his passion, is phonetics, the science of voice sounds, prelinguistic, purely oral; and he can utter 130 distinct vowel sounds, five times as many as his fellow expert Colonel Pickering. Shaw indicates that this professional involvement with the mouth suits his hero's character and has other manifestations as well. Higgins is described as "baby-like," and as an "impetuous baby." At one moment we see him chewing candy, at another munching an apple "noisily" with "a dreamy expression of happiness" on his face. He makes biting comments to the Eynsford Hills and grinds down on Eliza whenever he can. Shaw knows the symptoms if not our modern name for Higgins's regression to the oral phase, a phase that psychoanalysis has abundantly shown to be associated with sadism, at first in the form of biting. When Higgins tries to recreate a nursery world with Eliza, he understandably teaches her the very games he most enjoys; and, making her over in his own image, he concentrates on her mouth. Indeed he remarks that his interest in the teaching experiment slackened enormously once the phonetics aspect was concluded, when he was no longer "watching her lips and her teeth and her tongue," but had to concern himself with nonoral matters of deportment and the social graces. But then Eliza's public triumph confirms for him, among other things, that she is now orally skilled enough to graduate to the next stage, in which she can reverse roles with him, make him the victim, and bite into him, becoming the sadist as he turns masochist. To provoke her into accepting this extreme and sudden shift of roles, Higgins must be extremely cruel, which is not to deny him his hidden pleasure in his cruelty but to suggest that other lusts grip him as well. In truth his very pleasure in hurting Eliza makes him uneasy since it compounds his guilt, which must then seek the relief of punishment.

Exactly in this way, Shaw indicates, the sadistic phase flows into the masochistic one; but he also indicates the continuing fluidity of the total phenomenon, the continuing intermixture of the component impulses even though at any moment we can easily identify the predominance of either one. In the passage recently quoted, Higgins obviously defeats Eliza even though she has attacked him by hurling slippers and then her fists at his face; his sadism has momentarily triumphed over her and over his own masochism, for he had been inciting her to hurt him. Contrastingly, in the following passage, the second round of their fight, he succeeds in being wounded to the heart even though sporadically he still tries to hurt her; and Eliza will now be able to wound him because she finally senses that in this psychic game she must use his own oral weapons:

LIZA: Before you go, sir

HIGGINS [*dropping the slippers in his surprise at her calling him Sir*]: Eh?

LIZA: Do my clothes belong to me or to Colonel Pickering?

HIGGINS [*coming back into the room as if her question were the very climax of unreason*]: What the devil use would they be to Pickering?

LIZA: He might want them for the next girl you pick up to experiment on.

HIGGINS [*shocked and hurt*]: Is that the way you feel towards us?

LIZA: I dont want to hear anything more about that. All I want to know is whether anything belongs to me. My own clothes were burnt.

HIGGINS: But what does it matter? Why need you start bothering about that in the middle of the night?

LIZA: I want to know what I may take away with me. I dont want to be accused of stealing.

HIGGINS [*now deeply wounded*]: Stealing! You shouldnt have said that, Eliza. That shews a want of feeling.

LIZA: I'm sorry. I'm only a common ignorant girl; and in my station I have to be careful. There cant be any feelings between the like of you and the like of me. Please will you tell me what belongs to me and what doesnt?

HIGGINS [*very sulky*]: You may take the whole damned houseful if you like. Except the jewels. Theyre hired. Will that satisfy you? [*He turns on his heel and is about to go in extreme dudgeon*].

LIZA [*drinking in his emotion like nectar, and nagging him to provoke a further supply*]: Stop, please. [*She takes off her jewels*]. Will you take these to your room and keep them safe? I dont want to run the risk of their being missing.

HIGGINS [*furious*]: Hand them over. [*She puts them into his hands*]. If those belonged to me instead of to the jeweller, I'd ram them down your ungrateful throat. [*He perfunctorily thrusts them into his pockets, unconsciously decorating himself with the protruding ends of the chains*].

LIZA [*taking a ring off*]: This ring isnt the jeweller's: it's the one you bought me in Brighton. I dont want it now. [*Higgins dashes the ring violently into the fireplace, and turns on her so threateningly that she crouches over the piano with her hands over her face, and exclaims*]: Dont you hit me.

HIGGINS: Hit you! You infamous creature, how dare you accuse me of such a thing? It is you who have hit me. You have wounded me to the heart.

LIZA [*thrilling with hidden joy*]: I'm glad. Ive got a little of my own back, anyhow.

HIGGINS [*with dignity, in his finest professional style*]: You have caused me to lose my temper: a thing that has hardly ever happened to me before. I prefer to say nothing more tonight. I am going to bed.

LIZA [*pertly*]: Youd better leave a note for Mrs Pearce about the coffee; for she wont be told by me.

HIGGINS [*formally*]: Damn Mrs Pearce; and damn the coffee; and damn you; and damn my own folly in having lavished hard-earned knowledge and the treasure of my regard and intimacy on a heartless guttersnipe. [*He goes out with impressive decorum, and spoils it by slamming the door savagely*].

Eliza smiles for the first time; expresses her feelings by a wild pantomime in which an imitation of Higgins's exit is confused with her own triumph; and finally goes down on her knees on the hearthrug to look for the ring.

And with that vivid pantomime and unexpected act of kneeling, the curtain descends on one of the supreme dramatic passages in Shaw, a passage which mounts quickly to intense emotion and intense conflict, in which physical objects—slippers, necklaces, a ring, a fireplace, a piano, a door—become almost participants in the conflict, and in which the quick shifts of feeling render any analysis too schematic, all the more so because the imagery and the action are as fluid as the sadomasochistic phenomenon they express. But let us accept the difficulties and take note of a few points, starting with the dynamic completeness of the role reversal as Eliza now thrills over Higgins's suffering and drinks in his pain like nectar. He had been, we must remember, even more extensively scolded in the preceding act by his mother, whose rebukes "deeply injured" him. Why then, we may ask, need he create a cruel Eliza to gratify himself? Why will not his mother suffice? The difference between the two women, and his relationship to each, provides the answer. When he bursts in on his mother in the third act, she immediately berates him for coming and orders him to "go home at once." Eliza, in contrast, will be manifestly unable to command him to leave his own house; unlike his mother, she will be at home and available at all times. Moreover, with Eliza (and surely not with his mother) he will be able to choose both the occasions for his humiliations and their degree. Inside that large area of control, again, he can allow himself to be uncontrolled as he certainly cannot be with his mother; even while Eliza is wounding him, he can verbally counterattack and threaten to hit her, giving vent as it were to the lingering sadistic impulses within the masochistic phase. And lastly, in a blend of sadomasochistic pleasures, he can sense Eliza's "hidden joy" in wounding him—a joy he could never allow himself to ascribe to his mother; he can identify with Eliza and can thereby intensify the pleasures of his humiliation. As an authority on the subject of masochism, Theodor Reik, has remarked: "It is not always obvious with whom the phantasying person identifies. Certainly with the victim, the passive person of the scene, but also with the active, cruel figure."

Eliza is thus an "improved" mother for Higgins, and Shaw deftly reveals the ways in which Higgins's mother fixation governs his relations to other women, particularly when he finds in Eliza a girl willing to be remolded, one whom he can train to satisfy all his moods and to participate in all his infantile games, to be perverse yet undemanding, malleable and poundable yet quick to hit back. When Eliza achieves "her own triumph" in wounding Higgins, she does not realize that it is his triumph as well, the true fulfillment of all his endeavors. We observed earlier that Shaw omitted the scene of Eliza's public success because he was more interested in the relationship between his two principal characters. We can now see more specifically that from Higgins's viewpoint the deeper meaning of the public success lay in society's confirmation that Eliza was now a lady like his mother. Eliza can thereby pass for him from daughter to mother figure, and this decisive psychological moment corresponds to the pivotal point in the play's structure: he who at the beginning of the work had been concealed in darkness, godlike in self-sufficiency, in knowing people and dominating them, now becomes dependent (even for the whereabouts of his slippers), now becomes fully known to us and fully exposed, so that Eliza, maddened by his cruelties, can now provoke him and wound him, and thereby gratify him. He need not be conscious of his gratification. He undoubtedly will feel very much hurt by Eliza's treatment of him. Nevertheless, "if a masochist thus has succeeded in inducing his victim to injure him," Reik observes, "it not seldom occurs that he actually feels offended and hurt. This reaction, of course, is restricted to consciousness. But it does not exclude an unconscious satisfaction." That Higgins did take pleasure in the fight is apparent from his behavior the next day, when he hunts out the girl he damned as "heartless," immediately starts another fight with her in which he again provokes her to hurt him, and then after acknowledging that he likes her to behave in this way urges her to come back home and live with him.

And the process, Shaw further makes us realize, will be self-perpetuating and ludicrous because throughout the play Higgins wants nothing less than to punish himself for being a masochist! Or, to state it through his own behavior and his own words, to punish himself for being the sort of individual who provokes his mother and his housekeeper and his friend and his pupil into chiding him on various occasions for his immature behavior, who ruefully confesses his woodenness with women and retreats when threatened by them behind oral defenses, who confides that he has never been able "to feel really grown-up and tremendous like other chaps." Certainly in his relations with women he shows himself to be, underneath all the bluster, exactly the "shy, diffident sort of man" he claims to be. And of course his failed relations with his mother rankle most. All but announcing his kinship to Oedipus when he burdens his mother with the news that his idea "of a lovable woman is something as like you as possible," Higgins finds that she does not even allow him to kiss her without first finding fault with him. Thwarted by the only woman he is sure he loves, wanting her to mother him and then hating it when she treats him like a child, desperately showing off his professional skill by writing her postcards in an invented shorthand that he knows she cannot read, banned from meeting her friends at her home because he insults everyone in sight and stumbles over all available furniture, Mrs. Higgins's "celebrated son," as she grimly terms him, understandably solaces himself with warbling new vowels in private and slinking behind church pillars on rainy summer nights to catch the comforting sounds of human voices, wistfully sure that to place people is somehow to know them. But because he cannot really escape his sense of inadequacy, he creates situations that expose him to abuse, and fittingly enough he also seems to engage in direct self-abuse, which Shaw strongly hints at by making Higgins's most characteristic gesture a nervous playing with his hands in his trouser pockets, fingering his keys and his cash. In the wittiest suggestion of his hero's possible habits of masturbation Shaw juxtaposes word and deed as Higgins informs his mother,

I shall never get into the way of seriously liking young women; some habits lie too deep to be changed. [*Rising abruptly and walking about, jingling his money and his keys in his trouser pockets.*]

[III]

It is thus not surprising, in light of Higgins's infantile behavior, that he should unconsciously long for punishment and that the desired punishment should be a form of spanking. Accordingly, the climactic moment in the play comes exactly when Eliza scolds Higgins so sharply that he cries out that he has been "hit" and "wounded." Eliza has used only words to lash him, to be sure, yet this infliction may be more painful to Higgins than physical spanking because she thereby turns his own oral weapons against him. Nevertheless, Shaw would want us to be quite clear about the implications of the combat between them. In a letter written to Mrs. Campbell just before the opening of the play, he gave his first Eliza the following instructions:

If you have ever said to [your daughter] Stella in her childhood "I'll let you see whether you will . . . obey me or not," and then inverted her infant shape and smacked her until the Square (not to mention the round) rang with her screams, you will . . . know how to speak the line "I'll let you see whether I'm dependent on you."

There is no need to go beyond Shaw's indication of the flagellation motif in order to deepen our understanding of the sexual aspects of the play, though it perhaps validates Shaw's insight when we see how harmoniously the play supports some psychological theories of a later date, in particular the theory that the masochist desires a spanking as a gentler substitute for the more grievous castration punishment. Castration would certainly fit the law of retaliation for Higgins's incest desires and his guilt over his sexual deficiencies—the admitted inability to respond to women genitally, the possible onanism, and (in his mind, maybe consequential) failure to be "tremendous" like other men. Since the incest theme in the play is at once more elaborate and less focused than in *Candida*—being here divided between two women rather than centered on one—the castration threat can be similarly less direct. Higgins as an older Marchbanks has now learned discretion in announcing his desire to be mothered, and his castration anxiety is correspondingly reduced; he has also learned how best to be hit—by a woman, verbally—whereas Marchbanks takes risks of physical injury when he incites Morell to attack him. One might epitomize the difference between the two plays' treatment of the castration theme by noting that Shaw now obscures the presence of that very poker which in *Candida* so conspicuously suggested Morell's phallic superiority and his ability to destroy Eugene as a man.

The dramatic effectiveness of the fight between Eliza and Henry Higgins certainly does not depend upon our awareness of either a flagellation impulse or a castration anxiety. Indeed such an awareness might well weaken our support of Eliza's revenge. If we know that Henry, the poor dear, really wanted her to punish him, it might dilute the power of the scene and frustrate our own primitive satisfactions, since her hidden joy at getting her own back is entirely ours as well. She is the surrogate child-pupil taking revenge for endless self-denials on the forbidding parent-teacher, and as she acts on our behalf in hurting Higgins we must not perceive that he is somehow enjoying it: the pleasures of satisfying *our* Oedipal hostilities must not be thwarted by the recognition that he is busy relieving *his* Oedipal guilts. In short this is one of those amusing instances when too thorough a comprehension of a character's motives can perhaps damage our response to a play. What one hopes that future stage Higginses will convey is a hint of pleasure in Eliza's attack, which will in retrospect enrich our sense of the fullness with which Shaw has characterized the protagonist. Too broad a hint, however, will upset the superb balance of the play, for Shaw has worked hard along two parallel lines to draw us away from recognizing Higgins's perverse desire to be spanked. He has first of all made the early part of the play wholesomely risqué. He has created a not unpleasant sense of the orthodox temptations of the situation—the attractive and poor young woman living with the middle-aged bachelors. As Nigel Alexander has observed in an excellent critical commentary on the play:

The whole of the action of the second Act depends upon this doubt about whether Higgins' intentions are sexual or intellectual. Eliza assumes that they are sexual, and Pickering asks directly whether they are. Alfred Doolittle, Eliza's father, also arrives to investigate this dubious situation and extract what economic profit he can for himself. Audiences, therefore, are right to wonder about the relationship between Higgins and Eliza. It is certainly a major question of the play.

While the audience's mind is being teased by that question, Shaw allows the characters vaguely to suggest an additional perverse temptation—the whipping of Eliza. Higgins threatens her on three separate occasions with a walloping, until she finally calls him a great bully and insists that "I wont let nobody wallop me." When Doolittle arrives a while later, he acknowledges that the only method he used in training her was "to give her a lick of a strap now and again." And he assures Higgins, "If you want Eliza's mind improved, governor, do it yourself with a strap." Higgins's temptations with the girl are thus presented as normally carnal or familiarly sadistic. And Shaw has thereby veiled the masochistic cravings from the audience and from Higgins himself, even while demonstrating the connection between sadism and masochism and while showing that self-punishment is the sadist's ultimate goal.*

*Nigel Alexander, correctly seeing that Higgins has no ordinary sexual interest in Eliza, concludes that he has none whatsoever, that he is in no way "interested in her as a mistress but as a pupil" (*Shaw: Arms and the Man and Pygmalion*, p. 65). Most critics have drawn the same conclusion, and it has a degree of plausibility. Yet it cannot really cover even some of the most conspicuous surface phenomena, such as Higgins's uneasiness in Act IV when Eliza tells him she will leave, or his eagerness in the next act to have her return, or his statement that he will miss her. Clearly the "mistress or pupil" formula, while it may well express the choice Higgins thinks he has at the outset, does not account for his behavior or his words. Eliza is obviously more than a pupil if less than a mistress. The popular sentimental view is actually more perceptive in this matter than the usual scholarly one because at least it recognizes the mutual fondness. The present interpretation essentially elaborates on the popular view since it too insists that Higgins had more than a professional interest in Eliza from the very moment he accepted her as a pupil and possibly before he accepted her, while still testing her spirit. And insofar as he is capable of having a mistress, he has one in Eliza, who satisfies at first his personal brand of sadism (torturing of her mouth and lashing her verbally) and who then evolves into a mother figure who can be permitted to satisfy his masochistic needs.

The critics' failure to offer a view of the play as convincing even as the popular one stems perhaps from two sources. They have read more Shaw than the public, and in this case have studied the preface and the postscript, both of which take a far more favorable view of Higgins than does the actual play. Secondly, since these male critics are usually teachers, they have presumably trained themselves to keep their own relationships to their female students professional, and it is for them a beneficent professional myopia to ignore the sexual temptations inherent in the Higgins-Eliza relationship. We need not go to the absurd lengths indicated in Ionesco's *The Lesson* to recognize such temptations, but we should acknowledge that when an antiacademic writer like Shaw probes a professional teacher's motivations he might be less flattering than the teacher-critic would wish to perceive. Moreover, Higgins has some speeches and traits that make him especially appealing to fellow teachers (fondly thinking of himself as an unappreciated intellectual), and the teacher-critics seem therefore reluctant to scrutinize the credentials of a member of their guild. Perhaps, in an exchange of courtesies with Shaw, this reluctance can be overcome by remembering that the playwright himself, in his treatise on education written soon after *Pygmalion*, curiously reverts several times to the issue of flagellation and to the power that teachers and parents have to punish and violate the young, and Shaw himself seems throughout his life to

V

Let us return now to the question of Higgins's behavior, which originally prompted us to focus on Act IV. We have seen that Eliza was quite right to regard him as a bully but that she understandably neglected his motives. It seems that his emotional immaturity derives from a character warped from childhood and that instead of reviling him and taking pleasure in Eliza's victories over him, we should pity him as a man driven by impulses beyond his control, who may even be striving to keep himself unaware of the pain he feels compelled to inflict and the enjoyment he gains from it. Is this not perhaps what Shaw had in mind when he said that Higgins was "rather like a very impetuous baby" whose mischief was "unintended" and who was therefore "void of malice"? Surely then the question of whether Higgins was evil is now fully resolved in his favor, is now shown to be an artificial or at best an old-fashioned, nineteenth-century sort of question based on assumptions no modern mind, alert to the force of childhood conditioning, would ever entertain. Yet Bernard Shaw, it must be said, would not at all share our assurance, for though modern-minded he was also a man of the nineteenth century, admittedly non-Christian yet with a conscience still irradiated by the "aftershine" of Christianity, to use Carlyle's term. And perhaps nowhere else in Shaw's work can we see the conflict between the nineteenth- and the twentieth-century parts of his mind to be so productive as in this very play, written just before the curtain of gunsmoke in 1914 finally descended on the nineteenth century. For Shaw was unmistakably of two minds about Higgins. Indeed if the rationalist in Shaw declared that Higgins was merely babylike and void of malice, the artist in Shaw responded to the Victorian Christian view that adults bear responsibility for their behavior; and over against the rationalistic stage directions which palliate Higgins's character, and over against the humor which moderates our response to that character, there is the weight of Higgins's own words and deeds, which in fact show him to be nothing less than diabolically evil.

---

have had an uncommon, though well-controlled, interest in flagellation. Indeed the present play may from one angle be regarded as self-admonitory, just as from another it was doubly self-fulfilling because here he synthesizes his familiar conflict between the artist-man and the mother-woman by turning Higgins into an artist-mother to Eliza, and he proves that a virgin motherhood is in some sense attainable by allowing Higgins entirely on his own to create a "child" for himself.

Take for example something as apparently trivial as Higgins's habitual use of profanity. "You swear a great deal too much," Mrs. Pearce tells him, "damning and blasting, and what the devil and where the devil and who the devil"; and she forbids him to use his favorite word *bloody*.* These profanities, though casually overused by Higgins, are not therefore meaningless or only comic; they are akin to other of his dismissive and brutal phrases: "throw her out of the window"; "throw her into the gutter"; "what does it matter what becomes of you"; "[she] has no right to be anywhere—no right to live"; "[her] head will be cut off." Both single words and phrases bespeak an attitude, and they ironically underscore Higgins's belief that language gives people away, a truth he characteristically fails to apply to himself. His constant invocations to the devil, his direct and indirect vocabulary of damning, make us suspect that the devil is really his presiding deity, a suspicion shared by others in the play and amply confirmed by his actions. Mrs. Pearce is so incensed by his abuse of Eliza that she boldly intervenes: "Stop, Mr. Higgins. I wont allow it. It's you that are wicked." His mother berates him for his "brutal" treatment of his pupil and says that she would have thrown fire irons at him and not just slippers. And we know that Eliza is provoked into calling him a variety of hard names and is right in concluding that "you dont care a bit for me." Even his voice at the end of the play remains, we are told, "careless," and this basic carelessness derives from his utter self-absorption. Hence the very last lines read: "Higgins, left alone, rattles his cash in his pocket; chuckles; and disports himself in a highly self-satisfied manner." Not caring what he does to others, this diabolical figure—often amusing and seemingly guileless as any experienced devil should be—commits acts compatible with his blasphemous language. "His eyes suddenly [begin] to twinkle with mischief" reads one of the stage directions, and before this man's mischief is concluded Eliza has nearly drowned herself.

---

*Eliza's famous reply in Act III to Freddy's question whether she will be walking home across the park—"Walk! Not bloody likely"—caused a sensation for her listeners on and off the stage. Commentators have generally assumed that this merely capped her unconsciously funny accounts of how her aunt was probably murdered and how her father drank, both accounts rendered in slangy, ungrammatical language but with her newly acquired elegance of enunciation. The cream of the jest, however, lies in her thinking the word *bloody* perfectly acceptable in refined society because she has heard it all the time from her teacher's lips. Accent apart, Higgins is infinitely more foulmouthed than the pupil he undertakes to train.

Destruction is of course the devil's traditional specialty, and an individual qualifies as a member of the devil's party when he co-operates in his own destruction, his fall thereby duplicating the original Satanic fall. Satan may set the lure, as myth says he did for the angels who joined him, but the decision is finally the victim's alone. Now Eliza, we notice, lives in Angel Court, Drury Lane, and the lures Higgins sets out for her include some standard worldly items: "Think of chocolates," he urges her, "and taxis, and gold, and diamonds." And Eliza, protecting her virtue, replies: "No: I dont want no gold and no diamonds. I'm a good girl, I am." Mrs. Pearce tries to stop him: "Mr. Higgins: youre tempting the girl. It's not right." But the tempter wins, and the now perchless Eliza will find a few months later that instead of rising in the world she has fallen to the banks of the Thames, fearfully thinking of suicide. What neither Eliza nor we had foreseen, deflected by our suspicions about Higgins's possible designs on her body, were his graver designs on her soul. Pickering voices our suspicion when he warns Higgins that "no advantage is to be taken of her position." And the professor replies that Eliza will be "sacred, I assure you. You see, she'll be a pupil; and teaching would be impossible unless pupils were sacred." Despite the assurances, however, the girl from Angel Court is never sacred to him. He so completely violates her being that she becomes in the fourth act a creature with murder in her heart, reduced to a state of hopelessness. "What does it matter what becomes of you?" Higgins yells at her. "How the devil do I know what's to become of you?" he shouts, invoking the name of his deity at the very moment he finally crushes her spirit. And we may call to mind Morell's words to Eugene in *Candida*: "To break a man's spirit is devil's work. Take care of what you are doing. Take care." But Higgins, as we have seen, is thoroughly careless, except in the execution of his devil's work, and he has now left Eliza with the choice of living with him or drowning herself. That she finally chooses neither the devil nor the sea indicates merely the limits of Higgins's power. Retrospectively, if one keeps in mind that his goal is to possess her soul (as well as, in his fashion, her body), then the three stages of his plan, the three temptations, can now be discerned. The first was to have her join him in deceiving the public and prove herself a lady fit for a gentleman like himself. The second, occupying Act IV, was to make her even more like himself spiritually—destructive, hopeless—as well as sexually. The final temptation comes when he asks her to live with him as his assistant. No longer able to bait her with voice improvements, he now resorts to humility and flattery and then tells her with devilish frankness that he wants her soul even more than her body:

HIGGINS: . . . I have learnt something from your idiotic notions: I confess that humbly and gratefully. And I have grown accustomed to your voice and appearance. I like them, rather.
LIZA: Well, you have both of them on your gramophone and in your book of photographs. When you feel lonely without me, you can turn the machine on. It's got no feelings to hurt.
HIGGINS: I cant turn your soul on. Leave me those feelings and you can take away the voice and the face.   [V]

And Eliza's reply to this ultimate temptation shows that she recognizes at last the full truth about Higgins:

Oh, you are a devil. You can twist the heart in a girl as easy as some could twist her arms to hurt her. Mrs. Pearce warned me. . . . you dont care a bit for her. And you dont care a bit for me.   [V]

This is Eliza's high moment of illumination in the play. However Henry Higgins may have become the man he is, and however unconscious he may be of his own intentions, he is evil; and Eliza Doolittle barely escapes from his clutches, from going permanently to Higgins's realm from Angel Court.

Once we recognize this momentous spiritual battle, we can increase our appreciation of the defiance of great comedy (which capers on the edge of the tragic abyss) and also increase our delight in some of Shaw's most delicate effects. Regard Higgins as an unwitting devil having his tail salted, and a single word has comic reverberation:

PICKERING: Still, he taught you to speak; and I couldnt have done that, you know.
LIZA [*trivially*]: Of course: that is his profession.
HIGGINS: Damnation!   [V]

Yet even as Higgins affirms his damning profession he remains unaware of it, as a moment later he gives Eliza a nonchoice: "So you can come back or go to the devil: which you please." But not only are single words and lines given new meanings: the overall design is further clarified. Remembering what a profane man Higgins is, and that the root meaning of *profane* is "in front of a church," we see the fitness of the opening scene outside St. Paul's (with Higgins condensing from the darkness to terrify a simple flower girl), and of the offstage scene at the end as Doolittle heads for St. George's to be married, accompanied by all except Higgins, still the profane man and debarred from coming by his mother because "he cant behave himself in church." Bordered thus at either end by the realm of the sacred, the play alternates betweentimes in Higgins's laboratory and his mother's house: the realm of the devil's disciple which becomes a hell for Eliza, and the social realm to which she retreats for human comfort. And it is in this social realm, between heaven and hell, that she will try to work out her salvation. Viewed thus, in a somewhat Christian perspective, Mrs. Pearce's repeated warnings that Eliza "should think of the future" take on a more than mundane significance; and when Eliza says at the end, "I shall not see you again, Professor," she is turning away from a spiritual degradation that nearly drove her to suicide and from a tempter who had sought to capture her very soul.

VI

Pygmalion's richness of allusion in large part derives from Shaw's perception of Higgins as a true devil's disciple, and the allusions are functional as well as decorative, which is to say they contribute to the play's meanings by providing implicit and ironic contrasts. Shaw had in mind, when conceiving Higgins, two great predecessors who had also dealt with the devil figure, Milton and Goethe. Let us consider first the witty allusions to Goethe's most famous poem.

Henry Higgins, as befits his presence in a comedy, is in all respects a smaller figure than was Heinrich Faust. The latter kept among the scientific instruments in his study a full human skull, the former keeps among his instruments a sectional chart of half a human head; and this difference may conveniently indicate the contrast between the two scholars: Higgins is a considerably halved and flattened version of Faust. His knowledge is far less ample though he is within his field so much of a wizard that an awed member of the crowd exclaims, "Bly me! You know everything you do." Faust's despair over the futility of learning and the deadness of his heart is reduced to Higgins's wistful recognition of his own woodenness. Faust's restlessness is given a derisive modern image:

LIZA: I wont be passed over.

HIGGINS: Then get out of my way; for I wont stop for you. You talk about me as if I were a motor bus.

LIZA: So you are a motor bus: all bounce and go, and no consideration for anyone.

[v]

Both men first meet their young women in front of churches, and each of the women thinks she has been mistaken for a prostitute. Both men give jewels to the women. Margareta, though called an angel, feels very inadequate with the learned Faust and wonders "what he can see in a poor ignorant girl like me"; Eliza, from Angel Court, acknowledges to Higgins that "I know I'm a common ignorant girl, and you a book-learned gentleman." Flowers and dust provide contrasting symbolism in both works. Beheading and drowning, which figure so tragically in *Faust*, are also touched on in *Pygmalion*, untragically but not humorously. At other times, however, Shaw seems to be completely coating a grim event in Goethe's work with the brush of comedy: Eliza's amusing account of her poisoned aunt may have been intended to remind us of Margareta's poisoned mother, and Doolittle's eagerness to sell his daughter contrasts absurdly with Valentine's eagerness to defend his sister's honor.

Some of these resemblances—and there are several others—may be coincidental. Shaw did not keep his volume of Goethe at his elbow: his eye was on the play at hand. But he was fully saturated in the operatic and orchestral versions of the Faust legend, and in fact as a music critic had once boasted of having seen over seventy different performances of Gounod's opera. Much of *Pygmalion* bears no relationship to the Faust story, but much of it does shine forth more brightly if we allow Goethe's work to serve as a background.

A similar effect is achieved by Shaw's allusions to Milton. Higgins thinks of himself as something of a poet "on Miltonic lines," as he modestly informs Pickering. And one of his complaints against Eliza is that she does not appreciate his highly trained intellect: "I waste the treasures of my Miltonic mind by spreading them before you." Happily we are spared any samples of Higgins's poetic flights; they might not have attained even the level of that other self-styled poet Mendoza, the brigand chief in *Man and Superman* who puts Tanner to sleep with a verse that begins, "Louisa, I love thee, / I love thee, Louisa, / Louisa, Louisa, Louisa, I love thee." Undoubtedly Higgins's estimation of his poetic gifts is of a piece with his belief that he is well-mannered, soft-spoken, and shy. But if he is of uncertain quality as a poet, he is of specific value throughout the play as a walking joke "on Miltonic lines"—indeed a double joke. The first one is his talent for emulating none of Milton's many virtues but only his few lamentable faults—the severe egotism and the overbearing manner toward women, especially toward young women. Higgins admits that "the moment I let myself make friends with a woman, I become selfish and tyrannical," but he fails to see in his behavior toward Eliza an obvious example of his selfishness. He proposes to adopt her as his daughter because among other things he really wants her to continue as his servant, finding his slippers or his spectacles and keeping track of his appointments, just as Milton made slaves out of his own daughters. And Higgins waxes indignant at Eliza's apparent ingratitude just as Milton thought his daughters were unkind to him. The similarities extend even further. Higgins taught Eliza educated sounds, and Milton's most notorious exploitation of his daughters was almost identical: without ever teaching them a single foreign language he trained them to pronounce the words of several languages so that they could spend uncomprehending hours reading to him. In fact, just as Eliza did in the play, one of the daughters rebelled against the masculine tyranny and deserted her home. The first joke on Higgins, then, is that he unwittingly imitates his hero's character in the worst possible way. The second joke transports Higgins from life to literature as he demonstrates the influence on him of Milton's greatest poem, for with his eyes twinkling with mischief he first tempts the girl from Covent Garden with food in order to bend her to his will, then tantalizes her with visions of rising beyond her humble station, and finally comes near to destroying her though she at last gains enough knowledge of good and evil to reject him. Yes, Higgins may rightfully claim to do a little "on Miltonic lines" because he enacts the lines of the archvillain in *Paradise Lost*, quite unconsciously to be sure, and in his own inept way—eating the apple himself and finally controlling absolutely no one, especially himself. As we watch his antics, aware of the looming shadow of Milton's Prince Lucifer, we realize with amusement that vain old Henry Higgins is a failed devil; and we realize too that Shaw has adroitly fused the figures of Faust and Satan, demythologizing the composite figure and bringing it into the contemporary world.

Shaw's allusions to Goethe and Milton, besides lending contrast to his modern comic version of a diabolic man, also add weight to the underlying philosophical issues of the play. Those issues can now be seen to involve nothing less than the nature of human evil and of human responsibility. The converging significance of the allusions lies in their support of the doctrine of free will, since Faust and Eve *decided* to succumb to the devil's temptations and Satan himself *chose* to be evil. Higgins is evil, despite all the ways his conduct has been predetermined by character and conditioning, because he chooses to remain a naughty child in an adult body, chooses to ignore what others tell him, chooses to be cruel to Eliza, chooses to be incorrigible. Such a man, Shaw indicates, is a present-day devil's disciple, menacing to the limits of his power. In this case the limits are set by an extraordinary woman, Eliza Doolittle, even though she is nearly killed as a result of her association with him. The limits are also set by the pervasive humor of the play; and though Higgins is indeed as "wicked" as Mrs. Pearce declares him to be, the high comic tone reassures us of his ineffectuality and even manages to promote sympathy for him. Nevertheless, his ineffectuality and our sympathy must not obscure the evil power that in his limited and everyday way he embodies; indeed that power may be felt as more frightening exactly in proportion to its ordinariness. Shaw deliberately emphasizes the savage streak in his professor, noting that he sits down "savagely" and slams doors "savagely," and even making Higgins himself remark that "we're all savages, more or less," though of course without appreciating how much more of a savage he is than anyone else in the play. And once we perceive this streak in him, we can also see the connection between all the psychological probing of his character and the presentation of the social world in which he is an uncomfortable participant; for the manners and class distinctions of Mrs. Higgins's world, of that social world Eliza wants to enter, constitute even with their imperfections whatever civilization is available, and Higgins in his savagery is its enemy. There is not a class conflict in any traditional sense since Higgins and his mother are nominally of the same class; nor will any removal of the barriers between the classes terminate the true conflict, which at bottom is between civilization and savagery. It is a modern savagery, to be sure, armed with the presumptions of science and cunning enough to attack society's hypocrisies and to arrogate to itself the right of reform, perhaps claiming to advance society by eliminating, as Higgins proposes to do, the "gulf" between the social classes. One of the chief forms of evil in modern times, Shaw intimates, appears in the guise of a would-be benefactor, the blunt idealist disparaging mere manners, unregenerate man posing even to himself as a herald of enlightenment and higher civilization. When such a man as Higgins dismisses civility, we are forced to wonder whether civility is not a necessary even if insufficient condition of civilization, and whether manners do not make the livable world. If Higgins is the alternative to civilization, then that alternative is savagery, the scientist as the new savage, or any other reformer who patches his doctrine with scientific terminology and flaunts it as scientific truth. Who then, to revert to a question left unanswered earlier, is Caliban in the play? It is Professor Henry Higgins himself (who sometimes doubles as Prospero), Caliban decked out as a modern scientific reformer.

Shaw is understandably distressed by this insight, for if men like Higgins can really be savages—men of intellect, education, and wealth—then every scheme for improving the material conditions of mankind will only be of limited value; those who are possessed by a streak of savagery and who might be freed of material preoccupations in a prosperous society would simply have more time in which to exercise their destructiveness. To acknowledge thereby the reality of evil, and to locate it in man rather than in that abstraction known as society, is to weaken the foundations of socialist thought; and it is partly this threat to Shaw as a dedicated Fabian which calls forth the wonderful humor in the play, humor that seeks to disarm if not obliterate the menacing truth. But of course the truth also menaces Shaw even more directly since so much of his insight into Higgins's character is drawn from self-knowledge, and thus the humor is self-protective as well. Behind the manner of the play, behind its humor and its fairy-tale form, Shaw feels safe in delving far into the recesses of his own being, creating in the fullest sense a work of self-realization. Moreover the understanding he now shows of a world-betterer, and his ridicule of him, contrast totally with what we saw in our last chapter to be the laudatory treatment of Don Juan and of Juan's desire to promote a better world. Admittedly in *Man and Superman* Tanner is satirized, but not for being a revolutionary so much as a weak-willed one, an incompetent follower of Don Juan; and the only critic of Juan's motives is the Devil, whose position is therefore felt to be wrong. Yet in *Pygmalion*'s exposure of the savage destructiveness in the heart of a supposed idealist, and in the exposure of Higgins's facile contempt for the human world around him, Shaw for the length of an entire play illustrates the wisdom of the Devil's words: "Beware of the pursuit of the Superhuman: it leads to an indiscriminate contempt for the human." The later play thus rejects the "idealism" of *Man and Superman*, and incidentally the parallel "idealism" of *Major Barbara*, with its seemingly high-minded defense of war. In dealing with Henry Higgins, Shaw finds the courage to penetrate the dark soul of an idealist as he had not when creating Tanner, Don Juan, or even Undershaft, and it is from this courage that the superiority of the characterization ultimately derives. Shaw had once presented, it is true, a similar insight in the early work *An Unsocial Socialist*, where we recall Trefusis's remark that "with my egotism, my charlatanry, my tongue, and my habit of having my own way, I am fit for no calling but that of saviour of mankind—just of the sort they like." Yet this is a marginal comment in a work in which Trefusis as idealist is very much the admired figure. And when we also recall how in a late play like *The Simpleton of the Unexpected Isles* Shaw ignores the moral turpitude of his supposedly idealistic protagonists, then we are forced to conclude that he was unwilling to retain the disquieting knowledge of evil he had momentarily grasped in *Pygmalion*. The play is thus poised at the very crest of Shaw's work, its technical mastery equal to the courage and complexity of its insights, its ideas integrated into character and plot, and these in turn sustained by a variety of emotions and an ever-buoyant humor.

PART TWO

> Write the true story of *Pygmalion* and you will make all Britain and North America laugh uproariously, mostly at me. . . . But mind! it must be the utter grotesque truth.
>
> Shaw to Mrs. Campbell, December 1938

I

The creative power which fused the many elements of *Pygmalion* remains of course inexplicable, but some of the circumstances that stimulated that power can be identified. It is useful to do so because our preceding interpretation is thereby corroborated at many points, and Shaw's later relationship to the play is clarified.

Mrs. Patrick Campbell in 1911.

Furthermore, we can once again see the intimate connections between the dramatist's life and his art, for just as the play itself
deals with the interaction between life and art, the man-as-artist
creating a woman whom the artist-as-man then desires, so too the
events surrounding *Pygmalion* reveal a fascinating interplay between Shaw as artist and man.

The first major event that bears upon the work was the illness of Shaw's mother in 1912, the year *Pygmalion* was composed. She had suffered a stroke which was to lead to her death the following year at the age of eighty-three. In 1912 Shaw himself was fifty-five, the same age at which Vandeleur Lee had died. This double reminder of the nearness of death, and especially the prospective loss of a mother to whom he was still deeply attached, aroused many feelings about her as well as memories from childhood. In fact Shaw's mother probably served as one of the models for the admirable Mrs. Higgins; and in Henry's relationship to his mother, Shaw may well have been presenting with amused exaggeration a gloss on his own dealings with Mrs. Shaw: his idolizing of her, her refusal to be awed by his success, her continual correcting of his manners.

Less obvious, though convincingly argued by Philip Weissman, a psychoanalyst who has examined some biographic aspects of the play, is that Eliza as Higgins's student duplicates the student-teacher relationship between Lucinda *Elizabeth* Shaw and her teacher Vandeleur Lee. Weissman, however, simplifies the play a good deal to make it conform to Freudian categories, and he needlessly assumes Shaw's unconsciousness of the parallels between his mother and Eliza, and Lee and Higgins. Unconscious forces are no doubt present in the work, especially in the strength of the writer's involvement with particular characters, but there is ample evidence that far from repressing the main components of the family's ménage à trois, Shaw had reflected upon them often, no less so since the matter bore upon his own legitimacy. Indeed, viewed schematically these components may be said to be distributed in three concentric circles within the play. In the innermost circle is Mrs. Higgins, Shaw's tribute to his dying mother as she appeared to the world and to himself in her later years; and here Higgins and Mrs. Higgins are in part based on Shaw and his mother in their maturity. In the next circle outward (and back further in time) is Eliza, representing to some extent Mrs. Shaw as a gifted pupil who finally became a voice teacher herself. Here too there is a tribute to the playwright's mother, which does not exclude what we saw earlier to be some sympathetic identification by Shaw himself with Eliza's struggle for independence. In this circle Higgins is predominantly Lee; and we notice that Eliza lives in a ménage à trois, one which the dramatist takes pains to show is thoroughly innocent. Yet Shaw's apprehensions over that innocence could not be banished entirely, and they find expression, heavily buffered with humor, in our outermost circle. Here we may find Alfred Doolittle, who is not Shaw's father but does possess two of that father's characteristics, his enjoyment of drink and his negligence in business affairs. (Significantly, there is not even the slightest allusion anywhere to Higgins's father.) In this circle too we may place the shame that Doolittle creates for Eliza—as Shaw's father created shame for him also. Illegitimacy, too, is present in that Eliza is a bastard; in a simple reversal of her creator's situation she is certain of the identity of her father but not her mother. Doolittle is made to dismiss the importance attached to legitimacy as merely "middle-class morality," and in effect Shaw supports him by scoffing at the respectability of the middle-class Eynsford Hills and by demonstrating that the bastard Eliza is superior in every way to the "legitimate" young people, Clara and Freddy.

We have, then, in addition to Shaw's tribute to his mother in the person of the elegant Mrs. Higgins, which might be termed the positive charge of emotion attached to the innermost circle, a contrasting expression of anxiety about her and his father, and this forms the negative emotional charge of the outermost circle. The currents of feeling thereby created help to give the play its energy. But altogether those currents would also drive the work toward an ending that kept Higgins and Eliza permanently apart. Such an ending would presumably have reassured Shaw, allowing him to deny a romantic relationship between a pupil and a teacher who in critical respects resembled his mother and Lee. Yet Shaw seemed reluctant to pen that conclusive ending. Instead, he leaves open the possibility of Eliza's return. Nothing we have so far discussed explains this decision, but the motive becomes reasonably clear when we recall that the private fantasy underlying the play had not yet been fulfilled; for if Higgins-as-Lee is finally deprived of Eliza, so too, then, is Higgins-as-Shaw. Shaw the dramatist might win a delayed victory over Lee the voice teacher by creating through his imagination a pupil who enjoys a greater success than did any of Lee's pupils, and by creating a literary work that would endure beyond any of Lee's achievements, but, nevertheless, Lee apparently won the woman who followed him to London. To the extent that Higgins is Shaw, and the playwright is to complete an imagined triumph over Lee, then Higgins too must be allowed the possibility of having a woman for himself. And it was for that reason that Shaw left the ending of the play inconclusive. Or so we are driven to conclude when we come to consider that other critical event of 1912, in addition to the illness of Shaw's mother but distinctly related to it: the celebrated love affair with Mrs. Patrick Campbell.

II

"I saw you first in a dream 43 years ago. I have only just remembered it." Thus Shaw wrote to Mrs. Campbell at about the midpoint of their romance. It was a dream from his thirteenth year, long before he had ever seen the actress for whom he was to create the role of Eliza Doolittle. "You are a figure from the dreams of my boyhood," he told her in another letter; "let me have my dream out." And the first part of his having it out consisted of writing *Pygmalion* for her. Earlier I described the play as seeming to have been written with the rapid inevitability of a happy dream, and now we can see why it was composed so elatedly. It was a magnificent love offering to the woman he would soon be addressing in his letters as "Beatricissima," "Stella Stellarum," "Oh beautifullest of all the stars." If Shaw in creating Eliza drew upon his early feelings for his mother, he also and far more consciously drew upon his adult feelings for Stella Campbell.

These had been accumulating for nearly two decades. As a drama critic from 1895 to 1898 on the London *Saturday Review*, Shaw had witnessed many performances by the beautiful actress, who in 1893 at the age of twenty-nine had achieved her first great success in Pinero's *The Second Mrs. Tanqueray*, a story of a woman with a wicked past. One of Shaw's earliest reviews, in fact, dealt with Pinero's follow-up play *The Notorious Mrs. Ebbsmith* (1895), again starring Mrs. Campbell. It was, said the thirty-eight-year-old reviewer, a play whose badness was hidden by the "personal genius" of the "wonderful woman" who played the lead. "She creates all sorts of illusions and gives one all sorts of searching sensations. It is impossible not to feel that those haunting eyes are brooding on a momentous past, and the parted lips anticipating a thrilling imminent future, whilst some enigmatic present must no less surely be working underneath all that subtle play of limb and stealthy intensity of tone." A few months later, while condemning another work in which she was now appearing, Sardou's melodrama *Fedora*, he again commented on her "personal magnetism," and her creating the effect "of a magnificent woman with a magnificent temper, which she holds in or lets loose with exciting uncertainty." He succumbed along with the rest of the audience to her allure: "The moment she was seen, our reason collapsed and our judgment fled. Every time the curtain fell there was a delirious roar. If the play was not tragic, our infatuation was. I solemnly warn all and sundry that no common man's opinion of the artistic merits of that performance was worth a farthing after the first flash of the heroine's eyes. It was not Fedora; but it was Circe; and I, as sworn critic, must make the best attempt I can to be Ulysses." And attempt it he certainly did, at least to the extent of tying himself to the firmest critical standards and then finding that her performances in several later plays compared unfavorably to those of such famed older actresses as Sarah Bernhardt and Eleonora Duse, or else finding, like a proto-Higgins, that her diction was defective and required a greater phonetical awareness. But at times Stella overwhelmed his defenses, as when her playing of Ophelia pried from him a compliment to her mad scene with "its right tragic power and dramatic significance"; or when elsewhere he allowed that though she is "not yet a great actress, she is at any rate an artist"; or when momentarily he bowed to the futility of maintaining any critical standards whatever: "You will tell me, no doubt, that Mrs. Patrick Campbell cannot act. Who said she could?—who wants her to act?—who cares twopence whether she possesses that or any other second-rate accomplishment? On the highest plane one does not act, one *is*. Go and see her move, stand, speak, look, kneel—go and breathe the magic atmosphere that is created by the grace of all these deeds; and then talk to me about acting, forsooth!" Clearly the foundations of Shaw's latter-day romance with Stella were laid during those early years of exposure to her magic atmosphere.

Part of that magic came from her refined womanliness, but another and perhaps larger part came from a tigerish quality he thought he detected in her and which led him to call her Mrs. Pat-Cat to his friends. This was not said merely in disparagement, as has usually been assumed, since the aggressive woman with a touch of vulgarity had always appealed to him. Indeed one can see how fully Shaw centered his interest on this supposed facet of Mrs. Campbell's many-sided personality by noticing the roles in his own early plays for which he thought her suitable. These included Gloria, the heroine of *You Never Can Tell*, a passionate young woman with "a mettlesome, dominative character," as her creator put it; Mrs. Warren, the still "good-looking" and "domineering" prostitute of the famous play; Julia Craven, the fiery and brazen brunette of *The Philanderer*, who was based on Jenny Patterson, the aggressive woman who seduced Shaw on his twenty-ninth birthday and gave him his first experience of carnal love. Shaw's Cleopatra, of course, was fashioned with Mrs. Campbell directly in mind, and Cleopatra in Shaw's version is a dangerous young cat. By fancying Mrs. Campbell in these diverse roles the dramatist paid tribute to her capacity as an actress which the reviewer seemed reluctant to grant, even though all these women are varieties of the same prototypical siren: earthy, spirited, feline, and with claws that could tear.

Stella Campbell was thus a heady mixture of the two kinds of woman who most haunted Shaw's imagination, the other being the asexual angel-mother best typified by Lady Cicely Waynflete of *Captain Brassbound's Conversion*. In that mixture, Stella's sensual appeal unquestionably disturbed and fascinated Shaw more than her angelic grace; for in 1898, just as he was readying himself psychologically for marriage to the maternal and fairly sexless Miss Townshend, he made his Julius Caesar repudiate the lusty Cleopatra (as of course the historical Caesar had not done) and thereby himself repudiated, in a symbolic gesture soon to become a fact of his married life, that very principle of sexuality which Stella Campbell embodied for him. By 1900 he apparently found it necessary to fortify himself against sexual distractions emanating from the London stage by publicly denouncing Mrs. Campbell in all but name for playing roles of "violently oversexed" women in "voluptuous plays," and by privately complaining that her "overpowering *odor di femmina*" was a threat to the very health of—no, not Bernard Shaw, but the English theater! It was only after experiencing several more years of the frigid comforts of his marriage that he began to express indirectly, in such works as the 1908 *Getting Married* and the 1910 *Misalliance*, his yearnings for the sultry pleasures associated with the person of Mrs. Campbell; and when he created Eliza for her in 1912, suffusing the portrait with love and desire, he was now returning as a Caesar of the world of letters, to that woman whom age had scarcely withered. Stella Campbell need not have had half of her large intelligence to have discerned Shaw's emotional involvement with Eliza and indeed with herself, since as far as she could see they were one and the same. "She was flattered," the playwright wrote to a friend when recounting the first reading of the work to Stella; "she saw through it like a shot. 'You beast, you wrote this for me, every line of it: I can hear you mimicking my voice in it.'" She evidently saw through Shaw too, generously understanding what was implied by his bestowal of such affection on Eliza, and understanding also the shyly expressed longing in Higgins to be brought to life through love and the appealing self-mockery with which the talkative intellectual and critic of actresses' diction had created the talkative and intellectual teacher of phonetics. Though the playwright himself, doubtless fearing rejection, seemed reluctant to face up to the implications of a love gift in which he had so winningly humbled himself, and had also written an ending that showed himself bravely prepared for defeat, Stella was more self-confident. Shaw had given himself away—and she took him. The day after reading the work to her, he saw her again. "I went calmly to her house," he informed Ellen Terry, "to discuss business with her, as hard as nails, and, as I am a living man, fell head over ears in love with her in thirty seconds. And it lasted more than thirty hours. I made no struggle: I went in head over ears, and dreamed and dreamed and walked on air for all that afternoon and the next day as if my next birthday were my twentieth."*

Shaw stayed in love far longer than the thirty hours, longer even than the fourteen months during which the relationship ran a fairly untroubled course. The intensity of the "delightful dreams" varied as the reality of Shaw's married life asserted itself, and his "very wonderful lady," with her own dreams, did not always play the role his fantasy required. But Shaw was so eagerly in love that we have to go back thirty-one years to the Alice Lockett romance to find similar words of adoration. It is of course easy enough to smile at the effusions of the aging lover—the outbursts of verse, the baby talk, the twenty-nine repetitions of "Stella" with which he opened one excited letter of gratitude—or to dismiss it all, as have some nervous biographers, as "pseudo-romance" or "theatrical moonshine." Both parties were well aware of the comic aspects of middle-aged love (she verging on being a grandmother); yet this awareness made their feelings no less genuine. As she had the courtesy to respect his dreams it would be well for us to do so too, albeit without solemnity and with an eye to the light cast on

---

*During most of the period of the affair Stella was bedridden. She had been involved in a serious accident near the Albert Hall in July 1912, smashing her head through the window of her taxicab and nearly causing a brain hemorrhage. Her recuperation was lengthy, and she had to spend the early months of 1913 in a nursing home. To make visits to her less conspicuous to Charlotte, Shaw bought a motorbike and left the family Rolls at home. A few of his meetings with Stella took place at the home of his sister Lucy. Mrs. Campbell's husband, Patrick, had died in battle in South Africa in 1900, leaving her with two children. In June 1912, at the start of the affair, she was forty-seven and Shaw nearly fifty-six.

his writings, and especially at the moment on *Pygmalion*. Even
that perennial question of whether they had sexual intercourse
must be considered since it too bears upon our understanding of
the present play and of several later ones; in fact, since Shaw's life
and his work were so often intermingled, we may discover a fresh
solution to the question by approaching it through the play rather
than through the famous letters alone. For what becomes increasingly evident, and astonishing, is not only that the modeling of
Eliza on Mrs. Campbell was the beginning of a dream that Shaw
then completed by his affair, but that the course of the affair itself
was largely prefigured in the play. Had Shaw been out to prove
Wilde's theory that life follows art, he could not have done so
more convincingly.

The unusual number of similarities between Shaw's behavior
toward Mrs. Campbell and Higgins's toward Eliza is immediately
apparent once we bring the two couples into conjunction. Shaw
like Higgins quickly assumes the role of teacher, announcing to
Stella that "as you are always boasting of your ignorance, I take
you at your word and instruct you." She is far less malleable than
Eliza, however, and soon demands to know "why you go on scolding me because I am the woman I am and not the woman you
would have me be." Again like Higgins, who retreats from tender
emotions behind his professional concerns, Shaw retreats behind
his writing activities, frankly telling her that he must "work,
work, work, hurling off articles and despatching arrears of business, and writing volleys of letters" since he can "do nothing but
dream" when he thinks of her. "If I stop to think about myself
and you," he says elsewhere, "the situation becomes desperate."
Further like Higgins, he is tormented by the dangers of dependency, the fear of becoming "a parasite" upon her. "Stella, I must
break myself of this," he declares; "my soul can stand alone." Yet
he knows that being bound to her releases him into a "wild happiness." We recall that Higgins becomes apprehensive when Eliza
hints at her fondness for him and baits him to do something
about it, and Shaw writes one of his most remarkable letters
when after four months Stella finally intimates that she is falling
in love with him; alarmed, he warns her at the outset to "shut
your ears tight against this blarneying Irish liar and actor. Read
no more of his letters. He will fill his fountain pen with your
heart's blood, and sell your most sacred emotions on the stage.
He is a mass of imagination with no heart." At the end he pleads,
"Oh dont, dont, DONT fall in love with him; but dont grudge him

the joy he finds in being in love with you, and writing all sorts of wild but heartfelt exquisite lies—lies, lies, lies, lies to you, his adoredest."

Now these similarities between Higgins and Shaw have subtler manifestations, but before we deal with them, a few of the strictly verbal parallels may be conveniently indicated in the following columns:

Pygmalion	*Shaw to Mrs. Campbell*
[Stage description of Higgins]: "He is, in fact, but for his years and size, rather like a very impetuous baby."	"I am a mass of childish wants and dreams."
"Ive never been able to feel really grown-up."	"I shall be 56 on the 26th of this month and I have not yet grown up."
"I go my way and do my work without caring what happens to either of us."	"Being busy, I have no time to bother about being happy, no time to bother about other people being happy."
"Here I am, a shy, diffident sort of man."	"Men *are* fools, especially timid ones like me."
"I might as well be a block of wood."	"I have no heart." "I must leave myself no time and be a machine—all I am good for."
"I waste the treasures of my Miltonic mind by spreading them before you. So you can come back or go to the devil."	"I have treated you far too well, idolized, thrown my heart and mind to you. . . . Go then . . . seek some stuffiness that suits you."
"I said I'd make a woman of you, and I have."	"Shall I ever make a woman of you . . . ?"
"You infamous creature. . . . you have wounded me to the heart."	"What are you, miserable wretch, that my entrails should be torn asunder hour after hour?"
"If you come back, come back for the sake of good fellowship."	"I drag you out into freedom and fellowship."
"Eliza, youre an idiot."	["Stella,] you have no brain."

Given these resemblances, perhaps one must resist the thought that Shaw kept consulting his play as the relationship with Mrs. Campbell proceeded. Situational parallels undoubtedly gave rise to verbal parallels, yet the latter's total number does seem to be more than coincidence alone would supply. There are clearly many differences between Higgins and Shaw, and between the events in the play and those in the real-life romance, but the similarities are nonetheless striking reminders that both the play and the romance were created by the same man, who in this particular work was tapping a deeply rooted fantasy which he then tried to live out. Indeed he joked with Stella about giving incognito performances in which he would "play Higgins to your Eliza," and on another occasion asked her whether "earth or heaven [has] anything better to offer me than reading my plays to you (except perhaps living them with you?)." He truly wanted more than the "paper love" of the play and the letters—"that paper love is nothing: the real thing is in the marrow of my bones and the roots of my nerves"; "I want to live it." But like many another writer he was not fully able to separate his professional from his personal life, and even while living the real thing he continued to turn some of it into plays, much to Mrs. Campbell's annoyance. (*Overruled* and *Great Catherine* were both composed while the affair was in progress and show its influence.) He did warn Stella that he could be "treacherous," that he was the sort of man who "adores you with one eye and sees you with the other as a calculated utility"; yet he then found it hard to understand why such one-eyed adoration distressed her.

This mingling of his personal and professional interests should be distinguished from the mingled yearnings in the love itself: the desire to adore her at a distance and the desire to possess her. Shaw was not just pretending to be in love. There is, as one commentator rightly says, "a heartbreaking sincerity" in the letters and it was "his last chance at romance," but he still could not reconcile his conflicting impulses. Thus he hopes at one moment that she is "playing with him," for that will keep her at a safe distance; yet he will begin another letter with the angry injunction, "Stella; don't play with me." Small wonder then that the actress had, as she told him, a good deal to cope with and that she finally sought refuge in a seaside resort, notifying him that she "must be alone." Had she taken along the script of *Pygmalion* she might have been able to guess his next move, for he was following out the play's inner logic with extraordinary fidelity. To see this, let us return to some additional parallels between the play and its author's life.

In considering the text earlier we observed Higgins's desire to adopt Eliza as his daughter and have her live with him in "good fellowship." Yet we also observed that she finally is acceptable to him because she has become more of a lady, more like his mother. Shaw was thereby suggesting that the deeper meaning of the Pygmalion myth was the creation of a woman who would be simultaneously mother and daughter, and we extended this idea in analyzing the peculiar nursery games Higgins plays with Eliza in Act IV. Now this interpretation receives considerable support from the way Shaw acted out his relationship with the actress for whom he had created the part of Eliza, as may be indicated by a few further extracts from his letters to her. "You are such a jolly playfellow," Shaw exclaims in one passage, which follows a reminiscence about playing chess as a boy with his mother.

And such a child! an old fashioned child! I should like to spend an hour every day with you, in the nursery. I no longer want you to act for me. I cant bear the idea of your having to work: you are not grown-up enough. And you dont want me to be busy, but to come and play. I am so tempted that I must set up a barrier of engagements between us. . . . There are such wonderful sorts of relations, such quaint comforts and happiness, and close-together-nesses; and babes-in-the-woodinesses, besides being in love, which, as you point out, my diet and feeble nature forbid. I may have moments of being in love; but you must overlook them.

And now, having expressed myself with carefully punctuated moderation, I shall go to bed quite calmly, and sign myself, oh loveliest doveliest babiest

Your gabiest
G. B. S.

Elsewhere in the correspondence there is more baby talk, and Stella like Eliza occasionally falls into the nursery role assigned to her. Sometimes Shaw leaves the nursery and imagines her out-of-doors with him, as "two barefooted playmates on the hills," or as "a lad playing with you on the mountains and unable to feel where you begin and I leave off." We are again (as in the play) back in Marchbanks's fantasy world as he talks of romping with Candida on the mountains; and Shaw himself seems to have been reminded of his story of Eugene and Candida, and the gates of heaven that Eugene could not enter, in the following passage, remarkable in many aspects besides the explicit coalescing of mother and daughter which had been implicit in the play:

Oh, if only you were alarmed, and could struggle, then I could struggle too. But to be gathered like a flower and stuck in your bosom frankly! to have no provocation to pursue, and no terror to fly! to have no margin of temptation to philander in! to have a woman's love on the same terms as a child's, to have nothing to seize, nothing to refuse, nothing to resist, everything for nothing, the gate of heaven wide open as in my story, to have striven fiercely all my life for trifles and have treasures at last offered for nothing, to miss the resistance that has become to me what water is to a fish, to hear tones in a human voice that I have never heard before, to have it taken for granted that I am a child and want to be happy, to draw the sword for the duel of sex with cunning confidence in practised skill and a brass breastplate, and suddenly find myself in the arms of a mother—a young mother, and with a child in my own arms who is yet a woman; all this plunges me into the wildest terror as if I were suddenly in the air thousands of feet above the rocks or sea. The measure of that terror is the relief with which I felt the earth yesterday—as I felt the stone when I was swimming my last stroke. Yet here I am caught up again, breathless, with no foothold, at a dizzy height, in an ecstasy which must be delirious and presently end in my falling headlong to destruction. And yet I am happy, as madmen are. What does this sound like from me, the supersane man? I am not otherwise mad; yet I am stark raving mad in this matter unless you are indeed and in truth an extraordinary person, a genius, a half goddess, wonderfully lovely, wonderfully tender, and simply sincere and pitiful and—oh for the word: I am at last at a loss for one—when you take me up and say . . . . I cant write those two words: they can exist only in my holiest memory now.

The moving honesty and excitement of these lines need not be marred by prosaic comment, and we as readers can make what we will of its erotic undertones and of his breathless delirious ecstasy as on a dizzy height from which he will soon fall to his destruction. For our present purposes we need only see how the mother and daughter have become one, as in *Pygmalion* itself, and how here the wild terror of the double incest shows what is hidden behind Higgins's brass breastplate and what leads him to seek punishment. The echoes of *Candida* ring not only across the mountain imagery and through the gates of heaven references but also in other letters in which Shaw calls Stella his "Queen of Heaven," his "mother of angels," and tells her that "you must always sit enthroned in heaven for me." And Marchbanks's conflict is inherent in Shaw's relationship to Stella (as in Higgins's to Eliza) when he declares to her in another epistle: "I want my plaything that I am to throw away, I want my Virgin Mother enthroned in heaven. I want my Italian peasant woman. I want my rapscallionly fellow vagabond. I want my dark lady. I want my angel—I want my tempter." Since the Reverend Morell is now absent, however, Shaw is the only one available to enjoin himself to return to reality and everyday moral codes, to remind himself, if not of Candida's kitchen and onions, then of Charlotte's bossy insistence that he return punctually for dinner—a matter that

arouses Stella's ridicule and that even he ruefully alludes to
by calling himself a member of the firm of "Charlotte & Co."*
Higgins, as we recall, successfully guards himself against the
"Marchbanks" within except in those shy moments when he tells
Eliza that he will miss her; but Higgins too has his bossy Mrs.
Pearce who stabs him with scoldings for his domestic sloppiness.

Shaw wants Stella to be his tempter as well as his angel, and in
overtly teasing his "Stella Aphrodite" with the sexual possibilities between them (just as he had teased us in the play), he seems
unlike Henry Higgins, who remains outwardly immune to Eliza's
womanly appeal, casually assigning her future to some vaguely
mentioned titled officer. Yet despite this apparent difference, we
recall that when Freddy Hill turns out to be in love with Eliza and
wants to marry her, Higgins is "disagreeably surprised" and then
becomes enraged. Seemingly this is only because he regards Freddy as unworthy of Eliza, but jealousy is also involved, which leads
him to thrash out in several directions—to scold her, to cajole
her, to ask whether she wants him "to be as infatuated about you
as Freddy," to declare arrogantly that he can do without anybody,
yet also to ask her humbly to come back to him. Jealousy entered
as well into Shaw's affair with Stella, the Freddy Hill in this instance being Major George Frederick Cornwallis-West. When
Shaw discovered that he had a serious rival, he too seems to have
been disagreeably surprised and to have thrashed out in several
new directions—to scold her for having "jilted" him, to show her

*The senior member of "Charlotte & Co." was understandably disturbed by her
husband's romance and sought to rescue him from the temptations of London by
taking him on trips to the Continent and to Ireland, but he secretly sent back
yearning letters to Stella (Campbell Letters, pp. 27–31, 113–18). Charlotte also
sought to rescue herself from earthly cares by becoming a disciple of Dr. James
Porter Mills, who preached a soothing hodgepodge of parlor transcendentalism,
Christian Science, and proto-Jungian ancestral memory, with God conceived of as
the great Silent Partner (*Health: Abstract and Concrete* [London, 1908]). Charlotte
prepared an abstract of the master's doctrines in a little volume entitled *Knowledge is the Door: A Forerunner* (London, 1914). In this book she writes that
through knowing Dr. Mills's teachings, "we shall find that circumstances and objects which used to disturb us, have lost their power; that mental impressions
which were wont to get hold of and overwhelm us, no longer do so" (p. 24). "*There
is no need to give way to feeling,*" she insists, italicizing a sentence unemphasized
in Mills's text. "With intelligence above human feeling," she continues, "and with
determination, and the use of the method this book is written to explain, we can
gradually quiet the waves of emotion, and gradually do away with the tendency to
yield to that which is untoward" (p. 12). Charlotte helped quiet the emotion that
her husband's amorous diversions aroused by taking a voyage to America early in
1914 with Dr. and Mrs. Mills, and, perhaps pointedly, she did not return until well
after the London opening of *Pygmalion*.

that his love was genuine whereas hers had been frivolous, to ask with arrogant humility that she keep George West waiting "until I am tired of you."

Therefore, though I like George (we have the same taste) I say he is young and I am old; so let him wait until I am tired of you. That cannot in the course of nature be long. I am the most faithless of men, though I am constant too: at least I dont forget. But I run through all illusions and trample them out with yells of triumph. And about you I am a mass of illusions. It is impossible that I should not tire soon: nothing so wonderful could last. You cannot really be what you are to me: you are a figure from the dreams of my boyhood—all romance, and anticipation of the fulfilment of the destiny of the race, which is thousands of years off. I promise to tire as soon as I can so as to leave you free. I will produce *Pygmalion* and criticise your acting. I will yawn over your adorable silly sayings and ask myself are they really amusing. I will run after other women in search of a new attachment; I will hurry through my dream as fast as I can; only let me have my dream out.

It is not exactly a flattering plea and it is understandable that Stella was reluctant to wait until the dreamer awakened. It is understandable too that there were limits to Shaw's self-knowledge, for while gazing at the bright side of the dream he could not anticipate that his yells of triumph when trampling out the illusion would sound very much like shrieks of pain, or that the dark side of the dream had always included the craving for punishment. No woman, not even a great actress, could continue to immolate herself for him in the impossible role of virgin mother, and his dream knew this, as had the artist who created *Pygmalion*. But the man, especially when his mind was clouded by jealousy, forgot the retributive punishment that the artist had meted out to Higgins by having Eliza hurt him and walk out on him, and the man thereby was not consciously prepared when Stella did precisely the same thing.

Two months after writing the above letter, on August 10, 1913, Shaw sought to hurry through his dream by following Stella down to her hotel at Sandwich, where she had gone a short time before for rest and seclusion. He lodged at her hotel, and as soon as she discovered his presence she sent him the following note: "Please will you go back to London today—or go wherever you like but dont stay here—If you wont go I must—I am very very tired and I oughtn't to go another journey. Please dont make me despise you." She not only wanted to be by herself and to gain strength for a forthcoming theatrical engagement. She feared the scandal of staying for a week in the same hotel with the man everybody in London knew was in love with her—knew it because he had told everybody, including Charlotte. Stella realized that the scandal might ruin her relationship with Cornwallis-West. Shaw certainly realized this too, and at the least he was placing her in a difficult position. Perhaps jealousy blinded him to his cruelty, or perhaps he felt the cruelty was excused by the risks he himself ran. Possibly he was prepared to divorce Charlotte and to offer marriage to Stella. "I risked the breaking of deep roots and sanctified ties," he was soon to write to Stella in accounting for his sudden arrival at Sandwich. "I set my feet boldly on all the quicksands: I rushed after Will o' the Wisp into darkness: I courted the oldest illusions, knowing well what I was doing." But if he did know, he apparently did not tell Stella. Instead, during the single day they were together, he did not even talk to her about the note she had written to him in the morning asking for his departure, a note he kept in his pocket. He walked alone for miles and then worked on a short play. Like Higgins at the beginning of Act IV he seemed to forget all about the woman, and then again like Higgins he acted sleepy when he finally talked to her. Since he gave no sign of preparing to leave the hotel, nor any indication of what he really wanted, Stella paid her bill. And still the man said nothing to the purpose. Was he too sleepy to understand? Stella at first thought so, but when reviewing the incidents in a letter to him, she concluded that his inattention had been willed: "You *wouldn't* understand," she declared, emphasizing the word herself. Shaw was reenacting Higgins's behavior by being cruel to the woman and forcing her to leave, which she did quite as promptly as Eliza herself at the end of Act IV. But having seen that Higgins's cruelty was primarily a means of making Eliza wound him, we should not be surprised at Shaw's shrieks of outrage when he discovered Stella's absence:

Very well, go: the loss of a woman is not the end of the world. The sun shines: it is pleasant to swim: it is good to work: my soul can stand alone. But I am deeply, deeply, deeply wounded. . . . Bah! You have no nerve: you have no brain: you are the caricature of an eighteenth century male sentimentalist, a Hedda Gabler titivated with odds and ends from Burne Jones's ragbag: you know nothing, God help you, except what you know all wrong: daylight blinds you: you run after life furtively and run away or huddle up and scream when it turns and opens its arms to you. . . . you are an owl, sickened by two days of my sunshine: I have treated you far too well, idolized, thrown my heart and mind to you (as I throw them to all the world) to make what you could of; and what you make of them is to run away. Go then: the Shavian oxygen burns up your little lungs: seek some stuffiness that suits you. You will not marry George! At the last moment you will funk him or be ousted by a bolder soul. You have wounded my vanity: an inconceivable audacity, an unpardonable crime.

Farewell, wretch that I loved.
G. B. S.

It does not deprecate Shaw's suffering if we choose to hear overtones in this letter of a twentieth-century male sentimentalist secretly enjoying his grief. Shaw had not at all opened his arms to Stella at the hotel; had he done so instead of taking solitary walks and acting sleepy, she might even have stayed! Shaw's self-love had clearly been wounded but his love for her was best gratified at a safe distance. It might be all very well to visit her during her illness, when she was bedridden, but a healthy Stella Aphrodite might make some intimidating demands on her aging and talkative votary. Having now escaped these demands by forcing her to leave, he could minister to his injured ego throughout the day, and in the evening he sent forth this additional salvo:

Oh, my rancor is not yet slaked: I have not said enough vile things to you. What are you, miserable wretch, that my entrails should be torn asunder hour after hour? . . . Oh, may you be bored until in desperation you ask the waiter to walk out with you! You are worse than that fiend of a woman: she could at least hate and stick to it: you are neither love nor hate. Wretch, wretch, how well I, an Irishman, know this Roman Catholic product, this precociously forced erotic sentimentality, this narrow mind, this ignorance, this helplessness that longs to be forced because it can imitate nothing, will nothing, change nothing, that has no power except the power of endearment and no appeal except the appeal of beauty. These are the things you set up against the appeal of beauty. These are the things you set up against me when I drag you out into freedom and fellowship. Give me, oh my critical mind and keen eye, a thousand reasons for treating this light creature as she deserves, if such a monstrous retribution is possible. Come round me all the good friends I have neglected for her. Even her slanderers shall be welcome: I shall say: "Spit your venom; heap up your lies; vomit your malice until the air is poison: you will still fall short of the truth."

Let us interrupt the Lear-like imprecations with a reminder that the freedom and fellowship he had offered her was merely the fellowship of the nursery, where he could enjoy what we heard him earlier call the "quaint comforts and happiness, and close-together-nesses; and babes-in-the-woodinesses." Here perhaps we should also note that he would call his very next play, with the part of Mrs. Hushabye written for Stella Campbell, his "Lear" play.

Stella, how could you [the letter concludes], how could you? What micrometer could measure the shallowness that prevents you from knowing what you have done. Even if I had been secretly bored to distraction I would have stayed on in fire rather than have dealt you the enormous blow of deserting you. But at least the order of nature is restored to my imagination. It is I who cared, you who didn't. That is as becomes me. I no longer look up to the queen of heaven: I tower mountainous to the skies and see a pretty little thing wondering at me. How is it that this infinitesimal nothingness yet drags at my midriff and causes me strange pangs and makes me write wild nonsense? Oh, the world itself is too light to carry the reproach you deserve. You are more cruel than a child.

Enough, I will go to bed. I am still sleepy.

He may have slept the sleep of the innocent, having now established that the blame was entirely hers, and he may have dreamt of mounting high horses. The next day, refreshed, he hurled forth another missive, full of self-righteousness and anger:

Another day that might have been a day! What have I shrunk into? In all these years I have hurt many people as the Doctor hurt your thumb, sometimes sorely perhaps, but never maliciously, never desiring to hurt, never without such anodynes as my wit and address could devise. I have never said anything false or unjust or spiteful, and never wanted to. And now give me anything that is false, malicious, spiteful, little, mean, poisonous or villainous, and I will say it only if it hurts you. I want to hurt you because you hurt me. Infamous, vile, heartless, frivolous, wicked woman! Liar! lying lips, lying eyes, lying hands, promise breaker, cheat, confidence-trickster! . . . I think I shall stay here where my heart's blood has been spilt in the sand. I walk well here. I sleep well here. I suffer well here. . . . oh wretch, I could tear you limb from limb.

The sadomasochistic streak which we have seen in Professor Higgins manifests itself here in Shaw as well, and the pattern of the climactic fourth act of the play is now duplicated, from the initial sleepiness of the man to the provoked departure of the woman. Shaw seems no more conscious of having sought pain than did Higgins; yet his strongest emotion at Sandwich came not from the pleasure of Stella's company but from the suffering he managed to create for himself. Like Higgins, he "suffers well," and like Higgins he appears blind to the cruelty of his behavior. Higgins too thought that he wanted to hurt the woman simply because she had hurt him first. Both men hide their masochistic cravings behind a screen of self-righteousness, and both derive a secret satisfaction from having canceled the opportunity for any normal lovemaking and provided for themselves instead some of the satisfactions of sadomasochistic love.

Thus the play helps us to understand the affair with Mrs.

Campbell quite as much as the affair amplifies the meanings of the play. Higgins's mother fixation was akin to Shaw's own, and the relation of both men to women other than their mothers was governed by this fixation. Higgins tells his mother that his "idea of a lovable woman is something as like you as possible," and he tries to mold Eliza to this ideal. Similarly, in Shaw's romance with Stella—which spanned the period of his mother's last illness and death—there is a repeated association of the actress with his early childhood memories and desires: the cozy security of the nursery, the baby talk, the references to her as a "mother of angels," as "a figure from the dreams of my boyhood," as "a young mother" in whose arms he "suddenly find[s] himself." The point need not be labored, but it does make luminously clear why Shaw had to break off the relationship and why his behavior toward her became sadomasochistic as their intimacy increased. He was driven toward punishing himself—and to goad her into becoming the agent of that punishment—because the dream he was living included, as we heard him call it earlier, "the wildest terror" as the price of his ecstasy, "an ecstasy which must be delirious and presently end in my falling headlong to destruction." And it is because the hidden incestuous craving is accompanied by the hidden terror of the castration punishment that we can hear in those letters he hurled at Stella an undertone of satisfaction, like the histrionic whimpers of a man who finds himself saved from a fall down a mountain by a protruding ledge, on which he now sits bruised but achingly relieved.

Shaw's relief, however, had to be largely unconscious to be effective. His suffering could not be adulterated by any recognition that he hurt Stella first or that the responsibilities for the failed romance were mutual. His suffering verified his love, as is seen in his proudly grieving declaration, "It is I who cared, you who didn't. That is as becomes me. . . . I tower mountainous to the skies and see a pretty little thing wondering at me." Stella had once baited him by reporting a friend's verdict that "his love is epistolary," and Shaw had retorted that "it is past letter writing with me." Now his suffering showed that he had lived his love rather than merely fantasized it. Stella had also baited him for his reluctance to be seen with her, for his fear of Charlotte, for hiding behind the barrier of his work. She had hurled at him the word "Coward!" But by following her to Sandwich, even if spurred on by jealousy, he had boldly countered her charge and his own occasional admission that he was "timid." Courage, will, decisiveness, depth of emotion were now proven by his swooping down upon her and by the later intensity of his suffering. Now she could be accused of having "no nerve," of being a "sentimentalist" who would "run after life furtively and run away or huddle up and scream when it turns and opens its arms to you." With each pang of pain, with each letter he aimed at her, he towered higher into the sky. And from that height he was also able to render invisible his anxiety over the need to prove himself as a lover. The crisis with Stella had, after all, been delightfully delayed by her semi-invalidism: he had courted her in a sickroom. When she recuperated he began to be apprehensive, as he admitted to her in one of his letters: "When you said you were writing in bed, and for a moment I thought you might be ill again, I asked myself was it a wild hope or a wild fear. Oh the Life Force never laid a deeper trap than that illness that gained for me the entry to the sanctuary. I shant know what to do now that you are up." Higgins avoided such dilemmas by keeping Eliza at arm's length, but Shaw had already lived beyond this part of the script and his solution was lamely improvised. He apparently exhausted himself as a man of action by descending upon his beloved in Sandwich, because when there he had acted sleepy and she was "rather bored." He left her alone for many hours, and when with her he talked and he talked. "You blind man," she was to call him in her first response to his accusations. "You weaver of words, you . . . you poor thing unable to understand a mere woman. My friend all the same. No daughters to relieve your cravings—no babes to stop your satirical chatterings, why should I pay for all your shortcomings. You in your broom-stick and sheet have crackers and ashes within you." It was unkind, but still a temperate rejoinder to all Shaw's fulminations against her, and the remark about the cravings that would be relieved by daughters was acute, since Shaw was really following Higgins in wanting a combined mother and daughter, the comforts of the nursery, rather than a woman to take pleasure with in a bedroom. But he could not quite admit this to himself: he thought he wanted his tempter as well as his angel; and the problem of what to do with his Stella now that they were staying at the same hotel had to be faced. A hint of his solution, beyond the convenient sleepiness, is given in a passage from one of his first letters after she had left:

And now there is that desolate strand, and the lights of Ramsgate that might have been the camp fires of the heavenly hosts on the Celestial mountains. I said "There are seven stars and seven sorrows and seven swords in the heart of the Queen of Heaven: and for myself I want seven days." They began; and I held back: I was not greedy: for I wanted the last to be the best. And you yawned in my face, and stole the last five to waste in some desolate silly place with your maid and your chauffeur.

Stella may have yawned in sympathy with his sleepiness, or because she foresaw several days like the first one, though it is not clear whether Shaw had actually waxed poetical to her or only to himself. He now implies, however, that he had been fiercely holding himself back and was planning some sort of consummation on the last day. Possibly he believed it, and we may like to accept it. But he did manage to make sure that the lady was gone long before that last day arrived.

Back in London soon afterward, Shaw continued to indulge his ego-restoring grief, opening his next letter to Stella with the words: "Back from the land of broken promise. I might ring you up and say this; but I am too proud. Oh shallow-hearted thing!" and ending with: "Useless, these letters; the wound will not heal." But he quickly learned how to keep the wound from view, and he continued to write to her, though now in jaunty rather than amorous tones. The Shaws soon departed for a holiday in France where Charlotte, knowing that her husband's romance was over, let loose a blast of pent-up fury and then subsided into amiability. Stella wickedly expressed her hopes that "your honeymoon has been a success," and within eight months she was married to Cornwallis-West.

III

Shaw could never permit himself to savor the comedy he had lived. Had he done so he could have turned it into a fine successor to *Pygmalion*. But perhaps only a writer with different skills, a playwright like Pirandello, could have successfully woven together the crossing threads of theater and life which were present in the events, and rendered the confusions of its participants. Comedies are rarely funny to those who live them, and Shaw had a vested emotional interest in sustaining his grief. He did dip his pen into the wound and write some works which show the bitter aftereffects of his romance (as will be traced in our next chapter), but the actual comedy of that romance was too painful for him to contemplate. When we look back on it now, with a detachment he understandably was not able to possess, we can see that its final design was predictable because he had been unconsciously patterning it on his own *Pygmalion*. He had told Stella that he wanted to live his plays with her, but he had not told her or himself which one he was going to try to live first. As the romance proceeded he was perhaps drawn toward enacting the happy outcome of the love affair in *Man and Superman*, but Stella was no Ann Whitefield determined to catch a protesting male, and Shaw was no longer an unattached Tanner. Besides, that was Charlotte's play. Stella's was *Pygmalion*, and a much older Shaw had written it, a man whose character was more set in its mold. He was not altogether pleased with that mold—he often bemoaned to her his "heart of stone," his "marble heart"—and he tried to alter it by living a new play with her, a sequel to *Pygmalion* which would show Higgins and Eliza fulfilling their nascent romance. But the grip of the personal fantasy underlying *Pygmalion* was too strong to overcome, which is to say that Shaw's own mold was too firmly set. The unresolved ending of the play was psychologically right because it reflected hardened ambivalences in Higgins's character. His feelings for Eliza, as substitute daughter and mother, were doubly incestuous and therefore doubly inhibiting, even more so because the unappreciative Mrs. Higgins aroused his resentment, which was then displaced on to Eliza. Opposed to these inhibitions was a strong though timidly expressed yearning for normality, for a relationship with a woman which would allow him to be a lover as well as a father and son: he wanted Eliza to bring him to life as a man. These ambivalences were very much Shaw's own, as the affair with Mrs. Campbell demonstrates. And the dramatist's personal conflict was as unresolvable as his protagonist's for a similar reason: Stella, his Eliza, became too closely identified with his mother. In terms of the private fantasy underlying the play, we had hypothesized earlier that Shaw did not completely close the door on a future relationship between his fictional man and woman because he still longed for a woman for himself, especially one who could serve as a substitute for his mother. The Campbell affair conveniently confirms that hypothesis. But the very fulfillment of Shaw's longing created unhappy challenges for him. Stella did not want to be only a mother, and he thus felt obliged to make gestures as a lover. These had their limits, which were reached in the culminating events in Sandwich. There he tried to step beyond the script of *Pygmalion* and to remake himself, but the chains of his past finally grew taut and dragged him back into his Higgins self, compelling him to finish the script he was living in the same way

as he had finished the playscript, to force Stella to leave as Eliza
had been forced to leave, and to provoke her, as Eliza had been
provoked, into becoming a means for a man to punish himself.
He thereafter ignored the ways in which his own inhibitions had
contributed to the outcome of the affair. He put the blame entirely on Stella just as years earlier he had blamed Alice Lockett
for breaking up their romance and, later, had blamed Charlotte
for maneuvering him into marriage and keeping it unconsummated. The rationalizations then and now served their usual purpose of protecting the ego from the truth.

We have suddenly arrived at an answer to the question of
whether the Shaw-Campbell affair was sexually consummated,
and we may now realize, probably with disappointment, that the
answer seems to be negative. Such disappointment springs from
exactly the same source as the popular hope that Eliza will return
to Higgins and marry him. We want love to triumph and be fulfilled so that nature can triumph and we too can be vicariously
fulfilled. We want to banish the incestuous implications of Higgins's love just as we want to overlook the incestuous yearnings
in Shaw's devotion to Stella. But the mother fixation which possessed both Higgins and Shaw seems to have created similar asexual behavior in their relations with women. A protective uncertainty about the romantic outcome had always been intrinsic to
the fantasy at the heart of the play and of its lived enactment. The
fantasy was a tribute to a possibility, unimpeded by the demands
of reality, by the incompatibility between a woman as temptress
and as angel. To the extent that Eliza and Stella became obtain-
able, their desirableness decreased. Like a star whose beauty requires distance to appreciate, Stella Campbell had a shriveling
effect on her admirer when he came too close. But of course these
are ways of talking only about Shaw's psychic restraints. He may
also now have been impotent, and he certainly faced legal constraints. Stella wanted to be a wife rather than a mistress, and
Shaw was married, the "slave of an establishment," as he called
it. If he had seriously thought of divorce, it was not his aging
bones alone that may have given him pause: in the closet of his
establishment was the skeleton of an unconsummated marriage.
The world did not yet know of this and Shaw was not at all eager
to have it known. In his 1910 treatise on marriage and divorce he
had most insistently advocated a legal reform which would have
met his personal needs, the availability of divorce whenever either party requested it, and without the disclosure of any reason

whatsoever. But given the existing divorce laws, there was no way of predicting what an infuriated Charlotte might have disclosed; her husband's romance with Stella, as Shaw himself had observed, had driven her sick with jealousy and rage. Shaw as a great admirer of John Ruskin was nonetheless aware of the ridicule Ruskin had had to endure during his later life because of the scandal of his unconsummated marriage to Effie Gray. Shaw's masochism may have required its satisfactions—but in ways of his own choosing. In sum, there were more than enough inner and outer obstacles in the romance with Stella to have precluded its successful outcome, and perhaps we should finally be impressed by the lengths to which Shaw in fact managed to carry it.

Beyond this our disappointment can also be cushioned in three other ways: one small, one medium, and one very large indeed. Shaw in a small way, though to him a significant one, did go beyond Higgins in fulfilling his love for his Eliza. Though sexual consummation was probably not attained, there was quite likely a certain amount of dalliance, especially when Stella was still bedridden. And even on their first meeting in her house she must have made herself extremely captivating in response to the love gift of the play, for Shaw himself soon told her and others that he had fallen head over heels in love with her. A touching moment from that first meeting, which Shaw long remembered, was her taking his hands in hers, in enthusiasm and affection, and drawing them to her, with the knuckle of one of his fingers brushing against her bosom. An accident? Poor Shaw apparently wondered much over it, finally deciding that it had been intentional. But let us acknowledge that Higgins had never gotten even that far with Eliza. The final extent of the physical involvement is perhaps accurately summed up in a few of the verses Shaw once wrote to Stella during the height of the romance:

28th Feb. 1913

Who mashed Stella? Who made her smile? Who is her friend?
I, that rejoice Dis very chile Stella's true friend?
In a nice Irish voice With my wink and my wile. World without end
I mashed Stella *I* made her smile *I* am her friend.

Who kissed her toes? Who clasped her tight?
Who d'you s'pose? That wasn't right.
And also her nose? Oh, the delight!
I kissed her toes *I* clasped her tight.

This charming outburst of song from our distinguished man-of-letters, and the whole intriguing correspondence in which it is preserved, may be said to offer us a permanent, medium-sized consolation. Yet our largest comfort is simply the glory of having *Pygmalion*. The play was written, as we have seen, from the depths of Shaw's own being, and the fantasy satisfactions it provided for him, and ultimately for the world, required him to be a man who could not enjoy a fully consummated romance with a Stella Campbell. He of course might have preferred to possess Stella rather than to write a play for her—but then we would not have possessed *Pygmalion*.

Pygmalion is thus the loveliest of Shaw's plays because it is a double gift of love, to his mother and to Stella Campbell. It draws its ebullient energies from those loves, from honoring the most important woman in his past and yearning for another woman to replace her in the future. The structure of the play was created to accommodate this double gift of love, and through this structure, and the arrangement of incident within it, the latent conflict between the two loves was kept hidden. The protagonist's devotion to his mother could be shown as a fact from the past living on in the present. The protagonist's yearning to have another woman, a woman from the present who would carry him into a better future, could be kept muted because that woman was for most of the play only potentially inherent in Eliza, who had first to be shaped into a lady before she could become acceptable as a woman. Unlike the flawed romance in *Man and Superman*, where the love between Tanner and Ann remains somewhat unconvincing, *Pygmalion* creates a situation in which the possibility of romance can be left half submerged until near the end, can be treated as only a possibility since the primary relationship is between teacher and pupil. And this submerging of the romantic issue, and the removal of the need for any traditional love scenes, paradoxically released Shaw's own feelings of love and allowed him to express them safely. The play's form protected the desires from the threat of their fulfillment; and it allowed both loves to be expressed while tempering the conflict between them. What Shaw discovered in his affair with Stella Campbell was that only in his art could he give gifts to two women and avoid the need to choose between them. He thereby confirmed the old truth that among the reasons man creates art is that it allows him to express desires which are irreconcilable in life.

And now the private drama surrounding the play had one final scene which Shaw had to endure and which was to serve as the lived prologue to his next work.

Pygmalion

The English premiere of *Pygmalion* took place on April 11, 1914, eight months after the romance with Stella had collapsed. Sir Herbert Beerbohm Tree, the famous actor-manager, played Higgins to Mrs. Campbell's Eliza. The several weeks of rehearsal had been very straining, with Shaw unable to achieve his usual ease with his casts. He badgered the leading lady, scolded her for her accent, and so infuriated her that at times she insisted that he leave the theater and convey all further instructions through an intermediary; and on at least two occasions Shaw himself stomped out of the theater on his own. This irritability perhaps arose from more than the usual tensions of rehearsal. A defeated lover, coaching for opening night the woman who he thought had jilted him, Shaw seems to have behaved like Higgins at his most savage preparing Eliza for her debut as a duchess. But where the romantic outcome of the play had been ambiguous, Stella Campbell was now engaged to her Freddy; and indeed, almost as if Shaw by his behavior were unconsciously willing further pain for himself, Stella abruptly suspended her rehearsals five days before the opening and went off to marry Cornwallis-West, returning after a brief honeymoon full of glowing praise for her new husband, her "golden man" as she called him. Shaw released his vexation by further criticizing the actress right up to the night of the premiere, when he sent her a stern set of instructions headed FINAL ORDERS.

We can only surmise the playwright's feelings as he sat in the crowded theater on that famous evening. There as the scene opened was the portico of St. Paul's church in Covent Garden, protecting from the rain a lady and her daughter who had just come from the theater and were waiting for a cab. Soon a bedraggled flower girl hurries in for shelter—and the great first act is under way. Shaw had designed this method of beginning his work to show that the lady and her daughter would soon be involved in a drama with the flower girl more extraordinary than any play they had just seen. Drama was everywhere around us if we would only use our eyes. But now, as *Pygmalion* moved along, the eyes of the audience were riveted to the stage as Beerbohm Tree came forward to address Eliza with his opening words: "There, there, there, there! who's hurting you, you silly girl?" And unseen by that audience, an intense personal drama was transpiring between the famous actress in front of them and the quiet figure of the playwright sitting out amongst them. Did the actress's eyes and voice at times search him out in that darkness, we may wonder, as the play unfolded a story he had written lovingly for her, a story they partly reenacted during their abortive romance? "I'm a good girl, I am," sobs Eliza from the stage—and memories may have crossed the author's mind of his torment on the sands of the Channel after Stella, protecting her good name, had deserted the hotel. "I'm going away," Eliza later announces. "He's off his chump, he is. I dont want no balmies teaching me." And did the playwright recall those first words Stella wrote to him after she had left the hotel: "You blind man. . . . you poor thing unable to understand a mere woman. . . . You in your broom-stick and sheet have crackers and ashes within you"? And from the stage Eliza moaning her "Whood marry me?" while the playwright was still rankled by Stella's choice of a new husband, and had nearly broken up his own marriage to be with her. And on it went—line after line carrying special overtones for the actress and the play-wright, ironic echoes of their own romance. Higgins may have been tormenting Eliza up on stage but that was after all a make-believe world, of simulated emotions, whereas beyond the foot-lights one person had cause for real suffering. "Oh, you are a devil," Eliza calls out as Higgins tries to lure her back to him; "you can twist the heart in a girl as easy as some could twist her arms to hurt her." And Shaw himself, vainly attempting to lure Stella back after she had left him, had received from her the words, "You are trying to break my heart with your letters." But now another heart was perhaps being broken. And if the question had occurred to him, "Who's hurting you, you silly man?" he would have had to answer that he was hurting himself because Stella was simply sending forth into the theater the words that he himself had written for her. "You wanted to get rid of me," Eliza was presently declaring, and soon, asserting her independence, she bids Higgins a firm goodbye. Eliza had been getting her own back in the fairy tale up on stage, but the actress, now Mrs. Corn-wallis-West in real life and giving a magnificent performance, was more than getting her own back from the man who had caused her anxiety as a vacillating lover and a belittling director. And certainly no actor, Beerbohm Tree or his many successors, will ever again find a listener in the audience who could respond with as much feeling as the playwright himself that night when, to-ward the end, Higgins says softly, "I shall miss you, Eliza."

The play was over. Pygmalion's statue was alive. The sculptor had been turned to stone. As the audience thundered out its cheers, the playwright's success was complete. But Shaw did not hear the applause. He had hurried from the theater just before the final curtain, not waiting to see Eliza walk out on Higgins. He was too disturbed to concern himself with the insult to the cast of not attending the reception or congratulating the principals. He went home and read in bed for an hour until his nerves and his heart were calm enough to allow him to sleep. Yet that evening new impetus was given to the play he had conceived shortly after the romance with Stella broke up, the play he was to call *Heartbreak House.*

7

The Playwright's Revenge

That in black ink my love may still shine bright.

Shakespeare, Sonnet 65

Overleaf: Shaw in 1914.

$\mathcal{T}$HE OPENING NIGHT of *Pygmalion* brought to a climax the drama of Shaw's romance with Stella Campbell. It also spurred him to conduct a campaign of revenge against her, sometimes openly but more often from behind a literary smoke screen. The most accomplished expression of Shaw's anger was in the 1916 *Heartbreak House*, a work that lies outside the scope of this study. What does concern us here is the completion of the *Pygmalion* story, the strange way in which Shaw harmed his masterpiece by adding a postscript, and then a preface, and finally several new scenes, all of which appear in current editions of the text and have led critics astray. To understand why he was willing to damage the play, it is necessary to review all six chronological acts of his campaign. It forms a little psychodrama which may be called "The Playwright's Revenge," and of course it stars Bernard Shaw and Stella Campbell.

I

The lengthy postscript to the 1916 edition of *Pygmalion* was the opening salvo in Shaw's campaign. Here he invents an improbable sequel to the play's story and adopts an entirely new attitude toward both Eliza and Higgins. We now learn with some surprise that Eliza gives up her ambition to become a teacher and instead marries the penniless Freddy Hill. After a period of floundering they set up a flower shop with money supplied by Colonel Pickering. The venture is initially a failure because of the young couple's incompetence—Freddy not even knowing the meaning of a bank account—and Eliza repeatedly has to beg Pickering for more money. She who had once passed as a duchess also has to endure "a period of disgrace and despair" while studying at commercial schools alongside of prospective junior clerks. And further humiliating herself, she has to request that Higgins teach her how to write properly. At last, with additional backing from Pickering and Higgins, the shop somehow attains a modest success despite the inefficiency of its youthful owners. Then they apparently

253

start a family although absolutely nothing is said about their children. Instead we are told at the end that Higgins remains one of the most prominent people in Eliza's life and that she spends a good deal of time visiting him, no doubt to relieve the boredom of living with Freddy, who is portrayed as an "ideal errand boy" suitable only for fetching her slippers.

Let us pause to consider this story before proceeding to the postscript's equally changed viewpoint on Higgins. Most noticeable is the constant degrading of Eliza. She is "humbled in the dust" as one phrase puts it; and connecting these words to a central metaphor in *Pygmalion* we can see that whereas the writer of the play transformed the grimy daughter of a dustman into a human flower, the writer of the postscript tries to grind her back into the dust. He now changes Eliza's character in a variety of ways, robs it of essential aspects he had so expertly delineated in the play, and abolishes all of her growth from Act II onward. Suddenly we are informed that Eliza is "by no means easily teachable"! Suddenly all of her independence of spirit is taken from her. Now she keeps crawling back to beg for favors, and she renounces teaching in deference to the wishes of that same Higgins she had gloriously defied in the play. Suddenly she becomes a very ordinary girl whose only talent lies in exploiting Higgins and Pickering for her material benefit. In sum, the Eliza of the postscript is no longer the Eliza of the play, and Shaw has patched together a dummy figure into which he takes great pleasure in sticking pins.*

This strange treatment of Eliza is by no means clarified by Shaw's professed reasons for writing the postscript. He wanted, he declared, to prevent audiences from assuming that the play's two principal figures would eventually marry. He wanted to prevent Higgins from acting "like a bereaved Romeo." Yet these intentions did not require Eliza's debasement. Nor did they require her to marry Freddy Hill. Nor did they even require the writing of a postscript at all. A few emphatic sentences in the preface could have made the essential point that Higgins remained a bachelor.

---

*He also has a few pins left over to stick into Clara Eynsford Hill. Among the many oddities of the postscript is Shaw's long digressive account of Clara—"an utter failure, an ignorant, incompetent, pretentious, unwelcome, penniless, useless little snob"—whose existence Shaw somehow finds saved from futility by her determined reading of the novels of Wells and Galsworthy and a job in a furniture shop. Shaw may have sensed that hostility directed only toward Eliza would have been suspect, and by attacking Clara he ends up with an evenhanded display of misogyny.

Or, better still, they could have preserved the fine ambiguity of the play's ending by insisting on the unpredictability of Eliza's later relations with Higgins. Shaw's stated intentions, in a word, hardly justify the document's contents, and thereby license us to seek other motives for its composition.

These motives are easily found when we regard the postscript biographically. It tells us little about *Pygmalion* apart from confirming Shaw's emotional involvement with the play. And since that involvement included the actress who had inspired the work, the outcome of the romance with Stella Campbell determined the nature of the postscript and probably its very writing. Eliza now serves as a substitute target for Stella, and Shaw uses his potent pen to attack indirectly the woman who had seemingly rejected him as a lover. "I want to hurt you because you hurt me," he had written to her after she had left him alone at the hotel in Sandwich. "Give me anything that is false, malicious, spiteful, little, mean, poisonous or villainous, and I will say it only if it hurts you"; and through the postscript he at last finds a way to take his mean little revenge, spiteful, malicious, and totally false to the letter and the spirit of his great play. Indeed, he was so eager to have Stella read the wounding document that he mailed her an advance copy immediately upon receiving it, along with a hint that her new husband would find it interesting as well. For Shaw had also been using his potent pen to take revenge (as best he could) on his successful rival, and this explains why he now heaps scorn on Freddy Hill and turns him into the chief agent of Eliza's humiliation. In brief, it was Shaw himself rather than Henry Higgins who was acting like a bereaved Romeo—an elderly, jilted, and very angry one.*

Apparently Shaw's anger had to be powerful to help him forget his inadequacies as Stella's lover and his own responsibility for the affair's termination. Directed fiercely outward, the anger gave him time to mend his ego and to replace his lost love object with another one, namely, himself. This process had begun immediately after Stella departed from Sandwich, when he then boasted to her, "I tower mountainous to the skies and see a pretty little thing wondering at me." The process continued not only in the postscript's diminution of Eliza but also in its elevation of Hig-

---

*It should be noted that the anger did not wait until 1916 to be expressed. Shaw actually began drafting the play's addenda as early as 1913, the year the romance ended. He first informed Stella of the postscript's existence on Dec. 19, 1915, and sent her an advance copy five months later.

gins from the lowly state in which the play had left him. Higgins's characteristics are not changed, as were Eliza's. Rather, his faults are omitted or else treated indulgently. His selfishness and cruelty now go unmentioned, his bullying is regarded as harmless. He is portrayed as a superior man of "philosophic interests," a trifle eccentric but thoroughly decent. His yearning in the play to be more than a block of wood is now forgotten, as is his confession that he learned things from Eliza. Moreover, the writer of the postscript now defends him for the same sexual immaturity and mother fixation for which the writer of the play had ridiculed him. Higgins is now a "predestinate old bachelor" who has happily effected "a disengagement of his affections, his sense of beauty, and his idealism from his specifically sexual impulses." His cultivated mother, we are told, sets for him a standard against which very few women can compete, and certainly not the now commonplace Eliza. When Shaw recalls words in the play contradicting the new perspective on Higgins, the difficulty is removed by verbal legerdemain:

The very scrupulousness with which [Higgins] told [Eliza] that day that he had become used to having her there, and dependent on her for all sorts of little services, and that he should miss her if she went away (it would never have occurred to Freddy or the Colonel to say anything of the sort) deepens her inner certainty that she is "no more to him than them slippers"; yet she has a sense, too, that his indifference is deeper than the infatuation of commoner souls.

The final clause was added to a late draft of the postscript, and its specious profundity suggests Shaw's willingness to forget the true profundity of some words he had written at an earlier date: "The worst sin towards our fellow creatures is not to hate them, but to be indifferent to them; that's the essence of inhumanity." Yet despite Higgins's deep indifference, Eliza supposedly remains "immensely interested" in him and even has sexual fantasies of getting him alone on a desert island so that she can "just drag him off his pedestal and see him making love like any common man." Higgins is in fact turned into an exemplary man even while Eliza is being ground into the dust.

In this attempt to repair his own ego under the guise of talking about Higgins, Shaw sadly entangles himself in rationalizations that grow like an octopus's arms. For on the one hand, it now appears that Higgins [read Shaw] is simply "too godlike" for Eliza [read Stella], and that he has "formidable powers of resistance" to her charms. Yet on the other hand, he really was available had she wanted him: she alone was responsible for rejecting him and for marrying a lesser man. But on the third hand, maybe it was just as well since Eliza would have been a very difficult woman to manage; she still "stands up to him so ruthlessly that the Colonel has to ask her from time to time to be kinder to Higgins." But then again, on the fourth hand, the man is at bottom truly indifferent to the woman, and this indifference is somehow to his credit. In fact, on still another hand, the loss can really be viewed as entirely the woman's, and the poor thing will have to content herself with frequent visits to Higgins's house and futile fantasies of seducing him. Thus Shaw consoles his phonetician in far too many ways and then shows himself unconvinced by continuing the attack on Eliza and her husband. His words may formally commend her choice of Freddy Hill, but his contempt for that choice is nonetheless pronounced.

While constructing this elaborate defense for Higgins, Shaw embraces the Higgins element within himself. Yet with unintended irony he embraces the worst side of Higgins and shows the same savage temper and destructiveness for which he had ridiculed the professor in the play. He ignores the best side—the yearning to be more than a block of wood, to be brought to life and to receive love, the willingness to acknowledge his gratitude to Eliza and his need for her. That need for a woman to revivify him had been Shaw's very own, as the letters to Stella fully substantiate. But when she was no longer available he sought to deny that the need had ever existed, and he does this by portraying his surrogate Higgins as commendably indifferent to women and self-sufficient. It had become intolerable for Shaw to face those truths about himself which his love for Stella had encouraged him to express in the play. Equally intolerable was it to accept the play's truth that Higgins had defeated himself. Shaw was enacting, more than he could bear to recognize, the fate of his protagonist who again turns into wood.

That Shaw flinched from those truths he had once perceived is readily intelligible, for they could be safely exhibited only within the fantasy of the play, and only there could he harmonize his love for Stella and his love for his mother. Had he been able to do this in reality, there would have been no pressure to write the play, whose form, as we noted earlier, protected his desires from the threat of their vicarious fulfillment. The very same emotional conflicts that had energized the play were responsible for the difficulties of the actual romance with Stella, and given Shaw's nature the longing for revenge was inevitable. By his nature I refer again to the formula which he himself once offered to Alice Lockett: "Beware. When all the love has gone out of me, I am remorseless: I hurl the truth about like destroying lightning." The destructive impulse is clearly evident in the postscript, and Shaw tries remorselessly to take back the love gift to Stella and to show that Mrs. Higgins could be the only woman in her son's emotional life. But beyond this, what is finally striking about the postscript is its duplication of Shaw's reaction to earlier crises in his relations with women. Allowing for differences of detail, the pattern is much the same as in *An Unsocial Socialist,* which incorporated his response to the unsuccessful romance with Alice, and in *Man and Superman,* which was written in response to the unconsummated marriage to Charlotte. In all three instances Shaw repairs his ego by attacking whoever he fancies had injured it and by intensifying his self-love. Just as Don Juan renounces women and dedicates himself to philosophic pursuits and his mission to enlighten mankind, so too Higgins renounces women and dedicates himself to philosophic interests and his mission to help mankind by reforming the alphabet. Both men escape into intellectuality and a narcissistic self-sufficiency. Both exhibit beneath their proclaimed altruism a disdain for people and a contempt for love. The ominous difference in Shaw's treatment of Trefusis, Don Juan, and Higgins is that the first is made to laugh at his pretensions as a reformer, the second is given an antagonist who can rebut some of his arguments, but the Higgins of the postscript is treated with esteem. Shaw blinds himself to his earlier exposure of the destructiveness in the heart of the world-betterer Higgins. He himself now crawls back up on his pedestal and glares down at the world, stonily.*

II

The second act of Shaw's revenge was the writing of a short and unintentionally funny preface for *Pygmalion*. Higgins now has the stage to himself as Eliza, dismissively, is hardly mentioned;

---

*The glare must have hardened even more when Shaw learned that Stella did not bother to read the postscript—or pretended that she had not read it; and he rebuked her angrily as late as 1917 (Campbell Letters, p. 217; Campbell, *My Life and Some Letters,* p. 269). Cornwallis-West, however, may well have read it if one is to judge by the playful revenge he himself took on Shaw in his 1933 novel *Fortune's Revenge,* for the volume includes a number of private jokes alluding to Shaw and to the *Pygmalion* situation.

and the fun lies in watching Shaw diddle with the spotlight and colored filters so as to make Higgins appear ruddy with virtue. Shaw flatters Higgins even more than in the postscript in an attempt to predispose the reader of the forthcoming play to view Higgins admiringly. After all, Shaw now implies, the professor belongs to a choice group of the most eminent English phoneticians—Alexander J. Ellis, Tito Pagliardini, Henry Sweet, Robert Bridges—and Higgins's portraiture, we are assured, has in it actual touches of character drawn from some of these men. Henry Sweet is discussed at length, and it is implied that Higgins resembles him more than the others and actually uses Sweet's notational system (an alternative to Pitman's shorthand) in penning his own indecipherable postcards. Sweet is presented as a soured genius whose temperament was ruined by lack of recognition from academic circles, and Shaw, waxing indignant, attacks Oxford for its supposed failure to do him justice. Having thus aroused our sympathy for Henry Sweet, Shaw hopes that it will carry over to Henry Higgins, and he declares that his serious purpose in writing the play was to make "the public aware that there are such people as phoneticians, and that they are among the most important people in England at present." Henry Higgins, with his usual braggadocio, would claim no more.

Now Shaw is undoubtedly accurate in naming Sweet as one of his models for Higgins, but he is also accurate in going on to say that the portraiture is only slight and that the adventure with Eliza would have been impossible for someone like Sweet. Yet since that adventure is the very substance of the play, and shows aspects of Higgins's character which Sweet did not possess, the resemblance between the two men is superficial (just as Tanner's had been to Hyndman), and we can learn little about the play's protagonist by receiving information about Henry Sweet. Shaw's effort in the preface is certainly not to throw any bright light on the Higgins of the play but rather to deflect attention both from his faults and from Shaw's once critical attitude toward him. Similarly, Shaw is quite right in contending that the work was "intensely and deliberately didactic," yet there is a wide difference between what he had in mind to say while he was writing the play and what he now declares he meant. In the play, as we have seen, Higgins's obsession with phonetics is correlated with his deficiencies as a human being, and he is anything but a hero. In the preface this viewpoint is reversed, and Shaw asserts that "the reformer England needs today is an energetic phonetic enthusiast: that is why I have made such a one the hero of a popular play."

Heroic Henry Higgins! Even Shaw at his most assertive cannot convince us or himself of such an absurdity, and therefore he emphasizes his hero's vocation rather than his person, hiding the man behind the mission. But in order to do this, he must now make extravagant claims for phonetics and assume as unarguable that changes in the way a language is spelled will vastly improve the way it is pronounced. Shaw had always been interested in phonetics, it is true, and indeed in the play he had simultaneously used his knowledge of the subject and teased himself for overrating its importance. As early as 1890, even while defending phonetics, he had fair-mindedly recognized that "most men become humbugs when they learn elocution" and "that the elocutionary man is the most insufferable of human beings." But now a quarter of a century later, under the compulsion to defend Higgins, he loses his balance and launches his own career as a famous crank on the subject. The very sounds of a crank, the ill-tempered exaggerations and the implied promise of a cure-all, are heard in the preface's opening paragraphs:

The English have no respect for their language, and will not teach their children to speak it. They cannot spell it because they have nothing to spell it with but an old foreign alphabet of which only the consonants— and not all of them—have any agreed speech value. Consequently no man can teach himself what it should sound like from reading it; and it is impossible for an Englishman to open his mouth without making some other Englishman despise him.

This has the true Higginsian ring, which will hereafter be heard in all of Shaw's declarations as a phonetical missionary out to prove in his own person that Henry Higgins was absolutely right. Even death itself could not stop Shaw from proclaiming the new gospel: in his will he left the bulk of his residuary estate to the furtherance of Higgins's scheme to save the English-speaking world through alphabetical reform, to the "launching, advertising and propaganda" of a new British Alphabet. The lengthy codicils in Shaw's last testament which deal with these matters seem to have been dictated by Henry Higgins himself, and they testify as it were to Shaw's persistence in defending Higgins and in seeking to cancel, even from beyond the grave, the mocking self-exposure that his love for Stella Campbell had once emboldened him to undertake.*

* A portion of the relevant codicils is reprinted in the Notes.

III

The next three acts of The Playwright's Revenge were not directly related to *Pygmalion*, but they nonetheless throw light on the play's final revisions. The first of these attacks was incorporated into *Back to Methuselah*, begun in 1918. It is a work which fulfills Shaw's warning to Stella that if she rejected him it would "turn me into rusty iron and cut me off for ever from what is common and young in my humanity," and that he would be able to relieve himself only with "hideous laughter, joyless, hard, dead." The laughter in this huge and misanthropic work is hideous indeed as Shaw sneers at love and youth and at the very method of procreating the human species. But from our present vantage ground we can see him almost giving away the reason for the hideous laughter when he introduces toward the end, in a utopia set twenty thousand years into the future, a little scene involving none other than a scientist named Pygmalion who is trying to create artificial people. Having finally succeeded in his experiments, he now brings forth for their debut two synthetic creatures, a man and woman from the twentieth century, "of noble appearance, beautifully modelled and splendidly attired." Pygmalion rejects an onlooker's contention that his creatures are merely automata. They are, he says, typical humans of a primitive early time, for they lie and they posture and they boast, they are craven and vicious; and during their brief appearance they demonstrate all these traits. "Can they make love?" someone asks. "Yes," Pygmalion replies, "they can respond to every stimulus. They have all the reflexes. Put your arm round the man's neck, and he will put his arm round your body. He cannot help it." "Have they feelings?" "Of course they have," says Pygmalion; "I tell you, they have all the reflexes." But Shaw does not stop with these sardonic comments on the human creatures he has bodied forth, lovely in appearance, repulsive in behavior. He makes the two figures start to fight, and the female picks up a stone to hurl at her consort:

Pygmalion, seeing what is happening, hurls himself on the Female Figure and wrenches the stone out of her hand.
All spring up in consternation.
ARJILLAX: She meant to kill him.
STREPHON: This is horrible.
THE FEMALE FIGURE [*wrestling with Pygmalion*]: Let me go. Let me go, will you [*She bites his hand*].
PYGMALION [*releasing her and staggering*]: Oh!

A general shriek of horror echoes his exclamation. He turns deadly pale, and supports himself against the end of the curved seat.

THE FEMALE FIGURE [*to her consort*]: You would stand there and let me be treated like this, you unmanly coward.

Pygmalion falls dead.

THE NEWLY BORN: Oh! Whats the matter? Why did he fall? What has happened to him?

They look on anxiously as Martellus kneels down and examines the body of Pygmalion.

MARTELLUS: She has bitten a piece out of his hand nearly as large as a finger nail: enough to kill ten men. There is no pulse, no breath.

[V]

This is one of the few vivid moments of action in an otherwise garrulous play, and an audience would welcome it despite its abrupt touch of horror. Yet what is suggestive about the incident in our present context is how fully Shaw departs from the Pygmalion story in having the life-giver killed by his female creation. Was this, we may wonder, meant to be an exaggerated parable of his own fate in his dealings with Stella? Was it meant to convey to her a private message when she saw the play? Surely in naming a character Pygmalion, Shaw had to have had in mind his famous play of that name and its many associations with Stella. He even is drawn to the imagery of biting which appeared in the confrontation scene in Act IV between Eliza and Higgins, and he now carries that scene's masochistic impulses to their psychological conclusion in Pygmalion's death. We recall too that Eliza's story had first occurred to Shaw when he was writing for Stella the role of Cleopatra, and appropriately enough the female automaton is here called Cleopatra-Semiramis. Eliza had turned against Higgins and hurt him just as Stella was to do to Shaw; now when the woman fatally bites the hand of her creator, Shaw seems to be indicating under a protective cover of fantasy that Stella Campbell had killed something important in him. But he was still surviving well enough, it should immediately be added, to see to it that the character who had destroyed her Pygmalion was then herself killed as well.*

* This killing of Cleopatra-Semiramis occurs in the last of the five parts of *Back to Methuselah*. In the first one, set in Eden, Shaw creates in the Serpent the most imaginatively and affectionately conceived figure in the entire work. The endearing traits of this figure were drawn from Mrs. Campbell, as Shaw acknowledged, demonstrating once again the durability of his love for her. Mrs. Campbell thus in some fashion appears twice in the work, in the first play and the last, and I believe that the bitterness pervading the entirety can still be partly ascribed to Shaw's defeat as a lover. In the death of Pygmalion (the maker of live performing puppets), and in the death of "The Elderly Gentleman" which occupies most of the action of

IV

Thus far Shaw's chief acts of revenge were literary, and only in fantasy could he obliterate the supposedly ungrateful woman. But now we come to a seriocomic episode in which Stella Campbell tried to strike back. Ever since the opening night of *Pygmalion*, Shaw had been doing what he safely could to hurt her although outwardly they still remained friends. He even acknowledged to her his professional indebtedness for the several characters he had gotten "out of your manifold nature": Cleopatra, Eliza, Mrs. Hushabye, the Serpent. "I exploited you, made money out of you," he admitted. "Why, oh why do you get nothing out of me, though I get everything out of you? . . . You are the Vamp and I the victim; yet it is I who suck your blood and fatten on it whilst you lose everything! It is ridiculous! There's something wrong somewhere." What was wrong, as Mrs. Campbell knew, was that Shaw would do nothing to help her even when the opportunity arose. He ridiculed her behind her back, made her fear that he would advise theater managers not to employ her, and refused to let her play the role of Mrs. Hushabye in *Heartbreak House* even though she had inspired the character, would have played it brilliantly, and was having difficulty finding parts suitable for an actress now in her mid-fifties. What Mrs. Campbell may not have realized was that she *was* playing a leading role as the victim in the unfolding drama of The Playwright's Revenge, and that Shaw's refusal to let her act in his plays was part of the scenario.

But he was not to have everything his own way. He found that other people too could retaliate verbally, not by fantasizing but simply by telling the truth. Stella, needing money, had begun in 1921 to write her autobiography, and when Shaw learned of this he nervously stretched forth a helping hand. He put at her disposal his professional skill in connecting her "tidbits into dignified paragraphs," he hinted at the need to be circumspect lest she damage her reputation, he advised her with seeming disinterestedness of the legal consequences of publishing letters without the permission of the sender. Her own dignity, he always implied, was uppermost in his mind. Yet he could not always maintain the guise of the serviceable friend, and occasionally his alarm showed through. "If you send me *all* the letters that survive," he sug-

---

Part IV, Shaw seems to be preparing himself for his own death; and this supposition is strengthened by the genuine, if premature, foreboding expressed at the end of the preface: "My sands are running out."

gested to her, betraying his concern by emphasizing the *all*, "it may be possible to work in quite a good deal of them harmlessly and amusingly." Stella teased him for his anxiety, for putting on his "suburban cap," for not realizing that his letters actually did credit to him as a man of feeling. Shaw then reacted angrily and warned her that she would have to "give up the idea of making any use of the letters once and for all." They would offend Charlotte and "make mischief in my household"; they would be construed as showing an "author who tried to seduce you when you were an unprotected widow"; in short, a woman who published "love letters from a married man to a woman who is not his wife . . . is a rotter and a courtesan." Stella refrained from quoting to the self-proclaimed superman the words he had used in an early play to show how a real hero dealt with such matters—the Duke of Wellington's response to a woman who threatened to publish his letters to her: "'Dear Jenny: publish and be damned. Yours affectionately, Wellington.'" Instead, she tried to have her publisher release her from the understanding that she would include Shaw's letters. She also sent Shaw a bundle of letters to examine with Charlotte and make cuts of passages "that could hurt Charlotte." He did not let his wife look at the letters but, seeming to imply that he had done so, sent them back with extensive deletions indicated. Stella responded with the words: "It is a supreme pity that you have massacred the letters as you have done; they are now the only insincere thing in the book." Shaw also corresponded with her publisher to bring pressure on her, and in the end, after further surgery, the book finally appeared. It contained only a few of the most innocuous of the letters along with a handsome tribute to her friend's kindness.

Shaw had won. And the famous scoffer at bourgeois respectability, the dedicated advocate of truth, probably enjoyed his success in the role of the Reverend Bowdler, which he was to play throughout his lifetime with his several biographers and when writing his own reminiscences. Yet he knew that he had won only a temporary victory since the letters still existed, and so for the next eighteen years, until Stella's death in 1940, he continued to refuse her permission to sell or to publish any of them though she was facing actual poverty. His refusals were avowedly based on the desire to protect Charlotte from embarrassment, but that pretense of gallantry was exposed when even after his wife's death he still refused permission. Only after his own death was the correspondence allowed to appear.

V

To prepare the world for that posthumous day, Shaw eventually decided to give his own version of the affair with Stella. As a world-renowned author, and since 1925 a Nobel Laureate, he was exceedingly conscious of his place in history, and more than ever before he wrote with an eye to his future reputation. He advised Stella that "we must not be handed down to history by ignoble gossip and venomous slander" or, he might have added, by the unadorned portrait of himself that would someday appear in their letters. To touch up that portrait, and to take his most direct revenge, he decided in 1929 to amplify his notion of Stella as a courtesan by inserting into the middle of *The Apple Cart*, his next play but one after *Back to Methuselah*, a scene ostensibly drawn from the days of their romance. It was a scene without much relevance to the play, as he himself acknowledged by designating it "An Interlude," but he wrote it anyway because he wanted to influence posterity's judgment of his romance and wanted also the immediate satisfaction of humiliating Stella publicly—he broadcast the fact that she alone was the model for Orinthia, the play's courtesan.

The play as a whole is set in England in the latter twentieth century and deals with a power struggle between King Magnus, a dedicated and urbane ruler, and his Prime Minister. Each of the play's two acts features an argumentative meeting between Magnus and the Cabinet; and in the end he preserves his power by threatening to abdicate and become leader of a new political party. During the Interlude between the acts he visits the beautiful Orinthia in her rooms in the palace. She immediately starts a quarrel with him, complains of being neglected, and attacks his Queen Jemima:

ORINTHIA: . . . Everyone knows that I am the real queen. Everyone treats me as the real queen. They cheer me in the streets. When I open one of the art exhibitions or launch a new ship they crowd the place out. I am one of Nature's queens; and they know it. If you do not, you are not one of Nature's kings.
MAGNUS: Sublime! Nothing but genuine inspiration could give a woman such cheek.
ORINTHIA: Yes: inspiration, not cheek. [*Sitting as before*] Magnus: when are you going to face my destiny, and your own?
MAGNUS: But my wife? the queen? What is to become of my poor dear Jemima?
ORINTHIA: Oh, drown her: shoot her: tell your chauffeur to drive

her into the Serpentine and leave her there. The woman makes you ridiculous.

MAGNUS: I dont think I should like that. And the public would think it illnatured.

ORINTHIA: Oh, you know what I mean. Divorce her. Make her divorce you. . . . Everybody does it when they need a change.

MAGNUS: But I cant imagine what I should do without Jemima.

ORINTHIA: Nobody else can imagine what you do with her. But you need not do without her. You can see as much of her as you like when we are married. I shall not be jealous and make scenes.

MAGNUS: That is very magnanimous of you. But I am afraid it does not settle the difficulty. Jemima would not think it right to keep up her present intimacy with me if I were married to you.

ORINTHIA: What a woman!

[Interlude]

They continue in the same key, with Shaw giving Orinthia self-damning speeches on a variety of topics. She exhibits vanity and triviality, financial extravagance and mental narrowness. She loathes women who take an interest in politics, and she urges Magnus to be the sort of king who will "wipe [his] boots on common people." When Magnus finally tries to leave to take tea with his wife, Orinthia forcibly restrains him. They struggle on the settee and then she drags him to the floor, where they wrestle with each other until the King's secretary enters and Magnus can effect his escape.

Shaw did all he could do, while treading the edge of the libel laws, to make clear that Orinthia was modeled on Stella Campbell. He toyed with the astral image of her name and made allusions to her autobiography's account of their relationship. He made reference to her two marriages and imputed to her sole responsibility for their failure. He tastelessly alluded to her only son, Alan, who had died in battle in 1918. He also let it be known that the grappling on the floor was based on an incident years earlier at Stella's house, when supposedly she tried to restrain him from rushing back to have a punctual tea with Charlotte. There are of course details that differentiate Stella from Orinthia, and, even more, King Magnus from Shaw; yet the King's relations with Orinthia are manifestly intended to epitomize Shaw's own with Stella. Magnus is portrayed as a well-meaning, patient man, exploited by an exceptionally beautiful siren, but firm in his loyalty to his wife. He defends that wife's workaday value even while justifying his relations with another woman.

The portrait of Stella as Orinthia is suavely devastating. But it is not dramatically convincing. Given Orinthia's inadequacies of mind and character, and her appetite for quarreling, it is hard to credit the King's remarks that she is his "queen in fairyland" and that he goes to see her "to enjoy talking to you like this when I need an hour's respite from royalty: when my stupid wife has been worrying me." Physical beauty is all that Orinthia has to offer, and sexual pleasure is the only imaginable reason for keeping her; yet even while Shaw encourages this supposition he also hints at its negation. Orinthia is apparently resisting Magnus until he marries her:

MAGNUS: My dear Orinthia, I had rather marry the devil. Being a wife is not your job.

ORINTHIA: You think so because you have no imagination. And you dont know me because I have never let you really possess me. I should make you more happy than any man has ever yet been on earth.

MAGNUS: I defy you to make me more happy than our strangely innocent relations have already made me.

ORINTHIA [rising restlessly]: You talk like a child or a saint [Turning on him] I can give you a new life: one of which you have no conception. I can give you beautiful, wonderful children.

[Interlude]

Orinthia, we are startled to realize, is kept in the palace and pensioned by the state to serve as a nagging *platonic* mistress. What prompts the King to have such unnatural tastes, and to expend public funds on so sterile an enterprise, is left discreetly obscure.

Shaw's reasons for creating the obscurity are clear, however, and we can appreciate the difficulty he faced. He had to include the words "strangely innocent relations" because that was what he had assured Charlotte his relations with Stella had actually been. He also had to include the words to avoid legal proceedings from Stella, who wrote, as soon as she learned of the scene, "You have no legal right to put me in a play without my knowledge, or permission—damn you!" He had to include them, finally, because he was reluctant to tell an outright lie albeit quite willing to misrepresent in order to enhance his public image and to continue his campaign of revenge. The implication of the scene is that Orinthia is indeed the King's mistress, but the passing words "strangely innocent relations" allow Shaw the security of having it both ways. Nevertheless, with one eye on protecting himself, he is unable to focus on the implausibility of the scene even apart from its inorganic relation to the play as a whole. That implausibility derives more from what he leaves out than what he puts in. He includes part of the skeleton of his relationship with Mrs. Campbell, but he omits its heart. He excludes the overwhelming appeal that she had once had for him, an appeal based not only on her beauty but also on her "manifold nature," as he called it. He excludes her occupation; and, after all, it had been her gifts as a diligent, self-supporting actress which had first captivated him. Orinthia is merely a parasitic and self-indulgent trifler, devoid of Mrs. Campbell's strength of character. By portraying Stella in ways that allowed him to vindicate his hostility and to rationalize once again his past behavior, he ends up with a hollow woman who discredits her royal patron. Shaw thinks he is displaying the King's superiority and creating sympathy for a long-suffering male, but he forces us to conclude that Magnus is a fool to put up with the situation.

This error by the dramatist, as we may recall, corresponds to the one in *Man and Superman*, where the relative implausibility of the romance between Tanner and Ann can be traced to Shaw's need to avenge himself on Charlotte and to deny that he had pursued her. Now once again, in belittling a woman who had disappointed him, he leaves out the feelings that had drawn him to her. In both instances, his attempts to restore his ego lessened his ability to recapture the emotions that preceded the defeat. That here, in contrast to his earlier play, he scarcely disguised the identity of the woman, and in fact quickly made it known, indicates his eagerness to have people believe that the relationship between Magnus and Orinthia duplicated his own with Stella, so that their letters when published would be interpreted in ways favorable to himself; like Magnus, he would appear the victim of a scheming woman whose efforts to break up his marriage he had nobly resisted. And this interpretation is precisely the one that was later to be purveyed by some of Shaw's biographers, such as St. John Ervine.

There were also the more immediate satisfactions of humiliating Stella in person. At the end of March 1929, soon after finishing a draft of the play, Shaw wrote to taunt her with the Orinthia scene. "Perhaps you will never speak to me again when you have read it—or seen it," he said. He excused himself as "too shy" to read the scene to her, but urged her to learn its exact contents from a mutual friend who had recently heard him give a private reading. When that friend reported to Mrs. Campbell her recollection of the "Interlude" but apparently forgot its ending, Shaw gloatingly informed Stella that the ending was "of the red hot poker order: wildly disgraceful." (The ending of his preceding play, *Saint Joan*, was hotter, with Joan burning at the stake—but now

Shaw seems to have switched from the victim's side to the per-
secutor's.) To make sure that Stella had heard him correctly,
he wrote in another letter "that the scene is amusingly scandalous and even disgraceful." The scandal and disgrace, as they both
knew, would be entirely hers, and the amusement entirely his.
She was distressed by what she termed the "tricks" of her friend.
"You are out of tune with friendship and simple courtesy," she
told him, and urged him again to let her read the play. For three
months he managed to evade her, allowing the work to be pre-
miered intact in Warsaw. Then, when he finally visited and read
the scene, it seems to have been only to refine the game he was
making her play, for after inserting a few changes, far fewer than
she requested, he told her, "I shall now be able to say that you
revised it yourself, and dictated some of the best bits." Her continued protests against the "vulgarity and untruthfulness" of
the scene had no effect. But perhaps concerned over her threats
to charge him with libel, he kept assuring her that "of course
the scene isn't true." "There are no personalities in the narrower sense," he held. "Orinthia is not a portrait; she is a study
for which you sat as a model in bits only." These reassurances
brought no comfort since they were contradicted by an earlier
boast: "I have made a superb picture of you, God forgive me! and
you must play the game." When he also insisted on his privileges
as a writer—"I am an artist and as such unscrupulous when I find
my model"—she may have thought that he sounded remarkably
like his own Dubedat, the artist as scoundrel. King Magnus had
told Orinthia that he sometimes felt the impulse to kick her and
that he would even sign her death warrant without turning a hair.
But Shaw restrained Magnus's destructive impulses far more than
he restrained his own, and despite occasional qualms he allowed
the scene to stand without serious change. When the play held its
English premiere in Malvern in August, and then began a long
subsequent run in London, Stella Campbell had to bear the humiliation as best she could.

Yet although Stella's pleas failed to move Shaw, her final advice
to him before the play opened was right in all but one particular:
"Tear it up, and re-write it with every scrap of the mischievous
vulgarian omitted, and all the suburban backchat against Charlotte and suggested harlotry against me, and the inference of your
own superiority wiped out. People will only say that old age and
superhuman vanity have robbed you of your commonsense." Stella's mistake was simply that Shaw's common sense had long

since deserted him in his attitude toward her. His vindictiveness had first appeared several years earlier when he wrote the postscript to *Pygmalion*, and Eliza's supposed hope of knocking Higgins off his pedestal and forcing him to make love to her was now partially fulfilled in Orinthia's grappling on the floor with a reluctant Magnus. Similarly, Eliza's debasement in the postscript was paralleled by the debasing of Orinthia. "The Interlude" in *The Apple Cart* was thus merely the latest and most direct of Shaw's attacks on Stella, and it was not to be the last! For the final act of Shaw's revenge, at once the strangest and most self-defeating of them all, came when he altered *Pygmalion* itself; and having witnessed the other phases of the campaign we are now ready to view the spectacle of the artist desecrating his own living masterpiece.*

V I

The revisions to Pygmalion were made during the 1930's, chiefly in 1934 for the following year's German film produced by Eber-

---

*Before moving on, however, it is worth noting that the revenge taken in *The Apple Cart*, though structurally intrusive, is connected in spirit to much else in the play. If Stella cruelly suffered from the Orinthia portrait, Charlotte Shaw must also have winced at the portrait of herself as the prosaic Jemima; and Stella's concern over the play's "suburban backchat against Charlotte" seems reasonable as well as generous. The treatment of the two principal women is symptomatic of the play's general callousness. For the first time in his career as a dramatist, Shaw now fails to give strength to both sides in a conflict: Magnus is always cleverly right, his opponents stupidly wrong. All the male Ministers are grossly dehumanized. Moreover, the playwright's present contempt for human beings extends in some sense to his audience, if one may judge by his unprecedented degree of indifference to coherent dramatic form. He realized that the long opening conversation between the secretaries had been rendered superfluous after he later changed his mind about the play's direction, but he let that conversation stand anyway (Pearson, *Bernard Shaw: His Life and Personality*, p. 381). He let stand the irrelevant "Interlude," and also the irrelevant visit of the American Ambassador in Act II. The play dangles with loose ends, as Shaw quickly padded what is essentially a one-act work. King Magnus is the only character that the dramatist is imagining with any care, and the King is most likely, as Eric Bentley has suggested, another Shavian attempt at partial self-portraiture, this time incorporated with a power fantasy (*Bernard Shaw*, p. 206). Thematically, the play ridicules democracy and praises autocracy. It is part of the propaganda effort of Shaw's later years on behalf of dictatorships. These several aspects underlying the play—the callousness, the contempt for people and for democracy, the self-glorification, the approval of the political Strong Man—are interrelated. And if in this syndrome we would be right to expect our author's homicidal impulse to manifest itself also, he does not disappoint us. In the very first act, King Magnus complains that his restricted power prevents him from issuing "death warrants for a great many people who in my opinion ought to be killed." Clearly if Shaw's hero had absolute power, the state executioner would be a busy man. And it is hardly surprising that ex-Kaiser Wilhelm II was one of the play's most ardent admirers (Ervine, *Bernard Shaw*, p. 110).

hard Klagemann, and then again for the 1938 English film produced by Gabriel Pascal. Shaw drew on this material, especially the 1934 additions, when he issued in 1941 a revised text of the play designed to support his changed attitude toward Eliza and Higgins. We will briefly attend to the five added scenes and to some of the small verbal changes. Almost all of this new material expresses the same mood that had incited the attack on Stella as Orinthia. With Eliza Doolittle now once again the substitute target for Stella, as in the postscript, the campaign of revenge reaches its culminating cruelty. Shaw torments Eliza as soon as he can get his hands on her, putting her into three separate torture chambers in the very first three of the added scenes.

In the first of these, at the end of Act I, we follow Eliza's taxi to her lodgings and hear the taximan humiliate her by refusing to accept her money and by laughing at her. She then trudges up the alley to her small room, which is lined with "very old wall paper hanging loose in the damp places." A broken window pane is mended only with paper, an empty birdcage hangs in front of it, and "the rest is the irreducible minimum of poverty's needs: a wretched bed heaped with all sorts of coverings that have any warmth in them, a draped packing case with a basin and jug on it and a little looking glass over it, a chair and table, the refuse of some suburban kitchen." The scene ends as Eliza removes her skirt and shoes and climbs into bed to keep warm. Years earlier Shaw would have presented these details in order to comment on the misery of the poor under capitalism; but now the description is at best neutrally offered and, more likely we may suspect, with some joy in Eliza's predicament.

Our suspicions are confirmed when we see Eliza arrive in the next act at Higgins's house, and the added scene shows Mrs. Pearce preparing the terrified girl for a bath. Eliza protests with tears when she sees the tub, and Mrs. Pearce—no longer protective as in the original version—further humiliates the girl by calling her a "dirty slut" and a "frowsy slut." Commanded to undress, Eliza briefly disappears from view while Mrs. Pearce fills the bath and readies it for "her prisoner"; she lathers from a ball of soap "a formidable looking long handled scrubbing brush," and then:

Eliza comes back with nothing on but the bath gown huddled tightly round her, a piteous spectacle of abject terror.

MRS. PEARCE: Now come along. Take that thing off.

LIZA: Oh I couldnt, Mrs. Pearce: I reely couldnt. I never done such a thing.

MRS. PEARCE: Nonsense. Here: step in and tell me whether its hot enough for you.

LIZA: Ah-oo! Ah-oo! It's too hot.

MRS. PEARCE [*deftly snatching the gown away and throwing Eliza down on her back*]: It wont hurt you. [*She sets to work with the scrubbing brush.*]

Eliza's screams are heartrending. [II]

One may wonder if the old playwright's heart was rent at all. Perhaps some other part of his body was in small measure stirred as he vicariously snatched the gown from the nude girl, threw her down on her back, and set to work with that stiff, formidable looking, long handled brush lathered from its ball of soap! (Elsewhere in the play, and unchanged from the original version, reference is made to the bath's "wooden bowl of soap"; Shaw misremembers this as a "ball" while creating a disguised act of rape; and the "long handled" brush may carry an unintended personal conjunction with Higgins's possible onanism.) Yet even if the cleaning up of Eliza's body does not hint at impurities in Shaw's own mind, whatever appeal the scene may have is manifestly sadistic; despite Shaw's announcements of a "heartrending" and "a piteous spectacle," we are not really meant to feel sympathy for Eliza's plight. And curiously, the last spoken line of the scene, assuring Eliza that she won't be hurt, is practically the same as Higgins's first line of the play ("Who's hurting you, you silly girl?"), and we saw earlier that this disclaimer in no way prevents Higgins from tormenting Eliza. The sadism that Shaw had once exposed in Higgins is now practiced by the playwright himself, who shows again as he had in the postscript how much he is embracing Higgins's worst traits. Indeed, one almost fancies that Higgins is now the playwright, and a careless one too, for in Shaw's lust to torture Eliza in the hot bath he forgets that later on in the play, and left intact from the original version, Eliza describes her bath as having been a treat for her, with "soft brushes to scrub yourself," "woolly towels," and soap "smelling like primroses." The inconsistency is not in itself of much importance, but the difference between these two versions of Eliza in the bath—the once pleasant experience turned into the opposite—underscores the change in Shaw's attitude.

The third added scene carries us to yet another torture chamber, the professor's laboratory, as Eliza receives her initial lesson in pronunciation. Shaw again sees to it that she is quickly brought to tears:

HIGGINS: . . . Now do you think you could possibly say tea? Not ta-yee, mind: if you ever say ba-yee ca-yee da-yee again you shall be dragged round the room three times by the hair of your head. [*Fortissimo*] T, T, T, T.

LIZA [*weeping*]: I cant hear no difference cep that it sounds more genteel-like when you say it.

HIGGINS: Well, if you can hear that difference, what the devil are you crying for? Pickering: give her a chocolate.

PICKERING: No, no. Never mind crying a little, Miss Doolittle: you are doing very well; and the lessons wont hurt. I promise you I wont let him drag you round the room by your hair.

HIGGINS: Be off with you to Mrs. Pearce and tell her about it. Think about it. Try to do it by yourself: and keep your tongue well forward in your mouth instead of trying to roll it up and swallow it. Another lesson at half-past four this afternoon. Away with you.

Eliza, still sobbing, rushes from the room.

And that is the sort of ordeal poor Eliza has to go through for months

[II]

Higgins clearly need not drag her by her hair since the playwright secures the same effect on her by the ordeal he has staged, and it is equally clear that her tears differ from the crocodile tears which drip from Shaw's eyes. So intent is he on hurting Eliza that he unwittingly turns Higgins into an inept teacher who depends on Pickering to prevent her from running away. This we may feel cannot be the Henry Higgins who had taught scores of American millionairesses to speak English.

The same regrettable coarsening of Shaw's taste and judgment, if not the same display of sadism, is also evident in the two other added scenes—the Embassy scene at the end of Act III and Eliza's meeting with Freddy at the end of Act IV. Neither need detain us, and Higgins might well have been the playwright here since neither scene rises above a pedestrian level. At the Embassy reception, for example, the professor meets a bewhiskered former pupil and present rival named Nepommuck:

NEPOMMUCK: I am your pupil: your first pupil, your best and greatest pupil. I am little Nepommuck, the marvellous boy. I have made your name famous throughout Europe. You teach me phonetic. You cannot forget ME.

HIGGINS: Why dont you shave?

NEPOMMUCK: I have not your imposing appearance, your chin, your brow. Nobody notice me when I shave. Now I am famous: they call me Hairy Faced Dick.

[III]

And so in the same vein. When Shaw has to bid for a laugh with a "Hairy Faced Dick" we feel a strain which distresses all the more for the contrasting ease of the humor in the original version. Feeble in itself, the scene also damages the great midnight encounter between Eliza and Higgins in Act IV, robbing it of its suspense.

Also damaging is the revision of the end of that act, which had once concluded with a superb bit of pantomime showing the complexity of Eliza's feelings after she had infuriated Higgins and driven him from the room:

Eliza smiles for the first time; expresses her feelings by a wild pantomime in which an imitation of Higgins's exit is confused with her own triumph; and finally goes down on her knees on the hearthrug to look for the ring.

And then we later learn that she spends most of the night wandering the streets of London alone, depressed to the verge of suicide. In the new version Eliza is not allowed to enjoy her moment of triumph:

Eliza goes down on her knees on the hearthrug to look for the ring. When she finds it she considers for a moment what to do with it. Finally she flings it down on the dessert stand and goes upstairs in a tearing rage.

At this point Shaw adds a two-part scene as Eliza goes to her room, changes her clothes (with Shaw arranging for the third time in the new scenes to disrobe her), sticks out her tongue at herself in a mirror, and then leaves the house. Outside she runs into the lovelorn Freddy Hill who had been standing vigil beneath her window. They chat briefly, embrace and kiss, are interrupted by a police constable, flee to Cavendish Square, embrace and kiss, are interrupted by another constable, flee to Hanover Square, embrace and kiss, are interrupted by a passing taximan, and then ride off to spend the rest of the night apparently in the cab. The effect of this facetious scene, replete with improbabilities, is to lessen Eliza's dignity and to make Freddy a fool. In turning Eliza's once desperate flight from Higgins into farce, Shaw exposes how completely he has withdrawn from her the sympathy of the original version and has substituted the hostility of the postscript. Scenes free of such hostility might have been added to the play, but the ones we are given are not merely inferior in quality but upset the fine balance of the entirety. It attests to the strength of the play that it still can bear the weight of these gross additions.

Shaw also tinkers with the play in smaller ways, guided by the determination to embarrass Eliza, to rehabilitate Higgins, and to make the work conform to the changed perspectives of the postscript. Higgins now condemns Eliza's future husband Freddy as a fool not even good enough to get a job as an errand boy—exactly the same term as was first used in the postscript. The end of Eliza's line, "I'll marry Freddy, I will, as soon as he's able to support me," is changed to "as soon as I'm able to support him." New words of abuse are heaped upon Eliza as she is called a "squashed cabbage leaf" and an "incarnate insult to the English language." Contrastingly, Shaw now deletes Higgins's boast that he writes poetry "on Miltonic lines" and also deletes Higgins's words that "we are all dependent on one another, every soul of us on earth," while leaving intact his claim that he could "do without anybody." These niggling alterations—and there are others—are merely symptomatic of the change in Shaw's outlook and damage the play far less than the added scenes. But Shaw's final bit of tinkering, at the very end of the work, does create a significant shift in the audience's response. We recall that in the original ending Eliza bids farewell to her professor and tells him that she will not see him again; but when his mother offers to shop for the tie and gloves he had just ordered Eliza to buy for him, he confidently tells her not to bother:

HIGGINS [*sunnily*]: Oh, dont bother. She'll buy em all right enough. Goodbye.
They kiss, Mrs. Higgins runs out. Higgins, left alone, rattles his cash in his pocket; chuckles; and disports himself in a highly self-satisfied manner.

This ending leaves open the possibility of Eliza's return. But if she does not return then the joke would be on the smug Higgins. In the new ending, however, Shaw tries to turn the joke against Eliza, who is now to be burdened with the incompetent Freddy Hill:

LIZA: What you are to do without me I cannot imagine. [*She sweeps out*].
MRS. HIGGINS: I'm afraid youve spoilt that girl, Henry. I should be uneasy about you and her if she were less fond of Colonel Pickering.
HIGGINS: Pickering! Nonsense: she's going to marry Freddy. Ha ha! Freddy! Freddy!! ha ha ha ha ha!!!!! [*He roars with laughter as the play ends*].

The contemptuous laughter, hard and dead, is Shaw's very own. And with this change in the ending, similar in mood to all of the other revisions, the playwright completed his work of superimposing on the play an entirely different attitude toward his leading characters. Not a single one of the changes had improved the script in the slightest; all had damaged it in greater or lesser measure; and actors today who perform the play might be well advised to stay with the marvelous original version rather than to follow the angry old dramatist in profaning it. A work of art written in love cannot be successfully revised in hate, and Shaw's latter-day hostility to the play shows through in every touch he added. It had become an accusing mirror reflecting his past self, and to meet his current personal needs he splattered the mirror with ink. He may have sensed that he was abusing the play but he did not care. What he might have cared about, had he been able to recognize it, was the degree to which his own sensitivity to language had hardened; for if one compares any of the new dialogue to that of the original, the discordance between the two—the vulgarization of the rhythms and the diction—is immediately apparent. Thus the most damning price Shaw paid for his changed attitude toward Eliza was his inability to hear the sound of her voice, and it is ironic indeed to find the man who in later life was so concerned with phonetics becoming almost stone-deaf himself to the music of language.

At the beginning of this chapter I said that the various acts of what was dubbed "The Playwright's Revenge" constituted a little psychodrama, and this suggests that we might hazard a psychological interpretation of Shaw's behavior. Other men, after all, suffer defeats in love and recover; other men express anger against a woman and then feel purged. What accounts for the extraordinary durability of Shaw's anger? What allowed that anger to root itself with an almost pathological intensity? What caused it to increase over the years instead of subsiding? A psychoanalyst, looking back to the beginnings in 1912 of Shaw's romance with Stella and venturing a purely conjectural analysis, might perhaps tell us that Shaw as he then neared his sixtieth year was undergoing something more than the usual difficulties of a man reconciling himself to old age and to the likelihood that this was the last time he could hope for a love relationship with a woman. He was also feeling the stress of his mother's last illness and then her death, and the death of a mother typically arouses in her son an unconscious sense of grievance at her apparent desertion of him, which in Shaw's case duplicated her emotional desertion of him during the Dublin years of her absorption with Lee, and then her physical desertion of him when she followed Lee to London. The grievances stirred up by her death now awaited a new person on whom to fasten themselves, and Stella was especially qualified because Shaw's feelings toward her had been deeply ambivalent long before their romance began. And during the course of that romance, as the nursery imagery of the letters indicates, Shaw sought in her an alternative mother. When she then failed him in that role and made him feel, as he said, like a "cast-off," he had again become the abandoned child, emotionally alone and seething with rage. "Wretch, I could tear you limb from limb," were among the words he had hurled at Stella, and the triteness of this phrase should not mislead us into underestimating the extent to which Shaw's defeat mobilized his destructive impulses. Thus the anger was directed not only at Stella as a woman but as a lost second mother as well, on whom he could also vent his grievance over the desertion by death of his real mother, and could recapitulate his anger in childhood at that real mother's neglect of him and her devotion to Lee. If *Pygmalion* incorporated his love for his mother and for Stella, the subsequent acts of revenge show the other and hate-filled side of these attachments, for as Freud has remarked, the loss of a love object provides an excellent opportunity for the ambivalence in love relationships to come into the open. Furthermore—our psychoanalyst might continue—exactly as Shaw had lost out in childhood to another man, here again he was defeated by a rival. This had not been a feature of his relationship either to Alice Lockett or Charlotte Townshend, the romance with Alice having terminated well before her marriage and he himself having won Charlotte. A successful rival appeared only twice in Shaw's life, in the person of George Vandeleur Lee and then of George West. And however much hostility Shaw as a child may have felt toward Lee, it had been more than counterbalanced by his admiration for him as an ideal father figure. But now he had lost to a man who he felt was his inferior. His resentment therefore did not simply take root in him—the roots were already there from childhood; and the feelings now directed to Stella Campbell were a continuation of all that he had once felt toward his mother, intensified by contempt for West. It was as if the boy within him had finally proven himself by his accomplishments to be fully worthy of regaining a mother's love, only to find that she again chose another and far lesser George.

But not entirely lesser, our analyst would remind us, moving on to the one still unmentioned element in the situation—sex. West was not, as Shaw well knew, inferior to him sexually. Stella had happily implied that her new husband, her "golden man," was a fine lover, and Shaw was aware of his own inadequacies in that regard, having demonstrated to himself the modesty of his sexual needs in the course of his platonic marriage to Charlotte and his "strangely innocent" relations with Stella. Hidden within his contempt for West was a rankling masculine envy, which entered into the rage against Freddy Hill, the avoidance of the sexual aspect of Eliza's marriage to Freddy, and the reticence about their children. Since envy springs from discontent with the self, the rage against Freddy suggests the strength of Shaw's rage against himself. The sex hatred in Shaw's work after *Pygmalion*, so much more intense than in his earlier work, is the legacy of defeat in his last attempt at romance.

Yet the "innocent" relationship does not mean that libidinal energies were absent in Shaw. On the contrary, his sadomasochistic tendencies had from the outset entered into the romance with Stella and were strengthened by its termination. "I want my plaything that I am to throw away," he had said to her at the height of their romance. And after he threw her away he wanted her again—to throw away again. Stella might ask him, *nine* years after the romance had ended, "Aren't you tired of knocking me about?" but she did not realize that Shaw was simply following the same sadomasochistic pattern that had always been present in the relationship. Both in fantasy and in reality he continued to play Higginsian games with her: in the humiliations inflicted on Eliza in the postscript and in the revisions, in the death inflicted on the woman in *Back to Methuselah*, in the demeaning portrait of Orinthia with its "red hot poker" ending, in the battles over the love letters, in the perpetual disparagement of her in conversation, in the refusal to cast her for parts in his plays. Every time he attacked Stella, directly or vicariously, he appeased not only his sadism but also, by reawakening the agony of his defeat, his masochism as well—those self-inflicted pains which helped give him a sense of being alive even while they expiated his guilts. Disloyalty to his mother in transferring his affections to Stella was one source of guilt. A more important source was the very hostility he directed at his mother in the person of Stella; and even his knowledge that Stella was not at all his mother could be used to loosen the restraints on his hostility to his actual mother. Eliza-Stella is made into a "dirty slut," Orinthia-Stella into a courtesan: both are dirty for him, which is to say sexual for him, and thus available for abuse. Attached to them both were the forbidden thoughts about his own mother's sexuality in her possible relations to Lee, and his own Oedipal desires for her, tinged with the wish to hurt her for her rejections of him. And in his early eighties, when his attacks on Eliza in the revisions are most directly sadistic, there is more involved than a weakening of inhibitions that mark old age, for in its perverse way the heightened sadism was a tribute to his mother which simultaneously served an octogenarian need. It was a way of keeping alive his mother's memory and hence of preserving the continuity of his ego. It was a way of denying the reality of death, of quelling his fear of it and his longing for it.

So might our analyst attempt to explain Shaw's motivations, repeating at the end that this merely begins a depth analysis which must inevitably remain conjectural. And although I entirely agree with these conjectures, readers who are not fully persuaded may yet now possess enough evidence to construct an alternative account for what is surely one of the most curious vendettas in literary history, and one that variously affected Shaw's life and his work.

AFTERWORD

I am a man of the most extraordinary hardness of heart.

Bernard Shaw, 1927

*W*ITH THE ANALYSIS of the 1930's changes in *Pygmalion*, we have returned to our starting decade and thereby completed our present journey. We set out, from *The Simpleton of the Unexpected Isles*, by identifying a basic and hitherto unrecognized conflict in Shaw between his humane and his destructive impulses, with the latter seen to possess homicidal and sadomasochistic features. We then faced the task of locating some earlier expressions of this conflict and of accounting for its intensification over the years. Simultaneously, we sought to discover how Shaw made literary use of his homicidal and sadomasochistic tendencies; for we accepted that he, like any other significant writer, becomes interesting not by virtue of his possible neuroses but by his ways of responding to them. In the course of our inquiry we avoided the usual rationalistic approach to Shaw (which reduces him to a disembodied consciousness and attends in the main to those thinkers who supposedly gave him his ideas), and concentrated instead on a few central works that drew on important personal experiences and incorporated their deeper meanings. The varied effects of Shaw's difficult childhood were noted, as were the effects of his failed relations with women—with his early love, Alice Lockett, with his wife, Charlotte, and with his late love, Stella Campbell. In the course of each of these failures, Shaw's destructive impulses were aroused, even as he used his pen to take revenge on Alice in *An Unsocial Socialist*, on Charlotte in *Man and Superman*, and on Stella in *The Apple Cart* and elsewhere. These private calamities, moreover, had consequences for his thought; and we saw that the philosophy he enunciated in the Hell sequence of *Man and Superman*, though replete with idealistic phraseology and invocations to the "Life Force," really aimed to justify murder and the elimination of most of the present human race. In response to the trauma of his unconsummated marriage, Shaw thus elaborated a creed that could accommodate his future enthusiasm for the worst brutalities of European dictators.

281

Shaw's defeats as a lover obviously cannot account for all of the changes in his outlook. Other frustrations, both professional and political, also played their role. But his rejections by women were of crucial significance in loosening the restraints on his destructive urges, which were then allowed to circulate far more freely in his work. Indeed, as we have seen, he had shrewdly diagnosed this condition in himself, warning Alice in 1885 that he would turn remorseless when love was taken from him, and warning Stella twenty-eight years later that he would turn into rusty iron if she rejected him. The very length of Shaw's vendetta against Stella Campbell, lasting a quarter of a century, reveals how deeply he had been hurt by the termination of the romance, and the misogyny and bitterness that appear in nearly all his plays after *Pygmalion* are the legacy of that defeat. We may therefore reasonably connect Shaw's annihilation of the beautiful girl who represents love in *The Simpleton* of 1934, or his torture of Eliza Doolittle in the revisions to *Pygmalion* of 1934–38, with his defense of Mussolini's 1935 bombings of Abyssinia and of Stalin's bloodthirsty purges of the 1930's.

This increased expression of destructive impulses, equally apparent in Shaw's plays and his politics, is to some extent measurable. For example, in the first seven of the full-length plays, up through *The Devil's Disciple* (1896), Shaw uses the word "kill," along with its variants "killed" and "killing," thirty-four times. In the last seven plays, *On the Rocks* (1933) through *Farfetched Fables* (1948), the number goes up to eighty-six, a dramatic increase. Similarly, the word "blood" is first used eighteen times and then goes up to forty-four times. These figures suggest that Shaw's destructive yearnings became more than twice as powerful—or the control over them less than half as strong—after 1930 than before 1900. (Figures for the intervening decades show that the rise was generally steady but climbed sharply after the collapse of the Campbell affair and under the stimulus of World War I.) The statistics confirm the appropriateness of what we may see as contrasting symbols of Shaw's early and late work: the hero's unloaded pistol in *Arms and the Man* (1894) and forty years later, in *The Simpleton*, the death ray that disintegrates vast numbers of the world's population.

The origin of Shaw's homicidal and sadomasochistic tendencies must remain problematical. There may have been a constitutional predisposition, but his parental situation appears to have been critical in developing it. Although Shaw could drop "George" from his name, he could never drop from his mind the question of which George he had been named after: George Carr Shaw, his legal father, or George Vandeleur Lee, his mother's possible lover. The triangle of these two men and his mother plagued Shaw's life and was reflected both in his plays and his politics. And in his mind, the individual who principally caused all his heartache, an ache still deep enough for Shaw at the age of ninety-three to say that he would exult to see his old Dublin house "blown to smithereens," was his drunken father. He "hated and despised" him, according to the words of a close childhood friend. The father moved about the house, according to Shaw's own words, "full of self-reproaches and humiliations when he was not full of secret jokes and . . . either biting his moustache and whispering deep-drawn damns or shaking with silent paroxysms of laughter." Young Shaw laughed also as he helped his staggering father up to bed—but that laughter hid humiliation and rage. Not a single illegal act could be proven against this father even though his son thought him "a hypocrite and dipsomaniac" who brought bitter shame to the family. In a properly run country, however, such a situation would not be tolerated:

If we desire a certain type of civilization and culture we must exterminate the sort of people who do not fit into it. . . . It may be quite impossible to convict a [man] under a criminal code of having taken a single illegal step, but quite easy to convince any reasonable body of judges that he is what the people call "a wrong one." In Russia such a conviction would lead to his disappearance and the receipt by his family of a letter to say that they need not wait up for him, as he would not return home any more.

Thus Bernard Shaw at the age of seventy-seven justified exterminations in his ideal country. It is hard not to hear his click of satisfaction at the disappearance of this man. And if it seems reasonable to assume that the disappearing figure is a father, it may also be reasonable to assume that this father's name, had the writer brought it to consciousness, would be none other than George Carr Shaw. At the dark center of the playwright's obsession with extermination, I suggest, was the yearning to destroy that father who had caused him and his mother so much grief. And remembering that the rules of logic and the categories of time are suspended in the unconscious, we may say that the criminals whom Shaw in his penology tracts advocated killing were in some sense substitutes for his father; and that for Shaw the ultimate virtue of Stalin and Hitler and Mussolini was precisely their power to round up "wrong ones" and make them disappear, thereby vicari-ously satisfying his patricidal longing and, by making the practice routine, assuaging his guilt. As Shaw unconsciously hoped that the dictators would favor him with that ultimate murder, they became omnipotent surrogate fathers with whom he could si-multaneously identify himself and play the child, and to whom he could offer noisy support in repayment. It has long bewildered critics to find Shaw defending both Nazism and Communism, but the puzzle is quickly solved when we remember, as Shaw fully apprehended, that Hitler and Stalin were blood brothers.

Yet the roots of Shaw's homicidal passion, and the guilt that produced the attendant sadomasochism, are necessarily of only minor interest to the literary commentator, who is more properly concerned with the branchings and flowerings of these destruc-tive impulses. Such impulses when guided by talent have their uses in art, both for the creator and for his audience, and it must be reiterated that however Shaw's uglier emotions damaged him as a political analyst, they contributed vitally to his drama. *Pyg-malion*, as we have seen, was written by someone with an excep-tionally intimate knowledge of the sadomasochistic personality, and the play's greatness derives in part from such knowledge. *Candida*, as we have also seen, was written by someone who could convey from his heart the Oedipal pleasures of wounding a father. Shaw would probably not have created those fascinating figures Andrew Undershaft, the munitions magnate, and Captain Shotover, the old man trying to invent a death ray, had he himself not been abnormally interested in lethal weapons; nor would he have created an antimilitaristic Caesar or a pacifistic Androcles had he himself not been struggling to erect model barriers against his own homicidal inclinations. And had these inclinations di-minished over the years, we probably would not have obtained a *Saint Joan* of equal power. It was by knowing in his own bones the inquisitional spirit that Shaw could defend it with sympathy and thereby give enough human substance to Joan's enemies to transform the play far beyond melodrama.

The particular characters just mentioned were not among those discussed in this study. That they nevertheless fit so easily into the new framework we have been using may indicate its value in reconsidering Shaw's other dramatic works. His philosophy too, as well as his politics, can be profitably reviewed, I believe, in the light of the fundamental conflict explored here. Even Shaw's cele-brated style and his humor are by no means unrelated to his destructive impulses. On the style, briefly, we can notice an unusual congruence in the way critics describe his prose while praising it. One writer speaks of its "biting overemphasis," another of its "pugnacity," and a third says that its violence of assertion bludgeons us into acquiescence. Dixon Scott, in the course of a superb tribute to Shaw's style, nevertheless declares it to be a "pitiless prose" which "pelts the brain with stinging drops like driving hail" and can induce "limp obedience" and complete surrender. And the humor, also, frequently has a sadistic aspect, ranging from the joyful discomfiture of certain pompous or inept individuals to the reduction, especially in the later plays, of almost everyone to cartoon-like absurdity. Shaw's masochism clearly was part of his pleasure in making the Shavian man of words—Charteris, Morell, Tanner, Higgins, Aubrey, Chavender, or Iddy—the butt of the humor. And even Shaw's homicidal impulse can often be seen at play, for example in the funniest of the one-acters, *Passion, Poison and Petrifaction*, or in the opening of *The Man of Destiny*, or in *The Philanderer*'s most marvelous moment when Dr. Paramore learns with horror that his patient is *not* going to die, or in *The Devil's Disciple*'s best joke—General Burgoyne's reply when Dick Dudgeon insists that as a captured American rebel he should at least be honored with a firing squad rather than crudely hung on a gallows.

> BURGOYNE [*Sympathetically*]: Now there, Mr. Anderson, you talk like a civilian, if you will excuse my saying so. Have you any idea of the average marksmanship of the army of His Majesty King George the Third? If we make you up a firing party, what will happen? Half of them will miss you: the rest will make a mess of the business and leave you to the provo-marshal's pistol. Whereas we can hang you in a perfectly workmanlike and agreeable way. [*Kindly*] Let me persuade you to be hanged, Mr. Anderson? . . .
>
> RICHARD: . . . Thank you, General: that view of the case did not occur to me before. To oblige you, I withdraw my objection to the rope. Hang me, by all means. [III]

This gallows humor is not uncommon in Shaw, and it demonstrates one of the ways in which he successfully exploited the same impulse that, in politics, led him to defend the extermination practices of dictators. We may rightly welcome the humor and abhor the political position, but only by acknowledging the connection between them can we finally develop a coherent view of Shaw. Such a view has been obstructed by the critics' acceptance of Shaw's legend of himself as an intellectual man much like themselves—a humane and rational fellow, sensibly leftist, and wholly devoted to the true, the good, and the beautiful. Courteously ignoring Shaw's flattery, the critics have generally eyed their subject through the pleasing haze of this legend, all the more difficult to dispel because it contains part of the truth. Yet Shaw must be allowed his darker side as well, because in its shadow lurks his *daimon*, the source of most of his creative energy. He must be allowed, in other words, the full psychological bents that enabled him to write his comedies. By recognizing these bents we are in a sense giving Shaw back his humanity. And he in turn may reward us, for in our very act of seeing him as a man who used his writings to mediate the stresses of his life and to fight against his own inner demons, we may gradually find ourselves with an even greater Bernard Shaw, one whose work can still hold surprises for us, and more complex pleasures, too.

APPENDIX

APPENDIX

THE PREFACE TO *MAN AND SUPERMAN*

*M*AN AND SUPERMAN's preface, cast in the form of an Epistle Dedicatory to the critic Arthur B. Walkley, is a fascinating document which shows how fully John Tanner and Don Juan, though independent dramatic entities, also serve as Shaw's spokesmen. To be sure, not every idea in the play is touched on again in the preface, but the central ones are repeated, sometimes more briefly, sometimes with greater explicitness, and often in the same jeering tone. The Epistle restates what has been said on the conflict between the sexes and the aggressiveness of women, on the desirability of having ideas worth dying for, on the high mission of philosophers, on the need for eugenics. Like Don Juan, Shaw attacks romantic love, democracy, the common man, and the pursuit of pleasure. And just as Don Juan's self-assured manner has deflected the attention of commentators from his muddled thinking, so too Shaw's jaunty assertiveness throughout much of the Epistle, along with the brilliance and erudition of many of its passages, has masked his often fallacious reasoning.

Yet beneath all its inconsistencies and braggadocio, the essay also reveals a truthful impulse striving for expression and momentarily gaining its victory in the form of a caveat to the reader to distrust everything that the play says on the relations between men and women. Since this is of course the play's cardinal subject, Shaw has in effect dismissed his own pretensions as a reliable philosopher; and when he attempts to avoid this conclusion he falls into fresh difficulties and finally gives up with a gasp of futility. In sum, the preface shows the author struggling with exactly the same grievances that underlay the entire play, but now he hints more openly at their nature.

Let us take a closer look at the Epistle, starting with Shaw's conflicting remarks about the meaning and intention of his drama. He first speaks of having created "a perfectly modern three-act play," but soon afterward declares that he was "not producing a popular play for the market." He asserts in one sentence that his play will be "at least intelligible and therefore possibly suggestive to the Philistine," yet four sentences beyond declares that it will "pass at a considerable height" over the "simple romantic head" of the playgoing public. In one paragraph he announces that the opinions of all the characters are "right from their several points of view" and that these are, for the dramatic moment, his as well. In the next paragraph, however, he denies having subordinated his own opinions to those of his characters and asserts instead that he has planked down his own view of the relations between the sexes. He then claims that it is merely "a view like any other view and no more, neither true nor false," but he goes on afterward to ally himself to didactic writers whose work is filled with "constructive ideas."

Similar uncertainties also inhere in his conception of his protagonist. Even after writing the work, Shaw has still not decided how far his hero resembles the traditional Don Juan. He admits to "anxiety" over presenting a Don Juan play in which "not one of that hero's *mille e tre* adventures is brought upon the stage"; and he grants that he has created "a figure superficially unlike the hero of Mozart." He notes that his Don Juan is "the quarry instead of the huntsman," and says he is, in fact, "more Hamlet than Don Juan." Yet he nevertheless insists that this Don Juan is a true one, "defying to the last the fate which finally overtakes him"—which would of course make him similar to half a dozen other defiant Shavian heroes, from Dick Dudgeon to Saint Joan. But even if we accept defiance as a distinguishing trait of this modern Don Juan, we see that Shaw fails to hold to it consistently. Instead, he maintains that his hero has voluntarily renounced his "profligacy and his dare-devil airs" and altogether discarded his love affairs "as unworthy of his philosophic dignity and compromising to his newly acknowledged position as a founder of a school. Instead of pretending to read Ovid he does actually read Schopenhauer and Nietzsche, studies Westermarck, and is concerned for the future of the race instead of for the freedom of his own instincts." (The reference to a school is puzzling since neither Tanner nor Don Juan declares himself to be a founder of any school. But Don Juan Shaw had now become a recognized leader of that school of socialism known as Fabianism, had read the authors just mentioned and recently advised a friend to study Westermarck, and had sacrificed the freedom of his sexual instinct.) Don Juan is further said to be cast in the traditional mold as a "true Promethean foe of the gods," although this modern Prometheus will not even pull "the Nonconformist Conscience by the beard" since these days "prudence and good manners alike forbid it to a hero with any mind."

Now whatever incongruity there may be between a well-mannered Prometheus and the mythic one, or between Shaw's hero and Mozart's, there clearly does exist a correspondence between Shaw and his surrogate in the play. And this is evident in their similar manner of reasoning as well as in their shared opinions. Shaw effortlessly enmeshes himself in those non sequiturs and contradictions that had made Don Juan so singular a reasoner. Consider, for example, this sneering reference to modern London life:

The ordinary man's main business is to get means to keep up the position and habits of a gentleman, and the ordinary woman's business is to get married. In 9,999 cases out of 10,000, you can count on their doing nothing, whether noble or base, that conflicts with these ends; and that assurance is what you rely on as their religion, their morality, their principles, their patriotism, their honor and so forth.

But this criticism, momentarily appeasing the urge to attack, is immediately countered at the start of the next paragraph:

On the whole, this is a sensible and satisfactory foundation for society. Money means nourishment and marriage means children; and that men should put nourishment first and women children first is, broadly speaking, the law of Nature and not the dictate of personal ambition.

This truth, perceived disinterestedly by his intelligence, does not however satisfy Shaw's scorn or his need to defend himself, since if ordinary people are indeed following the law of Nature then he himself does not have Nature's backing for his unusual marriage. Hence a few sentences further along he resumes his attack, and what had just been declared to be "a sensible and satisfactory foundation for society" is now rescinded: "What is wrong with the prosaic Englishman is what is wrong with all prosaic men of all countries: stupidity. The vitality which places nourishment and children first, heaven and hell a somewhat remote second, and the health of society as an organic whole nowhere" is ruinous in the twentieth century. (It might be deemed odd for the secularist Shaw to imply that heaven and hell should be placed before nourishment, but apparently he will use any available weapon when on the attack.) He now twists praise into abuse by changing the statement "that men should put nourishment first" to "the determination of every man to be rich at all costs"; and by changing the statement that "women [put] children first" to the determination "of every woman to be married at all costs." And these determinations, he bleakly prophesies, "must, without a highly scientific social organization, produce a ruinous development of poverty, celibacy, prostitution, infant mortality, adult degeneracy, and everything that wise men most dread." Such a many-sided disaster can be avoided, he argues, only if men become socialists—almost as if socialism were not concerned with nutrition and healthy children. And though this advocacy of socialism momentarily gives Shaw a stick with which to beat the ordinary man, a few pages further on he rejects socialism and all meliorative social change in order to strengthen his argument for eugenics: "I do not know whether you have any illusions left on the subject of education, progress, and so forth. I have none. . . . Progress can do nothing but make the most of us all as we are, and that most would clearly not be enough even if those who are already raised out of the lowest abysses would allow the others a chance." Thus the prosaic man's stupidity keeps him from advocating a political faith that Shaw himself declares inadequate!

Shaw's animus against the common man seems to be dictated by social and intellectual snobbery, sexual jealousy, and the need to justify eugenics. This animus warps his judgment of democracy and lands him in further inconsistencies. At one moment he maintains that capable voters are those "who, if they cannot govern in person for lack of spare energy or specific talent for administration, can at least recognize and appreciate capacity and benevolence in others, and so govern through capably benevolent representatives." One might conclude that the voters' desire to be thus governed would make them indifferent to the mere class of their representatives. But Shaw affects to find this indifference reprehensible. Adopting Burke's phrase, he condemns "the swinish multitude" for electing so few members of its own class and for electing these "only under the persuasion of conspicuous personal qualifications." Thereby, according to Shaw, the multitude "admits itself unfit to govern."

Yet however shabbily he reasons when traducing the common man, he is perfectly willing to praise that self-same man when attacking other social groups. The aristocratic and commercial classes might seem to be the alternative to the masses as the governing organ, and in criticizing "the promiscuously bred masses" Shaw does momentarily uphold the "selected class bred by political marriages" which earlier had administered the country. But then he denounces this class as well, noting that "our very peasants have something morally hardier in them that culminates occasionally in a Bunyan, a Burns, or a Carlyle." This might seem to leave only one "class" available as a source of wisdom and governmental ability, namely, the geniuses. But Shaw displays greater hostility toward the geniuses than toward the masses, even though this leaves no one to run the country and also undermines his argument for eugenics. Indeed in talking against the "man of genius," Shaw commits his most flagrant lapses in logic; and here his grievance is at its most intense and his emotional conflict at its fiercest pitch.

At first, in speaking of the men of genius, he simply repeats the contentions of Don Juan that they have been "selected by Nature to carry on the work of building up an intellectual consciousness of her own instinctive purpose," that they incarnate "the philosophic consciousness of Life." But then he adds that they distinctively are "free from the otherwise universal dominion of the tyranny of sex." And this leads him to the following conclusion:

That art, instead of being before all things the expression of the normal sexual situation, is really the only department in which sex is a superseded and secondary power, with its consciousness so confused and its purpose so perverted, that its ideas are mere fantasy to common men. Whether the artist becomes poet or philosopher, moralist or founder of a religion, his sexual doctrine is nothing but a barren special pleading for pleasure, excitement, and knowledge when he is young, and for contemplative tranquillity when he is old and satiated. Romance and Asceticism, Amorism and Puritanism are equally unreal in the great Philistine world.

The world shown in books, he continues, is not at all the main world; rather, it is only "the self-consciousness of certain abnormal people who have the specific artistic talent and temperament."

And since what we call education and culture is for the most part nothing but the substitution of reading for experience, of literature for life, of the obsolete fictitious for the contemporary real, education, as you no doubt observed at Oxford, destroys, by supplantation, every mind that is not strong enough to see through the imposture and to use the great Masters of Arts as what they really are and no more: that is, patentees of highly questionable methods of thinking, and manufacturers of highly questionable, and for the majority but half valid representations of life.

The schoolboy who uses his Homer to throw at his fellow's head makes perhaps the safest and most rational use of him; and I observe with reassurance that you occasionally do the same, in your prime, with Aristotle.

Although there is a certain amount of hedging in these lines, the dominant intent of the paragraph is obviously one of disparagement, a Macaulayean disdain for the pretty truths purveyed by art, its "mere fantasy," its "imposture," its "highly questionable methods of thinking" and "half valid representations of life." Shaw ironically sounds like that very Max Nordau whose philistine attack on modern art he had powerfully rebutted in 1895, three years before the marriage to Charlotte. Certainly the charge that art is the "barren special pleading" of "abnormal people" sums up the essential philistine indictment of the artist, and both the words and the tone of the passages indicate that Shaw himself would like to heave Homer out. (Elsewhere in his writings, his contempt for Homer is explicitly voiced.) And this anger at art's supposed falsity blinds Shaw to the flagrant contradiction of claiming that the artist is both free of the "dominion of the tyranny of sex" and yet engages in a barren special pleading for his own sexual needs.

It also involves the more serious contradiction of claiming that the artist incarnates "the philosophic consciousness of Life" and builds up the "intellectual consciousness of [Nature's] own instinctive purpose," yet destroys young minds with its highly questionable methods of thinking and its highly questionable representations of life. This last contradiction Shaw perceives, and in the lines immediately following those we have just read, he tries to restate the matter.

Fortunately for us, whose minds have been so overwhelmingly sophisticated by literature, what produces all these treatises and poems and scriptures of one sort or another is the struggle of Life to become divinely conscious of itself instead of blindly stumbling hither and thither in the line of least resistance. Hence there is a driving towards truth in all books on matters where the writer, though exceptionally gifted, is normally constituted, and has no private axe to grind. Copernicus had no motive for misleading his fellowmen as to the place of the sun in the solar system: he looked for it as honestly as a shepherd seeks his path in a mist. But Copernicus would not have written love stories scientifically. When it comes to sex relations, the man of genius does not share the common man's danger of capture, nor the woman of genius the common woman's overwhelming specialization. And that is why our scriptures and other art works, when they deal with love, turn from honest attempts at science in physics to romantic nonsense, erotic ecstasy, or the stern asceticism of satiety.

Shaw's attempt to resolve the confusion only compounds it further. By his reasoning, the common man who is in danger of capture by a woman would not be susceptible to romantic nonsense or erotic ecstasy—a deduction belied by human experience as well as the popularity of love stories. By this reasoning, again, the man of genius, supposedly free of the common man's danger of capture, should have no axe to grind and should be able to drive toward truth in sexual matters. But somehow Shaw draws the opposite conclusion and finds that the man of genius inevitably produces romantic nonsense.

If such peculiar reasoning defies logical comprehension, it is nevertheless understandable in light of the sharply conflicting impulses in Shaw himself. One part of him needed to believe in the supreme importance of geniuses, and another to denounce their "romantic nonsense." As a self-proclaimed genius, he wished to ally himself in outlook and purpose with the acknowledged luminaries of the race, all the more so because of his disdain for all other human groups. Thus he momentarily recruits Shakespeare in support of his own position on relations between the sexes, absurdly declaring it a "Shakespearean law" that "women always take the initiative." This reassures him of the typicality of the Tanner-Ann Whitefield relationship and reinforces his private myth that he was not responsible for his marriage or for its failure to be sexually consummated. He also finds it reassuring to think that geniuses are free of the otherwise universal tyranny of sex (a claim which might have amused Bach's twenty children and Victor Hugo's many mistresses), and that the brains of geniuses are not deflected by mere bodily appetites from carrying on the work Nature had selected them for, the work of building up an intellectual consciousness of her own instinctive purposes. Shaw had to console himself for the termination of his sexual manhood by placing a higher value than ever before on his intellectual life, giving it a cosmic significance and flattering himself that all geniuses were just like him.

Now Don Juan, as we recall from our analysis of the dream sequence, adopted at first the same high-minded asceticism; and Shaw finds it as inadequate here as he did there. The ego may think it is strong enough to control the sexual impulses, but those impulses can at least complain; and just as the dream sequence attacks romance as a substitute for sex, here again Shaw goes on to attack those geniuses who made the idea of romance so compelling. Through the voice of Don Juan he had argued that the sexual and procreative purposes of marriage were being hidden "in a mephitic cloud of love and romance and prudery and fastidiousness," of "romantic vowings and pleadings" and other "unbearable frivolities." Now in his own voice he inveighs against the "abnormal people" who use their artistic talent to advance these "highly questionable representations of life." They rationalize their own predispositions and damage those who accept their outlook. In particular, they damage women who believe their notions of romance and love and then find that sex is incompatible with romance. Shaw could see through all this—but not Charlotte! And his personal grievance against geniuses seems to be that their romantic nonsense had not properly prepared Charlotte for her wifely obligations in bed, and had indeed given her prestigious arguments for avoiding sex entirely.

Thus Shaw's contradictory statements on genius spring from the attempt to fortify his ego in opposite ways, first by yoking the work of a genius like himself to Nature's most sacred purposes, and then by blaming his apparent sexual inadequacies on the romantic notions that misguided his wife. Geniuses give mankind truth and not simply special pleadings—or else his own artistic efforts might be suspect; yet on sex relations they had to be purveying lies—or else his own manhood might be suspect. The telltale example of the damage done by romantic nonsense he was not able to present without immense embarrassment to Charlotte and himself, and the frustration of not being able to state the truth may also have contributed to the aggrieved tone of his attack on the fictions created by geniuses. But something else was nagging him as well. He had no right to sneer at the fictions of "abnormal people" while pretending to be perfectly normal himself. He knew that his relations with his wife were far from normal. He knew that the huge play he had written was filled with special pleading. This truth at least could be told.

And tell it he does. For after seemingly leaving the subject and moving on to the impersonal world of political issues, where he can regain his composure and sound superior, he unexpectedly returns to the issue a few paragraphs later and surprises us with an admission. He had seemed until then to be dealing with writers other than himself, and attacking them for their highly questionable representations of life. But now he suddenly announces that he too is in the camp of the special pleaders:

You may, however, remind me that this digression of mine into politics was preceded by a very convincing demonstration that the artist never catches the point of view of the common man on the question of sex, because he is not in the same predicament. *I first prove that anything I write on the relation of the sexes is sure to be misleading;* and then I proceed to write a Don Juan play. [Italics added]

He had not of course proved that what he wrote was sure to be misleading. He had not seemed to be talking of himself at all. But some vein of humanity and honesty in him compels him to blurt out the truth. He issues a warning to his readers, after siphoning off his vexation of spirit in intemperate and inconsistent attacks, just as he had made the Devil warn the audience at the end of the dream sequence to beware of the inhumanity of Don Juan's doctrines.

It was a handsome admission and a courageous inclusion of himself among the artists who supposedly mislead the rest of mankind. But he nevertheless leaves himself squirming on the horns of a dilemma: although as a genius he must incarnate Life's philosophic consciousness, he admits that what he writes "on the relation of the sexes is sure to be misleading." He fully recognizes the dilemma and tries to answer the obvious question of why he has written a play on the subject. But his answer is lame and full of confusion:

Well, if you insist on asking me why I behave in this absurd way, I can only reply that you asked me to, and that in any case my treatment of the subject may be valid for the artist, amusing to the amateur, and at least intelligible and therefore possibly suggestive to the Philistine. Every man who records his illusions is providing data for the genuinely scientific psychology which the world still waits for. I plank down my view of the existing relations of men to women in the most highly civilized society for what it is worth. It is a view like any other view and no more, neither true nor false, but, I hope, a way of looking at the subject which throws into the familiar order of cause and effect a sufficient body of fact and experience to be interesting to you, if not to the playgoing public of London. I have certainly shewn little consideration for that public in this enterprise; but I know that it has the friendliest disposition towards you and me as far as it has any consciousness of our existence, and quite understands that what I write for you must pass at a considerable height over its simple romantic head. It will take my books as read and my genius for granted, trusting me to put forth work of such quality as shall bear out its verdict. So we may disport ourselves on our own plane to the top of our bent; and if any gentleman points out that neither this epistle dedicatory nor the dream of Don Juan in the third act of the ensuing comedy is suitable for immediate production at a popular theatre we need not contradict him. Napoleon provided Talma with a pit of kings, with what effect on Talma's acting is not recorded. As for me, what I have always wanted is a pit of philosophers; and this is a play for such a pit.

Shaw seems willing to terminate the discussion at this point, patting himself on the back at the end after having stumbled through some strange assertions: that his work is both intelligible to the philistines and must pass over their heads; that this very epistle might even be considered for theatrical production; that his view of the relations of men and women is neither true nor false but nevertheless records his illusions, and these would somehow be of interest to philosophers. He then moves into an apparent peroration, acknowledging the authors from whom he has borrowed—but suddenly he seems to sense the inadequacy of his recent comments on the artist's relation to truth, and he readdresses himself to the issue with another four thousand words. We need not dwell on this section for more than a closing moment, for though it includes some of the best writing in the entire essay it does not at all resolve his self-created problem.

In saying that the play presents "a view like any other view and no more, neither true nor false," indeed one which "is sure to be misleading," Shaw realizes that his work may be regarded solely as entertainment or as belletristic. He is not, however, a follower of art for art's sake. He is not even content to be thought of as a "mere artist." He had to regard himself as an artist-philosopher. "The artist-philosophers are the only sort of artists I take quite seriously. . . . For art's sake alone I would not face the toil of writing a single sentence." But neither would he face the toil if he were only giving a view like any other and no more, neither true nor false. He sets up a contrast between Bunyan on the one side and Shakespeare and Dickens on the other. The first wrote because he identified himself "with the purpose of the world as he understood it." The latter, in contrast, offer no philosophy or religion, and "Shakespeare's pessimism is only his wounded humanity." Neither one of the latter writers imparts any thought or inspiration for which any man could conceivably risk his life.

Shaw is clearly seeking to reestablish the artist's high mission as a teller of truth, a bringer of vision. And to find such truths and visions is the goal of the artist-philosopher and the ideal for all of mankind. Thus we have Shaw rising to the eloquence of his famous lines:

This is the true joy in life, the being used for a purpose recognized by yourself as a mighty one; the being thoroughly worn out before you are thrown on the scrap heap; the being a force of Nature instead of a feverish selfish little clod of ailments and grievances complaining that the world will not devote itself to making you happy. And also the only real tragedy in life is the being used by personally minded men for purposes which you recognize to be base. All the rest is at worst mere misfortune or mortality: this alone is misery, slavery, hell on earth; and the revolt against it is the only force that offers a man's work to the poor artist, whom our personally minded rich people would so willingly employ as pander, buffoon, beauty monger, sentimentalizer and the like.

He himself will not be a beauty monger or a buffoon; he will be a force of Nature and serve a mighty purpose. He boasts that he is one who has railed against "the theistic credulity of Voltaire, the amoristic superstition of Shelley, the revival of tribal soothsaying and idolatrous rites which Huxley calls Science . . . [and at] the welter of ecclesiastical and professional humbug." He is a didactic writer with something to teach, and he has "contempt for *belles lettres.*"

But however strongly Shaw insists on his high mission, he has still not explained how his play can disseminate universal truth or promote Life's philosophic consciousness of itself if everything he writes on the relation of the sexes is sure to be misleading. His renewed statements about the seriousness of artist-philosophers are impressive but do not meet the issue. He almost seems to be trying to make the very impressiveness of his statements distract himself and his readers from his failure to solve the dilemma. At the very end he escapes into an argument by analogy and compares himself to a wire which can turn an electrical current into heat and light but can also go out and go wrong. As a "luminous author" he must "take myself as I am and get what I can out of myself." It is a modest and sound statement, yet on the matter at hand an expression of futility as well. It was never a question of the author's shedding light or not but of the kind of light he shed, and of the range of validity of one man's truth.

Thus the preface to *Man and Superman*, albeit unable to resolve the issue it raises, does suggest a development in Shaw's understanding of the darker currents of his play, especially in its relation to himself. He here makes explicit that uneasiness over sexuality which is pervasively implicit in the play. And in his calling the writer an abnormal person whose sexual doctrines are a barren special pleading, he shows an insight into Don Juan's speeches which he probably could not have allowed himself when seeking to make those speeches convincing. But he does retreat from the more threatening insight that an abnormal person's idealism may be quite as flawed as his beliefs on sexuality. In this regard his comments on Shakespeare are especially revealing. He condemns Shakespeare's alleged pessimism and lack of identification with the purpose of the world, yet he shows a surprising blindness to his own extreme pessimism, which sees mankind in its present biological state as utterly incorrigible. Shakespeare is made to possess something of the same futile willlessness of the Devil in the play, and against both Shaw upholds a philosophy of the will, oblivious here as in the play of the dangers of such a philosophy. Why he so desperately needed to enthrone the will, and to condemn the pursuit of happiness, the preface does not say. But perhaps it gives the necessary clue when it says that Shakespeare's pessimism was "only his wounded humanity." The phrase forcibly recalls all the images of wounding in *Man and Superman*, with its castrating women and shamed men and its hero who "collapses like a pricked bladder." If the play showed the author variously responding to the disorienting effects of his unconsummated marriage, then the preface, at its deeper reaches, shows that the response was still being made.

NOTES

NOTES

Unless otherwise indicated, all play references are to the one-volume *Complete Plays of Bernard Shaw* (London: Odham's Press, 1950). Preface references are to *Prefaces* by Bernard Shaw (London: Odham's Press, 1938). The following books are cited in shortened form:

Campbell Letters	Alan Dent, ed., *Bernard Shaw and Mrs. Patrick Campbell: Their Correspondence* (London, 1952)
Chappelow	Allan Chappelow, *Shaw—The Chucker-Out* (London, 1969)
Collected Letters	Bernard Shaw, *Collected Letters*, ed. Dan H. Laurence, 2 vols. (New York, 1965–72)
Crompton	Louis Crompton, *Shaw the Dramatist* (Lincoln, Neb., 1969)
Evans	T. F. Evans, ed., *Shaw: The Critical Heritage* (London, 1976)
Rattray	R. F. Rattray, *Bernard Shaw: A Chronicle* (Luton, 1951)
Rosset	B. C. Rosset, *Shaw of Dublin: The Formative Years* (University Park, Pa., 1964)
Self Sketches	Bernard Shaw, *Sixteen Self Sketches* (New York, 1949)
Terry Letters	St. John Christopher, ed., *Ellen Terry and Bernard Shaw: A Correspondence* (New York, 1932)
Valency	Maurice Valency, *The Cart and the Trumpet* (New York, 1973)

I: INTRODUCTION

The bibliographical references here and elsewhere are selective and the evaluations strictly personal. Both are intended for the use of Shaw's future students, who can easily become bewildered by the vast and still growing mass of critical commentary on him. Such students will quickly go beyond the core of suggested reading and discover the many helpful items I have perforce omitted.

3 gratitude for his unexpected silence: Archibald Henderson, *Bernard Shaw: Playboy and Prophet* (New York, 1932), p. 744.

3 "mankind's friend": Thomas Mann, "He Was Mankind's Friend," in Louis Kronenberger, ed., *George Bernard Shaw: A Critical Survey*

(New York, 1953), p. 257. Mann's article first appeared in *The Listener,*
Jan. 18, 1951.

3 Pirandello, O'Casey, and Brecht: For Pirandello, see his review of *Saint
Joan* in the *New York Times,* Jan. 13, 1924, reprinted in Evans, pp.
279—84. For O'Casey, see "A Whisper About Bernard Shaw," *The
Green Crow* (New York, 1956), pp. 197—205; and *Sunset and Evening
Star* (London, 1954), pp. 210—51. For Brecht, see "Ovation for Shaw,"
Berliner Börsen Courier, July 25, 1926, reprinted in English translation
in *Modern Drama,* 2 (1959): 184—87. For an American playwright's re-
sponse, see Elmer Rice's comments in *The Shaw Bulletin,* vol. 2, no. 1
(1957), p. 6. For an assessment by a later British playwright, see James
Bridie, "Shaw as Dramatist," in Stephen Winsten, ed., *G.B.S. 90* (New
York, 1946), pp. 98—118.

3 Shaw festivals at Malvern: For a brief description of the Malvern
scene, see H. W. Nevinson, "Shakespeare's Rival," in Evans, pp. 317—
18.

3 Stephen Spender: "The Riddle of Shaw," *The Nation,* Apr. 30, 1949,
reprinted in Kronenberger, ed., *Shaw: A Critical Survey,* pp. 236—39.
Spender grants that Shaw is also more than an entertainer but admits
to difficulty in saying what that more amounts to.

4 since the days of Sheridan: Wilde's effect on the theater in the mid-
1890's was probably too short-lived (and too soon darkened by the
cloud of scandal) to initiate the new movement. It was the Royal Court
seasons under Vedrenne and Barker that established Shaw as a major
new dramatist. Though works by other new British playwrights were
shown, 70 percent of the total number of performances during the
1904—7 seasons were of plays by Shaw.

4 Shaw became a culture hero: Rupert Brooke's reaction at 19 may be
cited as not untypical. Of *John Bull's Other Island* he wrote to a friend,
"It is unspeakably delightful. . . . exquisite, wonderful, terrific, an un-
approachable satire on everything." To another correspondent he declared the following year that "*Candida* is the greatest play in the
world" (*The Letters of Rupert Brooke* [London, 1958], reprinted in
Evans, p. 163). The philosopher C. E. M. Joad, in his *Shaw* (London,
1949), engagingly recounts Shaw's impact on his generation. When as
an Oxford student he first saw Shaw in person, he "gazed with rapture," "glowing with hero-worship" (p. 29). The educational innovator
A. S. Neill concurs: "When I first discovered his plays and prefaces in
my student days, a new world was opened to me. He was the oracle.
. . . I had and still have a G.B.S. complex" ("Shaw and Education," in
Winsten, ed., *G.B.S. 90,* p. 183).

5 influential critics of the time: For a fair sampling, see Evans, pp.
48—53, 55—58, *passim.*

6 Shaw's most able recent defenders: There are of course significant differences in the approaches and achievements of these particular critics. J. L. Wisenthal's book, *The Marriage of Contraries: Bernard
Shaw's Middle Plays* (Cambridge, Mass., 1974), seems to me the best
single book on Shaw as playwright. A. M. Gibbs's *Shaw* (Edinburgh,
1969) is a pithy summing-up and deserves to be more widely known.

Although Eric Bentley in his deservedly popular volume *Bernard Shaw* (Norfolk, Conn., 1947) is sometimes willing to notice Shaw's shortcomings, both he and Louis Crompton write avowedly as partisans.

6 his own meaning in *Candida*: In a letter to James Huneker, Apr. 1904, reprinted in Stephen S. Stanton, ed., *A Casebook on Candida* (New York, 1962), p. 166. For some of his other comments on his inspiration, see the preface to *Buoyant Billions*, p. 4; the preface to *Farfetched Fables*, in the Constable edition of *Buoyant Billions, Farfetched Fables, and Shakes Versus Shav* (London, 1950), p. 66.

7 his work was confessional: Stanley Weintraub, ed., *Shaw: An Autobiography* (New York, 1969), I, p. x.

7 "a chaos of contradictions": Stephen Winsten, *Shaw's Corner* (New York, 1952), p. 118.

7 sharp fluctuations in quality: For example, *Great Catherine*, a weak short play, appears right after *Pygmalion*; and *Back to Methuselah*, in my opinion a weak long play, falls between the heights of *Heartbreak House* and *Saint Joan*.

8 compulsive addiction to writing: Frank Harris, *Bernard Shaw* (London, 1931), p. 82.

8 His alcoholic father. *Self Sketches*, p. 27.

9 Writing plays became a necessity: Preface to *Buoyant Billions*, p. 3.

9 "the unscrupulous moral versatility": Eric Bentley, ed., *Shaw on Music* (New York, 1956), p. 85.

10 use the prefaces warily: For the guidance of future students of Shaw, and with due affront to my modesty, I shall here set forth the Silver Rule for using the prefaces. When examining play "Y," attend as much to the preface to the preceding play "X" as to "Y"'s own preface. This rule, a local application of something known as chronology (usually overlooked in Shaw scholarship), reminds us that Shaw explored his own meanings while writing a play and frequently had begun that exploration in an earlier piece of writing—often in the preface that was then attached to the preceding play. The rule is of course of greater applicability in some instances than in others, depending mostly on the time span between the "X" preface and the "Y" play. A sometimes useful variant of the rule calls for special attention to the preceding play itself rather than to its preface.

10 supervised by Shaw himself: The first two: *George Bernard Shaw: His Life and Works* (London, 1911); and *Shaw: Playboy and Prophet*.

11 Frank Harris: See Shaw's own postscript to Harris, *Bernard Shaw*, pp. 387–96.

11 admit of one exception: Daniel Dervin's *Bernard Shaw: A Psychological Study* (Lewisburg and London, 1975) is perhaps another exception. It concentrates on Shaw's infancy and very earliest years and is thereby necessarily speculative. But it is well worth reading for its provocative insights and, even more, for its bold willingness to treat Shaw as a human being rather than a demigod or a sprite. The chief shortcomings of the book, in my opinion, do not at all lie in the application of Freudian categories (though these are sometimes handled too rigidly) but in the reluctance to give weight to Shaw's later experiences—hence the

unwarranted dismissal of Rosset's findings—and in the often deductive approach to the plays. These last provide the deepest well for understanding Shaw, and it is finally from them that the most secure generalizations about Shavian psychology must be drawn.

11 "I can only imagine": *Self Sketches*, p. 27.

11 "tragedy": Rosset, p. 68.

11 "salvation came through music": *Self Sketches*, pp. 30–31.

11 "at last became a member": *Ibid.*, p. 31.

11 "certainly no unpleasantness": Preface to *London Music, 1888–1889*, p. 16.

11 "blameless *ménage à trois*": Archibald Henderson, *George Bernard Shaw: Man of the Century* (New York, 1956), p. 37.

12 "blessed relief": *Self Sketches*, p. 148.

12 the work of an earlier scholar: The scholar was T. D. O'Bolger of the University of Pennsylvania. The letters between the two men (British Museum Add. MS. 50565), written between 1910 and 1922, indicate that when O'Bolger proved too independent as a biographer, Shaw turned difficult, forced him to write several revisions, and then finally made trouble with more than one publisher in order to block publication.

12 Catholics: Rosset, pp. 113, 34–38.

12 Mr. Shaw was appallingly submissive: *Ibid.*, pp. 115–16.

12 lived in very close proximity: *Ibid.*, p. 72.

12 the music lessons: *Ibid.*, pp. 75, 79–80.

12 cottage overlooking Galway Bay: *Ibid.*, p. 120.

12 house which Lee had already owned: *Ibid.*, p. 123.

12 rent was paid by Lee: *Ibid.*, p. 125.

13 father certainly did not like Lee: *Ibid.*, p. 105.

13 references to illegitimate births: *Ibid.*, pp. 139–74.

13 discreet inquiries: *Ibid.*, p. 30.

13 Shaw hated his mother: *Ibid.*, pp. 135, 347–48.

13 "discovery that [his father]": *Self Sketches*, p. 28.

13 "I have never believed": Terry Letters, p. 196.

14 "impecunious and unsuccessful" father: *Self Sketches*, p. 30.

14 "full of self-reproaches": Rosset, p. 4.

14 "a conductor of genius": *Ibid.*, p. 48.

14 his hair worn long: *Ibid.*, p. 40.

14 "despised his weak and inefficient father": *Ibid.*, p. 101.

14 "volubility of language": *Ibid.*, p. 40.

14 men for him to emulate: Shaw liked to imply that his uncle Walter Gurly was as important an influence as Lee. "I had a natural father and two supplementaries, making three varieties for me to study," he wrote in *Self Sketches* (p. 31). And as if to emphasize the point he devotes three times the space to Gurly as he gives to Lee, who in fact receives a scant 15 lines. But Gurly, a ship's surgeon, and a visitor only between voyages, was hardly Lee's equal as a household presence or model, and Shaw's attempt to elevate his importance seems to confirm in a curious way the actual importance of Lee.

14 "mesmeric vitality": *Ibid.*, p. 146.

14 Lee's influence: *Ibid.*, p. 31.

15 teaching voice control and enunciation: See, for instance, Vincent Wall's *Bernard Shaw: Pygmalion to Many Players* (Ann Arbor, 1973), pp. 52–67, *passim.*

15 system of spelling English: Abraham Tauber's anthology, *Shaw on Language* (London, 1965), traces this Shavian cause over its 50-year span.

16 Shaw's ambivalence as a literary artist: As late as 1948 he was publicly wondering whether he was not "a pathological case" (preface to *Farfetched Fables*, p. 64). Elsie B. Adams charts Shaw's ambivalences in her pioneering study *Bernard Shaw and the Aesthetes* (Columbus, Ohio, 1971).

16 claims made for a Heavenly Father: Rosset, p. 149.

16 Rosset conjectures: *Ibid.*, p. 77.

16 contempt for her husband: *Self Sketches*, pp. 27–28.

16 "horribly ugly": Terry Letters, p. 58.

16 "detestable": Stephen Winsten, *Days with Bernard Shaw* (London, n.d.), p. 13.

17 heroes invariably were foundlings: Harris, *Bernard Shaw*, pp. 71, 203–4.

17 idolization of the devil: Preface to *Immaturity*, p. 666; preface to *Misalliance*, p. 79.

17 mother he worshiped: Preface to *London Music, 1888–1889*, p. 13.

17 "a devil of a childhood": Terry Letters, p. 196.

17 "Except in my secret self": Letter to Adda Shaw Tyrrell, in Rosset, p. 87.

17 "or rather not brought up!!!": *Ibid.*

17 "I would see it": *Ibid.*, p. 88.

17 talks about his childhood with amusement: See, for example, preface to *Immaturity*, p. 669.

17 laughter could check tears: *Ibid.*, p. 668.

18 the hero Tanner: Rattray, p. 149.

18 H. D. Hyndman: Crompton, pp. 82–83.

18 sense of humor: According to Stephen Winsten, "Hyndman held all laughter suspect" (*Days with Bernard Shaw*, p. 79).

19 Maurice Valency and Bernard Dukore: Valency is more willing than Dukore (*Bernard Shaw: Playwright* [Columbia, Mo., 1973]) to notice the biographical roots; but despite several shrewd insights in passing, he manifestly prefers to approach his subject through theatrical and intellectual history even though at times such an approach seems quite tangential.

19 "My plays are interludes": Paul Green, *Dramatic Heritage* (New York, 1953), pp. 125–26.

20 "eludes our grasp": Jacques Barzun, "Bernard Shaw in Twilight," in Kronenberger, ed., *Shaw: A Critical Survey*, p. 159. It should be added that this essay significantly improved our grasp of Shaw at the time. A revised version has appeared in Barzun's *Energies of Art* (New York, 1956).

21 Stanley Weintraub: *Journey to Heartbreak* (New York, 1971).

22 he did not throw himself: Preface to *The Irrational Knot*, p. 687.
23 "His ability to transform": Robert Brustein, *The Theatre of Revolt* (London, 1965), p. 89.

2: THE SIMPLETON OF THE UNEXPECTED ISLES

The literature on this play is sparse and understandably one-sided. Those who find little merit in it, like Edmund Wilson and Maurice Valency, give it a bare passing word. Desmond MacCarthy is the only one who dismisses its worth yet devotes a few able pages to it. At the other end are the laudatory articles by Bernard Dukore and Raymond S. Nelson, the former in "Shaw's Doomsday," *Educational Theatre Journal*, 19 (1967): 61–71, the latter in *"The Simpleton of the Unexpected Isles*: Shaw's Last Judgement," *Queens Quarterly*, 76 (1969): 692–706. Both of these are indebted to an earlier eulogistic appraisal by Frederick P. W. McDowell, "Spiritual and Political Reality: Shaw's *The Simpleton of the Unexpected Isles*," *Modern Drama*, 3 (1960): 196–210. Margery M. Morgan deals respectfully and at length with the play in *The Shavian Playground* (London, 1972), and Martin Meisel is briefer but equally admiring in *Shaw and the Nineteenth-Century Theater* (Princeton, N.J., 1963).

A comparable situation prevails in the critical commentary on Shaw's latter-day politics, although here excuses replace approval. Shaw's enthusiasm for dictators embarrasses his devotees twice over, both in itself and in its incompatibility with their prettified image of him. Accordingly, denial, evasion, distortion, and other anxiety symptoms flare forth in the writings of otherwise responsible scholars, such as Katherine Haynes Gatch, Paul Hummert, Richard Nickson, and Gerard Anthony Pilecki. The greatest value of St. John Ervine's biography, *Bernard Shaw: His Life, Work and Friends* (London, 1956), lies perhaps in the author's willingness to dissect Shaw's more egregious political pronouncements (for example, pp. 533–44). Allan Chappelow is intermittently critical in his invaluable compilation of Shaw's political and social positions in *Shaw—The Chucker-Out*. Forthright comments are also available in Arland Ussher's chapter on Shaw in *Three Great Irishmen: Shaw, Yeats, Joyce* (New York, 1953), and Erich Strauss's *Bernard Shaw: Art and Socialism* (London, 1942). James Redmond's short critique is incisive: "William Morris or Bernard Shaw: Two Faces of Victorian Socialism," in J. Butt and I. F. Clarke, eds., *The Victorians and Social Protest: A Symposium* (Newton Abbot, Eng., 1973), pp. 156–76. Although Martin Meisel's important essay ranges widely, it also has bearings on Shaw's later views: "Shaw and Revolution: The Politics of the Plays," in Norman Rosenblood, ed., *Shaw: Seven Critical Essays* (Toronto, 1972). For purposes of contrast, Shaw's earlier position is deftly summarized by Leonard Woolf in "The Early Fabians and British Socialism," in C. E. M. Joad, ed., *Shaw and Society* (London, 1953); and in more detail, with great discrimination, by Willard Wolfe, *From Radicalism to Socialism* (New Haven, Conn., 1975). Gerard Anthony Pilecki's extended survey of Shaw's politics is useful but entirely uncritical (*Shaw's Geneva: A Critical Study* [The Hague, 1965]); E. J. Hobsbawm's "Bernard Shaw's Socialism," *Science and Society* (Fall 1947), views its subject through Marxist lenses and is too dismissive of Shaw's reformist impulses. On international matters, the best brief introduction is William Irvine's "Shaw, War and Peace: 1894 to 1919," *Foreign Affairs*, 25 (1947): 314–27. The two most authoritative books on the whole subject are A. M. McBriar, *Fabian Socialism and English Politics, 1884–1918* (Cambridge, 1962), and Wolfe's *From Radicalism to Socialism*.

27 chief value of Shaw's late plays: I am not persuaded by the claim that *The Simpleton* and some of the other late works are precursors of Absurdist drama. See, for example, Daniel J. Leary, "About Nothing in Shaw's *The Simpleton of the Unexpected Isles*," *Educational Theatre Journal*, 24 (1972): 139–48. Rather, they are reversions, as Meisel has shown, to the Burlesque-Extravaganza, a very popular form in the 19th-century theater, and still familiar through the work of W. S. Gilbert (*Shaw and 19th-Century Theater*, pp. 380–428). Of course, insofar as Absurdist drama itself uses devices from the Burlesque-Extravaganza tradition, it shares a common heritage with Shaw's late work. (It was in keeping with this heritage that *Waiting for Godot* starred that great burlesque clown Bert Lahr in its New York run.) But then again, many of the absurdities in Shaw's late plays derive simply from failing powers and reflect the same wavering coherency of the late political tracts. See also Albert H. Silverman, "Bernard Shaw's Political Extravaganzas," *Drama Survey*, 5 (1966–67): 213–22.

27 "without any premeditation whatever": Ervine, *Bernard Shaw*, p. 555. Shaw picked up a few ideas in Jan. 1934 from the manuscript of a play by Cornwallis West, his one-time rival for Stella Campbell's affections. West's play "The Woman Who Stopped War" (Brit. Mus. Add. MS. 58432/64OE) deals with a women's antiwar league and was published as a novel the following year. Shaw also borrowed some of West's ideas for his 1934 "Whither Britain" broadcast, reprinted in *The Listener*, Feb. 7, 1934.

27 Edmund Wilson: "Bernard Shaw at Eighty," *Eight Essays* (New York, 1954), p. 164.

27 "to provoke a revulsion against silliness": Katherine Haynes Gatch, "The Last Plays of Bernard Shaw: Dialectic and Despair," in W. K. Wimsatt, ed., *English Stage Comedy*, English Institute Essays (New York, 1955), p. 144.

31 his advanced age: For example, Terry Letters, pp. 346–47. Or, in the 1932 lecture "In Praise of Guy Fawkes," he remarks, "You notice that I am an old man, exhibiting very distinct symptoms of second childhood. . . . I am an old man and my brain is failing" (in Dan H. Laurence, ed., *Platform and Pulpit* [London, 1962], pp. 247, 253).

32 a soured old man's regret: "The Sanity of Art," *Major Critical Essays* (London, 1930), p. 315.

32 weak-minded old age: Terry Letters, p. 356; Ervine, *Bernard Shaw*, p. 155; preface to *Geneva*, p. 16. See also note above (his advanced age).

32 simpleton's words are often identical to Shaw's: Compare for instance Iddy's "second sermon"—"Nothing human is good enough to be loved. . . . I cannot bear being loved, because I know that I am a

worm, and that nobody could love me unless they were completely deluded as to my merits" (II, p. 1237)—with the following words from Shaw's 1937 speech over the BBC: "But such a command as 'Love one another' as I see it is a stupid refusal to accept the facts of human nature. Why, are we lovable animals? . . . I find I cannot like myself without so many reservations that I look forward to my death, which cannot now be far off, as a good riddance" (reprinted in Chappelow, p. 393).

33 "We shall make wars": One may contrast this late praise of war with the younger and saner Shaw's statement of 1916, "War will cure nothing. The business of war is to inflict wounds, not heal them"; or his statement of 1918, "War is so dreadful a calamity that only half-witted men would engage in it, or countenance it" (Chappelow, pp. 369, 377).

37 "the most effective engine": *Ibid.*, p. 175.

37 "with Signor Mussolini": *The Sunday Referee*, July 21, 1935, p. 12.

37 "I don't really want to see": Chappelow, p. 202.

37 England had committed ten times the atrocities: *Ibid.*, p. 397.

37 "the present complete despotism": *Ibid.*

37 "Churchillism" as bad as Hitlerism: *The New Statesman*, Oct. 7, 1939, p. 484.

37 "Fascist dictator": *Ibid.*

37 "Western democracy": Chappelow, p. 321.

37 "the British Party system": Bernard Shaw, *Everybody's Political What's What?* (New York, 1944), p. 353.

37 "that British democracy is nothing but": *Ibid.*, p. 351.

37 parliamentary system "a sham": "Sixty Years of Fabianism," postscript to *Fabian Essays*, Jubilee Edition (London, 1948), p. 228.

37 "Hitler was right": Chappelow, p. 331.

37 impressed by *Mein Kampf: New York Times*, July 10, 1938, p. 18.

38 "intense resentment": *Ibid.*, Nov. 24, 1933, p. 14.

38 he excused Hitler's violence: Chappelow, p. 398.

38 "Heil Hitler": *Ibid.*, p. 396.

38 opposed all efforts at disarmament: *Ibid.*, p. 389.

38 "all the most diabolical means": "Are We Heading for War," BBC "Whither Britain" Series, 1934 (London, n.d.), p. 3.

38 recommended German move into Austria: *New York Times*, Aug. 30, 1935, p. 6.

38 "a highly desirable event": *Ibid.*, July 10, 1938, p. 18.

38 "joyful news": *Times* (London), Aug. 28, 1939, p. 11. The letter was written on Aug. 25, 1939.

38 "Mr. Hitler did not begin": Antony Weymouth, *Journal of the War Years*, I (Worcester, 1948), p. 261.

38 "we are not the terrified victims": Chappelow, p. 396.

38 "moral courage" and "diplomatic sagacity": Weymouth, *Journal*, I, pp. 262–63. H. M. Geduld's "Bernard Shaw and Adolf Hitler," *The Shaw Review*, vol. 4, no. 1 (1961), pp. 11–20, provides an informative survey of its subject and suggests some, but by no means all, of the reasons for Shaw's support of the dictator. While it is true, as Geduld writes, that Shaw "saw Hitler through the 'injustices' of the Versailles Treaty," I believe that his own grievances at having had his 1919 pamphlet "Peace Conference Hints" ignored, made him enjoy the prospect

of being a grimly accurate prophet, and one who could now see England further discomfited. Shaw did what he could to support Hitler within the limits of his own commitment to Soviet Communism—and sometimes beyond those limits—for in 1933 he opposed international protests against the Nazi trial of Van der Lubbe and the other Communists accused of setting fire to the Reichstag building, and he later approved the verdict against them. He was also undisturbed by Hitler's 1935 proposal to rearm Germany and by his later European conquests. He thought it would be "a lot of rubbish" to talk about bringing Hitler and other top Nazis to trial as war criminals since no "spotless men" could be found to try them—a point he invariably forgot to mention whenever he proposed that ordinary citizens should justify their existences before tribunals. Geduld and others claim that Shaw's appalling errors of judgment on Hitler were due to old age and a simple inability to comprehend the man's monstrousness. Perhaps so, but there was a *will* not to comprehend, and this needs explaining. Part of the answer, in my opinion, is that Nazi successes fed Shaw's antipathy to democracy and Nazi methods gratified his destructive urges. Finally, Shaw seems to have identified himself with Hitler, at least in the latter's earlier career. Notice what he chooses to mention about Hitler in the *Geneva* preface, keeping in mind that Shaw had come up to London as a poor young man with ambitions to be an artist, having left a dull commercial job, and that he then lived a mildly Bohemian life, joining debating societies and training himself as a speaker: "It happened that in Munich in 1930 there was a young man named Hitler who had served in the Four Years War. . . . He was poor and what we call no class, being a Bohemian with artistic tastes but neither training nor talent enough to succeed as an artist, and was thus hung up between the bourgeoisie for which he had no income and the working class for which he had no craft. But he had a voice and could talk, and soon became a beer cellar orator who could hold his audience. He joined a cellar debating society (like our old Coger's Hall)" (p. 18). It was surely not by oversight that Shaw's name was absent from a lengthy Nazi "Special Search List" that was to be used if a German invasion of England succeeded. The Nazi regime also allowed Shaw's plays to be performed throughout their reign (William L. Shirer, *The Rise and Fall of the Third Reich* [New York, 1960], pp. 783–84; postscript in Geduld, p. 20).

38 visit to Stresa in 1927: For Shaw's intolerance at this time of any criticism of his pro-Fascist stand, see Ignazio Silone's comments in the *Times Literary Supplement*, June 4, 1964, p. 485.

38 "Europe has begun to clamor": *The Intelligent Woman's Guide to Socialism and Capitalism* (London, 1928), p. 318.

38 Shaw's defense of Mussolini's torturing: Chappelow, pp. 187.

38 bombings of defenseless Abyssinians: Blanche Patch, *Thirty Years With G.B.S.* (London, 1951), p. 116; Chappelow, p. 391. John Rothenstein, in his autobiography *Summer's Lease* (London, 1965), offers this account of a Shaw visit: "One day Bernard Shaw and his wife came to lunch. The Abyssinian War was at its height, and Shaw, an impassioned advocate of the 'civilizing mission' of Italy, argued at length

that she deserved praise—in place of the blame that her aggression so widely provoked—for her self-sacrifice in attempting to put an end to the intolerable barbarism which prevailed in Abyssinia. I cannot recall a fine, in many respects a great, intellect arguing so crude a case and showing so little awareness—in fact none at all—of the moral or the political complexities of the issue" (p. 214). See also "G.B.S. on the White Man's Burden," *California Shavian*, 6 (1965): 1–4.

39 "the necessary intimidation": *Times* (London), Oct. 22, 1935, p. 12.

39 objected to imposing sanctions: *Ibid.* Shaw's continual advice to surrender to Italy and Germany all the territory they wanted cannot be viewed as merely a counsel of appeasement to prevent a major war. He was an enthusiastic supporter of the Fascist regimes and wanted those regimes to succeed. For strong contemporary attacks on Shaw's pro-Fascism, see E. Sylvia Pankhurst's "An Open Letter to G.B.S.," *The Sunday Referee*, July 14, 1935, p. 6, and her letter to the same weekly newspaper of Aug. 4, 1935, p. 6. See also the veteran anti-Fascist leader Carlo Rosselli's letter in the same paper of July 28, 1935, p. 13.

39 refused to sign the protests: *Ibid.*, July 14, 1935, p. 6.

39 Mussolini's "star was eclipsed": Preface to *Geneva*, p. 21. The full depressing story of Shaw's support of Mussolini has not yet been written. The exchange of public letters in 1927 between Shaw and the Austrian socialist leader Friedrich Adler, and between Shaw and the Italian historian Gaetano Salvemini, contains only part of the story. (A summary of the controversy appears in Chappelow, pp. 186–96.) Most of the letters are reprinted in a rare pamphlet published in London in 1927 and entitled *Bernard Shaw and Fascism*. A more complete documentation, edited and with notes by Salvemini, is available in Italian: *G. B. Shaw E Il Fascismo* (Palma, 1955). Salvemini's criticisms are devastating, and he clearly demonstrates that Shaw was not only ignorant of Italian affairs but willing to trim his words to suit the needs of Fascist propagandists (*Bernard Shaw and Fascism*, pp. 12–13, 15–16, 20–21). Richard Nickson's survey of the dispute ("GBS: British Fascist?", *The Shavian*, no. 16 [Oct. 1959], pp. 9–15) is far too indulgent to Shaw and avoids all the hard questions: Did Shaw flirt with the Fascists? Did he use a double standard and justify acts in Italy that he would have loudly condemned in England? Did he allow his written words to be changed for the Italian press so as to exculpate Mussolini of Giacomo Matteotti's murder? I also find it difficult to accept Nickson's reassurance that Shaw was not "so ready to get rid of democratic institutions" (p. 13) when most of the evidence points the other way, and when Nickson himself, in a later article, praises Shaw as a "terrorist" ("The Art of Shavian Political Drama," *Modern Drama*, 14 [1971]: 326, 330). It simply will not do to say that Shaw opposed only "sham-democracies." After World War I he on the whole opposed everything that is usually meant by democracy, and part of his continuing political importance is that he did so. Understandably he was cautious in throwing too many flowers to the dictators, for he did not want to undergo again the ostracism he had known during World War I. As Rothenstein remarked, Shaw's admiration for dictators was more freely expressed in conversation than in writing (*Summer's Lease*, p. 72). Ap-

parently Shaw learned nothing in 1927 from Salvemini, for in 1933 we find him writing to Lady Astor, "All these anti-Mussolinians are idiots" (in Hesketh Pearson, *Bernard Shaw: His Life and Personality* [New York, 1963], p. 381).

39 the greatest man alive: Pearson, *Shaw: Life and Personality*, p. 458.

39 "a good Fabian": *Ibid.*

39 He took credit for many Soviet policies: Paul Hummert, *Bernard Shaw's Marxian Romance* (Lincoln, Neb., 1973), p. 167.

39 "I do not want the catastrophe": Laurence, ed., *Platform and Pulpit*, p. 257.

39 championing Russia's attack on Finland: *New York Times*, Dec. 2, 1939, p. 4.

39 "there are no democracies": Chappelow, p. 322.

39 "the freest civilized people": *Ibid.*, p. 213.

39 "the only country in the world": Pearson, *Shaw: Life and Personality*, p. 458.

39 "men are so constituted": Chappelow, p. 314.

40 "the dictatorship of the proletariat": *Ibid.*, p. 308.

40 "the ignorant, the incompetent": *Ibid.*, p. 310.

40 "elect and remove their lawgivers": *Ibid.*, p. 337. In 1918 he had known what liberty was: "Liberty is the right to think and choose for oneself" (*ibid.*, p. 343).

40 gratified by dictatorships: To George Orwell, so far as I can determine, belongs the credit for first perceiving the secret appeal that dictatorships had for Shaw. In the 1944 piece entitled "Raffles and Miss Blandish," appearing in *Horizon*, he remarked: "I believe no one has ever pointed out the sadistic element in Bernard Shaw's work, still less suggested that this probably has some connection with Shaw's admiration of dictators" (reprinted in Sonia Orwell and Ian Angus, eds., *The Collected Essays, Journalism and Letters of George Orwell*, III [London, 1968], p. 222). Orwell's courageous insight has proven difficult to assimilate into Shaw scholarship. Even Allan Chappelow, writing a quarter of a century after Orwell's comment, and patiently assembling a great deal of material that bears on the issue, is reluctant to bring the two sets of facts together, that is, Shaw's reverence for dictators and his obsession with liquidation. Chappelow boldly recognizes the latter to be "an important and central quirk in Shaw's character" (p. 403), but he entirely insulates it from Shaw's political views, talking elsewhere of Shaw's "fundamental concern for mankind" (p. 412), of his "fundamentally religious and indeed mystical nature" (p. 343), and deeming it significant that Shaw wanted all the liquidation to be done "in a gentlemanly way" (p. 403). Nor does Chappelow make any further mention of the "central quirk" in his long *Times Literary Supplement* letter on Shaw's politics of Apr. 23, 1971. I believe that the only other scholar to sense the importance of the destructive element in Shaw's work has been Lawrence C. Keough, whose short but acute essay in *The Shavian*, vol. 3, no. 6 (Winter 1966–67), pp. 12–17, entitled "The Theme of Violence in Shaw," nevertheless limits itself to a few of the plays and says nothing of the politics.

40 Hitler should have given him credit: Chappelow, p. 403.

40 idea of liquidation: Hummert, *Shaw's Marxian Romance*, p. 168.
40 sympathized with Stalin's extermination: Chappelow, p. 403.
41 "I would like to take everyone": Patch, *Thirty Years*, pp. 168–69.
41 "ruthlessly exterminating the poor": Chappelow, p. 323.
41 Russia's "ultra-democratic system": Shaw, *Everybody's Political What's What?*, p. 35.
41 "who want to be free": Chappelow, p. 201.
41 "what the Russians can do": Hummert, *Shaw's Marxian Romance*, p. 202.
41 "a great part of the secret": *Ibid.*, p. 169. Shaw's attitude toward the Soviet Union has been examined in Hummert's book and in Katherine L. Auchincloss's article "Shaw and the Commissars: The Lenin Years, 1917–1924," *The Shaw Review*, vol. 6, no. 2 (1963), pp. 51–59. Both are factually informative but veer toward facile and flattering pro-Shavian explanations for his conversion from Fabianism to Communism. Despite Auchincloss's contentions to the contrary, there is evidence that Shaw's conversion came very early after the Russian Revolution and that he remained dedicated to the Russian cause throughout the rest of his life.
42 "a Totalitarian Democrat": Chappelow, p. 322. Shaw does not have in mind J. L. Talmon's later usage of the term in *The Origins of Totalitarian Democracy* (New York, 1960), for Talmon's "totalitarians" affirm the supreme value of liberty.
42 would be done "scientifically": Preface to *On the Rocks*, p. 357.
42 "put on a scientific basis": *Ibid.*, p. 353.
42 "an up-to-date Vision of Judgment": Preface to *The Simpleton*, p. 642.
42 "the special inquisitionary work": *Ibid.*, p. 641.
42 "people were public spirited enough": *Ibid.*, p. 639.
42 "The planners of the Soviet State": Preface to *On the Rocks*, p. 363.
43 "the notion that persons": *Ibid.*, p. 360.
43 "But the most elaborate": *Ibid.*, p. 361.
43 "It may be quite impossible": *Ibid.*, p. 362.
43 "Note, however, that a sentence": *Ibid.*
43 "the practice of extermination thereupon disappear": *Ibid.*, p. 357.
43 "might continue much more openly": *Ibid.*
43 "become a humane science": *Ibid.*, p. 362. The critic Katherine Gatch adopted the convenient defense against this preface of denying that Shaw meant what he said. For her it is an ironic essay in the manner of Swift's *Modest Proposal;* Shaw shows only "seeming approval of cold-blooded Russian methods," for he "could not, like the rigid Hegelian or Marxist, countenance cruelty" ("Last Plays," in Wimsatt, ed., *Stage Comedy*, p. 174). Although few would go that far in denial today, the impulse to block out or ignore or isolate this strain in Shaw continues to bedevil the intellectual honesty of Shaw criticism.
44 "unfortunate Commissar": *Ibid.*, p. 361.
44 "gentle Djerjinsky": Preface to *The Simpleton*, p. 639. The photograph of Djerjinsky stands next to one of Gandhi!
44 "It is true": Preface to *On the Rocks*, pp. 365–66.
44 "free to say and write": *Ibid.*, p. 368.
45 "Without sedition and blasphemy": *Ibid.*, pp. 375–76.

45 "a salutary severity": *Ibid.*, p. 374.

45 "If it is your will": *Ibid.*, p. 373.

46 "letting life come to you": It is usually assumed that Shaw is satirizing the Young Woman-Mrs. Hyering's "Let life come to you" tag line, but Prola's last speeches—we are here "to wrestle with life as it comes"—are patently elaborations of the same creed.

47 humor of Shaw's prime: Fred Mayne's short volume, *The Wit and Satire of Bernard Shaw* (London, 1967), ably ventures into the realm of Shaw's humor, which, however, still requires a good deal more exploration.

49 as he declared afterward, a "phantasm": Preface to *The Simpleton*, p. 643. He later referred to the four children as "four lovely phantasms." It is equally pointless to take at all seriously (as Paul Hummert apparently does) Shaw's claim toward the end of the play that the four children represent "Love, Pride, Heroism and Empire" (II, p. 1244). Apart perhaps from Maya as the representative of love, the actual characterization of the others hardly rises to symbolic distinctness. Hummert's view can be found in "Bernard Shaw's Marxist Utopias," *The Shaw Review*, vol. 2, no. 9 (1959), p. 20.

49 "I feel apologetic for my existence": Campbell Letters, p. 346.

49 "people with any tenderness of conscience": Preface to *On the Rocks*, p. 377.

50 "Greet the unseen with a cheer!": "Epilogue to Asolando."

3: AN UNSOCIAL SOCIALIST

Critical study of the novels has made good beginnings though much yet remains to be done. The major articles are Claude T. Bissell, "The Novels of Bernard Shaw," *University of Toronto Quarterly*, 17 (1947): 38–51; Stanley Weintraub, "The Embryo Playwright in Bernard Shaw's Early Novels," *University of Texas Studies in Literature and Language*, 1 (1959): 327–55; and Robert Hogan, "The Novels of Bernard Shaw," *English Literature in Transition*, 8 (1965): 63–114. Of the two book-length studies, R. F. Dietrich's *Portrait of the Artist as a Young Superman* (Gainesville, Fla., 1969) is superior to E. Nageswara Rao's *Shaw the Novelist: A Critical Study of Shaw's Narrative Fiction* (Masulipatam, 1959). Comments on the novels are particularly helpful in the following books: Alick West, *George Bernard Shaw: "A Good Man Fallen Among Fabians"* (New York, 1950); Homer E. Woodbridge, *G. B. Shaw: Creative Artist* (Carbondale, Ill., 1963); Morgan, *Shavian Playground*; Adams, *Shaw and the Aesthetes.*

55 originally called "The Heartless Man": Rattray, p. 45.

55 "depicting capitalist society in dissolution": *An Unsocial Socialist*, Standard Edition (London, 1932), foreword, p. v.

55 "the poor gets poorer": *Ibid.*, p. 90.

57 "that grand public rejection": "Introductory Note," Dan H. Laurence, ed., *Selected Non-Dramatic Writings of Bernard Shaw* (New York, 1965), p. ix.

57 his "selfish nature": *Unsocial Socialist*, p. 11.

57 "natural affection": *Ibid.*
57 "the curiosity of the vivisector": *Ibid.*, p. 167.
57 "With my egotism, my charlatanry": *Ibid.*, p. 104.
58 "Death seemed to have cancelled": *Ibid.*, pp. 127–29.
59 "Jansenius can bear death": *Ibid.*, p. 125.
59 "their feelings for the living": *Ibid.* I do not share Alfred Turco's opinion that Shaw is ridiculing Trefusis for his behavior toward Hetty's parents (*Shaw's Moral Vision* [Ithaca, N.Y., 1976], p. 64).
59 "socialism is often misunderstood": *Unsocial Socialist*, p. 79.
59 he intends to "harrow" the feelings: *Ibid.*, p. 205.
59 he regards the poor as slaves: *Ibid.*, p. 149.
60 "an international association of creatures": *Ibid.*, p. 96.
60 "is not to be despised": *Ibid.*, p. 249.
60 "the poor man who loves you": *Ibid.*, p. 252.
61 "a genial partner": *Ibid.*, p. 248.
61 "a consoling dash of romance": *Ibid.*
61 "I amuse myself": *Ibid.*, p. 114.
61 "love is an overrated passion": *Ibid.*, p. 249.
61 "The first condition of work": *Ibid.*, p. 77.
61 "only a pleasant sort of trifling": *Ibid.*, p. 239.
61 his "natural amativeness": *Ibid.*, p. 201.
61 "A glance at my lost Hetty": *Ibid.*
61 "was not made for domestic bliss": *Ibid.*, p. 102.
62 most rapidly composed of Shaw's novels: The manuscript, in shorthand, bears the date 9.7.82 at the top of the opening page and 4.11.83 as the date of completion (Brit. Mus. Add. MS. 50656).
62 "Forgive me": Collected Letters, I, p. 64.
62 "May I ask": *Ibid.*, p. 65.
62 "That is right": *Ibid.*, p. 67.
63 "Am I a dancing bear": *Ibid.*, p. 72.
63 "I will be your slave": *Ibid.*, p. 70.
63 "I am sorry": *Ibid.*, p. 68.
63 "You are dancing through my head": *Ibid.*, p. 73.
64 "Let Miss Lockett beware": *Ibid.*, pp. 65–67.
64 "The expanse of stars": *Unsocial Socialist*, pp. 191–92.
65 her "dual identity": Collected Letters, I, p. 72.
66 "to express her feelings": *Unsocial Socialist*, p. 155.
66 "hopeless discontent was her normal state": *Ibid.*, p. 172.
66 "cold, mistrustful, cruel": *Ibid.*, p. 178.
66 "contemptuous by nature": *Ibid.*, p. 27.
66 "too proper to be pleasant": *Ibid.*, p. 184.
66 "plumed herself on her condescension": *Ibid.*, p. 81.
66 "was resolved to die": *Ibid.*, p. 154.
66 a portrait etched in acid, a revenge: It has, I believe, escaped notice that Shaw probably also used Alice Lockett as a model for Alice Goff in his preceding novel, *Cashel Byron's Profession* (Shaw met Miss Lockett in 1881 and *Cashel* was begun in Apr. 1882). Alice Goff's sister Janet is a teacher, as was Alice Lockett's sister Jane. Alice Goff is 23, and Alice Lockett was 23 when Shaw met her. Moreover, the fictional

Alice distinctly resembles Gertrude Lindsay, who was admittedly based on Miss Lockett. As the young novelist describes her, Alice Goff is tyrannical toward men, rigidly proper and supercilious, stiffly self-conscious and snobbish, haughty and disdainful. A milder version of Gertrude Lindsay, Alice Goff is instructed in true breeding by her employer Lydia Carew; and one can easily fancy Shaw using Lydia—whom Stanley Weintraub once termed a petticoated projection of the author—to correct faults in Alice Lockett's behavior. It is not known whether Miss Lockett ever had the benefit of Shaw's earlier portrait of her while their stormy romance was in progress. She would have had to have seen the manuscript itself since the story was not published until its serialized version in 1885. And, to carry the speculation one step further, Shaw may even have put her in another book because she had not been able to see herself in the earlier one.

66 "she counted the proposals": *Unsocial Socialist*, p. 189.
66 "encouraged him with more kindness": *Ibid.*, p. 172.
66 conscious "of her murderous impulse": *Ibid.*, p. 110.
66 "I don't care": *Ibid.*
67 "that wishes for the destruction": *Ibid.*, p. 96.
67 "a sound thrashing": *Ibid.*, p. 185.
67 "an occasional slapping": *Ibid.*, p. 186.
67 "get a big stick": *Ibid.*, pp. 184–85.
67 "quickness of wit": *Ibid.*, p. 240.
68 her "flippancy": *Ibid.*, p. 48.
68 "half cajoling, half mocking air": *Ibid.*, p. 3.
68 her spirit of "insubordination": *Ibid.*, p. 48.
68 "as serious and friendly": *Ibid.*, p. 84.
68 "I am selfish": *Ibid.*, p. 106.
68 "We are too cautious": Collected Letters, I, p. 76.
68 a woman he never addressed: Preface to *Immaturity*, p. 678.
68 projections of his own character: Even upon Alice Lockett, Shaw may have been projecting the idea of a duality of self, if not his own exact traits. In the very letter to her which first describes her double self (Sept. 11, 1883), he acknowledges his own doubleness: "Have I not also a dual self—an enemy within my gates—an egotistical George Shaw upon whose neck I have to keep a grinding foot—a first cousin of Miss Lockett!" (Collected Letters, I, p. 66). See also the letter of Aug. 19, 1886, where he admits to Alice that he has often told women of their two selves, and adds that the reason he knows so much about her and everybody else "is that at least ninetenths of me is a simple repetition of ninetenths of you" (*ibid.*, p. 158).
68 "much nearer akin than her own": *Unsocial Socialist*, p. 240.
69 "Erskine is a poor man": *Ibid.*, pp. 249–51.
70 he tells Gertrude to "sacrifice" herself: *Ibid.*, p. 252.
70 "you sometimes have to answer": *Ibid.*, p. 253.
70 "a very nice fellow indeed": *Ibid.*, p. 244.
70 "realized her conception": *Ibid.*
70 "and therefore a pronounced ass": *Ibid.*
71 Shaw wrote little poems to Alice: Collected Letters, I, pp. 62–63.

72 "When all the love has gone": *Ibid.*, p. 143.

73 Marxism is a quasi-religious ideology: "The Marxist Church," preface to *Farfetched Fables* (London, 1950), p. 77.

73 "made a man of me": Rattray, p. 43.

74 "drivelling sentimentality": *Unsocial Socialist*, p. 91.

74 he violates canons of sentiment: Weintraub, ed., *Autobiography*, I, p. 108.

74 even socialism itself: It is invariably assumed (as for example by Hummert or Rao) that Shaw was merely paraphrasing Marx in the novel's lectures. But in chapter 15, behind the joking about the exchange value of Donovan Brown's painting, one may detect that uneasiness with the surplus value theory which was soon to issue in Shaw's conversion to Wicksteed's and Jevon's views. See R. W. Ellis, ed., *Bernard Shaw & Karl Marx: A Symposium, 1884–1889* (New York, 1930), especially pp. 123*ff.*

74 Agatha threatens to kill Gertrude: *Unsocial Socialist*, p. 6.

75 *The Doctor's Dilemma*: I hope to present the argument for this claim in a subsequent volume.

4: CANDIDA

The most important articles on the play are Walter N. King, "The Rhetoric of *Candida*," *Modern Drama*, 2 (1959): 71–83; Elsie B. Adams, "Bernard Shaw's Pre-Raphaelite Drama," *PMLA*, 81 (1966): 428–38; and Betsy C. Yarrison, "Marchbanks as 'albatros': an interpretation of *Candida*," *The Shaw Review*, vol. 20, no. 2 (1977), pp. 71–82. In the books on Shaw, A. H. Nethercot's section on the play in *Men and Supermen* (Cambridge, Mass., 1954), pp. 7–17, has a firm thesis and argues it well; Crompton's chapter is especially useful on the play's background; and Valency's chapter (pp. 118–35) suggestively touches on most of the central issues.

79 "at this late date": Joseph Wood Krutch, "A Review of *Candida*," *The Nation*, CLXII (Apr. 20, 1946), p. 487, reprinted in Stanton, ed., *Casebook on Candida*, p. 213.

79 Marchbanks is the author's favorite: For example, Eric Bentley in *The Playwright as Thinker* (New York, 1946), p. 166; and Valency, p. 123.

79 competent and emotionally mature woman: William Irvine, *The Universe of G.B.S.* (New York, 1949), pp. 175–77; G. K. Chesterton, *George Bernard Shaw*, Dramabook Reprint (New York, 1965), p. 92.

79 a cruel and domineering philistine: See Edmund Fuller, *George Bernard Shaw: Critic of Western Morale* (New York, 1950), p. 27, reprinted in Stanton, ed., *Casebook on Candida*, p. 225; and Paul Lauter, "'Candida' and 'Pygmalion': Shaw's Subversion of Stereotypes," *The Shaw Review*, vol. 3, no. 3 (1960), p. 18, reprinted *ibid.*, p. 272. Nethercot analyzes her as a philistine in *Men and Supermen*, pp. 14–17. He is following Shaw's division in *The Quintessence of Ibsenism* of philistine, idealist, and realist attitudes to marriage. But Shaw was not, I feel, writing this play to sustain a critical formula devised to discuss

Ibsen, and to call Marchbanks "the realist," when he is clearly an "idealist" about marriage, weakens the position fatally.

79 the *Hamlet* of Shaw criticism: Nethercot, *Men and Supermen*, p. 8.

79 subtitled the work "A Mystery": The subtitle in the British Museum manuscript of the play reads simply "A Domestic Play" (Brit. Mus. Add. MS. 50603A).

79 "a counterblast to Ibsen's *Doll's House*": Raymond Mander and Joe Mitchenson, *Theatrical Companion to Shaw* (London, 1954), p. 43.

79 *The Wild Duck* and *The Lady from the Sea*: On *Candida* and *The Wild Duck*, see Jacob H. Adler, "Ibsen, Shaw and *Candida*," *Journal of English and Germanic Philology*, 59 (1960): 50–58, reprinted in Stanton, ed., *Casebook on Candida*, pp. 258–67. Henderson suggests the parallel (of the "auction scene") to *The Lady from the Sea* (*Shaw: Man of the Century*, p. 543, reprinted *ibid.*, p. 239).

80 "the whole truth": *Collected Letters*, II, p. 415.

83 actual touching: *Heartbreak House* runs a close second.

84 "I demand respect": "A Dramatic Realist to His Critics," *The New Review*, XI (July 1894), reprinted in E. J. West, ed., *Shaw on Theatre* (New York, 1958), pp. 38–39.

84 to follow Shaw's usage, simply "realists": This is the term he uses in *The Quintessence of Ibsenism*. It has of course caused much difficulty since it seems opposed to "idealist." Shaw's "realist" may best be thought of as a practical idealist—like Caesar.

85 "that the affections of their friends": "A Dramatic Realist to His Critics," in West, ed., *Shaw on Theatre*, p. 39.

86 he found himself being praised: See reviews by William Archer and A. B. Walkley in Evans, pp. 61–68. Walkley, in differentiating between Gilbert and Shaw, seems to have had the benefit of Shaw's own formulation of that difference. He may have been shown Shaw's letter to Archer of Apr. 23, 1894 (Collected Letters, I, pp. 425–28), before writing his Apr. 28 review, for his argument clearly resembles Shaw's own.

86 "I had the curious experience": Collected Letters, I, p. 462.

87 "My dear fellow": *Ibid.*, p. 433.

87 "the old categories of good and evil": *Ibid.*, p. 427.

87 "as a monstrously clever sparkler": *Ibid.*, p. 462.

87 "The stage world": "A Dramatic Realist to His Critics," in West, ed., *Shaw on Theatre*, p. 20.

87 "I created nothing": *Ibid.*, p. 38.

87 "no class is more idiotically confident": *Ibid.*, p. 20.

87 conversations with a couple of Slavs: Stepniak and Screbriakov. For Shaw's amusing comments on the Bulgarian locale as an afterthought, see his "Interview" in *The Pall Mall Budget*, Apr. 19, 1894, reprinted in *Arms and the Man*, ed. Louis Crompton (New York, 1969), pp. 77–80.

88 Bulgarians back from residence in England: See, for example, the conversation in Act II where Petkoff hurries down the steps to welcome Bluntschli.

88 *The Land of Heart's Desire*: Yeats's play had originally opened with John Todhunter's *A Comedy of Sighs*, but the adverse critical reaction to the latter compelled the manager Florence Farr to ask Shaw to sub-

stitute a play of his own for Todhunter's. He complied by putting the finishing touches to *Arms and the Man*, and it went into rehearsal shortly thereafter. Yeats's account of the opening is given in his *Autobiographies* (London, 1955), pp. 280–81.

88 shared a wary mutual respect: Yeats met Shaw in 1888 at William Morris's house and wrote to a friend that Shaw was "certainly very witty. But like most people who had wit rather than humour, his mind is maybe somewhat wanting in depth" (Allan Wade, ed., *The Letters of W. B. Yeats* [New York, 1955], p. 59).

88 productions beyond the makeshift ones: *Mrs. Warren's Profession* ran into licensing troubles and was not seen in any form until 1902.

88 "art is art": Yeats, *Autobiographies*, p. 279.

89 "the ugly thing": Russell K. Alspach, ed., *The Variorum Edition of The Plays of W. B. Yeats* (London, 1966), p. 198. All other references to Yeats's plays are from this edition.

89 "ride the winds": *Ibid.*, p. 208.

89 "moves out of a red flare": *Ibid.*, p. 185.

89 actors' occasional mismanagement of their lines: Collected Letters, I, p. 435; Yeats, *Autobiographies*, pp. 282–83.

89 "I listened to *Arms and the Man*": Yeats, *Autobiographies*, p. 283.

90 Florence Farr: Yeats says in the *Autobiographies* that he often walked homeward with Florence Farr and talked of Shaw (pp. 283–84). Shaw and Florence Farr had been having an affair since 1891. That Shaw apparently accepted the essential image is seen in his occasional rueful reference to himself as a mere "writing machine" (Terry Letters, p. 232).

90 his opinion of *Land of Heart's Desire*: Late in life, in an introductory note for the 1942 edition of Florence Farr's letters to himself and Yeats, Shaw remarked that *Arms and the Man* had been first shown with Yeats's play serving "as an exquisite curtain raiser" (Clifford Bax, ed., *Letters of Florence Farr, Bernard Shaw, W. B. Yeats* [New York, 1942], p. xi). I do not believe that we can take this gracious remark, made so soon after Yeats's death by a fellow Nobel Laureate, as indicative of Shaw's view of the play nearly fifty years earlier. Back in 1898, in the preface to *Plays Unpleasant*, Shaw, without commenting directly on Yeats's play, called him "a genuine discovery" among the "New Dramatists" (p. 728).

90 the latter is often parodied: Louis Crompton was the first to suggest that in *Candida* Shaw "was presumably reacting to Yeats's play, and indeed, using it as a point of departure" (p. 30). Although Yeats is mentioned in other parts of Crompton's discussion, I am not sure if this critic would agree that Yeats served in any respect for the portrait of Marchbanks.

91 "the ruler of the Western Host": Yeats, *Land of Heart's Desire*, p. 205.

91 "bear children": *Ibid.*, p. 206.

91 mimicking Yeats's description of fairyland: It may be significant that Yeats used the word "shallop" only once, in his early unproduced playlet *Mosada*, written in 1884 and published in *The Dublin University Review*, June 1886. It is possible that he showed the play to Shaw,

who may have picked up the word as characteristic of the young poet's early style. When we read the "shallop" passage from *Mosada*, we can see how well Shaw was imitating Yeats's current idiom, even if he had not been shown the actual play. The monk Ebremar says to the lady Mosada: "We'll fly from this before the morning star. / Dear heart, there is a secret way that leads / Its paven length towards the river's marge / Where lies a shallop in the yellow reeds. / Awake, awake, and we will sail afar / Afar along the fleet white river's face— / Alone with our own whispers and replies— / Alone among the murmurs of the dawn" (p. 1276). Shelley also used the word "shallop" only once, in "Alastor," at the beginning of the Poet's famous voyage: "A little shallop floating near the shore / Caught the impatient wandering of his gaze" (ll. 299–300).

92 miracle plays: Richard Ellman, *Yeats: The Man and the Mask* (New York, 1958), p. 128.

92 Desmond MacCarthy. *Shaw: The Plays* (Newton Abbot, Eng., 1973), p. 25.

92 Proserpine Garnett and Lexy Mill: Proserpine's name may have been vaguely suggested by the supernatural elements in Yeats's play. In any case Shaw doubtless wanted an audience to savor the irony of that little secretary devoted to her clerical boss flaunting the magnificent name of the pagan queen of the underworld, and competing futilely against the "Virgin Mother" Candida. With the Rev. Alexander Mill's name, the irony again juxtaposes the secular with the religious, since the most celebrated bearers of that surname in 19th-century England were the utilitarians James and his son John Stuart. For further speculations on the names, see Morgan, *Shavian Playground*, pp. 78–79; and James Mavor Moore, "Why 'James Mavor' Morell?" *The Shaw Review*, vol. 23, no. 2 (1980), pp. 48–51.

93 a touch of early De Quincey: Shaw said that "when I began writing the part of the young poet, I had in mind De Quincey's account of his adolescence in his *Confessions*" (Mander and Mitchenson, *Theatrical Companion*, p. 43). Barbara Peart argues well for the validity of Shaw's claim in "De Quincey and Marchbanks," *The Shaw Review*, vol. 17, no. 3 (1974), pp. 139–40. It further substantiates her position to record that in the first draft, under "Persons in the Play," Shaw lists "Eugene Marjoribanks" and then adds "Marchbanks" in a parenthesis (Brit. Mus. Add. MS. 50603A, f. 1). De Quincey in the *Autobiography, 1785–1803* discusses the merging of the pronunciation of the two names (*Works* [Edinburgh, 1863], XIV, p. 129n). For a full review of Marchbanks's prototypes, see Arthur Nethercot, "Who *Was* Eugene Marchbanks?", *The Shaw Review*, vol. 15, no. 1 (1972), pp. 2–20.

93 a view Shaw had publicly corrected: In "Shaming the Devil about Shelley," *The Albermarle Review*, Sept. 1892, reprinted in *Pen Portraits and Reviews* (London, 1932), pp. 236–46.

93 several touches of early Yeats: Colin Wilson sees Marchbanks as drawn entirely from W. B. Yeats, but I do not think Shaw would have wanted to be that direct—or insulting (*Bernard Shaw* [New York, 1969], p. 138).

93 "the sole refiner of human nature": *Unsocial Socialist*, p. 165.

93 Shaw's own actual overpayment: Rattray, pp. 102–3.
93 haunting of the Embankment: Pearson, *Shaw: Life and Personality*, pp. 56–57.
93 a mockingly exaggerated version: Rattray says that in creating Marchbanks "Shaw drew upon his own nature and youth" (p. 102), but does not at all regard that treatment as satiric.
94 "distil the quintessential drama": Preface to *Plays Pleasant*, p. 729.
94 "In my 'Land of Heart's Desire'": Quoted in Ellman, *Yeats*, p. 181.
94 "spirits of evil": Yeats, *Land of Heart's Desire*, p. 210.
97 contemporary Christian Socialist ministers: Mander and Mitchenson, *Theatrical Companion*, p. 43. Crompton sees Morell as representative of the Anglo-Catholic Socialists who manned the Church of England slum parishes and were ardent sacramentalists who "made much of the cult of the Virgin" (pp. 31–32). I cannot see any of the ardent sacramentalism in Morell, and it was Marchbanks rather than Morell who gave Candida the print of Titian's Assumption of the Virgin.
97 "readiness to boss people spiritually": Collected Letters, I, p. 611.
97 "certainty that his own idea": *Ibid.*
97 "facile, cheery": *Ibid.*
97 he did not throw himself: Preface to *The Irrational Knot*, p. 687.
97 guilt over this still continuing dependency: See also the letter to Ellen Terry of Nov. 4, 1896, Terry Letters, p. 107.
97 his Fabian lecturing: "What troubled me most was that my Socialist lectures were mostly received like Christian sermons except that there was loud applause instead of reverent silence. I preached every Sunday for twelve years; and every Monday my crowded and enthusiastic audiences went back to their capitalistic routine as if I had merely played the organ to them" ("Fabian Successes and Failures," Brit. Mus. Add. MS. 50689, f. 196). See also Weintraub, ed., *Autobiography*, II, p. 179.
101 "repudiate duty altogether": *Quintessence of Ibsenism*, in Laurence, ed., *Selected Non-Dramatic Writings*, p. 230.
101 "[Candida] is straight for natural reasons": Letter to James Huneker, Apr. 6, 1904, Collected Letters, II, p. 415. Eric Bentley surely misstates the matter when he says that Shaw "attacked" Candida in this letter, and when he says that "outside the play, Shaw is against Candida" (foreword to his Signet edition of *Plays by Bernard Shaw* [New York, 1960], p. xxii). Nor am I able to see the pattern of increasing disparagement over the years that Charles Berst discerns in Shaw's remarks on Candida (*Bernard Shaw and The Art of Drama* [Urbana, Ill., 1973], pp. 40–41). Shaw was partly reacting against the excesses of what he termed the Candidamaniacs, and was also undervaluing an earlier acclaimed piece, as writers usually do to protect their more recent and their future works. Now that he was married to a kind of mother figure, he may also have been less fervent toward maternal types. Withal, the letter to Huneker contains far more praise than criticism of Candida.
101 "a very immoral female": Letter to Huneker, Collected Letters, II, p. 415.
101 "I have written THE Mother Play": Terry Letters, p. 34.
101 Candida "is the Virgin Mother": *Ibid.*, p. 26. That description was

used in the British Museum manuscript of the play as well. Under "Persons in the Play," Candida was described as "thirty three. A beautiful woman, with the double charm of youth and maturity. A true Virgin Mother" (Brit. Mus. Add. MS. 50603A, f. 2).

103 Candida's actual children: Traces of Shaw's initial uncertainty over whether Candida had any children remain even in the present text, where in Act III Marchbanks says that she wants "somebody to give her children to protect, to help and to work for." Only when he resolved the matter of her offspring could Shaw add the clever touch of Morell sitting in a child's chair in Act III; in the early manuscript version it is called merely an ordinary chair (Brit. Mus. Add. MS. 50603C, f. 45). References to the children were first added in 1897—three years after the completion of the first draft—while the play was in rehearsal (Bodleian MS. Don d. 161).

103 "The secret is very obvious": In George A. Riding, "The 'Candida' Secret," *The Spectator*, Nov. 17, 1950, reprinted in Stanton, ed., *Casebook on Candida*, pp. 168–69.

104 archetypical pattern of human development: Robert Whitman's account of Marchbanks's growth in *Shaw and the Play of Ideas* (Ithaca, N.Y., 1977), pp. 196–201, is admirably attentive to its complexities.

104 *Candida* and the Ibsen plays: Ellida is of course younger than her doctor husband in *The Lady from the Sea*, but her former lover is not a young man and is about her own age.

107 "Man can climb to the highest summits": Interestingly, in the original draft Shaw allowed Marchbanks a humbler reply:

MORELL: Man can climb to the highest summits; but he cannot dwell there long.

MARCHBANKS [*thoughtfully—with a sort of terror*]: So you can say things that strike home, after all. Perhaps it *is* possible for a woman to love you. The moments on the highest summits are only moments, then, after all. What is their price?

MORELL: Their price is a thousand moments [cancelled: moralizing and preaching to people who are not poets] in the scullery, slicing onions and filling lamps (Brit. Mus. Add. MS. 50603C, fs. 16–17)

108 The castrating instrument: Marchbanks is of course citing scripture to Morell—"a flaming sword which turned every way, to keep the way of the tree of life" (Gen. 3:24). That the young man identifies Candida with the tree of life as well as the angel supports the incestuous implications I have been emphasizing.

110 "Everyone is quoting Stevenson's dictum": Collected Letters, I, p. 472. Bentley also interprets Eugene's rejection of happiness to mean that he will learn to live "without women" (*Playwright as Thinker*, p. 167).

110 small triumph of having a secret: In the first draft Shaw did not include that line over which so much ink has subsequently been spilt: "But they do not know the secret in the poet's heart." The phrase preceding it, "They embrace," is the final one (Brit. Mus. Add. MS. 50603C, f. 53). The added, mystifying line is actually contradicted by Candida's perceptive remark that "he has learned to live without happiness"—though it is doubtful if she or even Shaw himself recognized

the completeness of the sexual renunciation involved. Shaw became aware of the inaccuracy of his final line, for in the famous letter to Huneker he says that Candida's line shows that "she has a little quaint intuition of the completeness of his cure" (Collected Letters, II, p. 415). "Quaint" or not, what Candida said remained the substance of what Shaw himself said whenever he disclosed the supposed secret.

111 Beatrice Webb: Terry Letters, p. 232.

113 a profit of £341: Collected Letters, I, p. 447.

114 the growth of a latent tendency: MacCarthy also sees *Candida* as marking a shift in the author's outlook (*Shaw*, p. 25). Though this critic's way of phrasing the matter is different from mine, our sense of Shaw's change is much the same.

114 "What business has a man": Stanton, ed., *Casebook on Candida*, p. 169.

5: MAN AND SUPERMAN

The most significant articles on the play are Frederick P. W. McDowell, "Heaven, Hell, and turn-of-the-century London: Reflections upon Shaw's *Man and Superman*," *Drama Survey*, 2 (1963): 245–67; Julian L. Stamm, "Shaw's Man and Superman: His Struggle for Sublimation," *American Imago*, 22 (1965): 250–54; and A. M. Gibbs, "Comedy and Philosophy in *Man and Superman*," *Modern Drama*, 19 (1976): 161–75. Of the books on Shaw, William Irvine's *The Universe of G.B.S.* and J. L. Wisenthal's *Marriage of Contraries* contain the best discussion of the play. But A. W. England's commentary, *Man and Superman*, Blackwell's Notes on English Literature Series (Oxford, 1968), remains the most balanced analysis that the work has yet received.

119 Maurice Valency: *Cart and the Trumpet*, pp. 200–236.

119 Louis Crompton: *Shaw the Dramatist*, chap. 6.

120 Mozart's *Don Giovanni*: On *Don Giovanni* and *Man and Superman*, see Gibbs's article, "Comedy and Philosophy," *Modern Drama*, 19 (1976): 170, 173; and Eileen Dombrowski's "Shaw's Mozartian Ana: *Don Giovanni* and *Man and Superman*," *The Shavian*, vol. 5, no. 2 (1975), pp. 15–21. The most important discussion is Charles Loyd Holt's "Mozart, Shaw and *Man and Superman*," *The Shaw Review*, vol. 9, no. 3 (1966), pp. 102–16. On Shaw and Mozart more generally, see E. J. West's "Disciple and Master: Shaw and Mozart," *The Shavian*, vol. 2, no. 3 (1961), pp. 16–23.

120 Don Juan's story: An interesting side issue concerns the degree to which Shaw's hero can properly lay claim to the name of Don Juan or be at all regarded as his legitimate descendant. Shaw himself struggled with the issue in the Epistle Dedicatory but (as I show in the Appendix) without resolving it. One student of the Don Juan legend, noting that Shaw's Don Juan is no longer a libertine but a moralist, concludes that the change from Tirso de Molina's 17th-century hero to Shaw's involves the "most strange and complete transformation that any character of the stage has ever undergone" (John Austen, *The Story of Don Juan* [London, 1959], p. 200). A later student of the legend, Leo Wein-

stein, agrees that with Shaw "the extreme reversal of Tirso's Burlader was accomplished. . . . when [Juan] runs away from a woman he has not possessed, he has lost his *raison d'être*—he has become the anti-Don Juan" (*The Metamorphoses of Don Juan* [Stanford, 1959], p. 153). Another scholar, Oscar Mandel, similarly concludes that Shaw's play "has really nothing of the Tenorio legend *in its action*" (*The Theatre of Don Juan* [Lincoln, Neb., 1963], p. 548). The most thoroughgoing critique of Shaw's handling of the figure is by Robert J. Blanch, "The Myth of Don Juan in *Man and Superman*," *Revue des langues vivantes*, 33 (1967): 158–63. Blanch observes that Juan was originally an exemplar of masculinity, a courageous man with vital sexual urges, a hedonist who enjoyed life. In Shaw's play, however, "the archetypal myth of Don Juan is inverted" (p. 161). The opposing position has been best developed by Carl Henry Mills, "*Man and Superman* and The Don Juan Legend," *Comparative Literature*, 19 (1967): 216–25. Mills maintains that Tirso and Shaw actually were not far apart in their intentions, both condemning amorism and sensuality. Further, by the time Shaw entered the scene, the Don Juan figure had become progressively more bored with amorism "until he rejected it outright, as Faust did. Adoption of a serious philosophy of life was the next and logical step." Thus Shaw "did not transform Don Juan . . . [but] brought him up to date" (p. 224).

My own position in this argument follows two quite distinct lines. First, while a writer can of course give any name whatsoever to his creatures, there is value in having certain human types permanently embodied in mythic figures—a Don Quixote, a Romeo, a Faust, an Oblomov; and stretching the type beyond recognizable limits, as Shaw apparently does, deprives us of Juan's archetypal importance. But secondly, if the analysis developed later in this chapter is persuasive, the dispute I have just sketched out must now move to entirely new ground. Shaw's Don Juan, as I perceive him, is still as obsessed with sex as was his original, but is now forced to disguise that obsession. His nature has not at all been changed, only its opportunities and mode of expression. The issue that now emerges is whether the behavior of Shaw's caged and emasculated Don Juan is psychologically true to type.

120 one of his most tedious plays: Among the play's depreciators, one might cite James Huneker, *Iconoclasts* (New York, 1905), pp. 256–66; Ussher, *Three Great Irishmen*, p. 15; Marvin Mudrick, *On Culture and Literature* (New York, 1970), p. 115. See also reviews by William Archer and Max Beerbohm in Evans, pp. 102–5, 116–19.

120 Act II: Act II falls off considerably, and it was perhaps an impulse to liven it up for the reader that prompted Shaw to add the huge stage description of young Hector Malone.

121 interlude is "totally extraneous": Epistle Dedicatory, *Man and Superman*, Standard Edition, p. xv. See also the preface to *Back to Methuselah*, where he remarks that the interlude was a dramatic parable of Creative Evolution. "I surrounded it with a comedy of which it formed only one act, and that act was so completely episodical (it was a dream which did not affect the action of the piece) that the comedy

could be detached and played at full length owing to the enormous
length of the entire work" (pp. 545–46).

121 his academic defenders: Critics are by no means united in praising
the work without qualification, though the usual academic view is ful-
some. Representative of this latter school is Frederick P. W. McDowell's influential article which vigorously and adroitly defends the
play's unity and philosophy ("Heaven, Hell, and turn-of-the-century
London," *Drama Survey*, 2 [1963]: 245–67). But this scholar, in my
opinion, slides over all the difficult questions we might put to the
work and actually ends up conventionalizing Juan's doctrines. Thus he
finds that Shaw is not really condemning music nor beauty nor patriotism but only their sham forms (pp. 248, 255). What a neutral observer
might regard as contradictions, McDowell regards as the "two directions" in which Juan's philosophy works (p. 258). Thus though the Life
Force is called "irrational in essence," Juan is admired as a philosopher
who will reason out its meaning (pp. 258–59). J. L. Wisenthal, who is
more willing to spot the weaknesses in Juan's position, argues forcefully for the unity of the entire work, including the Epistle Dedicatory
and the "Handbook." His observations are often astute. But he resists
conclusions to which his own reasoning seems to lead him. For instance, he sees that some of Juan's argument is "not entirely convincing," that it is "by no means a refutation of what the devil has just
said," yet he nevertheless concludes that "there can be no doubt that
Juan is the victor" in the debate (*Marriage of Contraries*, pp. 42, 43).
Further, in his quest for the unity of the work, Wisenthal inadvertently
undercuts Juan's supposed victory—his claim that philosophy is vital
in shaping the future—by arguing that "Tanner's qualities of thought
and intelligence are of value" only in Hell, "where the real world no
longer exists" (p. 40). Alfred Turco is another of the rare critics who
grapple directly with the play and bring to it an appetite for subtle-
ties. He is the first to perceive one of the crucial changes in Shaw's
thought as embodied in *Man and Superman*—the shift from the *Quintessence*'s attack on idealism to a celebration of it (*Shaw's Moral Vision*, pp. 156–57). But for all his generous impulse to harmonize
Shaw's contradictions, Turco does not in my opinion succeed. He attempts to distinguish among various kinds of idealism, but he does not
extricate Shaw from the hole that Shaw had himself dug earlier with
his own sharp criticism of all idealisms, for example: "The origin of
ideals [is found] in unhappiness, in dissatisfaction with the real."
Turco quotes this line from the *Quintessence* without bringing it to
bear on Don Juan's and Shaw's current pretensions. Nor does Turco
successfully reconcile what he calls the "antirationalistic stance" of
Man and Superman with Juan's praise for contemplation and the philosophic mind (p. 158).

Among those who accept a degree of disunity in the work, one may
instance Robert Brustein's remark that "the central action does develop some of Shaw's philosophical themes, but in a highly circum-
scribed and limited manner" (*Theatre of Revolt*, p. 217). Bentley says
that "whatever his initial intentions Shaw has given us the lower biological comedy in which we have not an impasse, not two irresistible

forces, but the snapping up of a clever young man by a shrewd young woman" (*Bernard Shaw*, p. 154). A. W. England finds "some lack of coherence between the philosophy expounded by Tanner and the demonstration of this in dramatic terms by Shaw." The dramatic action "does not conveniently fit the formal philosophical scheme" (*Man and Superman*, p. 14). This critic grants (as I do) that there is some continuity between the play and the Hell scene, with "characters from the one being reincarnated in the other, and themes from the one being expanded and developed in the other. But both these factors together are not sufficient in themselves to constitute a unity of action. What we must ask ourselves is whether the Hell scene adds anything to the imaginative scope and depth of the play proper" (p. 58). He finds that the Hell scene, though it enlarges on the topics raised in the play, "fails to add a further dimension to the comedy of manners; nor does it really make us see the love-chase as the operation of universal forces and Tanner's capitulation to Ann as a world-shattering event." Yet finally he perceives a coherence between the two sections by redefining the dramatic theme as "the helplessness of the intellectual in the face of a determined attack by practical instinct. What happens in the dream of Hell is that the talker who fails in the realm where some actions are more effective than words succeeds in the realm where ideas are the weapons. . . . it is perhaps an ironic reflection on the intellectual that having the right ideas ensures victory only in a dream" (p. 58).

This last argument parallels Wisenthal's and is open to the same objection. It assumes that Juan is victorious in the debate. But his "victory" can only mean that the "right ideas" he espouses overcome the Devil's objections to them. Juan's central contention is that the power of thought can help life in its upward struggle. The Devil doubts that this can be done; for him it is not at all a "right" idea. When critics echo the Devil's own doubts by saying that Tanner's qualities of intelligence and his ideas can be of value only in a dream, they are robbing Don Juan of the victory they claim for him. And they are controverting Shaw's avowed intention of celebrating the value of intellect. One wonders whether Shaw would welcome a view that unites the two parts of his play at the cost of demolishing his philosophy!

121 title is misleading: As A. H. Nethercot has remarked, "Shorn of the third act, the title has no meaning" ("The Schizophrenia of Bernard Shaw," *The American Scholar*, 21 [1952]: 463).

122 platform of costumed debaters: That Shaw counted heavily on "cunning costumes" to make the scene endurable is evident in a letter to Florence Farr in Collected Letters, I, p. 590.

122 "a pit of philosophers": Epistle Dedicatory, p. xxvii.

122 the philosopher: The philosopher C. E. M. Joad seems to have left his professional equipment at home when he saw the play, for there is no criticism of this aspect of Shaw's work in Joad's interesting book *Shaw*. But it is also possible that Joad simply heard what he wanted to hear. His own philosophy (as expressed in *Matter, Life and Value* [London, 1929]) was for a time an elaboration of Shaw's own. John G. Demaray, in a penetrating critique, finds that the two men "turned the irrational, instinctive forces of the cosmos to an end which would have

scandalized the nineteenth-century vitalists." Though Shaw and Joad "claimed to be in general agreement with the views of Bergson, Schopenhauer, Nietzsche, and Samuel Butler, the pair used vitalism to reintroduce the Cartesian realm of mind against which the philosophers of the irrational had revolted" ("Bernard Shaw and C. E. M. Joad: The Adventures of Two Puritans in Their Search for God," *PMLA*, 78 [1963]: 263).

123 "The pattern of action": Valency, pp. 211–12.

124 hack playwrights: See, for example, Peter Ustinov's *Who's Who in Hell*, a characteristically trivial comedy with heavy borrowings from Shaw and others.

126 "he collapses like a pricked bladder": This image of "the pricked bladder" seems to be a tolerable displacement by Shaw of the real target of Ann's attack, and the image clearly supports my contention that Shaw is portraying Ann as a castrater.

126 "the marked-down quarry": Roebuck Ramsden's name doubly reinforces this animal imagery. And even Octavius or Ricky, sometimes called "Ricky-ticky-tavy," makes his contribution also, for his name was probably drawn from the mongoose in one of Kipling's *Jungle Books*, "Rikki-tikki-tavvi." But a mongoose can defeat a snake, and ironically, despite himself, it is Ricky in the end who escapes from Ann's coils. See Brian Foster, "A Shavian Allusion," *Notes and Queries*, vol. 8, no. 3 (Mar. 1961), pp. 106–7.

126 "The joke on Tanner": Brustein, *Theatre of Revolt*, p. 219.

128 Ann's putative appeal: Shaw later claimed in the Epistle Dedicatory that Ann had been suggested to him by a performance of *Everyman*: "I said to myself: Why not Everywoman? Ann was the result; every woman is not Ann; but Ann is Everywoman" (p. xxi). Opinions differ widely on whether he achieved his supposed end. Max Beerbohm scoffed at the notion that Ann adequately represented women; he found her merely "a minx" (*Around Theatres* [London, 1953], p. 271). At the other end, she has been applauded as nothing less than "the Mother Goddess" (Daniel J. Leary, "Shaw's Use of Stylized Characters and Speech in *Man and Superman*," *Modern Drama*, 5 [1963]: 478). I agree with Beerbohm.

129 W. S. Gilbert: Meisel, *Shaw and 19th-Century Theater*, p. 178. I am happy to acknowledge a general debt to this excellent study. Strindberg may also have been in the back of Shaw's mind though I think that, if anyone, Gilbert, who was a better-known figure at the time, would have been in the forefront. Shaw knew of some minor Strindberg pieces as early as 1892, and he may have read an English version of *The Father* in that year. (No Strindberg was shown in England until 1906.) But although Shaw was later one of the Swedish writer's most devoted supporters, I believe that *Man and Superman*'s attitude about the sexes draws mostly on Shaw's own earlier work and on his own temperament and experiences. Margery Morgan has made a significant start in tracing the relations between the two men in "Strindberg and the English Theatre," *Modern Drama*, 7 (1964): 161–73. Colin Wilson's contrast between the two dramatists seems to me superficial:

"Strindberg is the necessary antithesis of Shaw. Shaw stands outside his works; he very seldom descends from his mountain top" ("Shaw and Strindberg," *The Shavian*, no. 15 [June 1959], p. 24).

130 "an Irish Don Juan": Collected Letters, I, p. 278.

130 he was called Don Giovanni: Crompton, p. 92.

130 "Don Giovanni Explains": Shaw's story conveniently confirms his early identification with Don Juan. It also bears a few resemblances to the later Hell scene. Both are "framed" visions: the former as a ghost story and the latter as a dream. In both, Don Juan is on good terms with the Commandant. In both, Shaw illustrates the voluntary nature of residency in Hell by the same image of men who prefer the racecourse to the more ennobling concert hall. Also, the two Don Juans are somewhat alike physically and temperamentally, as are to a lesser extent the two Devils.

However, the differences are too critical for us to regard the early story as merely an embryonic version of the Hell scene, as have some commentators. The attack on aestheticism is not in the early story. Neither is the later Don's idealism. Above all, the creed that Shaw said he included in the Hell scene, "the dramatic parable of Creative Evolution" as he would later call it, is totally absent.

Shaw's movement away from the early story, which he probably recollected or consulted when he began to compose the Hell scene, may perhaps account for one of the latter's major inconsistencies: the Devil in both versions at first wants the Don to leave Hell, but then further along Shaw seems to forget this or to change his mind, since he makes the Devil react to Juan's departure gloomily and term it a political defeat.

130 H. M. Hyndman: Crompton, p. 82. Crompton's emphasis on the Tanner-Hyndman resemblance, which Bentley also prefers, seems a little inconsistent with his later (and, I think, correct) identification of Don Juan with Shaw (pp. 92–94). If Tanner is related to Don Juan, and the latter is a version of Shaw, then to some extent so is Tanner as well. R. F. Rattray's opinion that Tanner is a combination of Hyndman and Shaw seems to me a safe compromise (p. 146). For Shaw's opinion of Hyndman, see *Pen Portraits*, pp. 125–41. Since Tanner is given to confessional moments with Ann, it is perhaps pertinent to notice Shaw's comment in 1911 on one of Hyndman's volumes: "This is no book of confessions. Confession is not a Hyndmanesque attitude" (*ibid.*, p. 126).

Shaw's identification with Tanner has probably become too fixed to sever, and it is not at all arbitrary. For instance, Frank Swinnerton declared Tanner to be an "embodiment of his creator's coyness and garrulity" (*The Georgian Literary Scene* [London, 1935], p. 60). A later critic observes that "it is obvious that John Tanner is, even more than usual among Shaw's more talkative heroes, largely Shaw himself" (Alan Reynolds Thompson, *The Dry Mock: A Study of Irony in Drama* [Berkeley and Los Angeles, 1948], p. 105). And Erich Strauss, author of one of the most probing books on Shaw, remarks shrewdly that "we have to accept Tanner as a revolutionist in Shaw's image" because in the play itself the political side of his character, which is supposed to be the most important side, is actually quite rudimentary (*Bernard Shaw: Art and Socialism* [London, 1942], pp. 44–45).

130 "in which the hero revolts": *Self Sketches*, pp. 199–200. And he adds that "Tanner, with all his extravagances, is first hand." Although Shaw may playfully exaggerate in the "How Frank Ought to Have Done It" chapter of *Self Sketches*, there is no reason to doubt the claim of the personal experience behind Tanner's struggle against marriage, especially since Shaw always said that Charlotte had captured him when his poor health made him too weak to escape.

130 "an Irishman's habit": Collected Letters, I, p. 278.

130 memory of their dead father: Janet Dunbar, *Mrs G.B.S.: A Biographical Portrait of Charlotte Shaw* (London, 1963), pp. 26–27, 32, 61, *passim*.

131 Charlotte's handsome eyes: Collected Letters, I, pp. 676, 709, 723, 831.

131 description of his heroine: In the family names White*field* and *Town*shend we may if we wish see a subtle allusion by opposites to the connection yet contrast between the two women. Perhaps Shaw also intended another ironic private message to Charlotte: although Ann Whitefield carries the virginal surname, she most conspicuously differs from Charlotte in her healthy determination to lose her virginity and to become a mother. Shaw's simple technique in *An Unsocial Socialist* of devising a negative surrogate for Alice Lockett in the person of Gertrude Lindsay, and then a contrasting ideal in Agatha Wylie, now achieves greater complexity as he creates a figure with desired as well as criticized qualities.

131 Charlotte's initiative: See, for example, Dunbar, *Mrs G.B.S.*, p. 171; and Patch, *Thirty Years*, p. 240.

131 his mother's house: See "How to Become a Man of Genius," in Laurence, ed., *Selected Non-Dramatic Writings*, p. 344.

131 *The Devil's Disciple*: On Apr. 11, 1898, he reported to Webb that his royalties for that play "are now well into the third thousand" (Collected Letters, II, p. 30). On Apr. 4, he told Charlotte that he had just received £68 from America for four nights of the play's production in St. Louis. "I am supposed, it appears, to be taunting you with my independence. Well, then, I *will* taunt you" (*ibid.*, p. 27). Earlier he had realized £829 from the production of *Arms and the Man*.

131 "I am old and breaking up": *Ibid.*, p. 26.

132 "Wrote article": *Ibid.*, p. 27.

132 "I have no news": *Ibid.*, p. 29.

132 "My troubles all over": *Ibid.*, p. 38.

132 "Yes, I *might* have telegraphed": *Ibid.*

133 "This time we have been joined": *Ibid.*, I, pp. 645–46.

133 "marry my Irish millionairess": *Ibid.*, p. 693.

133 "And must a woman": *Ibid.*, p. 702.

134 "have the nerve to use me": *Ibid.*, p. 700.

134 "unless you deliberately": *Ibid.*, p. 714.

134 "there are two laps": *Ibid.*, p. 691.

134 "Curse this cycling": *Ibid.*, II, p. 27.

134 "Not until I was past forty": *Self Sketches*, pp. 178–79.

134 "singularly unfair to her": R. J. Minney, *Recollections of George Bernard Shaw* (Englewood Cliffs, N.J., 1969), p. 50; Ervine, *Bernard Shaw*, p. 317.

134 "as for Shaw abandoning his philanderings": Minney, *Recollections*, p. 50. C. G. L. DuCann is also skeptical on this point in *The Loves of George Bernard Shaw* (London, 1963), pp. 184–85.

135 "It is almost certain": Ervine, *Bernard Shaw*, p. 316.

135 Shaw "in his old age": *Ibid.*, p. 315.

135 "was a man who delighted": *Ibid.*

135 Charlotte announced her decision: Laurence's statement on the matter, coming after his description of the early months of the marriage, seems to imply that the decision was made subsequent to the marriage: "Charlotte, too, probably had never been more content. Aided by Shaw's fortuitous injuries she had succeeded in obtaining a marital arrangement that entirely excluded sex" (*Collected Letters*, II, p. 4).

135 ambivalence toward sexuality: For example, in *Mrs. Warren's Profession* and *Candida*. Vivie and Eugene, apparently with their creator's approval, turn their backs on any sexual involvements.

135 Charlotte's fortune: In *The Millionairess*, which contains many autobiographical overtones, one of the heroine's admirers says to her: "You are so rich, Epiphania, that every decent man who approaches you feels like a needy adventurer. You dont know how a man to whom a hundred pounds is a considerable sum feels in the arms of a woman to whom a million is mere pin money" (I, p. 1261). See Arnold Silver, "*The Millionairess*: A Confessional Comedy," *The Shavian*, vol. 5, no. 1 (1975), p. 4.

138 a distinctive limp: Rosset, p. 36. There may be further psychoanalytical significance in Shaw's injury. He would later tell the prospective biographer T. D. O'Bolger and then repeat to Frank Harris that one of Lee's legs had been "very much" shortened by an injury sustained after falling off a banister (*Bernard Shaw*, pp. 59–60). Now when Shaw fell over a banister 17 days after his marriage, he further disabled himself and perhaps made it even more reasonable to postpone discussing sexual relations with Charlotte. Through the fall, he succeeded in very much shortening, as it were, his "middle leg," and in that sense lamed himself for the rest of his life, just as Lee had literally lamed himself for life. At any rate, when Shaw in later life talked about Lee's injury he would curiously conjoin it to Lee's sexuality, and thereby he may have been foisting his own experiences on Lee. As Harris writes, of a man he did not know, in a book finally polished by Shaw: "Lee always walked about with a limp of studied elegance. Possibly this handicapped him completely in a matter of sex" (*ibid.*).

138 only forty-one: *Self Sketches*, p. 177. A number of biographers have somehow settled on 42 as Shaw's age at the time of the marriage, though he was still nearly two months shy of his 42d birthday. That Shaw was not using some private system of age notation is indicated, for instance, in Aug. 1903, when he rightly referred to himself as 47 (*Collected Letters*, II, p. 342). I suppose that he consciously pushed his

age forward to make it seem that he was more middle-aged when he married (and therefore presumably less in need of sex) or that he had had a longer period of sexual activity, that is, from 29, when he lost his virginity, to "43," when he married. These justifications are neither mutually exclusive nor incompatible with an unconscious identification with Lee.

138 "the mother of a child": Dunbar, *Mrs G.B.S.*, pp. 72, 283.

138 Beatrice and Sidney Webb: *Ibid.*, pp. 121, 141–42.

139 1914 preface to *Misalliance*: The date in the collected *Prefaces* is given as 1910, when *Misalliance* (written in 1909) was first produced. But internal evidence (p. 75) indicates that 1914 was its date of composition.

139 "The dogmatic objection": Preface to *Misalliance*, pp. 60–61.

140 1910 preface to *Getting Married*: Internal evidence (p. 32) indicates that the date of writing was 1910.

140 "the licentiousness of marriage": Preface to *Getting Married*, p. 5.

140 "incompatible with the higher life": *Ibid.*

140 "every thoughtful and observant minister": *Ibid*

140 "It was certainly a staggering revelation": *Ibid.*

141 never spent a night with a woman: Shaw adroitly has it both ways and sidesteps any attempt to pin him down on personal experience. He can claim shock at the supposed intemperance of married men but, by saying that he was one of the "young" sociologists present, can half imply that he is no longer shocked and no longer finds the questions of windows and blankets insoluble.

141 "Please remember": Preface to *Getting Married*, pp. 5–6.

141 "marriage will have to go": *Ibid.*, p. 7.

142 Shaw's postmarital writings: For example, in the preface to *Androcles and the Lion*, pp. 583–90.

143 financially dependent on his wife: Collected Letters, II, p. 5.

143 advised by friends: *Ibid.*, p. 3.

143 Charlotte's "broken heart": *Ibid.*, I, p. 696.

143 "All this time": *Ibid.*, II, p. 28.

143 prime obstacle to their marriage: *Ibid.*, p. 50.

146 passage adds nothing: Shaw himself early recognized that much of this scene between Tanner and Ann could be safely cut (*ibid.*, pp. 375–76). James Agate called it "a never-ending desert of purely irrelevant talk" (in Herbert Van Thral, ed., *James Agate: An Anthology* [London, 1961], p. 33).

148 began writing the philosophic section: Collected Letters, II, pp. 5, 275.

153 "Beware the pursuit": David J. Gordon remarks that this line of the Devil's "has in one thrust toppled the magnificent edifice erected by Don Juan" ("Two Anti-Puritan Puritans: Bernard Shaw and D. H. Lawrence," *Yale Review*, 56 [1966]: 89). The only flaw in this fine article is the ubiquitous one in Shaw scholarship: the failure to recognize the changes in Shaw's thought.

155 other (unnamed) philosophers: Nietzsche is named toward the end of the scene, but Shaw cannot afford to specify many other past or present philosophers without destroying his case, for the claim that phi-

losophers are unanimously giving Nature a greater understanding of her instinctive purposes collapses as soon as one names particular philosophers and their mutual disagreements. Even Shaw at one time or another disagreed with dozens of thinkers, including Schopenhauer, Rousseau, Marx, Mill, Bergson, Russell, Freud, and himself. Indeed the earlier Shaw would have scoffed at anyone who talked as he and Don Juan now talk of discovering "the purpose of Life," life for the earlier Shaw having been entirely an end in itself.

157 "mating such couples": "The Revolutionist's Handbook," *Man and Superman*, pp. 175, 177–178.

158 "State Department of Evolution": *Ibid.*, pp. 204, 205.

158 "a conference on the subject": *Ibid.*, p. 207.

159 a thousand and one platonic nights: "The Revolutionist's Handbook" was not written until 1902.

159 success in London as a playwright: It must again be remembered that Shaw did not begin to be accepted as an important dramatist until the 1904–7 Barker-Vedrenne seasons at the Royal Court. The first London performance of *Man and Superman* did not take place until 1905, and "Don Juan in Hell" was not performed until 1907.

161 Shakespeare's 130th sonnet. Perhaps this is especially evident when he goes on to speak of "a creature of coral and ivory."

161 "overpowering *odor di femmina*": Collected Letters, II, p. 219.

162 tribunals "from which worthless people": *The Simpleton*, II, p. 1245.

163 the sake of making war: *Ibid.*, p. 1247.

163 "make war on war": *Major Barbara*, III, p. 501.

163 They will still be "riff-raff": "Revolutionist's Handbook," p. 207.

164 purpose scarcely advocated again: This is not to say that Shaw did not continue to advocate birth control. His 1919 article on "Morality and Birth Control" has been reprinted in *The Independent Shavian*, vol. 10, no. 3 (1972). The idea of separating conjunction from marriage also appears occasionally in his late writings, for example, in the preface to *Good King Charles's Golden Days* and in *Buoyant Billions*.

164 elimination of the "unfit". I of course do not claim that such advocacy first began in 1900. Well before his marriage, in 1882, Shaw was laying the philosophical groundwork for the elimination of defectives in an unpublished speech on "The Sacredness of Human Life" (Brit. Mus. Add. MS. 50702). My point is that Shaw's emotional involvement with killing greatly increased, as did the frequency of his advocating it, after the sexual frustrations of his marriage had begun to take hold on his thought. It was then that he proceeded to blur the critical distinction between the physical and mental defectives, on the one side, and what he regarded as the morally unfit on the other. I doubt that Shaw before 1900 would have said what he did in an address to students of political economy in 1905: "Will the subject become more and more pressing as the time goes on, so that in the end you will be prepared to kill anyone who attempts to stand between you and political economy? I fear not?" ("Life, Literature, and Political Economy," *The Shaw Review*, vol. 8, no. 3 [1965], pp. 104–10).

164 "I should make each citizen": Collected Letters, I, p. 128.

167 *Heartbreak House*: Act III, p. 801.

167 a single active principle: Years ago Montgomery Belgion offered a related objection when he wondered whose human will could be said to be most in tune with the Life Force, given the vast variety of human wills (*Our Present Philosophy of Life* [London, 1929], p. 102). Those Shavians who innocently talk of the Life Force notion as if it were a precious and unassailable contribution to 20th-century philosophy might benefit from confronting the strictures of a man like Belgion, whose lengthy chapter on Shaw tends to go unmentioned in discussions of Shaw's thought.

168 denied the attribute of benevolence: Bertrand Russell remarks that the Webbs "used to divide mankind into A's and B's. The A's were artists, anarchists, and aristocrats; the B's were bourgeois, bureaucrat, and benevolent. They always used to add that Shaw was an A and they were B's" ("George Bernard Shaw," *The Virginia Quarterly Review*, 27 [1951]: 2). It is pertinent in the present context to note that Russell said that Shaw "could be very cruel when his vanity was involved" and that "his kindness and his cruelty were equally essential parts of his incredibly vigorous personality."

172 Nietzsche's doctrines: Shaw's relation to Nietzsche still needs further examination. A. C. Ward's comment in the introduction to his edition of *Man and Superman* (London, 1956) indicates the accepted and superficial distinction between the two men: Nietzsche's Superman is "the embodiment of Might," whereas Shaw's is "the embodiment of Right" (p. 209). A. N. Kaul in his astute essay on Shaw suggests that the playwright may in fact have been in part ridiculing Nietzsche's idea of the Superman as well as Bergson's *élan vital* "by having them offered as justification for such everyday facts as love, marriage, and the prospect of offspring" (*The Action of English Comedy* [New Haven and London, 1970], p. 311). Shaw's own early reviews of Nietzsche are not without their ambivalences. See *Pen Portraits*, pp. 217–20. Julian Kaye offers some useful distinctions in his valuable study *Bernard Shaw and the Nineteenth-Century Tradition* (Norman, Okla., 1955), pp. 100–108. Arthur Nethercot voices his skepticism about Shaw's grasp of Nietzsche in "Bernard Shaw, Philosopher," *PMLA*, 69 (1954): 57–75, especially 66–67; and William Brashear is even more critical in "O'Neill and Shaw: The Play as Will and Idea," *Criticism*, 8 (1966): 161–62. Carl Levine's piece is marred by too much indulgence to Shaw, who is for instance called at one point "an ardent democrat" ("Social Criticism in Shaw and Nietzsche," *The Shaw Review*, vol. 10, no. 1 [1967], p. 13). Patrick Bridgewater's discussion is adequate but not up to the level of his other chapters in *Nietzsche in Anglosaxony: A Study of Nietzsche's Impact on English and American Literature* (Leicester, 1972). David S. Thatcher is both discriminating and thorough in his analysis of the two men in his *Nietzsche in England 1890–1914: The Growth of a Reputation* (Toronto, 1970), pp. 180–212. Yet in light of my own analysis, which sees Shaw's position as more problematical and certainly less innocuous than has been hitherto believed, the question of Nietzsche and Shaw invites some basic reconsideration.

173 "Beware": Collected Letters, I, p. 143.

173 a paramount ethical tenet: Reviewing a production of *Hamlet* in the *Saturday Review*, Oct. 2, 1897, Shaw wrote: "And, indeed, there is a sense in which Hamlet is insane; for he trips over the mistake which lies on the threshold of intellectual self-consciousness: that of bringing life to utilitarian or Hedonistic tests, thus treating it as a means instead of an end" (in James Huneker, ed., *Dramatic Opinions and Essays* [New York, 1907], II, p. 315).

173 existed alongside it: Collected Letters, II, p. 203.

175 seeking almost to humiliate the men: He may also have wanted to create a measure of suffering for the audience by the sheer length of the play. The correlation between Shaw's oppressively long plays and their misanthropic attitude is evident also in *Back to Methuselah*.

175 a captured bird: Shaw picturesquely indicates the danger of being a captured bird by having Violet's hat decorated by a dead one.

6: PYGMALION

Critical commentary on this play is surprisingly meager and is usually pulled awry by the preface and the postscript. Their misleading effects were spelled out in Milton Crane's "*Pygmalion*: Bernard Shaw's Dramatic Theory and Practice," *PMLA*, 66 (1951): 879–85. Crompton, however, argues against Crane in his chapter on the play, and he proceeds to interpret the work largely from Higgins's viewpoint. Valency's pages show the strain of worrying too much about the postscript's supposed realism. Desmond MacCarthy and Eric Bentley, attending directly to the play, make acute brief observations in their respective books on Shaw; Charles Berst is fresh and provocative in *Shaw and the Art of Drama*; and Nigel Alexander's analysis is unfailingly thoughtful in *Shaw: Arms and the Man and Pygmalion* (London, 1968).

179 piece of commercial theater: St. John Ervine, for example, while granting that it has great "entertainment value," maintains that it "is not a major play" (*Bernard Shaw*, pp. 459, 460). Margery Morgan says that it is not one of Shaw's "heavyweight" plays (*Shavian Playground*, p. 63). The extent to which the work is considered irrelevant to Shaw's philosophy is indicated in its neglect by Alfred Turco and Robert Whitman in their recent studies of Shaw's thought.

179 "shameless potboiler": Weintraub, ed., *Autobiography*, II, p. 68. He also calls it a potboiler in a letter to Mrs. Campbell of Apr. 26, 1913 (Campbell Letters, p. 123).

179 the "lucky" hit: Maurice Colborne, *The Real Bernard Shaw* (New York, 1949), p. 173.

181 Shaw's mastery over the play's structure: For me the play's only flaw is Doolittle's second appearance, in Act V. One may grant the amusing double switch on the Cinderella legend of having fortune descend, all too heavily, on the heroine's father rather than on herself. One may also grant that Doolittle's fall into the grip of middle-class morality has its thematic point. Still, his transformation ruptures the level of semiprobability that the play has established, and Shaw has to

suspend all action and give Doolittle the play's longest speeches to try to overcome his audience's likely incredulity.

182 "a socialist parable": Dukore, *Shaw: Playwright*, p. 288.

185 snobbery to selfhood: It could be argued that this growth, too, is relative rather than absolute, and that Eliza may still have her traces of snobbery; for example, witness her angry response in Act V to Doolittle's announcement of his forthcoming marriage.

185 manners were so gauche: Pearson, *Shaw: Life and Personality*, p. 63.

185 his family traced itself: Henderson, *Shaw: Man of the Century*, pp. 3–4.

185 he gave himself away: Pearson, *Shaw: Life and Personality*, pp. 56–57.

185 studied hard to change: Wall, *Bernard Shaw*, pp. 41–42.

187 "If Forbes Robertson": Preface to *Great Catherine*, p. 812.

188 only remark available on the play: Terry Letters, p. 234.

189 *The Tempest*: There are some other stray resemblances between the two plays. Caliban says to Prospero in Act I: "You taught me language; and my profit on't / Is, I know how to curse. The red plague rid you / For learning me your language." Ariel was a creature whose noises made the wolves howl before Prospero came to the rescue. Prospero calls Caliban a devil, and Eliza uses the same term for Higgins. Eliza says it was her sixth stepmother who turned her out, and Miranda remembers that four or five women tended to her. Doolittle, perhaps in a parodistic enactment of Ariel's song, suffers a sea-change into something rich and strange. In Act V Prospero says to Ariel, "I shall miss thee"; and Higgins says in Act V, "I shall miss you, Eliza." Claribel married the King of Tunis and Higgins tells Eliza he has made her a consort for a king; and Higgins's line about Eliza as a consort battleship may have been distantly prompted by all the talk of ships of war in *The Tempest*. Possibly these resemblances are coincidental, but we may wish to think that Shaw in these ways was variously hinting at the play the Eynsford Hills may have seen before they arrived for shelter under the portico of St. Paul's Church.

For Clara's name, I should like to add, Shaw's first source may have been entirely nonliterary. Clara was the given name of his housekeeper Mrs. Higgs. And the name of her husband, Henry, the head gardener, may have supplied Shaw with the given name of Professor Higgins, as well as that first syllable of Higgins's name which rhymes with Pygmalion's first syllable. Shaw was fond of inserting into his fictions the names of friends and family members.

On Shakespeare analogs, again, Lise Pedersen presents a suggestive case for *The Taming of the Shrew* in "Shakespeare's *The Taming of the Shrew* vs. Shaw's *Pygmalion*: Male Chauvinism vs. Women's Lib?," in Rodell Weintraub, ed., *Fabian Feminist: Bernard Shaw and Woman* (University Park, Pa., 1977), pp. 14–22. Although this critic argues her case well, and acknowledges that the motivations behind the bullying tactics of Petruchio and Higgins are different, she is impelled by her argument to minimize the equally important differences between Kate and Eliza, and to claim that Higgins rejects "the concept of male dominance over women" (p. 21). But surely the orders that Higgins issues to

Eliza at the end of the play, and his behavior in the postscript, indicate that he is as much of a male chauvinist as ever—as was Shaw himself when he wrote that postscript.

190 "On Parents and Children": Written in 1914; attached as the preface to *Misalliance*.

190 "white paper": John Locke, *An Essay Concerning Human Understanding* (London, 1846), Bk. II, chap. 1, p. 53, Bk. I, chap. 2, p. 15.

191 "violation of children's souls": Preface to *Misalliance*, p. 49.

191 "that submissiveness should no longer": *Ibid.*, p. 105.

191 "If you once allow yourself": *Ibid.*, p. 50.

193 this effort to teach the teacher: Peter Ure was the first critic to give proper emphasis to the "reversal of roles," with Higgins as "the educator who is himself educated by [his pupil]" ("Master and Pupil in Bernard Shaw," *Essays in Criticism*, 19 [1969]: 128).

195 *Love Among the Artists*: Letter by Stanley Weintraub, *Times Literary Supplement*, Nov. 13, 1959, p. 668.

196 Eliza's triumph at the party: Henderson, *Shaw: Man of the Century*, p. 730.

198 critics have overlooked these hints: Valency, for instance, asserts that the play has "nothing to do with the legend of Pygmalion and Galatea" (p. 319).

198 a collector of dirt: The extensive dirt imagery in the play, which splits off into Doolittle's profession and Higgins's attitude toward Eliza—"She's so deliciously low, so horribly dirty"—was probably as fundamental in Shaw's feelings when he created the play as was the opposing attraction of the floral imagery. It connects, too, I suspect, with Shaw's deep ambivalence toward sex, his frequent regard of it as dirty. Hence, if we pursue this conjecture one step further, the "dirt" Shaw is trying to rid himself of through ridiculing Higgins is in his own mind. And if, as I argue later, he is in writing the play preparing himself psychologically for a love affair with Mrs. Campbell, then he is seeking to cleanse his own attitude toward her. In his letters to her after the play was completed, he significantly resorts on several occasions to floral imagery; for example, he wants his "garden of lovely flowers," to be with her "in the magic gardens again" and enjoy "roses and rapture" (Campbell Letters, pp. 97, 101, 100). Back in 1900 he was condemning the "overpowering *odor di femmina*" which assailed him whenever he saw Mrs. Campbell act (Collected Letters, I, p. 219). In the hygienic activity of writing *Pygmalion*, we might say, Shaw was seeking to change Mrs. Campbell's effect on his nostrils.

199 father-daughter relationship: Shaw may have picked up the clue to the father-daughter relationship from W. S. Gilbert's *Pygmalion and Galatea* (1871), which touches upon this theme in Act II. Gilbert's play was the most popular treatment of the legend in the 19th century. Shaw may also have picked up one or two other items from Gilbert's version; for example, Colonel Pickering's implied military background may derive from Gilbert's secondary figure "Leucippe," a soldier; Higgins's apparent rejection of Eliza as a slave who will fetch and carry for him may have been suggested by the conversation of Pygmalion's slave at the opening of Gilbert's play, with its references to fetching

337

and carrying; and again, Eliza's lack of a proper mother and Higgins's sense of being a mother as well as a father to her may have derived from Galatea's insistence that she has no mother. The differences between the two plays, however, are more significant and instructive than their resemblances. Shaw may also have known William Morris's poem "Pygmalion and the Image," but I cannot detect any trace of this work in the play. Nor, obviously, did Shaw pay much heed to Ovid's version except for Higgins's casual misogyny.

Gilbert may also have inadvertently provided Shaw with the name Eliza. In the 1910 preface to *The Shewing-Up of Blanco Posnet*, Shaw reports Gilbert's statement to a Parliamentary Committee on Censorship: "In a novel one may read that 'Eliza slipped off her dressing-gown and stepped into her bath' without any harm; but I think if that were presented on the stage it would be shocking" (p. 430). (In Shaw's original version Eliza has her bath offstage.) Rattray suggests that the name derives ultimately from Somerset Maugham's story of a Cockney flower girl, *Eliza of Lambeth* (p. 184). But a later scholar notes that Eliza was the sister of a Pygmalion in another myth and that a 16th-century poem by Johan Jakob Bodmer borrowed this sister's name in dealing with the sculptor in "Pygmalion und Elise" (Meyer Reinhold, "The Naming of Pygmalion's Animated Statue," *Classical Journal*, 66 [1971]: 316–19).

Wherever Shaw first found the name, it captured him in ways he may have been only half-conscious of, for as indicated below, the play duplicated aspects of his own mother Lucinda *Eliza*beth's experiences with her teacher Lee. And once Shaw had adopted the name, other trains of association were probably created. I suggest, for instance, that the name Eliza was responsible for Higgins's address at 27A Wimpole St. since about a hundred yards further along is the house of that street's most famous resident, Elizabeth Barrett, who had also to escape from the domination of a father. (Shaw admired Browning's poetry and had been a sometime participant in the meetings of the Browning Society.) And such associations of thought may lead on to "My Last Duchess" and then on toward the impenetrable recesses of Shaw's inspiration.

205 "cruelty would be delicious": Mrs. Hushabye in *Heartbreak House*, II, p. 783.

209 "It is not always obvious": Theodor Reik, *Of Love and Lust* (New York, 1967), p. 190.

209 "if a masochist thus has succeeded": *Ibid.*, p. 220.

211 "If you have ever said": Campbell Letters, p. 179.

211 psychological theories of a later date: See Wilhelm Reich, *Character Analysis*, 3d ed. (New York, 1949), p. 222.

212 presence of that very poker: See *Pygmalion*, II, p. 735, V, p. 745.

212 "The whole of the action": Alexander, *Shaw: Arms and the Man and Pygmalion*, p. 62.

213n the issue of flagellation: That he was well aware of the perverse sexual aspect of flagellation is evident from his 1898 lecture on the subject, in which he termed it "a mania which is based on a *sensual* instinct." See "Shaw on 'Flagellomania': A Lecture and a Letter," *The Shaw Review*, vol. 20, no. 2 (1977), pp. 89–92.

214 the "aftershine" of Christianity: Thomas Carlyle, *Sartor Resartus: The Life and Opinions of Herr Teufelsdröck*, in *The Works of Thomas Carlyle*, XII (New York, 1897), p. 127.

216 "To break a man's spirit": *Candida*, I, p. 133.

218 *Pygmalion*'s richness of allusion: Shaw's allusions to the Cinderella story are, I assume, too familiar to require discussion, as is his probably unconscious borrowing from Smollett's *Peregrine Pickle*. (For the theatrical antecedents see Meisel's commentary in *Shaw and 19th-Century Theater*, pp. 169–76.) The Cinderella story of course supplied devices that Shaw could manipulate parodistically—the slippers that belong to the man rather than the woman, the transformed poor girl who walks out on her prince after a midnight confrontation, the older women who browbeat the hero rather than the more vulnerable heroine, the wealth from a "fairy" millionaire falling on the heroine's father and nearly crushing him, and so forth. The often menacing undertones of a fairy tale are also deftly maintained. Yet when he later emphasized the Cinderella theme in his critical comments, Shaw drew attention away from many of the other aspects of the play, including the allusions to Goethe and Milton. His reluctance to mention these may have been part of the same latter-day impulse to whitewash Higgins which reappeared in the preface and the postscript.

The Cinderella motif, however, does not generate much of the play's emotional appeal even though it creates some of the humor. Valency, who summarily dismisses the pertinence of the Pygmalion legend, is left only with the Cinderella story to account for the play's power, and this lands him in several difficulties and contradictions. Thus he finds Higgins "an unemotional man" with "no need of love" (pp. 317, 319), who nevertheless "feels some emotional need for the girl" and "would rather die than part with [her]" (pp. 320, 310). Clinging to the Cinderella story, he finds the last act "both superfluous and repetitious," especially since it lacks the supposedly obligatory love scene. Berst is on surer ground when he says that the two myths are "played off against each other," though he does not explain their basic contradiction (*Shaw and the Art of Drama*, p. 202). The emotional strength of the play, as I have argued, depends far less on the Cinderella than on the Pygmalion legend. Higgins is too old to be a prince, charming or otherwise, but he is the right age to be a father. The disguised incest appeal is therefore, I believe, fundamental, and it is this which gives even more force to Shaw's use of the Goethean and Miltonic allusions to the evil in Higgins.

219 wonders "what he can see": "Bin doch ein arm unwissend Kind, / Begreife nicht, was er an mir findt" (Johann Wolfgang von Goethe, *Faust, Part One*, trans. Philip Wayne [Harmondsworth, Middlesex, 1962], p. 144).

219 several other resemblances: For example: the plot of each play is precipitated by a wager; dustbins appear in both works; the sound of church bells gives each man pause; Margareta and Eliza are reduced to depression and to thoughts of suicide; Faust would like to give a present of a ring and Higgins does so; Faust renounces his scientific instruments and Higgins in Act V momentarily realizes their inadequacy. The resemblances of course multiply when we recall that Mephi-

stopheles, as Margareta comes to realize, is Faust's other self, which signifies in our present context that Higgins, too, coalesces with the Devil. Hence Higgins's command to "burn her clothes" is reminiscent of Mephistopheles' power over flames, and the latter's desire to capture human souls is duplicated in Higgins's craving for Eliza's soul.

223 "with my egotism": *Unsocial Socialist*, p. 104.

225 Shaw's mother as one of the models: According to Henderson, "She remained to the end mildly skeptical of George's success, and derived no end of amusement from the adulation showered upon him by 'disciples'" (*Shaw: Playboy and Prophet*, p. 181). Doubtless Mrs. Higgins was a figure fused from several models, from life as well as literature. But I think that Philip Weissman is correct in seeing Shaw's mother as one of the chief of these models (*Creativity in the Theater* [New York, 1965], p. 152). This contention seems to me further strengthened by recognizing that one component of the name of Mrs. Higgins's friend, Mrs. Eynsford-Hill, was probably drawn from the name of Shaw's childhood governess Caroline Hill. It appears reasonable to assume that Shaw would think of his mother when thinking of his governess.

225 Philip Weissman: *Creativity in the Theater*, p. 149. Weissman's essay is persuasive on a number of counts. However, he makes a consequential error in assuming that the play was written, not before, but during the romance with Mrs. Campbell. This leads him to assert—wrongly—that she was a "desexualized" object for Shaw and to interpret the ending of the play as a renunciation of the pursuit of Mrs. Campbell (pp. 169, 167). The exact opposite seems to me nearer the mark; as I argue later, one reason that Shaw kept the ending open was to allow in imagination for a personal union with the actress for whom he had written Eliza's part. The same argument militates against John O'Donovan's claim in his provocative little volume *Shaw and the Charlatan Genius* (Dublin, 1965) that Higgins is based *exclusively* on Lee (p. 60).

227 "I saw you first": Campbell Letters, p. 91.

227 "You are a figure": *Ibid.*, p. 131.

227 "Beatricissima," "Stella Stellarum": *Ibid.*, p. 15.

227 "O beautifullest of all the stars": *Ibid.*, p. 16.

227 "She creates all sorts of illusions": Huneker, ed., *Dramatic Opinions*, I, p. 42.

227 "The moment she was seen": *Ibid.*, pp. 117–19.

228 her performances compared unfavorably: *Ibid.*, II, pp. 2–3, 122–27.

228 her diction was defective: *Ibid.*, I, 118.

228 "its right tragic power": *Ibid.*, II, p. 320.

228 "not yet a great actress": *Ibid.*, I, p. 363.

228 "You will tell me": *Ibid.*, II, p. 6.

228 Mrs. Pat-Cat: Collected Letters, I, p. 622.

228 "a mettlesome, dominative character": *You Never Can Tell*, I, p. 177.

228 still "good-looking" and domineering prostitute: *Mrs. Warren's Profession*, I, p. 64.

228 Julia Craven based on Jenny Patterson: Rattray, p. 94.

229 "violently oversexed" women: Preface to *Three Plays for Puritans*, pp. 738, 739.

229 "overpowering *odor di femmina*": Collected Letters, I, p. 219.

229 "She was flattered": Terry Letters, p. 410.

230 "I went calmly to her house": *Ibid.*

230 the "delightful dreams": Campbell Letters, p. 14.

230 his "very wonderful lady": *Ibid.*

230 repetitions of "Stella": *Ibid.*, p. 87.

230 "pseudo-romance": Ervine, *Bernard Shaw*, p. 445.

230 "theatrical moonshine": Alan Dent, *Mrs. Patrick Campbell* (London, 1961), p. 245. Dent rightly takes St. John Ervine to task for his blatant bias against Mrs. Campbell; yet Dent's defense of her is almost as damaging as Ervine's attack since he robs her of any sincerity in the relationship. Clearly Mrs. Shaw herself did not regard her husband's affair as the "hilarious theatrical moonshine" or the "witty make-believe" that Dent believes it to have been. Valency's opinion of Mrs. Campbell is a sound corrective to Ervine's disparagement: "[She] was in every way an exceptional woman, highly gifted: at forty-eight still beautiful, notoriously difficult, and unusually intelligent" (p. 323).

231 "as you are always boasting": Campbell Letters, p. 137.

231 "why you go on scolding me": *Ibid.*, p. 145.

231 "work, work, work": *Ibid.*, p. 113.

231 "If I stop to think". *Ibid.*, p. 109.

231 "Stella, I must break myself": *Ibid.*, p. 90.

231 a "wild happiness": *Ibid.*, p. 91.

231 "shut your ears tight": *Ibid.*, p. 55.

232 The strictly verbal parallels: Pygmalion, II, pp. 721, 727, V, p. 749, II, pp. 727, 726, V, p. 751, IV, p. 742, V, p. 749; Campbell Letters, pp. 104, 19, 102, 109, 58, 110, 154, 144, 154, 153.

233 "play Higgins to your Eliza": Campbell Letters, pp. 114–15.

233 "earth or heaven [has] anything better": *Ibid.*, p. 50.

233 "that paper love is nothing": *Ibid.*, p. 117.

233 "I want to live it": *Ibid.*, p. 107.

233 *Overruled* and *Great Catherine*: Dent briefly mentions the autobiographical elements in *Overruled* (*Mrs. Patrick Campbell*, p. 249). I believe that the title figure of *Great Catherine* was created with Mrs. Campbell as well as the Empress herself in mind. Catherine is called "the little angel mother," practically the same term Shaw used upon occasion for Stella (Campbell Letters, pp. 149, 150, 173). Catherine is also termed a cat, as was Stella. The situation of Captain Edstaston bears some resemblance to Shaw's: he is caught between two women; he must try to prove to one of them that her jealousy is unfounded and that he is an innocent man who has been forced to use words of endearment. Catherine accuses him of timidity just as Stella accused Shaw of timidity. There is also a noticeable amount of violence, anger, and giddy sadomasochism in the play. It seems to have served Shaw as an outlet for the emotions churned up in the Campbell affair, as a means of chastening himself by ridicule, and as a preparation for his return to Charlotte. Indeed this therapeutic intention may help to account for the play's embarrassing badness: the experience had not yet been assimilated, and Shaw was attending to his own situation far more than to that of his characters. The shorthand draft of the play in the Hanley Collection at the Humanities Research Center of the University of

Texas at Austin is dated July 29–Aug. 13, 1913, which would mean that it was completed just after Stella left Sandwich.

233 "adores you with one eye": Campbell Letters, p. 55.

233 "his last chance at romance": Valency, p. 216.

233 "playing with him": Campbell Letters, p. 55.

233 "Stella; don't play with me": *Ibid.*, p. 143.

233 She "must be alone": *Ibid.*, p. 152.

234 "You are such a jolly playfellow": *Ibid.*, pp. 79–80.

234 "two barefooted playmates on the hills": *Ibid.*, p. 114.

234 "a lad playing with you": *Ibid.*, p. 116.

234 "Oh, if only you were alarmed": *Ibid.*, pp. 104–5.

235 "you must always sit enthroned": *Ibid.*, pp. 115, 149, 95.

235 "I want my plaything": *Ibid.*, p. 96.

236 "Charlotte & Co.": *Ibid.*, p. 69.

236 his "Stella Aphrodite": *Ibid.*, p. 90.

236 scold her for having "jilted" him: *Ibid.*, p. 145.

237 "Therefore, though I like George": *Ibid.*, p. 131.

237 "Please go back to London": *Ibid.*, p. 152.

238 "I risked the breaking": *Ibid.*, p. 154.

238 "You *wouldn't* understand": *Ibid.*, p. 160.

238 "Very well, go": *Ibid.*, pp. 153–54.

239 "Oh, my rancor": *Ibid.*, pp. 154–55.

239 his "Lear" play: *Shakes versus Shav*, p. 1404.

240 "Stella, how could you": Campbell Letters, p. 156.

240 "Another day": *Ibid.*, pp. 156–57.

241 "his love is epistolary": *Ibid.*, p. 101.

241 "it is past letter writing": *Ibid.*, p. 113.

241 hurled at him the word "Coward": *Ibid.*, p. 128.

242 "When you said you were writing": *Ibid.*, pp. 117–18.

242 "You blind man": *Ibid.*, p. 157.

242 "And now there is that desolate strand": *Ibid.*, p. 155.

243 "Back from the land": *Ibid.*, p. 159.

243 a blast of pent-up fury: *Ibid.*, p. 166.

243 "your honeymoon has been a success": *Ibid.*, p. 168.

244 "heart of stone," "marble heart": *Ibid.*, pp. 143, 134.

245 the "slave of an establishment": *Ibid.*, p. 109.

245 1910 treatise on marriage and divorce: Preface to *Getting Married*, pp. 31, 43.

246 sick with jealousy and rage: Campbell Letters, pp. 114, 128–29.

246 a certain amount of dalliance: *Ibid.*, pp. 87–88.

246 touching moment from that first meeting: *Ibid.*, p. 59.

246 "Who mashed Stella": *Ibid.*, p. 98.

248 her "golden man": Dent, *Mrs. Patrick Campbell*, p. 243. Shaw may have relented when he came to write out the stage directions for the play's publication, for he seems to allude handsomely to Stella's "golden man" by saying that Higgins enters in Act IV "half singing half yawning an air from *La Fanciulla del Golden West*." (Perhaps the desire to slip in the private reference to West made Shaw disregard precision, since Puccini's *Fanciulla del West* is of course the proper title and *The Girl of the Golden West* the name of the David Belasco play

from which the libretto was drawn.) It may also be noted that Stella would probably have gone off to marry West whatever Shaw's behavior had been like, for she married him on the same day that his divorce from Lady Randolph Churchill became absolute.

248 instructions headed FINAL ORDERS: Campbell Letters, p. 179.

249 "You are trying to break my heart": *Ibid.*, p. 158.

249 audience thundered out its cheers: Richard Huggett, *The Truth About Pygmalion* (London, 1969), p. 137. Huggett presents a gossipy account of the play's early history. But he underestimates the strength of Shaw's romantic involvement with Mrs. Campbell (p. 38), and thereby misses the inner drama of the play's rehearsals and the reasons for Shaw's irritability at the time.

250 *Heartbreak House*: Weintraub, *Journey to Heartbreak*, pp. 5–6.

7: THE PLAYWRIGHT'S REVENGE

Almost all of the commentary on *Pygmalion* has been influenced for the worse by the addenda. As Diderik Roll-Hansen was one of the few to perceive, the direction of the reader's sympathies is now changed toward Higgins ("Shaw's 'Pygmalion': The Two Versions of 1916 and 1941," *A Review of English Literature*, vol. 8, no. 3 [1967], pp. 81–90). Myron Matlaw's article, "The Denouement of *Pygmalion*," which regards Higgins as Shaw's ideal hero, illustrates the dangers of viewing the play through the lenses of its preface and postscript (*Modern Drama*, 1 [1958]: 29–34). Donald Costello's excellent study of Shaw and the cinema, *The Serpent's Eye* (Notre Dame, 1965), indirectly points out Shaw's error in mixing proposed movie sequences with play scenes in his new edition of the play. Roll-Hansen was quite right in 1967 in calling for a critical edition of what he termed Shaw's "most misunderstood play." The need has still not been met; and one hopes that when that edition does appear, the so-called "screen additions" will be dropped into notes and the great early version allowed to shine forth without encumbrances.

254 "like a bereaved Romeo": Meisel, *Shaw and 19th-Century Theater*, p. 117n.

255 "I want to hurt you": Campbell Letters, p. 156.

255n he mailed her an advance copy: *Ibid.*, p. 209.

255 "I tower mountainous": *Ibid.*, p. 156.

256 "The very scrupulousness": *Pygmalion*, p. 757.

256 a late draft of the postscript: "Pygmalion Preface and Epilogue, Early Draft, 1913," Hanley Collection, Humanities Research Center, University of Texas at Austin, p. 15.

256 "The worst sin": *The Devil's Disciple*, II, p. 230.

258 "Beware": Collected Letters, I, p. 143.

259 "the reformer England needs": Shaw was even more extravagant in an early typescript, which has "The Savior that England needs today" (Brit. Mus. Add. MS. 50628, f. 1).

260 "most men become humbugs": *London Music, 1888–1889*, p. 301.

260 "The English have no respect": Preface to *Pygmalion*, p. 807.

260 codicils in Shaw's last testament:

35 . . . (2) To employ a phonetic expert to transliterate my play entitled Androcles & The Lion in the Proposed British Alphabet assuming the pronunciation to resemble that recorded by His Majesty our late King George V and sometimes described as Northern English. . . . (4) To advertise and publish the transliteration with the original [established] lettering opposite the transliteration page by page and a glossary of the two alphabets at the end and to present copies to public libraries in the British Isles, the British Commonwealth, the American States North and South and to national libraries everywhere in that order.

36. I desire my Trustee to bear in mind that the Proposed British Alphabet does not pretend to be exhaustive as it contains only sixteen vowels whereas by infinitesimal movements of the tongue countless different vowels can be produced all of them in use among speakers of English who utter the same vowels no oftener than they make the same finger prints. Nevertheless they can understand one another's speech and writing sufficiently to converse and correspond: for instance, a graduate of Trinity College Dublin has no difficulty understanding a graduate of Oxford University when one says that "the sun rohze," and the other "the san raheoze" nor are either of them puzzled when a peasant calls his childhood his "chawldid." For a university graduate calls my native country Awlind.

37. It is possible that the ministry of Education may institute the inquiry and adopt the Proposed British Alphabet to be taught in the schools it controls in which event subsection I of Clause 35 foregoing and its relevant sequels will be contra-indicated as superfluous and Clause 40 come into operation accordingly but the adoption must be exact and *no account taken of the numerous alternative* spelling Reforms now advocated or hereafter proposed. [Italics but not the vanity added.]

38. I hereby devise and bequeath the balance of the income of my Residual Trust Funds . . . as follows:

(A) To remunerate the services and defray the expenses incidental to these proceedings and generally to the launching advertising and propaganda of the said British Alphabet.

(B) To acquire by employment purchase or otherwise the copyright and patents (if any) created by or involved in the designing and manufacture of the said Alphabet or the publication of the works printed in it without exploiting the said rights or for commercial profit.

(C) To wind-up the enterprise when the aforesaid steps have been taken or if and when its official adoption or general vogue shall make further recourse to my estate and action on the part of my Trustee in respect of this charitable Trust superfluous (From Weintraub, ed., *Autobiography*, II, pp. 237–39).

This is only about half of what the will has to say on the subject. Of course the younger and more pragmatic Shaw, not yet mounted on his alphabetical hobbyhorse, would have been able to entertain the hypothesis that if the spelling of a language has some significance in training the character of a people, as perhaps it does, then our old and much-criticized alphabet may have contributed to the unideological nature of the English-speaking race, its recognition that the printed word can be deceptive, that reality escapes the mesh of human constructs, and that compromise is therefore a part of wisdom. The making of ideologies and philosophic systems, with their faith in the adequacy of language, is surely not encouraged when an individual must learn from his earliest years that even the spelling of words is treacherous. Unfortunately, in his old age Shaw lived too much with words, lost touch with reality, and aspired to be a phonetical system-maker on a far more grandiose scale than Professor Higgins himself.

261 "turn me into rusty iron": Campbell Letters, p. 131.

261 "hideous laughter": *Ibid.*, p. 97.

263 "out of your manifold nature": *Ibid.*, p. 345.

263 "Why, oh why": *Ibid.*, p. 334.

263 made her fear: *Ibid.*, p. 289.

263 Mrs. Hushabye in *Heartbreak House*: *Ibid.*, p. 250.

263 "tidbits into dignified paragraphs": *Ibid.*, p. 269.

263 "If you send me all": *Ibid.*, p. 270.

264 "suburban cap": *Ibid.*, p. 271.

264 "give up the idea": *Ibid.*, p. 273.

264 "make mischief in my household": *Ibid.*, p. 269.

264 "author who tried to seduce you": *Ibid.*, p. 258.

264 "love letters from a married man": *Ibid.*, p. 274.

264 "Dear Jenny": *Mrs. Warren's Profession*, I, p. 68.

264 "that could hurt Charlotte": Campbell Letters, p. 271.

264 "It is a supreme pity": *Ibid.*, p. 281.

264 tribute to her friend's kindness: Mrs. Patrick Campbell (Beatrice Stella Cornwallis-West), *My Life and Some Letters* (London, 1922), pp. 249ff. The tribute was not unmixed with criticism; for instance, Stella noted: "His inflexible domesticity seemed absurd. . . . Strong feelings exalted him—but the slightest contretemps would turn his fantastic adoration into almost alarming abuse" (pp. 264, 268). She also expressed reservations about his playwriting and directing.

265 "we must not be handed down": Campbell Letters, pp. 331–32.

265 a scene without much relevance: The dominant critical view can be summed up in Nethercot's terming it "the completely extraneous Interlude" (*Men and Supermen*, p. 276). Frederick P. W. McDowell presents the best case for the minority position in his article "'The Eternal Against the Expedient': Structure and Theme in Shaw's *The Apple Cart*," *Modern Drama*, 2 (1959): 99–113. If the play is regarded merely as a portrait of a king, as seen through his day's activities, then of course the work has unity; but then the plot is rendered even more threadbare. Margery Morgan's claim that Granville Barker's play *His Majesty* (London, 1928) influenced Shaw is, I think, irrefutable (*Shavian Playground*, pp. 306–12). The issue of the King's abdication, his long interview with a representative American, his speech on the value of a ruler who is above party squabbles—all find their counterparts in *The Apple Cart*. Furthermore, the character of Barker's King Henry seems to have impressed Shaw greatly, probably because he fancied his likeness to the King, who is described as a charming, shrewd, courteous man with a "cordial simplicity of manner," "an ironic, a

mischievous sense of humour," and depths into which he withdraws himself (p. 3). Shaw sensibly ignored Barker's overloaded plot, but he hardly bothered to provide any plot to replace it. The heart of the play is Magnus's meeting with his Ministers and his threat to abdicate if they deprive him of veto power. Shaw simply divided the meeting into two sessions and then created the Interlude as a filler. (The stretching out of the thin material is of course cleverly done.) Significantly, *His Majesty* has nothing even vaguely resembling the scene with Orinthia. Shaw wrote a letter to Stella just after completing a draft of the play in which he suggested that she try to get a Civil List Pension (Campbell Letters, p. 312), and Orinthia, curiously, has a somewhat comparable pension. It is not inconceivable that Shaw was trying to have Stella create further resemblances between her situation and Orinthia's.

266 tastelessly alluded to her only son: Shaw may not have been aware of the tastelessness of his allusion any more than on a famous earlier occasion he had been aware of the heartlessness with which he dismissed the victims of the torpedoed Lusitania, or at another time, in *Back to Methuselah*, had callously alluded to Prime Minister Asquith's eldest son who had been killed in the battle of the Somme. See Weintraub, *Journey to Heartbreak*, pp. 202–3. The tastelessness is not in what is said about Orinthia's son but in saying anything at all about him. At least it was insensitive to refer to the son of the character that many knew to be Stella Campbell slightly disguised. In naming the son Basil, Shaw uses the same first initial of Alan Campbell's nickname, Beo. Eleven years earlier, before the fight over Stella's book had further embittered their relationship, Shaw had written her a letter of outraged grief upon hearing of Alan's death (Campbell Letters, p. 224).

266 incident at Stella's house: The incident bears some resemblance to one Shaw used in the novel *The Irrational Knot* (1880), as Ervine points out (*Bernard Shaw*, pp. 83–84). It also bears a generic similarity to an incident in *The Philanderer* (1893) in that there again a man and a woman are interrupted at an embarrassing moment by a third party. (It is of course an ancient dramatic situation, dating back to classical comedy.) Yet Shaw most likely drew the scene from life rather than from work he had written decades earlier. He told Ervine just before the Malvern opening that the real-life incident had occurred in Mrs. Campbell's house (p. 84), and he told Pearson exactly the same thing years later (*Shaw: Life and Personality*, p. 424). In Harris's biography, carefully supervised by Shaw, we read of the Interlude: "[It] has absolutely nothing to do with the plot. But it is not irrelevant to Shaw's private life, and that is how it absent mindedly got into the play" (*Bernard Shaw*, pp. 213–14).

267 "You have no legal right": Campbell Letters, p. 316.

268 Shaw's biographers: Ervine, *Bernard Shaw*, pp. 445–51. Pearson's account also reveals Shaw's controlling hand (*Shaw: Life and Personality*, pp. 284–93).

268 "Perhaps you will never speak": Campbell Letters, p. 314.

268 "of the red hot poker order": *Ibid.*, p. 316.

269 "that the scene is amusingly scandalous": *Ibid.*, p. 324.

269 "You are out of tune": *Ibid.*, p. 329.

269 "I shall now be able": *Ibid.*, p. 334.

269 "vulgarity and untruthfulness": *Ibid.*, p. 332.

269 "of course the scene isn't true": *Ibid.*, p. 316.

269 "There are no personalities": *Ibid.*, p. 331.

269 "Orinthia is not a portrait": *Ibid.*, p. 333.

269 "I have made a superb picture": *Ibid.*, p. 331.

269 "I am an artist": *Ibid.*, p. 333.

269 "Tear it up": *Ibid.*

271 "the rest is the irreducible minimum": *Pygmalion*, Standard Edition, I, p. 212. All quotations from the revised version are taken from this edition.

274 damages the great midnight encounter: There is also a small incon sistency between Pickering's final line added to Act III ("I am hungry. Let us clear out and have some supper somewhere.") and his remark near the opening of Act IV that they had attended a dinner party before the reception. On this matter of inconsistency, there is a curious and to me inexplicable one in the original version, which Shaw seems not to have perceived or bothered about when preparing his revisions. The play begins in the summer. Higgins says in Act II and again in Act III that he will pass Eliza off as a duchess in six months. Yet Act III seems to take place in the spring: the windows are open, Higgins gazes at the flowers in Battersea Park, Mrs. Eynsford-Hill fears that influenza may attack her family as it does every spring. Then at the opening of Act V, the night of the reception, we are told that "it is a summer night." Thus the play's time span seems about a year rather than six months. Since the romance with Stella lasted only a little more than a year, and ended in the summer, it is conceivable that in respect to time, too, the play foreshadowed a major feature of the romance.

274 "Eliza goes down on her knees": In the 1934 version, Shaw still al lowed Eliza a moment of sentiment: "She finds the ring; holds it up in triumph; and replaces it on her finger. She rises, and makes for the door, very determined and self-satisfied" (Brit. Mus. Add. MS. 50628, f. 29).

277 a "cast-off": Campbell Letters, p. 188.

277 "Wretch, I could tear you": *Ibid.*, p. 157.

277 as Freud has remarked: J. Strachey, ed., *Standard Edition of the Complete Psychological Works of Sigmund Freud* (London, 1957), XIV, p. 251.

278 "I want my plaything": Campbell Letters, p. 96.

278 "Aren't you tired": *Ibid.*, p. 289.

279 quelling fear of death: Shaw's fear of death and longing for it had ear lier been most fully manifested in *Back to Methuselah.*

279 a depth analysis: Further analysis would also have to attend to Shaw's shifting feelings toward his father during the course of the rela tionship and his ambivalent feelings toward Cornwallis-West. West for instance was something of a man of action who was to see service dur ing the war as Assistant Provo-Marshal of the 57th Division, and Shaw in his writings had often fantasized himself as a man of action. In addition, West's very name "George" provided still another positive emotional link and his very age provided another, for West was 18

years Shaw's junior (and 9 years younger than Stella), and thus by years alone was someone who could more easily conform to the son-mother relationship that Shaw himself had sought with Stella. As she became in some degree for Shaw associated with his own mother, so too West perhaps became associated with himself in the role of son; and when West's marriage to Stella finally broke up in the early 1920's, Shaw's anger against her may have received a fresh stimulus: once again the mother figure seemed to reject a boy-man with whom Shaw had been unconsciously identifying himself. (This anger would not at all have been lessened by Shaw's conscious knowledge that it was West who first walked out on Stella in 1919.) At any rate the unpublished letters from Shaw to West indicate that whenever Stella's name arose, Shaw mocked her or sympathized with West (Brit. Mus. Add. MS. 58433).

AFTERWORD

283 "blown to smithereens": Rosset, p. 88.

283 "hated and despised": *Ibid.*, p. 101.

283 "full of self-reproaches": *Ibid.*, p. 4.

283 "If we desire a certain type": Preface to *On the Rocks*, p. 362. A similar passage in the preface to *The Simpleton* points equally in his drunken father's direction: "But police measures are not enough. Any intelligent and experienced administrator of the criminal law will tell you that there are people who come up for punishment again and again for the same offence, and that punishing them is a cruel waste of time. There should be an Inquisition always available to consider whether these human nuisances should not be put out of their pain, *or out of their joy* as the case may be" (p. 643) [my emphasis].

284 Hitler and Stalin were blood brothers: George Orwell made a somewhat similar comment, in *The Road to Wigan Pier* (London, 1965), when he observed that to Shaw, "Stalin and Mussolini are almost equivalent persons" (p. 179).

285 "biting overemphasis": Edmund Wilson, *Classics and Commercials* (New York, 1950), p. 240.

285 "pugnacity": Chesterton, *George Bernard Shaw*, p. 182.

285 "violence of assertion": Mayne, *Wit and Satire of Shaw*, p. 14.

285 "pitiless prose": "The Innocence of Bernard Shaw," in Kronenberger, ed., *Shaw: A Critical Survey*, pp. 86–87. Richard N. Ohmann, in his thoughtful volume *Shaw: The Style and the Man* (Middletown, Conn.: 1962), finds that his posture of denial and condemnation, his attempt to outrage the reader, his "flaying" of complacency, raise the question whether Shaw's nay-saying did not spring from an emotional complex rather than a code of belief (p. 107). I obviously think that it did, though I would not want to assume that Ohmann would necessarily agree to the sadistic strain in that complex.

INDEX

Index